Carry Th

A Banker's Tale of Deceit and Consequence

Farooq Mohammad

Carry The Lie

Cover design by Woodbridge Publishers

Edited by Woodbridge Publishers

Printed in the UK by Woodbridge Publishers

ISBN Paperback (978-1-7394329-7-3)
ISBN Hardback (978-1-7394329-8-0)

*This book is dedicated to my family
who have inspired, supported, and
stood by me on my journey
through life*

*My special thanks to my wife
Yasmeen
who has been a warrior along
with me in every obstacle*

Carry The Lie

*Banking establishments are more dangerous
than the standing armies
Thomas Jefferson
Third President of the USA*

Author's note

This is the story of a **fictional bank**, inspired by scandals that have rocked the banking and financial world in recent times. The activities of the bank described in this book are not dissimilar to the activities of some of the major financial institutions as revealed recently. Some of these major financial institutions, when caught, pay large amounts as fines and continue to operate as if nothing happened.

This is a work of fiction. Names, characters, businesses, organizations, countries, places, and events are either the product of the author's imagination or are used fictitiously. Any resemblance to actual persons, living or dead, events or locales, and countries is entirely coincidental and has no relationship to any person, place, organization, or events that might have occurred or existed at any time.

Part I
Gathering Storm

Chapter 1

Karachi, Pakistan

Amir looked at his watch, 9 p.m. There was still time to make the flight to Geneva. Swissair left Karachi at 2.30 a.m. and reached Geneva via Istanbul at 7.30 a.m. Central European Time.

Amir was the youngest assistant vice president at Growth & Prosperity Bank, known as G&P Bank. The G&P Bank was the pride of the Pakistani banking industry. It was the only non-Western international bank with over two hundred fifty branches around the world. Twenty of those branches were in the UK alone. The bank's tag line was *"The bank that grows your business"*.

Only yesterday, Amir was asked to go to Geneva to help with the bank's operations.

Yesterday morning, Amir arrived at work at his usual time and had barely settled down at his desk when the phone rang. It was Samira, the Secretary to Azhar Alam, the head of global operations and second in command at the bank. He was a feared man and was known not to suffer fools.

'How are you?' chimed Samira. Amir was a very eligible bachelor, and Samira was not shy, often flirting with Amir.

'Good. And you?'

'Could be better if you kept your promise of treating me to a dinner,' Samira made an unabashed approach.

'Any time. Any time, sweetheart,' Amir was also not beyond flirting.

'Words! You should teach classes on charming girls. Okay, let's fix something after you return,' Samira responded.

'After I return? I'm not going anywhere, so how about tomorrow evening?'

'Well, let's deal with the first things first. Azhar Alam wants to see you in fifteen minutes, and I am not supposed to say anything further before you meet him.'

'What? Why does Azhar Alam want to see me? I am not being fired, am I?' Amir was shocked and afraid of this sudden interest in him by Azhar Alam.

'Relax. Nobody would dare touch our blue-eyed Amir. I'll see you in fifteen minutes.' And she was gone.

Fifteen minutes felt like fifteen hours. Amir could not concentrate. He combed his hair, straightened his tie, and was outside Azhar Alam's top floor office in thirteen minutes.

Samira was all smiles and full of charm. 'Go straight in. He is waiting for you. I have already ordered coffee.'

'Good morning, Sir.' Amir stepped into the luxurious office.

'Good morning! Come in, come in.' Azhar Alam was very welcoming. 'Please, have a seat. He pointed to the plush chair by his desk as Amir sat down. 'Well, how are you keeping up these days?'

'Busy, but I enjoy work.'

'Good. Good. Everybody fine at home?'

'Alhamdulillah *(praise be to Allah)*. Everybody is fine. I hardly see them, though,' Amir responded.

'I get excellent reports about you. You must not work so hard. We must see that you get a bit of relaxation, too.'

'There is so much to do. I am working on renewing facilities at TIG,' Amir replied.

Tanganyika International Group, commonly known as TIG, was the biggest client of the bank. They had a finger in every pie. The chairman of the group, Ismail Soothar, was a personal friend of the bank's chairman, Sheikh Tayeb.

'Oh, TIG is too big for one person to handle. You must have several assistants to manage it. Don't worry, I will organise it. My reason for calling you this morning is the urgent need for somebody very smart and talented to go assist our Geneva branch with the year-end closing. They are in a mess, and Masood is panicking.' Masood Qadir was the chief of the bank's Geneva operations. 'What I have in mind is that you go to Geneva on tomorrow night's flight, help Masood for a few days, and since you have been working too hard, take a week off, at the bank's expense, and enjoy the new year in Europe.' Azhar Alam beamed.

'Thank you, Sir. I am speechless. But who will look after the TIG? Their facilities are up for renewal early in the New Year. And there are many issues to resolve before we can renew. I fear we are very exposed. I also fear that the auditors might have difficulties with this account if the full facts are revealed. I have already sent a note to Mr. Abu Talib.' Although eager not to lose the opportunity to go to Geneva, Amir did not want to appear negligent. Abu Talib was the senior executive vice president directly responsible for TIG at the bank.

'Oh, don't worry. Saima in the corporate banking unit will look after it while you are away. I will personally keep an eye on her until you return. I suggest you brief Saima about the account and hand over all the documents to her,' Azhar Alam replied.

'Thank you very much, Sir. Unfortunately, travelling tomorrow may be too early. I don't have a Swiss visa, and it might take a few days to obtain one.'

'Visas should not be a problem. Give your passport to Samira. She will get the visa stamped for Switzerland and other neighbouring countries in no time. We have contacts at the embassies. Samira has already booked you a first-class ticket on Swiss Air for tomorrow night. You should also not worry about the expenses. Everything within reason will be taken care of. Enjoy yourself and relax. By the way, you won't have very heavy baggage, will you?' Azhar Alam asked.

'No. I will travel light. Why?' Amir enquired.

'We need to send some security papers and other stuff to Geneva. I thought it might be a good idea if you carried them with you. I hope you don't have a problem with that,' Azhar Alam explained.

'Of course not, Sir. I am more than happy to carry anything you want to be delivered to Geneva.' Amir was afraid that he might have offended Azhar Alam.

'Well, it's settled, then. Shakadir Khan will bring the stuff personally to you tomorrow evening. I hope this will not be an inconvenience.' Retired Major Shakadir Khan was the head of security and the personal assistant to the chairman. He was a powerful man at the bank.

'I don't have any plans for tomorrow evening. Mr. Shakadir can come by at any time.'

'I will ask Shakadir to phone you and arrange the time.' Azhar Alam got up and offered his hand. 'Good luck. I'll see you when you return.' The meeting was over.

That was yesterday. Amir had hurriedly organised his desk and handed over the documents relating to TIG to Saima. Visas for Switzerland, Italy, France, Germany, and the UK were miraculously stamped on his passport within twenty-four hours. The bank had friends in embassies and consulates.

Shakadir had promised to personally deliver the papers to Amir's home in good time for the flight. Amir again looked at his watch. Shakadir should be arriving any minute. With the time on hand, Amir could not help but think of the twists and turns his young life had taken so far.

He was the eldest child of Majid Ali Ramli and Raana Ramli, nee, Syed. Their other child was Seemi, now a beautiful twenty-three-year-old woman who was a final-year student at the Institute of Business Administration at Karachi University.

Majid's family came from a small town called Ramla in what is now the Madhya Pradesh state of India. It was common for prominent families in India to be named after the town in which they originated from. They had agricultural land there. Majid's father was a student at the Aligarh Muslim University and an active worker in the Pakistan movement. Majid moved to Pakistan in 1947 as a ten-year-old. His family's wealth was left in India.

The family settled in Karachi. With his Aligarh Students' Union connections, Majid's father got himself a job in the newly established Civil Service of Pakistan. In the friends-look-after-friends culture of post-independence Pakistan, he progressed quickly and became a senior government officer. After finishing his college degree and with the help of family contacts, Majid joined Altos Pharmaceuticals Limited, a small pharmaceutical plant manufacturing cough syrup and gripe water for children under a licence from a UK parent. With his father's connections and his ability to self-project, Majid progressed swiftly, and when the company's British general manager left Pakistan, Majid was selected to be the chief executive officer of the company.

Majid married the vivacious and cultured Raana, whose father was related to the Bhopal's ruling family in India. With his own family connections, his position in the company, and Raana's 'blue-blood' heritage, Majid and Raana soon became part of the Karachi elite. They had a membership in the Sind Club and were regulars at every notable social function in the city. Raana was also an ace bridge player who took part in international tournaments.

Amir grew up in this so-called upper-class Pakistani environment. He was never a bright student and could only just manage a low-grade Bachelor of Commerce degree in Karachi. This was not adequate. Like every other recent graduate in Amir's social circle, he also wanted to go abroad for further education, and he wanted to become a chartered accountant. CAs were highly respected and remunerated careers in Pakistan. Parents were proud to announce that their son or daughter was a chartered accountant. Children from upper-class families preferred to go to the UK to earn their qualifications.

Unfortunately, because of his low grades for his Bachelors, Amir was not accepted at any of the more prominent institutions in the UK. Also, there were some financial constraints. Majid Ali had lost some money playing the stock market and was having some financial difficulties. He told Amir that he would be able to bear the airfare, a reasonable tuition fee for the first year, and a few months' living expenses only. Amir would have to fend for himself after that. After considerable efforts, Amir obtained admission to Sunderland Polytechnic for the foundation course in Accountancy, a programme necessary for foreign graduates to register as CA trainees in the UK.

Amir's departure to the UK was given the widest possible publicity in Karachi's social circles by his parents. He was invited by his parents' friends to several farewell parties; a few hosts even hinted that upon returning to Pakistan, Amir would have a guaranteed job and a beautiful girl waiting to marry him. In Pakistan, parents did not miss any opportunity to find a suitable match for their daughters.

Amir's stay in the UK was another story. Despite his best efforts, he failed the foundation exams. He had no money, and none was coming from Pakistan. For a few months, he even took a part-time job at McDonald's in Sunderland, but that was not sufficient to cover his expenses.

At Sunderland Polytechnic, Amir befriended Shariful, a UK citizen of Bangladeshi stock, who offered to help Amir if he went to London. With no money and little prospect of furthering his education in Sunderland, Amir took up the offer. True to his word, the Bangladeshi friend helped Amir find a bed for a few nights only in a heavily crowded and cockroach-infested, one-bedroom apartment in Brick Lane. Amir's friend also assisted him in finding work as a shop assistant selling saris in the Lane.

Throughout this time, Amir's parents were proudly telling everybody they knew Amir was pursuing further education in the UK, but Amir was desperate. During his weekly calls home, he used to cry and beg his parents to let him return. The answer was always the same: 'Try a little more.' This was a matter of family honour. Raana and Majid Ali would be shamed if their son returned without a foreign degree.

During this period, Amir went to the London School of Economics to hear a lecture by Benazir Bhutto of Pakistan on Pakistan's political situation. At LSE, among other Pakistanis, he met Danial Rafi. Danny was an English chartered accountant who worked as an audit manager for Tolbert and Gibbs, a major accounting firm that also happened to be the auditors of G&P Bank in the UK.

Amir and Danny immediately became friends. Having suffered similar difficulties in his early days in the UK, Danny empathised with Amir and adopted him as a sort of younger brother. He asked Amir to move in with him in his Milton Keynes apartment. Amir gratefully accepted the offer. Using his contacts at G&P Bank, Danny arranged an interview for Amir at the bank's London headquarters at Knightsbridge.

Amir mentioned this happy development to his mother during one of their weekly calls. Raana was the bridge partner and friend of Shakila, the former personal assistant and current wife of G&P Bank's chairman, Sheikh Tayeb. Sheikh Tayeb had married his pretty and efficient secretary, who was thirty years his junior. Before falling for Shakila, Sheikh Tayeb's only passion in life was G&P Bank; now, he shared his love between Shakila and the bank, and rarely did anything without consulting her. Shakila was Sheikh Tayeb's closest behind-the-scenes adviser, and she was involved in every major decision at the bank. Raana assured Amir that his difficulties would be over and there would be a job waiting for him at G&P Bank in London.

As it turned out, a red carpet was rolled out for Amir when he arrived for his interview at G&P Bank. The head of human resources saw him immediately and offered him a job as a trainee officer in the corporate banking division.

***

In the UK-Asian circles, G&P Bank was viewed with respect and pride. The bank was popular among Asian businessmen in the UK. It was their bank. G&P Bank stood shoulder-to-shoulder with the more established banking giants of the world. It had an extensive network of branches around the world and even had a correspondent relationship with a US bank. G&P Bank was proud to provide highly efficient personal services and support small businessmen by extending facilities at much lower rates than the high street banks. It was a small man's bank with a conscious. Every branch manager personally knew and dealt with the bank's clients in his area. G&P was more than a bank; it was a community service centre for the Asian business community wherever it operated.

Amir was proud to be a part of G&P Bank. He eagerly adopted the culture of '*Your Banker is Your Friend*' and developed a flair for relationships with his clients.

After staying in the job for a while, Amir realised he had to obtain some sort of qualification to advance his position. He scoured newspapers and finally found a university offering MBA degrees based on experience – for a hefty fee. Amir immediately applied and now holds an MBA from the University of Cornfields. This was good news for his family. Raana and Majid immediately announced that their son was now an MBA and a very senior officer at G&P Bank and that he would return to Pakistan soon. Raana spoke to her friend, Shakila, and G&P Bank London was instructed to transfer Amir to the Karachi Office after promoting him to assistant vice president.

Amir returned to Pakistan as a handsome man, internationally qualified, and an AVP at G&P Bank. He was the target of every young girl and her parents hunting for a husband. There was nothing more in life he could ask for. During all this, Amir's friendship with Danny grew stronger. After Amir's return to Pakistan, Danny visited many times and stayed with Amir's family. Danny and Seemi formed a close friendship and spent time together. Raana and Majid hoped Seemi would marry Danny.

Amir smiled at the thought. Seemi and Danny! He thought they would make a wonderful couple.

Amir's reverie was broken by the ringing of the bell.

'There is somebody to see you, Sahib.' It was Amir's ancient watchman, Shahbaba. Due to frequent robberies and hold-ups, security guards and watchmen were a necessity in Karachi.

'I'm coming.' Amir rushed to the door and was surprised to find Shakadir Khan himself standing there with a suitcase.

'Oh, it's you, Sir. I thought you might send somebody else. Please come in,' Amir said, taking the suitcase from Shakadir's hands. It was heavy.

'I shan't stay. I have to go to one of those weddings. Because of the importance of the contents, I thought I should personally give the suitcase and key to you,' Shakadir handed over the suitcase and its key to Amir.

'Don't worry, Sir. I will deliver the suitcase and key to Masood Sahib in Geneva,' Amir replied.

'Well, good luck, and have a safe trip. By the way, if anybody bothers you at Karachi airport or while you are in transit, call this number and we will sort out the problem.' He gave Amir a small piece of paper on which there was a telephone number with the key.

'Thank you, but why would anybody bother me? Don't worry, Sir, I know how to handle people at the airport and such places,' Amir replied, but he took it anyway.

Amir lugged the suitcase inside. '*God, this is heavy*', he thought to himself as he wondered what it contained. He checked his watch again. It was past midnight. Seemi had insisted that she would drop him off at the airport, and she should be over any time now to pick him up. Amir had just enough time for another drink.

As he poured the drink, he heard his garage door open, and Seemi came in with his parents.

'What a wonderful couple!' Raana was saying as she walked through the door.

'Yes, they looked gorgeous. Our Seemi would also look marvellous in a wedding dress,' Majid Ali replied.

'Oh, Mama, Papa, stop it.' Seemi showed her annoyance at this continuous reminder for her to get married.

'You ready, Amir? Come on, you will be late, otherwise.' Seemi diverted the attention from the topic of her marriage to Amir.

'I'm ready. Let's go.'

'You have packed a lot of woollies, I hope? It will be cold in Switzerland,' Raana reminded him.

'I have packed a coat and some warm clothes. I'll buy some if I need,' Amir replied.

'Okay, *Beta*, have a safe trip and look after yourself. This is a very good opportunity for you. Good luck.' Majid Ali gave his parting advice to Amir.

'What is in this heavy suitcase?' Seemi was surprised as she lifted it from the floor, and enquired. 'This isn't yours, is it?'

'No. It's from the bank. Some papers they want me to take to Geneva.'

'I forgot you are now a very senior officer of the bank. They trust you with the family silver.' If only Seemi knew the truth of what she had said.

With that, Amir's bags were loaded into the car, and Seemi and Amir left for the airport. The traffic was thin that late at night, and it took only twenty minutes for them to reach the airport.

'Do you want me to wait for you?' Seemi enquired while she parked the car. A porter came running to take Amir's bags.

'No. You go ahead. It's already late. I'll call you from Geneva.'

'Calls will not be sufficient. You will have to bring a good gift for me. Maybe a Cartier.' Seemi did not want to miss out on an opportunity to get an expensive gift from her brother.

'A gift, sure. A Cartier, I'm not so sure.' Amir laughed and waved Seemi off.

Chapter 2

Jinnah International Airport, Karachi

With the porter in tow, Amir entered the airport's departure terminal. Karachi airport had a customs checkpoint before the airline check-in counters. A young customs preventive officer, Sajjad, eyed Amir as he strolled through the doors. *'A rich kid with a beautiful girlfriend',* Sajjad mistakenly thought when he saw Seemi waving goodbye to Amir. Although customs officers normally wave passengers through, Sajjad decided to check Amir, just to get out of boredom and to have some fun.

'Can I see your passport and ticket, Sir?' Sajjad confronted Amir.

'What for?' Amir asked, clearly annoyed. 'I am a first-class passenger to Geneva on Swiss Air, and I have all the correct papers.'

'I am sure, Sir, but it is my duty to check,' Sajjad insisted.

'Here they are. If that's what you're looking for, I'm not an illegal immigrant.' Amir practically pushed the documents under the customs officer's nose.

'Thank you, Sir.' Sajjad was having fun. 'Could you open this suitcase for me, please?' Sajjad pointed at the bank's suitcase.

'Look, you are harassing me. These are my bank's papers. I work for G&P Bank.'

'Sir, I am not harassing you. I am only doing my job. I need to see this suitcase.' Sajjad persevered.

'Oh, okay. Look, there is nothing here that might interest you,' Amir said, undoing the lock of the suitcase.

But Amir was completely wrong. Both he and Sajjad were stunned when the suitcase's top flipped open. The case was full of US dollar bills and documents that looked like security papers. There were also a couple of heavy pouches.

Sajjad could not believe his luck. He immediately called Jamal, the head of airport customs. 'Sir, please come over here. Quick, Sir.'

Everybody in the departure terminal knew something very important had been discovered. Other customs officers started looking in Amir's direction, and a couple of other senior officials also walked to where the examination was being conducted.

After looking at the contents of the suitcase, Jamal instructed Sajjad to take Amir and the suitcase to the Customs Enquiries Room. He also asked two senior officials to go with Sajjad, so there were witnesses to what was being discovered.

Amir protested. 'This suitcase was given to me by a very senior officer of our bank. I must catch Swissair to Geneva. I don't have time for this harassment. The bank will be very angry and will deal with you appropriately if you do not let me go.'

'You do not realise that you are in a lot of trouble, young man. Please go with the officers; otherwise, we will have to handcuff you and drag you to the interrogation room. Forget about travelling by Swiss Air or any other airline tonight,' Jamal responded.

'I need to make a telephone call.' Amir insisted.

'Not now. Let us see what we have here first.' Jamal rejected Amir's request.

The group proceeded to the Customs Enquiries Room. It was a bare room with one desk and four chairs in a corner of the departure terminal. Three of the chairs were placed behind the desk, and another, the one for the accused, was placed on the opposite side of the desk.

'Well, let us see what we have here.' Jamal opened the suitcase. He asked the two senior customs officers to carefully count the cash and prepare a list of the bills. He also asked them to look at the security papers. These appeared to be bearer bonds in various European currencies. Then, he spread a clean cloth on the desk and carefully emptied the contents of the two pouches. The room suddenly glimmered with light as hundreds of beautiful, sparkling diamonds were spread on the tablecloth.

'Gentlemen,' Jamal spoke to the customs team, 'this is beyond our normal enquiries and not possible to handle here. Let us seal everything and transfer the contents under an armed guard to the Customs House. We will all, including the gentleman here, go there with the suitcase and let the people more senior to us handle this. I will phone and let the head of Karachi customs know that we are on our way to the Customs House, and he should be there with an appropriate team.'

Amir was in tears. 'Please let me make one telephone call before we leave from here. Please. I need to tell my people that I might miss the flight.' He realised he was facing a disaster.

'Okay. I will let you make the call, but be very brief and do not mention any details of what is happening here. Just say that you have missed the flight.' Jamal tried to be kind to the young man who appeared to be nothing more than a courier or mule – the term used in customs language.

Amir quickly called the number Shakadir Khan had given him. Despite the late hour, his call was answered on the first ring.

'Hello.' A gruff voice responded.

'Sir, my name is Amir Ramli; I work for G&P Bank. I have been given this number by Mr. Shakadir Khan.'

'Just tell me where you are and who is with you,' the voice said.

'I am at Karachi airport with customs people. The senior officer's name is Jamal,' Amir replied.

'Okay, don't panic. We will sort things out.' And the telephone went dead.

In less than five minutes, and while the customs officers were still putting the contents back into the suitcase, Jamal's wireless phone started ringing.

Jamal switched the phone to receiving mode. 'Yes?' Upon hearing the caller's voice, he immediately stood at attention. Beads of perspiration started appearing on his forehead. 'Yes, Sir. As you say, Sir.'

The caller spoke some more, and when he was able to respond, Jamal said, 'Sir, we knew nothing about this. Nobody alerted us. I am very sorry, Sir. We should be able to put him on the Swiss Air flight. I will take personal responsibility to make that happen, Sir.' There was more talking from the party on the other end of the call. Jamal paled. 'Again, I am very sorry, Sir. Don't worry; nobody will know anything about this, Sir.'

After switching off his phone, Jamal wiped his face and forehead with a handkerchief. He was shaking like a leaf as he said to his team, 'Gentlemen, we have to put this gentleman on his flight without any further delay or formalities. These are our instructions. Let us all help in repacking everything.'

He then turned to Amir. 'Sorry for the confusion, Sir. We'll check you in for the flight. It should board soon, but we will manage.' Then he turned to Sajjad and asked him to rush to the Swiss Air counter and tell them a VIP passenger was still to check in and to get everything organised.

Amir was perplexed. He thought it was all a dream. He never believed that somebody could be so powerful and could do such things, and then he realised he was dealing with people in a different league.

Amir was now treated like royalty by the people at the airport. He was whisked aboard the plane, and with typical Swiss efficiency, the flight left Karachi for Geneva on time.

Chapter 3

Aboard Swiss Air Flight from Karachi to Geneva

Although it was a night flight, Amir could not sleep, nor could he eat or drink anything offered to him by the air hostess. He kept thinking of the nightmare and near disaster he had just faced. What was his role in all this? Was he simply a mule used to carry the money out of Pakistan? Or were they trying to remove him from his Karachi desk at the same time because he was looking into the affairs of TIG? That group stinks, and the bank was exposed to a loss of several hundred million dollars, at the least. Or were they killing two birds with one stone, sending Amir off to Geneva with the suitcase, and taking TIG away from him at the same time?

Amir was angry. He knew that his job at the bank was over. He could not work with such people, but he must take revenge for their using him. He was insulted by the bank. He must deal with this. He also started to worry about the Swiss. He was afraid he would be caught again by Swiss customs and nobody would be there to help him. He might be arrested and put in prison for years. The more he thought of the whole situation, the angrier he became and the sicker he felt from worry.

Life! What a joke it was. He had considered himself the luckiest person on the planet only a few hours earlier. Now, perhaps, he was the unluckiest person on earth. He had to tell somebody about this. Danny! He had to tell Danny about this. At least writing to Danny would take his mind off the worry.

Amir took a pad from his briefcase and wrote a detailed letter. In it, he described the entire episode, starting with when he was called in by Azhar Alam and sent on a quickly arranged trip to Geneva, including his involvement with and doubts about TIG, and ending with the ordeal at Karachi airport.

He concluded:

Danny, I am sorry to burden you with this, but I do not know what is going to happen to me. Although I am on the flight to

Geneva, I am not sure if I will remain free after I disembark from the aircraft. I am very worried.

I do not know whose money it is or where it is going. I do know that some very powerful people are involved. I may even be killed if the suitcase is not delivered safely to G&P Bank in Geneva.

I also believe that there is something seriously wrong at the bank, and I am afraid that I am in a deep mess.

I am furious with the bank for this insult, which may ruin my life and my family's reputation. I will get even, even if it is the last thing I do – but I must get out of this mess first.

Just so that you get the complete picture, I will ask Samira to send you a copy of the memo I wrote on TIG. I know that this is highly unethical and dangerous, but the situation is beyond these considerations. I am sure that Samira will oblige.

My friend, you are the only one I could turn to for help in this situation. Please do not disappoint me.

I hope to be in London before the New Year if I can get out of Geneva safely. I will let you know my exact plans. We will talk more about this, and you can guide me. As usual, I will take advantage of your kindness.

I look forward to seeing you in London.

With kindest regards,

Amir

Still, in the mood for writing letters, Amir wrote to Samira:

Samira,

I am on a flight to Geneva. I do not know if I should thank you for arranging everything so efficiently or curse my luck.

I had an amazing and nerve-wracking experience at Karachi airport, but everything was sorted out in the end and I was able to fly.

I have a request to make. You know my friend Danny in London. I need to send him the memo I wrote on TIG; he needs it to do some work for me. It is in the latest correspondence file. Please send a copy of this memo to him by courier. You know his address; he works for Tolbert and Gibbs in London. Please don't let anybody know of this. I am requesting it as a personal favour.

I am sorry to make such a request, but I know you will do it for me.

Take care.

Amir

Amir thought he should also let Seemi know of his difficulties. He wanted her to know that he may be stuck for a while if there was trouble at Geneva Airport. He drafted a letter to Seemi:

Little Sister,

Thank you for dropping me off at the airport. I am writing this from the plane on the flight to Geneva. Although I reached the airport well in time, I almost missed the flight because a customs officer took an interest in me.

I hope I will not face difficulties in Geneva. The Swiss are not known to be flexible if they believe their laws have been violated. I might find myself in that position, although through no fault of mine. If you do not hear from me, then assume that I am in the hands of the Swiss and facing legal difficulties. I will tell you more about it when I see you, which I hope will be soon.

I love you, little sister.

Amir

Amir called the air hostess and requested some envelopes. He also enquired whether she would post the letters for him. The air hostess said that she would be happy to mail the letters for him, so he put all three letters in separate envelopes, addressed each one carefully, and handed them over to her. She promised she would post them as soon as they arrived in Geneva.

Having unburdened himself, Amir felt completely drained and tired. He stretched out in the wide, first-class seat and was soon asleep. He was still fast asleep when he felt himself being shaken gently. He dreamt of Samira, and in his half-sleep state, he believed Samira was trying to wake him up. Actually, it was the air hostess, she was rousing him as they were about to land in Geneva and he must fasten his seatbelt.

Chapter 4

Geneva

Swiss Air flight 156 from Karachi to Istanbul landed without incident at Geneva International Airport. Shortly after the air bridge was connected and the first-class passengers were invited to disembark, Amir forced himself up from his seat, collected his hand baggage, and lumbered towards the exit. He knew that Geneva International Airport was on the border between France and Switzerland, and there were two separate exits: one for France and one for Switzerland. It seemed to Amir that there was no energy in him to move, but he had no choice. So, with the other passengers, he dragged himself toward the gate with the Swiss flag that said *Arrivals* in both French and English.

Passport Control was relatively quiet at the time of the day they arrived. Amir was third in the queue.

'Good morning,' he said, handing over his passport to the immigration officer.

'Good morning,' the polite, efficient Swiss immigration officer replied. 'Are you here on business or holiday?' The usual questions had to be asked.

'Business. I work for G&P Bank. We have a large office at Bel-Air,' Amir replied.

'And how long are you going to stay?'

'One week at the most. I will be off to London for New Year's.'

'Have a pleasant stay in Switzerland.' The immigration officer stamped and returned Amir's passport.

Amir knew he would not be able to go through the customs examination. He had no choice but to take his chances and go through the green channel, claiming that he had nothing to declare.

The ten minutes wait at the baggage carousel was the longest ten minutes in Amir's life. He recited several verses of the Holy Quran and prayed to Allah to get him out of this safely. Finally, the bags arrived. Amir loaded them on a trolley and walked towards the green channel. Every step was a trial.

He was halfway into the green channel zone when a uniformed officer stepped in and stopped Amir. 'Can I see your passport, please?'

Amir thought he would have a heart attack. He froze, but then managed to pull his passport from his pocket and hand it over to the officer.

'Where are you coming from today?' The officer enquired.

'Karachi, Pakistan.'

'What is your business in Switzerland?' The officer asked while thumbing through Amir's passport.

'I am an assistant vice president at the G&P Bank. We have an office at Bel-Air in Geneva. I'm here for a week on business.' Amir tried hard to keep his voice steady.

'Please open this bag.' The officer pointed at the handbag Amir had carried with him on the plane.

Amir felt as if he would faint, as if this were the end. He imagined the newspaper headlines in Karachi: Pakistani Banker Arrested at Geneva Airport for Carrying Millions of Dollars in Cash and Securities and Young Banker Charged by Swiss authorities for smuggling. The shame for his family would be unbearable.

Amir put his handbag on the examination table. The officer went through the contents carefully. These were Amir's items and nothing important. The officer closed the bag and pointed at the other two suitcases.

'What is in those?'

'One contains my personal stuff and the other some papers for the bank.' Amir tried very hard to sound casual. He was sure his voice was cracking. The officer thought for a second, then handed back the passport and said, 'Okay, pass.'

Amir was overcome with relief. He steeled himself to walk slowly, fearing that he might break into a run and be called back. Soon he was outside the airport in the crisp, cool air of Geneva.

'Thank you, Allah.' Amir looked skyward and felt like prostrating in gratitude to Allah.

A very smart-looking Pakistani in a cashmere overcoat and charcoal grey suit was waiting outside the terminal. 'Amir?' He enquired, coming toward Amir.

'Yes?' Amir responded, still in shock.

'Masood.' He offered his hand. Amir felt a wave of nausea and hatred, but he took Masood's hand. 'My car is just over there, so let's walk.' They walked to Masood's Mercedes S 500 and loaded the bags into the boot. 'You must be tired. You are booked at the Caravel, not far from the office. Let's go there first, and then we will talk about how you want to spend the rest of the day.'

Masood sat on the driver's seat in the car, and once they were both in the car, he turned to Amir and said, 'I am sorry that you had a little trouble at Karachi airport. That young customs officer was stupid. We have made arrangements for him to be transferred out to the Pakistan-Afghanistan border where he will suffer for the rest of his life, dealing with the petty smugglers and bandits.'

'He was only doing his duty.' Amir did not see the logic of punishing the young customs officer.

'If he does not know whom not to stop, then he should not be at the airport,' Masood replied. 'Anyway, I hope you didn't have any other difficulty on the flight or in Geneva.

'No problems on the flight. Customs at Geneva checked one of my bags. I almost had a heart attack.'

'They normally go through the hand baggage for passengers coming from Pakistan. They are looking for drugs. The Swiss rarely bother with the checked-in luggage. This was your first time, so you are rattled. You will get used to dealing with these situations with a little more experience,' Masood explained.

'You mean that I have to do this again?' Amir could not believe what he was hearing.

'Everybody senior in the bank has to do this. This is your baptism by fire. You are now part of the inner circle. You are one of us. Congratulations! Also, there is a generous bonus for performing this delicate task.'

Amir was speechless.

The hotel was not far. When they arrived, Masood accompanied Amir to the reception desk for check-in.

'G&P Bank has a junior suite booked for Mr. Amir Ramli for as long as he stays in Geneva,' he said to the receptionist.

'Yes, of course, Sir. We have all the papers ready. Mr. Ramli, if you'll just sign here and let us make a copy of your passport.'

Amir was checked into the hotel in no time. His personal baggage was taken out of the car, but Masood asked the porter to leave the bank's suitcase.

'Well, you rest now, Amir. It is now 10.30, which means 2.30 in Karachi. With the experience you have had on the flight, you must be very tired. You may want to take a light lunch in your room. The room service at this hotel is very good. I will leave you now to rest. If okay with you, I will pick you up at 7 this evening for dinner. Geneva is not Paris or London, but we will see what we can do.'

'I'll be ready at 7. A plain dinner will be fine. I'm a little tired, so don't worry about the entertainment,' Amir said, and he went to his room.

Once there, he called Seemi. She was happy to learn that he had a good flight and had reached Geneva safely. Amir did not mention his ordeal and asked her to destroy the letter he had written on the airplane. He promised to explain everything upon his return. Seemi was intrigued but did not insist. She again reminded Amir not to forget her gift.

After talking to his sister, Amir laid down, but he could not get his thoughts away from his recent experience. He wondered about the organisation he was working for. He felt there was something seriously wrong at the bank.

He was angry that he had been used. And, as if that wasn't enough, it was expected that he would repeat these trips. Amir wondered if the bank's management was aware of the risks people like Amir were exposed to. Sure, the bank had powerful contacts, but these could not guarantee safe passage in every country of the world. Suppose he had been caught by the Swiss. Would the bank have been able to get him out? And what would have happened to his family? He could not forget the episode at Karachi airport and the trauma of going through customs at Geneva.

The more he thought about the events of the last twenty-four hours, the angrier he became. Amir again swore that he would get even for the insult. He would dedicate all of his energy to learning about the bank's activities so he could expose them. For this, he would have to play the long game. He would try to find out as much as possible about the bank's not-so-legal operations in Geneva.

With his decision made, Amir relaxed. He got up, shaved and showered, put on fresh clothes, and strolled out for a walk. It was a bright, crisp, early afternoon. He walked towards Lake Geneva via the Rue du Mont-Blanc. He wanted to look at the famous Jet d'Eau. On the way, he looked into the souvenir shops, most of which were selling Swiss wall clocks in various designs. There were cuckoo clocks of every description. They looked lovely.

At the lake, he picked up a cheese sandwich from a stall, sat down on a bench, and ate it while admiring the famous fountain. He walked back to the hotel, feeling refreshed.

Back at the hotel, Amir changed into pyjamas and lay down, trying to sleep. He felt restless and could not fall asleep. To kill time, he switched on the news on CNN. The world continued to be in turmoil. There was trouble everywhere.

Just before 7, Amir donned his best Armani blazer, paired with his Brooks Brothers shirt and Armani trousers. At exactly 7 p.m., he stepped out of the elevator into the lobby. Masood was already there with two beautiful ladies. He walked toward Amir, full of warmth and smiling.

'Amir, I hope you were able to rest. I know you are tired from the flight and jet-lagged, but we could not abandon you on your first night as our guest in Geneva. I want you to meet Sylvie and Maria. They work in our guest relations department and are happy to look after our VIP guests. Sylvie, Maria, meet my friend Amir Ramli, the newest rising star at G&P Bank.'

Both Sylvie and Maria advanced toward Amir as if he were an old friend.

Sylvie said, 'Hi,' as she offered her hand.

'Hi.' Amir took Sylvie's hand and was surprised at her firm grip.

Maria walked straight to Amir and hugged him, murmuring, 'Darling, you are so handsome.' She offered her cheek for a kiss, to which Amir felt compelled to oblige. Maria also seemed to exert a little too much pressure when hugging him, and his nostrils filled with the scent of her perfume.

With introductions over, Masood said, 'We have reserved a table for the evening at Chez Geraldine. Swiss beef is the best. They really look after their cattle here. At Chez Geraldine, you will get the best beef in the world. I tell you this from the experience of a well-travelled man!'

'Dinner at Chez Geraldine will be fine,' Amir replied.

The group walked to Masood's car. Masood held the front passenger-side door open for Sylvie. Amir and Maria sat in the back. It was a bitterly cold but clear evening. In the car, Maria gently took Amir's hand and started caressing it. Amir was embarrassed. He did not want to appear rude, but he was not enjoying it. Maria noted Amir's discomfort and assumed that since he came out of Pakistan, he was shy. She did not mind shy people. It was her job to make people comfortable.

Chez Geraldine was only a couple of kilometres from the hotel. Masood handed over his car to the valet, and the group entered the restaurant. The maître d' saw them and came running over.

'Welcome, Sir. Your table is ready.'

Amir guessed that Masood and G&P Bank must be regular and lavish clients at Chez Geraldine. They were seated at a discreet corner table to offer privacy.

'I like Chez Geraldine because, besides serving the best meat in town, they know how to look after their clients,' Masood said, sitting down. 'So, what did you do this afternoon? Slept off and got ready for a long night out, I presume?'

'I walked up to the lake and had a sandwich there. The walk was very refreshing. Back at the hotel, I lay for a while but could not sleep, so I watched some television.' Amir responded.

'You know Geneva well, do you?' Masood asked.

'No. This is my first time here. I had heard a lot about Lake Geneva and the Jet d'Eau. I asked the concierge for directions and found out that it was quite near the hotel, so I ventured out for a walk. It was magnificent.'

'Wasn't it a bit too cold for a walk?'

'It was cold but clear and crisp. I enjoyed it. And Jet d'Eau is amazing,' Amir explained.

'Maria could show you a bit of Geneva tomorrow. This is a very international and modern city. It has its own history of several centuries. Julius Caesar talked about Geneva in one of his chronicles,' Masood said and looked enquiringly at Maria. 'I hope you have time, Maria.'

'But, of course. I would love to accompany Amir and show him our beautiful city,' Maria replied.

'You will enjoy Switzerland,' Masood said. 'It's a unique country. I love it. Everything works here. Nothing ever goes wrong. Did you know that Switzerland does not have a regular army but relies on its citizens to volunteer for emergency duties as and when required? Every Swiss gets Army training and is issued full Army paraphernalia, including an assault rifle, which is supposed to be kept ready in case there is an emergency need, but rarely are these weapons used illegally. The Swiss are the most law-abiding people in the world.

'They go home early, straight from work, and are a living example of the wisdom of "early to bed and early to rise." You are expected to take every care not to disturb your neighbours at night.

'There are four officially recognised national groups and languages here. There is complete harmony between these groups. They never fight with each other.

'The Swiss are very serious people. They do not like to express emotions. Everything is to be done professionally. If you are a private banking client of a bank, then you must enjoy total confidentiality and personal service. Of course, the level of service depends on the balance in your account. Small customers are not welcome here. The Swiss have the best lawyers in the world. They know their Swiss and international laws. And again, the confidentiality is guaranteed.

'For generations, the Swiss have maintained neutrality. They do not want to be a party to any conflict in the world. They are not concerned about your domestic laws or regulations. They have their own laws and they stick to them. A Swiss banker is not concerned with the source of money or whether or not transactions have any substance. As long as you do not violate Swiss law and pay your taxes in Switzerland – and there are heavy taxes, mind you – you are not bothered. This is an ideal place for the wealthy to keep their assets. Nobody will know about it or have access to it. The Swiss government would certainly not volunteer any information.' Masood was in an expansive mood.

'But aren't there some laws now that require banks to disclose information to the government and even freeze the assets of a suspect depositor?' Amir asked.

'Yes, this is a recent phenomenon, but it is applied only in very sensitive and publicised cases. The Swiss banks are now required to disclose the information when asked by the Swiss courts, who would only do so if there was clear evidence that the funds deposited in Switzerland were acquired through illegal means. This was applied for the first time in the case of certain African former heads of state. Nigeria was the first one, I believe, where the request for repatriation of ill-gotten wealth by one of their former presidents was submitted to the Swiss government.' Masood explained.

'And where does G&P Bank stand on this?' Amir was being provocative.

'Exactly where everybody else does.' Masood replied. 'Enough of this banking and financial talk. We are boring the ladies. Let's leave the serious talk for the office and order our drinks. They have one of the best-stocked wine cellars in Switzerland; it could satisfy the most discriminating connoisseur of wine.'

'I enjoy my glass but am no connoisseur. In Pakistan, we enjoy scotch. I like my Black Label, but I will take whatever you select,' Amir replied.

'And Sylvie, Maria, what do you prefer?' Masood asked as he referred to the wine list.

'You chose, Masood. You are the expert.' Sylvie said.

Masood consulted the wine list and ordered a bottle of very expensive French wine. The waiter brought the bottle to the table for Masood to inspect. Following Masood's okay, he uncorked the bottle with great ceremony and poured a sip for Masood to test. Masood rolled the wine around on his tongue and approved. Amir always wondered at this rolling of the wine in mouth ceremony and believed that this was a trick by the restaurant staff to increase the price of the wine and the tip.

The wine was served in crystal goblets. Masood raised his glass and toasted the health and prosperity of everybody and extended a warm welcome to Amir to the G&P Bank's Executive Club. Everybody looked at their menus while they enjoyed the wine.

'I would like the French onion soup, and for the main course, the Chateaubriand is the best here, but it is served for two people. You will share it with me, Amir, yes?' Maria asked.

Amir believed he had to agree, so he jovially said, 'You are the expert, Maria. If the Chateaubriand is good here, then the Chateaubriand is what I am going to have. And since I am sharing the main course with you, I will also have the French onion soup as a starter.'

The wine was out of this world, and the food was delicious. Amir had to acknowledge that Masood knew a thing or two about dining in Geneva. The ladies, as it turned out, had been with the bank for a couple of years each. Their primary duty was to make the bank's VIP visitors from overseas 'comfortable'. Over dinner, talk invariably turned to Pakistan and its politics. Masood was very pro-Zia-ul-Haq, the Military Dictator of Pakistan. Masood was proud that Zia, in Masood's opinion, had provided strong leadership to Pakistan.

Masood was still single. He moved in the high society circle of expatriate bankers and businessmen living in Geneva, and he was proud that, under his leadership, G&P Bank's Geneva operations were the most profitable in the entire bank. His only hero in life was

Sheikh Tayeb. According to Masood, Sheikh Tayeb was a saint sent from heaven to help the economically oppressed small men in developing countries – a true visionary who understood God's command regarding the use of money.

Amir was getting a little tired of the diatribe and was also worried about the effects of this Pakistan-cum-G&P Bank propaganda on the two ladies, but Sylvie and Maria appeared to be used to it and even took part in some of the talks. Amir thought they must get a lot of visitors from Pakistan.

Finally, even Masood tired of his monologue, declared that he was ready to go. 'I must get to bed. You are still young, so you can have some fun. I'm sure Maria would be more than pleased to enjoy the rest of the evening with you.' He said this without any embarrassment.

'I am also very tired from my flight. I'll also pack up.' Amir replied.

'Surely we could go out for a little while.' Maria sounded disappointed.

'I would love to, Maria, but my entire body is aching. I hope you will excuse me tonight.' Amir had had enough for one evening.

Reluctantly, the party broke up. The ladies were disappointed, as they were looking forward to a night out. Masood drove Amir back to the hotel.

With a twinkle in his eyes, he asked, 'Amir, are you sure you would not like to have a nightcap with Maria? She is looking forward to your company.'

'I am very tired, Masood. Sorry, Maria.' Amir replied.

'I'll send a car to pick you up at 8.30 tomorrow morning.' Masood said.

'I'll be in the lobby then. Good night, everybody.'

The ladies again followed the same pattern of saying good night. Sylvie shook Amir's hand, and Maria offered her cheek for a goodnight kiss.

Back in his room, Amir sighed with relief. He had enjoyed the meal but was not comfortable with the overtures of Maria and Masood's perception that Amir wanted to sleep with her.

Amir thought he should give Danny a call to let him know he was safe in Geneva and would descend upon him shortly. He dialled his friend's home number. Fortunately, Danny was home.

'Hey, Danny, did I wake you?' Amir asked when Danny answered after several rings.

'Hi, Amir. What a pleasant surprise. No, I was lying down but not asleep. What are you doing up at this hour? It must be quite late in Karachi.'

'I'm in Geneva. Came here this morning for some work at the bank.'

'Great! It looks like you are moving up in the bank,' Danny joked. 'You must be quite an important person for the bank to send you to Geneva.'

'It's a long story. I'm not sure if the bank has sent me here in recognition of my position or for diverting me from what I was doing in Karachi. Also, I have been used as a mule to carry some stuff that the bank wanted safely delivered to Geneva. I sent you a letter from the airplane. Please read it, but don't do anything 'til I see you in London. We have to talk.'

'Sounds mysterious. Sure. When are you coming to London?'

'Hopefully in the next couple of days. I should be there for Christmas.'

'We, Pakistanis are great bigots. We believe that Christianity is a superseded religion polluted over the centuries and has no relevance to the real religion as propagated by Jesus Christ or Muhammad (peace be upon them), yet we still don't want to miss out on celebrating in their festivities.' Danny teased Amir.

'Stop it. This is a never-ending debate. You know me. I am with everybody, particularly for the festivities.' Amir did not want to prolong this discussion about the conflicts in Pakistani society.

'You had a good flight to Geneva, I hope.' Danny enquired.

'Flight was very comfortable. There were other events which have shaken me a little. I'll talk to you in London.'

After a little more bantering and enquiring about each other's social life, Amir hung up.

Chapter 5

G&P Bank's offices, Geneva

Amir had a fitful night. He dreamt of being pushed and abused by tough-looking uniformed men who locked him up in a dark cell. He woke up in a sweat and was unable to sleep afterwards. He kept turning and twisting. He kept checking his watch and finally got out of bed around 6 in the morning. He shaved, showered, and took an early breakfast at the restaurant. He even had time to read the *International Herald Tribune* before it was time to go.

At 8.30 a.m. sharp, a smartly dressed gentleman approached him and asked if he was Mr. Amir Ramli.

'Yes,' Amir replied.

'I have the car to take you to G&P Bank,' the visitor advised. Amir was impressed. A gleaming new BMW 705 had been sent for him.

The bank was close to the hotel. Despite the morning traffic, Amir arrived there within 15 minutes. The bank occupied the entire building, with Masood taking up the entire fifth floor. Amir was dazed by the size and décor of Masood's office. It was tastefully furnished with antiques; paintings by some famous artists adorned the walls, and the floor was covered with Persian rugs.

Masood stood from his desk and came out to receive Amir. 'Come in. Welcome to the world of real banking.' Three young girls were working outside his office. 'Meet my assistants, Julia, Sabeen, and Natasha.' Masood introduced Amir. 'And ladies, this is Amir, our newest rising star in the bank.' The girls got up and shook hands with Amir.

'Coffee?' Masood asked.

'Coffee would be fine.' Amir replied.

Immediately, one of the girls went to the coffee machine in the corner.

'So, Amir, you had a good night's rest? Or did you surrender to the temptations of Geneva?' Masood enquired.

'I made a telephone call and then went straight to bed. I was exhausted, but I could not sleep.' Amir was truthful.

'You missed a good opportunity last night. I could see that Maria was looking forward to being with you. Well, there will be other opportunities. You might go out with Maria today to see a bit of Geneva. She also knows some good spots for shopping. I had a lovely night with Sylvie, and hardly slept a wink. That girl is a tornado, you know.' Masood was proud to share his experience.

'These things are not for me, I suppose. I have not yet adopted the Western lifestyle.' Amir wanted none of this nonsense.

'You guys in Pakistan are a very difficult lot. You lust after women, but when the opportunity arises, you chicken out. All sorts of excuses come out – religion, commitments, social barriers, and ethics. Live your life, man, while you can. That is my motto.' Amir let the sermon on the pleasures of spending nights with hostesses pass. 'Well, now to business,' Masood continued. 'We are in the middle of the closing. Some of our investments were very exposed, and we urgently needed to cover them, otherwise, there would have been hell to pay, as the regulators and auditors would have downgraded those investments and insisted on provisions. Do you know the suitcase you brought contained almost thirty million dollars' worth of stuff? Thank you for that. In the last two weeks, we have received almost five hundred million dollars from various sources in fresh deposits.'

'Who are these depositors? And if they had funds, why were their borrowings exposed?' Amir asked innocently.

'These depositors would like to remain anonymous. They are not connected with the exposed borrowers. The funds that came in will be credited against the exposed investments for the December closing. Hence, there will be no need to make any provisions.'

'The suitcase that I brought contained diamonds and bonds, in addition to hard cash. How are you able to convert these into legitimate money for crediting it into the debtors' balances?' Amir did not understand.

'For a banker, you are very naive. Do you know why Geneva is the world capital for private banking? I will tell you why. It is famous for private banking because banking is highly confidential here. The Swiss are famous for their banking secrecy. All sorts of facilities have been created here to keep wealth secret. Swiss banks have lockers full of jewellery, bullion, and other valuables worth billions if not trillions of dollars that have remained unopened since the last war. There are numbered accounts. The clients operate these banking facilities in complete secrecy. They deposit and withdraw the assets from these lockers and numbered accounts and do whatever they want to do with them without anybody watching or asking questions.

'It is very easy to dispose of jewellery and gem stones here. Jewellers are always   hungry for high-quality diamonds and heirloom pieces, which may become available at reasonable prices. We sell jewellery and other items, such as very expensive paintings, postage stamps, vintage cars, and antique watches, et cetera, to a select group of customers. Of course, everybody knows where these are coming from, and therefore the price is discounted appropriately.

'The system works well. The Swiss get a percentage of sales as tax. The jeweller is happy to get the jewels at lower than market value. The banker is happy as he makes a killing in handling fees for such transactions, and the client is happy to have been able to convert the asset into legal money.'

'Where do we come into this? You said that we had debtors who couldn't repay their balances. It looks as if the depositors and debtors are not the same.' Amir pressed on.

'We have financed certain parties and ventures that are facing temporary difficulties. Don't forget that a lot of our clients are new entrepreneurs. They don't get credit from the more established banks. The established banks, which are a part of a closed club of interested parties, like to keep their hegemony and push new entrants like ourselves down. Our chairman, Sheikh Tayeb, is a visionary. He realises that the only way developing countries can be truly independent is to be economically strong. We, as a bank, have a great responsibility to support and nurture the enterprises undertaken by the businessmen of these developing countries who have good projects and the ability to see them through.

'We look at the business plans and the capabilities of these businessmen carefully. Once satisfied with their plans and ability, we advance funds on favourable terms. Our financial charges are always lower than the so-called high street bankers because we do the financing for these projects as a duty.

'Now some of these projects, as I said earlier, suffer temporary difficulties and teething problems. We are fully convinced that they will pull through, but they require time. Time is not always your friend. We have the annual closing and will be examined by the regulators and external auditors. We must ensure that these accounts do not appear to be inactive or past due.

'To deal with this situation, we need deposits. We have clients who keep their funds with us and want to remain anonymous for their own personal reasons. They send the funds in cash or other convertible assets. We realise these assets and temporarily credit the exposed investment accounts. After 31 December we will credit these deposits to their correct owners' accounts.' Masood seemed exhausted from the lecture.

'Very interesting. But who keeps track of these deposits and ensures that they all get correctly sorted out in the end?' Amir persisted.

'There is a committee of five key executives in the bank who share this information and keep it absolutely confidential. I am a member of this committee.' Masood replied.

'Yes, of course, you would be. After all, you manage Geneva.' Amir was not beyond flattery.

'Well, now, let's leave these banking technicalities and deal with more important things.' Masood took an envelope from a drawer in his desk and gave it to Amir. 'Azhar Alam, we affectionately refer to him as AA, is very pleased with your support in transferring the funds to Geneva, and has instructed me to give you $20,000 as a Christmas bonus to show the management's appreciation.'

Amir took the envelope 'Thank you. You know I want to make a long-term career with the bank and understand the need to take part in special assignments. There was no need for any special gesture.'

'Of course, you are now one of us, and I am sure there will be a promotion for you. I think you should work in Geneva as you now know the bank pretty well and may become a good assistant to me. AA felt that a cash bonus might come in handy for shopping.'

'Thank you very much. The cash will be useful to buy some gifts. You know that we in Pakistan have to return laden with presents.' Despite his earlier experience, Amir was happy that he was being rewarded.

'We in Pakistan are still living in the eighteenth century. We are still expected to travel with loads of gifts for those we know and even those we don't know. We have to grow up if we want to progress.' Masood was not very kind to Pakistani society. 'So, what are your plans?' he asked.

'My plans?' Amir was surprised. 'I am here to do whatever you want me to do.'

'Well, we had this need for assistance for closing, but everything is under control now. I will introduce you to the department heads and find something for you unless you want to go off early.'

'I would like to use my time gainfully while I am here. I may learn something about the banking practices in Geneva. As of now, I have a reservation to London on December 23. With the holiday rush, it might be difficult to change my flight,' Amir replied.

'So, you have today and tomorrow. I suggest you take it easy today and go with Maria to see a bit of Geneva. Tomorrow you might want to spend time with our corporate banking division and learn how they are operating here in Geneva.'

'I am definitely interested in learning about the operations of the corporate banking division. I thought it might be useful if I were to get involved in the department dealing with our VIP customers.' Amir made the request gently.

'Those we call VIP clients are personally dealt with by myself and Rehmallah, our chief of corporate banking, with the direct involvement of our chairman and AA in Karachi. Rehmallah might be able to brief you about some of our more important clients. I'll give you a tour of the bank and introduce you to key people. The corporate banking division is on the fourth floor. Rehmallah also sits there. After that, you might want to go out with Maria.'

'I am sure going around Geneva will be interesting, and I do not wish to miss the offer. I would, however, like to take the opportunity to learn something about our operations here, which may become useful if I am more involved with Geneva in the future.'

'Fine by me. Give me ten minutes to clear up a few things. You can read some journals in our library while you wait. We'll have lunch at the executive cafeteria. Other senior officers of the bank will also be there. It'll be a good opportunity for you to meet them.' Masood's tone made it quite clear that he did not want Amir to snoop into any banking activities.

Amir parked himself in the library, which was adjacent to Masood's office. It held a lot of magazines and publications about the money market, investments, and banking, in addition to the day's editions of *Financial Times, International Herald Tribune,* and The *Wall Street Journal.* Amir browsed through the reading material for about ten minutes until Masood walked in.

'Let us go.' He beckoned Amir.

Masood led Amir on a quick tour of the bank. He was introduced to various department heads as a visiting VP from Pakistan. It seemed that most of the senior people were already aware of his visit and knew the background.

Rehmallah Soofi, the chief of corporate banking, welcomed Amir warmly. 'We have heard of you. I understand you are doing a great job in corporate banking in Karachi.'

'I believe Geneva is the leader in servicing the bank's corporate banking clients, and you are the guru of corporate banking,' Amir reciprocated.

'Sitting in Geneva, we have the full picture of our clients' affairs. That helps,' Rehmallah said modestly. 'You are welcome to spend time with us while you are here in Geneva. Masood has arranged for an office for you on this floor.'

'I would be delighted to.'

'Amir wants to see a bit of Geneva today. Maybe tomorrow,' Masood interjected.

'I don't want to bother Maria. I'll take a solo tour of Geneva tomorrow. In the meantime, I would like to spend some time here, if that is okay.' Amir did not want to lose the opportunity to learn more about banking operations in Geneva.

'Suit yourself. Maria will be disappointed.'

'I will apologise to her. But I would feel more comfortable being on my own. Geneva is a pretty safe and organised city. I'm sure that I won't get lost.' Amir wanted to ensure that he was out of Maria's clutches for the day.

'As you, please. I will inform Maria. You may also want to speak to her if you see her around.' Masood accepted the defeat.

'Oh, I certainly will.' Amir promised.

Chapter 6

G&P Bank's Offices, Geneva

Lunch at the executive cafeteria was a sumptuous five-course affair where the wine flowed freely. The bank did look after its executives.

Staff in officer grade normally had their lunch in the cafeteria. There were several tables where people were having lunch and chatting with each other. The very senior executives had a separate reserved table in a corner. Amir's place was at the senior executives' table with Rehmallah. Rehmallah introduced Amir to other executives. Everybody was very polite and welcoming.

Amir thought he saw Richard Bringsen with some people at a table in the middle of the hall. Richard and Amir had worked together during Amir's time in London. Amir got the feeling that Richard had seen and ignored him. Perhaps he had failed to recognise Amir. Amir did not think further about Richard and busied himself chatting with the people at his table. There were the usual discussions about holiday plans, the dollar's weakness, and the European economy – the type of talk bankers make when together. After lunch, Amir walked with Rehmallah to the fourth floor.

'This is your office.' Rehmallah led Amir to a small but comfortable and well-lit room. There was a desk and a swivelling executive chair. On the desk were a telephone and a couple of writing pads and pencils in case Amir wanted to make any notes.

'This looks nice.'

'My secretary, Pat, will be pleased to help you with anything that you may need. She sits outside my office. Her internal extension is 4107.'

'Thank you very much. I wonder if you would have time to chat a little. You might teach me a few things about corporate banking in Geneva.'

'Sure. Come over. The business has already slowed down for the holidays.' Rehmallah was pleased with this expression of respect from Amir.

They walked to Rehmallah's office.

'Care for a coffee?' Rehmallah asked as they entered his office.

'I would love one.' Amir said.

'Pat, could you organise coffee for Amir and me?' Rehmallah spoke over the intercom as he settled down in his chair.

'The bank has certainly done well in Geneva. It must have been a tremendous effort on the part of the senior team to achieve all this.' Amir was complimentary.

'Our chairman, Sheikh Tayeb, should get the most credit for this bank. And not only for this success in Geneva but all around the world. This giant organisation with over two hundred fifty branches around the world is the creation of his vision and untiring efforts. I don't know if you know the history of Sheikh Tayeb and the bank.' Rehmallah replied.

'I have a vague idea but wouldn't mind hearing it from you.' Amir was interested.

***

The Story of G&P Bank

'Money has no colour. There is no such thing as white or black money. A banker is the custodian and manager of the funds entrusted to him by his clients. He should not be concerned about the origins or source of money. He should only be concerned with making the most profitable and productive use of the money entrusted to him.'

Sheikh Tayeb, Chairman, G&P Bank

Rehmallah apparently loved narrating the story of G&P Bank. He cleared his desk and started telling the story that he believed should be known by every aspiring banker and should form a compulsory part of banking education.

'G&P Bank is the creation of our chairman, Sheikh Tayeb, and ably supported by his friend and second-in-command at the bank, Azhar Alam. Sheikh Tayeb is a visionary. AA is the engine. Sheikh

Tayeb is the life and soul of our bank. Without him, G&P Bank would never have come into existence, and without the able management of AA, it would not have reached the summit.

'Sheikh Tayeb was born in Delhi in 1918 into a venerated Sunni Muslim family. After completing his matriculation, he went to Aligarh Muslim University, where he earned his Bachelor of Arts degree.

'After his graduation, he joined the Bombay branch of the South Asia British Bank in Bombay. Sheikh Tayeb quickly rose through the ranks and became manager of the Indian Business Accounts Department. This was the senior-most position possible for a non-European to occupy at that time. Sheikh Tayeb was a friend of small businessmen. He supported them and extended credits when no established bank in India would give them any money. Sheikh Tayeb was very popular and became a favourite of the bank, as well as its Indian customers.

'After the partition of India, the South Asia British Bank transferred Sheikh Tayeb to its Karachi branch as the assistant country manager for Pakistan. Pakistan was a virgin territory with a complete vacuum in the banking and financial world. Local merchants sought out a bank to deposit funds and obtain overdraft facilities for day-to-day business needs.'

'With the reputation of a prestigious British bank supporting him, Sheikh Tayeb became one of the key players in the development of banking in Pakistan. He was an outstanding marketing man and knew how to get business for the bank. The bank's Pakistan operations' balance sheet became stronger every year. The bank had opened several branches in various cities in Pakistan.'

'In these early days of his banking career, Sheikh Tayeb would send his officers to merchants, promising very lucrative facilities if they helped the bank meet its deposit targets. Although there was strong growth in business, the bank was finding it difficult to post European officers to Pakistan. Pakistan's business was not very significant for the bank. In these circumstances, the bank promoted Sheikh Tayeb to general manager in Pakistan.

'It was then that Sheikh Tayeb started dreaming of owning and running his own bank. He started talking to the local businessmen about starting a new Pakistani bank. He took his proposal to Mr. Rais Kubair to be his partner and financier. The Kubairs were very rich and considered one of the top business groups in the country. Mr. Kubair was an admirer of Sheikh Tayeb. He agreed to team up, and with Rais Kubair as the principal investor and other businessmen supporting the idea, Sheikh Tayeb made an offer to the South Asia British Bank to sell its Pakistan unit at the net book value of the assets in Pakistan. Since the bank was finding it difficult to provide active management support to the operations in the country, they were happy to sell the operations to Sheikh Tayeb, who had already incorporated a banking company under the name Tijarat Bank.

'Tijarat Bank was new, but it had the infrastructure and customer base of the South Asia British Bank. This was a good opportunity for Sheikh Tayeb to achieve his vision of becoming the prime banker of Pakistan. As the banking control laws were still in their infancy in the country, Sheikh Tayeb moved aggressively.'

'Tijarat Bank competed with other local banks by giving higher than normal returns on deposits and extending overdraft and loan facilities at lower than market rates. The bank went out of its way to create personal relationships between the bank's officers and customers. The bank's officers were instructed not to shy away from any initiative that would ingratiate them with customers. The bank would send expensive gifts at the weddings of customers' family members. A major customer falling sick would be visited by a senior vice president with flowers and an offer to pay the medical bills. The bank's slogan was '*Our Customers Are Our Family and Family Stands Together.*' In addition, the bank hosted several parties and conventions at locations both inside and outside Pakistan where the bank's major customers, along with their families, would be invited to all-expenses-paid trips.

'In his quest to expand the bank, Sheikh Tayeb began to look outside Pakistan.' One of the locations he looked at was the small island of Banjar, which means barren land in the local Banjari language. Banjar is an arid island located in international waters just outside territorial waters of Iran. It now has a much larger population than it did when we first went in there. At that time, it was inhabited by about one thousand families of Baloch descent, originally from the desert of Balochistan (in Iran and Pakistan). The ruler of Banjar is called Khan. The main language is a dialect of Balochi called Banjari, but Farsi and Urdu are also commonly used. Prior to the current economic boom, the Banjari Baloch were mainly involved in fishing or plying motor launches for the transport of goods to and from the neighbouring countries.

'Banjar was a trading post and centre of currency exchange business through a system of informal money transfers called *hawala* or *hundi* in the Indo-Pakistan subcontinent and Iran. These countries had very severe restrictions on the import of goods and exchange controls for the remittance of funds outside their countries. The enterprising Balochis, Iranian and Asian businessmen developed informal money exchange channels to deal with these restrictions.

'The Asian and Iranian merchants had warehouses in Banjar where they would store goods such as cloth, electronics, food items, and jewellery imported for shipping into Iran, India, and Pakistan. These goods were transported by motor launches. Shipments of gold were extremely profitable, as a launch could carry a very high-value consignment with a lucrative fee for the *Nakhooda* (captain of the boat) and sailors. There was always a very strong demand for yellow metal in India and Pakistan.

'In addition, the pilgrims from India and Pakistan going on the annual pilgrimage of Haj to Makkah required Saudi riyals and US dollars for their journeys. These countries had strict exchange controls and only allowed very small sums of money to their citizens for travelling abroad. Pilgrims would carry handwritten pieces of paper, commonly known as 'chits' (*hundis*) addressed to merchants in Makkah from their counterparts in Banjar to pay the pilgrims the requested amount in Saudi riyals and dollars.'

'There was a very sophisticated system of clearing for the settlement of these transactions. There were several techniques to achieve this. Invoices for goods exported from India and Pakistan showed a much lower value than the actual one. The difference was settled outside of these countries with exchange houses in Banjar. Similarly, goods exported to India and Pakistan showed much higher value than the actual. The difference was retained in Banjar for use in the exchange transactions. In addition, many workers needed to remit funds to their families back home. They would deposit these funds with the local *hawalawalas* (money dealers), who would notify their correspondents in Afghanistan, Iran, India, or Pakistan to send the money there.

'Sheikh Tayeb was aware of these operations and wanted to use this for the benefit of his bank. Since Banjar was not considered an important business location, not many international banks or multinationals had operations there. Sheikh Tayeb cultivated a relationship with Banjar's ambassador to Pakistan. He showered him with expensive gifts and invited him to lavish parties where there was no dearth of beautiful hostesses ready to look after guests.

'Through the ambassador, Sheikh Tayeb arranged to visit Banjar and meet Bulund Khan, the Khan of Banjar. Sheikh Tayeb landed in Banjar in a chartered plane accompanied by senior directors of Tijarat Bank and beautiful lady secretaries. He carried expensive gifts of jewellery and other valuables. By nature, Bulund Khan was a kind, generous, and affable man, a true Baloch. Bulund Khan and Sheikh Tayeb became friends immediately. The Khan appreciated the gifts and respect Sheikh Tayeb had shown.

'Bulund Khan was a much-married man. Over the years, he married twelve women from various Balochi tribes from Pakistan and Iran, although never more than four at a time, keeping with the Islamic injunctions. He had twenty-two sons and a similar number of daughters. Of these children, Prince Sitara Khan was the eldest and heir apparent. His second son was Prince Taj Khan, from a different mother. Unfortunately, none of Bulund Khan's wives were very educated or sophisticated. They came from a tribal-cultural background, which required ladies to be secluded and refrain from participating in any activities involving men. Bulund Khan always found them wanting when he dealt with the international community, and he desired a more ladylike companion. Recognising this need of the Khan, Sheikh Tayeb asked his Iranian secretary, Farah Naz, to stay on in Banjar to help the Khan deal with Western connections and to select and train lady assistants for his personal staff. The Iranian secretary liked being a companion and adviser to the Khan of Banjar. Over time, she took on a very important role in the Khan's court and eventually surrendered to the Khan's charms and married him. Today, Farah Naz is one of the stronger wives of Bulund Khan, and Sheikh Tayeb now has a friend and confidante in the Khan's bedroom.

'At Sheikh Tayeb's request, the Khan issued a banking licence to Tijarat Bank with permission to open branches anywhere in Banjar. The first account was opened by Bulund Khan himself with a deposit of one million US dollars gifted by Sheikh Tayeb.'

'Over the next years, the friendship between Sheikh Tayeb and Bulund Khan grew, and they became close friends. Sheikh Tayeb also took on the role of the chief financial adviser to the Khan.'

'With Tijarat Bank nicely set up and prospering, Sheikh Tayeb set his eyes on creating a presence in international banking. At that time, the Kubair family was under a cloud due to the political changes in Pakistan and was not able to support Sheikh Tayeb's ambitions. He decided to go at it alone.'

'Sheikh Tayeb left Tijarat Bank and persuaded Bulund Khan to be a principal shareholder and patron-in-chief of the Growth & Prosperity Bank, to be commonly known as G&P Bank, that he planned to establish. Soon thereafter, G&P Bank was incorporated in the Cayman Islands as a banking corporation. Prince Sitara Khan, the eldest son of Bulund Khan, was appointed the first chairman of the bank. Sheikh Tayeb took the positions of deputy chairman, president, and chief executive officer. G&P Bank's first branch was opened in the city of Banjar, where it also acted as the personal bank of the Khan.'

'Over the years, Sheikh Tayeb had acquired the reputation of being a very shrewd and capable banker. With his aggressive personal relationship campaigns and the ability to shower gifts and massage the egos of senior players in the world of politics and finance, he had developed excellent personal relationships with a lot of influential people, including members of the Iranian and other powerful regional families, senior politicians, and ruling establishments around the world.

'As the luck would have it, just about the time G&P Bank was formed, a huge offshore oil and gas field was discovered in the territorial waters of Banjar. An American company, Texas Oil & Mineral Inc. (TOMI), under a concession from the Khan, struck pay dirt. Sheikh Tayeb had encouraged Bulund Khan to award concessions to TOMI, for which he earned a hefty fee and the personal gratitude and friendship of Bernard Schlom, President of TOMI. Bernard Schlom later helped Sheikh Tayeb establish connections in the power corridors of the USA.'

'Banjar was now an important economic player in the region. A huge construction boom started on the hitherto neglected and barren island. Many foreign companies flocked to Banjar looking for a share in the prosperity. Senior company executives visiting the island were made aware that the door to the *Durbar* (court) of the Khan was through Sheikh Tayeb and G&P Bank.

'The oil boom in Banjar came as a gift for the initial survival of G&P Bank. Sheikh Tayeb cleverly used his connections with Khan to position G&P Bank as the government's main banking arm. All foreign companies had to open accounts there. Banjar's government would only accept payment for any official levies and charges through G&P Bank's branch in Banjar. Contractors were required to pay wages to their workers through G&P Bank, and the workers were required to open accounts with G&P Bank to remit funds outside Banjar.

'Following the Arab-Israel war of 1973, oil prices skyrocketed. This was a bonanza for all the oil-producing countries, and Banjar was no exception. Lucrative contracts for projects to develop and upgrade the oil and infrastructure facilities were offered and signed regularly. Foreign contractors never had better.'

'All this activity necessitated the import of a large number of workers from the Asian subcontinent and other neighbouring countries. Hundreds of thousands of workers were recruited to work on the projects in Banjar. In the absence of any reliable and developed banking channels for the remittance of money to their home countries, these workers used the services of the *hawala walas*.

The workers also faced the difficulty of leaving their worksites and going to the city to make the remittance. Often, this required a few hours' journey and leave from the employer. Sheikh Tayeb realised the opportunities provided by the prospering oil economy, particularly in the field of providing banking facilities to contractors, citizens, and expatriate workers. Leveraging his contacts, Sheikh Tayeb managed to open G&P Bank branches in all the countries in the region. To capture the expanding oil boom business, Sheikh Tayeb used to offer support fees and send lavish gifts to the project managers, encouraging them to open accounts with G&P Bank and use the bank's facilities. He also created the concept of the 'Bank on Wheels'.

'G&P Bank's mobile bankers would visit project sites and offer full banking facilities to the contractors, as well as to the employees. Workers were able to remit funds to wherever they wanted without leaving their work location. The G&P Bank managers were also very relaxed about advancing loans to workers if they obtained their employers' commitment to transfer the borrower's salary to the bank. This novel idea of 'Bank on Wheels' was a great success. Soon, G&P Bank was recognised as a major bank providing top quality service to the small man.

'As the funds were remitted from Banjar primarily to Afghanistan, Iran, India, Pakistan, Sri Lanka, and Bangladesh, G&P Bank opened branches in every major city of these countries and became a household name.

'Sheikh Tayeb recognised that he needed a strong foothold in the Western world to be accepted as a respectable bank. Initially, he entered into correspondent arrangements with a high street clearing house bank in the UK. Once that relationship was working well, with the help of his influential friends, he managed to obtain a licence to open banking business in the UK.

'The first branch of G&P Bank in the UK was opened in Knightsbridge in London, near Harrods. This was the area where the rich and influential had residences. The opening ceremony of the bank was conducted by His Royal Highness, Bulund Khan. Among other dignitaries present at the ceremony, senior officials of the British political establishment along with the mayor of London were also present, seated in the front row. Each VIP invitee was presented with a gold Rolex as a thank you gift. The event was covered by every major newspaper in the UK, with the *Financial Times* printing Sheikh Tayeb's photograph and praising him as a visionary banker from Asia.

'With the financial resources and influence of the government of Banjar behind him, Sheikh Tayeb started acquiring real estate in prime areas of the UK. Large branches were established on the bank's own property in several parts of London, Manchester, Birmingham, and Glasgow. True to his commitment to serve the small working man, Sheikh Tayeb also opened small branches in towns like Bradford, Hull, Leeds, Leicester, Cardiff, and Newcastle upon Tyne, where large middle and working-class Asian populations resided, and encouraged them to use G&P Bank for their personal banking needs and remit funds back to the lands of their ancestors without hassle.

'G&P Bank immediately made a mark on the UK banking industry. The small businessman was treated as a VIP and was able to get loans and other banking facilities without difficulty. G&P Bank's clientele in the UK included many large contractors with contracts in the Middle and Near East, large and small Asian business houses, and a lot of individuals with personal accounts.

'With the principle of helping the small businessman, Sheikh Tayeb also believed that the bank should follow the money. Money had no colour, and money had power. G&P Bank was structured to help people with money who wanted to remain anonymous. With this in mind, Sheikh Tayeb opened a very large banking facility in Geneva. The Swiss banking laws guaranteed confidentiality and were ready to grant a banking licence to any foreign banking entity that could bring deposits into Switzerland.

'With facilities in the UK and Switzerland, the bank started scouting countries where it was possible to secure large deposits. Workers' deposits and remittances were not sufficient. G&P Bank needed large sources of funds to be able to expand. Certain countries in Asia, Latin America and Africa looked interesting. Most of these countries were ruled by dictators, and there was a culture of corruption in these countries.

'In pursuit of his goals, Sheikh Tayeb visited several countries in the Americas and Africa. He went with strong references from his customers and friends, such as the South and East Asian and Iranian aristocracy, as well as Bernard Schlom of TOMI. TOMI had strong connections with the people who had the money and power in these countries. Soon, G&P Bank opened branches in several parts of East Asia, Africa and Latin America, including Malaysia, Burma, Indonesia, Kenya, Nigeria, Zaire, Central African Republic, Brazil, Argentina, Venezuela, Panama, Columbia, Haiti, and Nicaragua. G&P Bank had rich and powerful clients in these countries.

'G&P Bank also opened branches in various European and Asian countries to support its international banking transactions. To this day, some of the major depositors of the bank are located in the Asian subcontinent, Iran, Africa, and Latin America. Most of them want to remain anonymous for their own personal reasons. In order to facilitate the anonymity of the depositors, the bank has created an elaborate and fool proof security system to protect their identities. The Bank's top management are experts in handling numbered accounts whose owners are known to only the chairman and two very senior executives.'

'The G&P Bank is now an international bank with a very wide network of branches.'

'The bank had another stroke of luck that helped it achieve further prosperity. This time, the Soviet Union had committed the folly of occupying Afghanistan, which prompted the US government and its allies to encourage and support the religious-minded Afghans and other Muslim zealots to fight against the Soviets. These people called themselves *Mujahideen* (religious warriors*)*. Since the Soviet Union was perceived as a Godless country, the war in Afghanistan was fought with religious fervour. As Pakistan is next door to Afghanistan, the Pakistan government played a major role in supporting these warriors.'

'With its strong presence in Pakistan, G&P Bank was ideally suited and selected by US government agencies and other anti-Soviet players to channel funds to the Mujahideen.'

'Unfortunately, with the defeat of the Soviet Union in Afghanistan, the US funds dried up, but the departure of the Soviets from Afghanistan has not brought peace there. The Mujahideen, who were fighting the Soviets, are now fighting among themselves for power in Afghanistan. Their needs have opened up new funding requirements and sources. Afghanistan is the world's largest producer of poppy, the plant that produces opium which is converted into heroin. Dealing with heroin provides ready cash for its dealers. As the Afghans have already been dealing with G&P Bank and have established contacts with the bank for a long time, the money arrangements for their operations are routed through G&P Bank.'

'The success of the G&P Bank and its ability to adjust to the changing business conditions encouraged the chairman to give something back to society, particularly the underprivileged Muslim youth. He established the G&P Bank Foundation. The Foundation grants educational assistance to thousands of deserving students. In addition, the Foundation has established medical facilities in thirty countries in Asia and Africa.'

'Today, the G&P Bank can boast that it operates in more than 50 countries and has over 250 branches. Our total assets are in excess of tens of billions of US dollars. We are the envy of every high street bank in the West, and all this was achieved in a very short period of time. Imagine the possibilities. *Insha Allah* (God willing), G&P Bank will be the world's biggest bank one day.'

It was almost 5 p.m. when Rehmallah finished his narrative, and Amir felt tired.

He thanked Rehmallah for letting him know the history of G&P Bank and asked his permission to leave for the day. 'I feel tired; maybe it is the jet lag,' he said.

'Sure. I'll arrange for a car to take you back to the hotel.' Rehmallah offered.

'No. Please. I would like to walk. I enjoy walking. It's not far, is it?' Amir asked.

'No, it's not far. It takes less time to walk than to drive. Fifteen minutes. What are you doing this evening? My wife, Rehana, and the girls would be delighted to see you at dinner if you have nothing else planned.'

'I would love to join your family for dinner, but I'd like to do some shopping before, though.' Amir could not say no to a dinner offer from this nice man and his family.

'You have the whole day tomorrow for shopping. I suggest that you get some rest today. You do look tired. Should I pick you up at, say, 7.30?' Rehmallah asked.

'I'll be in the hotel's lobby at 7.30.' Amir said.

Amir walked out of the bank into the cool Geneva air and onto Rue du Mont-Blanc, facing the lake. He continued to be amazed by the height of the jet, and he sat down on a bench near the lake. He started thinking about his experience over the past three days, particularly his day at the bank.

Obviously, the bank had no scruples. They were involved in money laundering, arms smuggling, window dressing of financial statements and reports, false and fraudulent accounting, and God knew what else. The bank did not mind playing with the lives of its staff. Amir could have very easily landed in a jail.

He needed the plan to stop the bank. They should not be allowed to expose innocent people and violate all the moral, ethical, and legal standards of the banking business. Banking was an honourable profession. With dirty bankers awash with money, it may be one of the most dangerous professions in the world. A dirty banker could do more damage to society than a drug baron. He needed further information about the operations of the bank, particularly the dealings of the special accounts. Once he had the information, he would approach the relevant authorities.

Relevant authorities? Where? Amir asked himself. He did not know enough about the laws and the operations of authorities in other countries. He was not rich enough to hire lawyers. Maybe Danny would help. Yes, Amir decided, Danny was the answer.

Amir should gather enough detailed evidence to convince Danny and others to act. He would start preparing a dossier of all the illegal activities of the bank. He would have to be very clever to do this. Amir was sure that he and his family would be in serious trouble if the bank found out about his activities. He needed to do it with stealth.

He would start with TIG. There was certainly something very fishy there. This one account could give him a lot of information, as well as a starting point. Most of the information about TIG was likely to be in Pakistan and Geneva.

He would not achieve much in Geneva in his present trip, as the time was too short, and everything was closing for Christmas and New Year's. He planned to go to Pakistan and return here as soon as possible. He would have to convince AA to give him another chance to come to Geneva, maybe for a short secondment of at least a month. In the meantime, he would talk to Danny during his trip to London and gauge his reaction. He would try to enlist the support of Samira. She certainly had access to a lot of confidential information.

With a game plan in his head, Amir started to relax. He said aloud, 'I swear, I will get you, you bastards. You cannot buy me for twenty thousand dollars and a first-class trip to Europe.' A couple of people passing by looked at him with surprised expressions, as if wondering whether he was sane.

After deciding on a course of action, Amir felt refreshed and energised. He stood up and started walking back toward the hotel. On the way, he looked into the shops selling souvenirs and bought a lovely cuckoo clock. By the time he reached the hotel, it was nearly 7 p.m.

He quickly showered and changed and was in the lobby at 7.30. True to his word, Rehmallah was there exactly on time.

'My car is in the hotel parking lot,' Rehmallah said as he led Amir to his car. Amir was impressed; he had the latest Mercedes S 500. 'We could actually walk to my apartment from here, but I thought you may be tired and prefer the car.' he added.

'It is also a little cold now, so going by car would be better.' Amir replied.

Rehmallah lived on Eaux-Vives, not far from the lake and Amir's hotel; they arrived in ten minutes. He lived on the third floor of a very nice late-nineteenth-century building.

At the entrance to the building, Rehmallah pressed the doorbell to let his wife know they were coming up. She was waiting for them at the door.

'Meet Rehana,' Rehmallah said to Amir, then he turned to his wife. 'And Rehana, this is Amir from our main office in Karachi.' Rehmallah introduced them without much formality.

'*Assalam Alaikum.*' Rehana welcomed Amir with the traditional greeting.

'Waalekum Assalam,' Amir replied.

As he was about to enter the apartment, Amir saw Rehmallah taking off his shoes. This was a practice more religiously inclined Muslims adopted to keep their houses clean and pious. Amir also took off his shoes and left them near the door.

'Come on, girls, meet Uncle Amir.' Rehana called Rehmallah's daughters. In Pakistani culture, everybody who was a friend of their parents was called an uncle or aunt. Age was not a criterion.

Amir was immediately struck by the religious atmosphere in the apartment. There were prints of Quranic verses on the walls. Rehmallah's wife and daughters were heavily covered in the traditional shroud (*chador*), and they walked around the place with bare feet.

'This is Sana, and this is Saba,' Rehmallah said, introducing his two daughters. 'Sana is sixteen and studying O Levels. Saba is fourteen. Both of them go to the British School and plan to go to British universities for further education. In spite of living in Switzerland, we remain very strong in our religious practices. Both Sana and Saba pray five times each day and learn the Quran from a Jordanian lady.'

'Assalam Alaikum, Uncle.' Both Sana and Saba said in unison.

'Waalekum Assalam, *Beta,*' Amir replied in Urdu.

'How do you find the school in Geneva?' Amir asked to start the conversation.

'The school is very good. We have a mixture of nationalities. All our teachers are British. Our school has one of the highest passing rates in O and A Levels,' Sana, who was more extroverted, replied.

'In this, we are lucky. Education in Pakistan has really deteriorated. My children are lucky to be able to live in Geneva and go to this school,' Rehmallah remarked.

Rehana was busy in the kitchen organising the dinner.

'Girls, go help your mother,' Rehmallah directed his daughters.

Immediately, the girls rushed off and got busy setting up the table and bringing in the food from the kitchen.

'What would you like to drink?' Rehmallah asked. 'I'm afraid in our house you will get only a soft drink.'

'A Coke will be fine,' Amir replied.

Sana brought out a big bottle of Coke and passed it to her father, who poured it into a glass and handed it over to Amir.

'Since you and your family are so religious, how do you reconcile working with the G&P Bank?' Amir could not resist the question any longer.

'What is wrong with working with the G&P Bank?' Rehmallah appeared not to understand Amir's question.

'Well, to start with, it is a bank and deals in interest, which, at best, is controversial under *Sharia* (the Islamic legal code), if not outright banned. In addition, some of the practices of the bank may be on the fringes of the prevailing laws.' Amir said.

'You talk like those uneducated mullahs,' Rehmallah replied vehemently. 'The G&P Bank is not a bloodsucking lender like some of the Western banks that are interested in supporting only Western business. It does not indulge in usury. The G&P Bank is a holy place that acts as a guardian of money for those who do not know how to invest their money. The bank channels these deposits for the development of businesses for third-world entrepreneurs who are not able to obtain a single Swiss franc from traditional banks. Look at the business houses like Tanganyika Investment Group, TIG, which have risen only with the help and support provided by the

G&P Bank. There are several *fatwas* (religious edicts) that clearly state normal bank interest is not usury and therefore not forbidden in Islam.' You should also look at the good work that the G&P Bank has done for the development and education of people in developing countries. We talked about that this afternoon.

'As for the laws, these are man-made edicts created to protect the Western civilisation and its financial and legal systems. There is no compulsion for us to follow these man-made laws if we see that a common good may be achieved by finding ways around them. I find nothing un-Islamic in what the G&P Bank does. As a matter of fact, I feel like a soldier fighting for the economic emancipation of small businessmen from developing countries.'

Amir was taken aback by Rehmallah's diatribe, and he did not know what to say next. Fortunately, Rehana came to his rescue.

'Come on guys, the food is getting cold.' She called them to the dining table.

Amir and Rehmallah walked to the table. It was very informal. Sana sat next to Amir. She seemed to be developing a genuine liking for him.

'Mama has prepared *Hyderabadi biryani* (rice with spiced meat, a famous Pakistani-Indian dish) and *aloo gosht* (mutton with potatoes). You must first try the biryani and then the aloo in the second round.' Sana said as she passed a large dish filled with meat and rice to Amir.

Amir passed on the dish after taking a substantial portion of biryani. Biryani was his favourite dish, and nobody made it better than people from Hyderabad.

'Mm. Delicious.' It was really good.

Rehana blushed and said, 'You must take some more.'

'I will. I will,' Amir assured her.

'When did you come to Geneva?' Sana asked.

'Yesterday afternoon.' Amir replied.

'Seen anything of Geneva? It is a lovely town.'

'Only a little. I hope to go around tomorrow.'

'I have school tomorrow, otherwise, I would have come. We are having Christmas and New Year's parties at the school. I must be there.' Sana was apologetic.

'Not to worry. I'll find my way around. I might do a bit of shopping, too,' Amir said.

'You are in one of the best shopping districts in the world right here,' Sana replied. 'There are some very nice department stores and shops across the Rade on Rue du Rhone and Rue du Marche.'

'I will make sure that I visit them,' Amir replied.

'And if you want to see real Geneva, then you must not miss the Old Town. We call it Vielle Ville. The Old Town has the grand Cathedral St-Pierre built in the thirteenth century. It is lovely.' Sana loved Geneva.

'I would definitely like to go there. Thank you for the tip.' Amir replied and turned his attention to Rehana, who was very quiet and appeared interested in serving the food and making sure that everybody had plenty.

'How do you like Geneva?' He asked to engage her in the conversation.

'It is a very nice city. Unfortunately, I do not enjoy it much. I spend most of my time at home looking after the family. These girls don't do anything for themselves. I have to worry about everything. I also miss life in Pakistan.'

Amir regretted that Rehana was not happy. To change the subject, he said, 'Where do you guys go for vacation?'

'Most of the time to Pakistan, as Rehana and I like to spend time with the family back home. The girls, however, want to go skiing and on holidays in Europe. Sometimes we spend half the time in Pakistan and half in Europe,' Rehmallah replied.

'Try the aloo gosht.' Rehana passed on the bowl to Amir.

'Thank you, everything is so delicious,' Amir said, serving himself the aloo gosht. 'I am afraid I will not have the energy to get back to the hotel if I stuff myself like this.'

'Don't worry, you have a chauffeur to take you to the hotel; I'll drop you there. But you must eat. Rehana will feel unhappy otherwise,' Rehmallah said.

Rehana went into the kitchen and brought in two casseroles, each one filled with a separate dessert. 'I have made *gulab jamun* (sweet balls submerged in sugary syrup) and rasmalai (sweet cream cakes in milk) for you. You must try both."

'Wow. You are getting special treatment, Amir,' Rehmallah commented. 'We have to fight with Rehana to make one sweet, gulab jamun or rasmalai. Because of you, today we are going to enjoy both.'

Amir took one piece of each. 'These are really magnificent,' he said truthfully.

After dinner, Rehmallah and Amir sat in the sitting room in front of the television. The girls went to their rooms, and Rehana busied herself in the kitchen. As it was almost 9 p.m., Rehmallah switched on the TV and tuned into CNN for the news. The headlines reported continued fights among the Mujahideen groups in Afghanistan.

'You know, our bank was at the forefront of fighting the Soviets in Afghanistan.' Rehmallah was proud of the fact that G&P Bank was involved in facilitating the covert war.

'How did the bank do that?'

'The Mujahideen required money and supplies. The bank got them both. There was a special department headed by a senior executive vice president to manage such matters. The department made arrangements with various parties and ensured that all the efforts were coordinated and the Mujahideen did not suffer because of the lack of money or materiel. We are very proud of our role in the conflict.' Rehmallah had strong views on the subject.

'Tea?' Rehana walked in with a tray.

'Thank you. I would love some,' Amir replied.

Rehana poured each a cup and sat down with a cup for herself. 'You always watch the news. Let's watch something more interesting,' she said, taking hold of the remote control.

'Please excuse me. I am a little tired and would like to go to the hotel.' Amir stood up.

'I will drop you.' Rehmallah also stood up. 'Are you coming?' he asked Rehana.

'I'll stay on,' Rehana replied.

'Rehana gets a little homesick occasionally,' Rehmallah commented.

'I understand. It might be very lonely for her in Geneva.'

'There is a Pakistan community here, but most of the people, particularly the women, are snobs. In the Pakistani community, you should belong to one of the groups to get any recognition. Diplomats are considered the most exalted. They behave as if all the Pakistanis here are their subjects and should give them the royal treatment."

'This is our story everywhere. It was the same in London, and in Pakistan, your social rank is the most important. In Pakistan, you won't get attended to by a doctor if you aren't considered of appropriate status. It's sickening.' Amir agreed.

Soon they reached the hotel. Amir thanked Rehmallah for the lovely evening and quickly went to his room.

Chapter 7

Geneva

Opening the door to his hotel room, Amir noticed an envelope that had been slipped under the door. It was a letter addressed to Mr. Amir Ramli at the hotel address, and it had a Geneva postmark. It did not indicate the name of the sender.

Intrigued, Amir opened the envelope and read:

Dear Amir,

I hope you remember me, Richard Bringsen. We used to work together at the bank's Knightsbridge branch not so long ago.

I saw you at lunch today. Please excuse me for acting as if I did not recognise you. I did so intentionally. I will explain when we meet.

I was transferred to Geneva last year. They asked me to work directly with Masood Qadir in the Special Accounts Department. I must say that one comes across some very interesting transactions when dealing with these accounts.

I understand that you are here for a very short period of time and may be leaving soon. I will be going away for Christmas and New Year's with my girlfriend, Ursula, to see her parents, Otto and Else Huber, in Speyer. I understand that it is a historical town just across the border in the Rhine Valley in Germany. Several German kings are said to be buried there, and the town has a lovely cathedral.

I understand that you had some problems when you travelled to Switzerland. Frankly, I am not surprised. In grave personal danger, I have done some research on the bank's activities and accumulated a lot of information. I am afraid that the bank appears to have found out that I was snooping into the confidential information and making copies. I fear that Oshko, the security officer, is on me, and I may be in danger. Well, I am in it now, and there is no way I can extricate myself from this mess.

Fearing for my safety, I am taking the dossier with me to Speyer and will request that Otto Huber keep it safe for me or give it to somebody I authorise to collect it (I felt that it would be safer to keep the information outside of the bank and my home). It makes for a very interesting read. I will show you when we meet, which I hope will be sometime soon.

In the meantime, enjoy your holidays and accept my best wishes for a very happy new year.

Richard

Amir was puzzled. Richard's letter was certainly strange. He did not understand why Richard could not say hello to him when he saw him at the cafeteria, nor did he understand the information about the bank that was so sensitive that he had to keep it with his girlfriend's parents. Amir knew the bank was involved in money laundering, but that was true for many other banks, too. This certainly did not pose a personal threat to the likes of Richard or Amir himself.

He was exhausted and needed rest. Without thinking much further, he jumped into bed and was soon asleep. The next day, he woke up early and was at the bank before 8 a.m.

'Assalam Alaikum.' He peeked into Rehmallah's office.

'Waalekum Assalam. You are already getting into the bad habit of coming in early. Come in and have a coffee.' Rehmallah was happy to see Amir.

'I came to thank you and your family for the lovely evening yesterday. Rehana is a fantastic hostess. The food was out of this world – the best I've ever had. My mother would be upset if she heard me saying this.' Amir was very complimentary.

'Yes, she does cook well, but yesterday you got special treatment.'

'I used to know a chap by the name of Richard Bringsen when I was in London. I thought I saw him here yesterday. I'm not sure if it was him, though.'

'Richard works in Masood's department. He sits just across from here, on the other side, next to Roberta, the blonde girl. It's early. He normally comes in around nine.'

After coffee and small talk, Amir went to the office assigned to him, and he busied himself with the day's newspapers and economic reports.

'Hey, what are you doing here? I thought you were going shopping today.' It was Masood. He was also an early bird at the bank.

'I got up early, so I thought I would come to the bank and go out a little later when the shops open.' Amir replied.

On impulse, he said to Masood, 'Geneva is a great place, and you run a fantastic operation here. If possible, I would like to spend a few weeks working with you here.'

Masood was flattered. 'As a matter of fact, I need somebody like you to help me here. Let me see. Have you got too much on your desk in Karachi?'

'Nothing much. I handed everything over to Saima in the corporate banking unit. I'll have to start afresh when I return.'

'Good. I suggest that you spend your vacation as planned. I'll talk to AA and convince him to let you stay here for a few more weeks. I hope this will be agreeable to you and your family.'

'Of course. This will be a great learning opportunity for me. I'm sure my parents won't miss me much during this period. I would like to go to Karachi during the holidays, though. I need to pick up some more clothes and personal items as I'll have to stay here for some time.'

'Well, then it's settled. I'm sure AA won't say no to me. Go ahead and do some shopping and see Geneva. I'll call you in Karachi as soon as Azhar approves my request.'

Amir was delighted at this development. He would now get an entry into the bank's inner-working circle in Geneva. This could only help him achieve his objectives. He looked at his watch. It was past nine, time for shops to open. He decided to give himself a little more time, so he requested a coffee and busied himself in the technical journals. There was an article in *The Banker* about the cut-throat competition among banks and some of the sharp practices prevailing in the business.

After finishing the article, Amir walked over to Julia and said, 'Good morning, Julia.'

'Hey, enjoying Geneva?'

'I haven't seen much of it as yet. I am planning to go out today. I understand there are some great Christmas and New Year's bargains going on in London. I have received a bonus, which should come in handy to do some shopping here and in London.' Amir replied.

'Masood mentioned that you want to spend your bonus on shopping. You must be very rich. Do you want me to join the party?' Julia joked.

'You don't know how the folks back home are waiting for me to return with presents. There will be little personal shopping for me. The shops must be open by now, mustn't they?' Amir enquired.

'Oh, yes. Shops open early in Geneva. What do you want to buy?'

'I would like to buy a few shirts and other things for me. I would also like to look at some handicrafts.'

'For shirts and other such things, go to Rue du Rhone. There are some nice department stores there. The most famous is Globus-Grand Passage. You should be able to find almost everything there. However, for handicrafts, Place de la Fusterie is the best. It is just off Rue du Rhone. You could walk there.'

Julia got up and showed Amir a pocket map of Geneva. 'We are here. And you want to get there. It shouldn't take you more than fifteen minutes. Take the map so you don't get lost,' she said, marking the locations of the bank and Globus-Grand Passage on the map.

'Thank you. It is very kind and helpful of you.' Amir thanked her.

On the way out, Amir passed near the section Rehmallah had pointed out where Richard worked. The desk was empty. Amir wondered why Richard had not turned up at work but decided not to enquire.

Chapter 8

Geneva

Amir followed the map and soon found himself on Rue du Rhone, a long street with shops on both sides. He soon located the famous Globus-Grand Passage. It was a large store spread over several floors.

Amir went to the men's clothing section and asked the sales lady to show him some nice shirts. She asked for his size and immediately produced several shirts for him to consider. After buying a few things, Amir was ready to leave when he heard a sexy voice. 'I thought you might be here.'

Amir looked toward the source of the voice and found himself looking at a stunningly beautiful lady dressed in slim-fit shirt and trousers and carrying a Hermès bag. He realized the lady was Rehana. She had completely transformed. The long sheet covering her from head to toe at dinner had disappeared, and in front of him stood a very nicely dressed, exceedingly beautiful lady with a dazzling smile on her face.

'Oh, hello. Sorry, I didn't recognise you. You look totally different from yesterday.'

'Yesterday, I dressed the way Rehmallah wanted me to. Today, I am the way I like to be. He does not know that I dress like this or that I am here. I was getting bored at home. I came here hoping to find you.' She was frank.

Amir was mesmerised. This was not the Rehana of yesterday. Yesterday, she looked average. Today she was stunning.

'So, what do you want to buy? This is a good place to shop for high-quality items. They are expensive, but they last.'

'Well, I wanted to buy a few shirts, ties, and personal items. I would like to see some handicrafts, as well.'

'Not buying anything for your family?'

'My sister has asked for a Cartier, so I'll go to Cartier's boutique for that. I'll also pick up something for my mom and dad. I'm not married, so there is nobody else to buy for.' Amir did not know why he mentioned that he was not married. Perhaps Rehana was appearing at the shop, especially for him, and the way she was dressed was affecting him. His head was spinning.

'Knowing Pakistan's environment, I would have thought unmarried girls and their parents would be swarming all over you. You are lucky to be single. I would have bet that you were already married with several children. I'm very pleasantly surprised.' Rehana was being provocative, and Amir found himself blushing. 'So, what are you looking at?' she asked, intertwining her fingers in his.

Amir was taken by surprise. He did not know how to react to Rehana's move, but he did not withdraw his hand.

Rehana asked the sales lady to show them some high-quality German and Swiss shirts and ties. 'The quality of the German and Swiss textiles is much better than that of the UK or USA,' she said.

Amir quickly selected a few shirts and ties. He bought a couple of each for his father, as well. While he was settling the account for his purchases, Rehana joined him with a beautiful Louis Vuitton gold colour tie in her hands.

'I bought this for you. Please accept this as a gift from me.'

'Oh, no. I cannot accept this, Rehana. You cannot buy me this expensive tie.'

'Why not? Can a friend not give a gift to another? Or, in our culture, ladies should not give gifts to men? Don't tell me you are one of those backward-minded Pakistanis.' Rehana was in no mood for resistance. 'Anyway, I have already paid for this. And since I do not feel like giving a gift to Rehmallah, I'll have to throw this away. This will remind you of me.'

'Okay, but you are spoiling me.'

'You are worth spoiling and adoring,' Rehana replied without missing a beat.

'I am done with the shopping for myself and my father. I need to buy some ladies' accessories for my sister and mom.'

'Okay, let's go to the ladies' section and then have lunch. There is a nice family-run Lebanese restaurant near here called Al Bustan.' Rehana suggested.

They walked hand-in-hand to the ladies' section. This time, Rehana walked very close to Amir – so close that he could smell her perfume.

In the ladies' section, Amir bought some designer jewellery and make-up for his sister and mother. Then, he saw a Tiffany boutique in the corner. He led Rehana into the shop and started looking at pendants.

'What do you think of this?' Amir asked, picking up a pendant designed as a flower with a small diamond in the centre on a thin gold chain.

'This is beautiful. Your sister or girlfriend would love it.'

'Please gift wrap this,' Amir told the sales lady, and he quickly paid for the pendant. As they left the store, Amir said to Rehana, 'Okay. Let's go to lunch.'

'This way,' Rehana said, leading Amir toward the restaurant, again hand-in-hand.

True to its billing, the restaurant had a lovely atmosphere. There were only a few tables, and an old Lebanese man, Karim, was manning the reception and seating the guests. The kitchen seemed to be looked after by Madam Mona, the wife of Karim. There were very few waiters serving the guests. The restaurant was almost full, with a couple of tables available. Rehana and Amir were quickly shown to a corner table set discreetly at the back of the room. They ordered some *mezze* (Lebanese starters) and two *shistaou* (grilled pieces of marinated chicken).

'You may drink if you wish. I don't drink,' Rehana said, putting her hand on Amir's and caressing it.

'I will also pass. I'm fine with plain water.'

The food was served quickly, and after the main course, they declined dessert but ordered Turkish coffee.

With her cup of coffee in her hand, Rehana, with complete serenity said, 'You must think very poorly of me, chasing you like this.'

'I'll admit to being a little surprised, but this does not mean that I'm not attracted to you or do not like you meeting me like this.'

'Ever since I saw you last night, I felt as if I was pushed your way by a strong force. I hardly slept a wink and stayed up the whole night thinking about you. I couldn't wait until the morning to see you. I didn't care if you were married, here for a couple of days only, or might be a strict fellow who might not want to see me. I had to come. I didn't care what you might think of me. I knew where you would be.

'Please understand that this is the first time I am out on my own in a restaurant with another man. Of course, I dress up and go out for shopping and walks alone, but this is the first time I am with a man other than Rehmallah.

'I know you will leave tomorrow, and I might never see you again. But I want these few minutes we spend together to be remembered as cherished moments in my life. I do not ask anything of you. Just remember me as someone who adores you and would swim across any ocean to be near you.

Amir was deeply moved. 'I do not know, Rehana. You hardly know me. You are married with children. I don't want to ruin your life, and I believe that your attraction to me may be a result of your boredom with the life here.'

'It's true that I live a very boring life here, but I have been doing that for years. Wives of Pakistani expatriates living outside their own country suffer invariably as we miss our culture, family, and the luxurious lifestyle that we had back home. There, we had several servants and maids. Here, we do everything by ourselves. We live in gilded cages. Our lives revolve around our husbands and children. But we Pakistani women are used to living a double and triple life. We are opaque and difficult to read. It is almost impossible to read a Pakistani woman.

'Our husbands and male relatives hardly know us or what we are doing. They don't care. For them, we are there at their bidding. My husband is blind toward me. He hardly notices me or cares what I do.

'I hate Rehmallah. He goes out with several women and has a regular girlfriend. He drinks when he's at parties or with his friends. He says that he has to do this for business. He insists that as a man, he is entitled to have his fun, but wants to protect his family from the bad effects of Western society. He therefore imposes strict rules for me and my children. We are not allowed to wear anything other than Pakistani clothes, except for the uniform the girls wear at school. We should not come in contact with other men, unless permitted or introduced by him, and that should only happen in his presence. I also know that the bank gets involved in a lot of illegal activities. Rehmallah is personally involved in many of these activities. He brings papers home and keeps a filing cabinet there for confidential papers. They talk about Islam but do everything against the Islamic injunctions, claiming that they do this for a higher purpose. I hope someday I will be able to take out my revenge against Rehmallah.

'My life is very complicated. I'll tell you all about my married life some other time. Suffice it to say, it is only a façade. Let's leave my husband and children out of this. This is my problem, and I will deal with it in my own way.

'I am not asking anything of you. I know that you have your own life, and there may be no room for me there. I do not want any commitments or promises from you, not even an acknowledgment or acceptance of my feelings. I will pray for you. Please call me once in a while if you remember me and consider me worth communicating with. Here is my telephone number.' She handed Amir a piece of paper with her number scribbled on it.

Amir quickly pocketed the number and said, 'Well, I may not go out of your life completely, as there is a strong possibility that I might have to return here on a longer-term assignment. Masood will speak to Azhar Alam. I have some unfinished business here. Actually, I may need your help when the time comes.'

'Oh, please don't build my hopes. I know this is not true, and you are telling me this to make me feel better. Please don't play with me like this, otherwise, I will wait for you to come back forever. As to me being able to do something for you, please know that I would do anything – anything – even at the risk of losing my life for you.'

'Let's say there is a possibility at this stage for me to return here. I don't know if and when it will happen. I'll let you know one way or the other as soon as possible, which may be in the next few weeks. In the meantime, I would like you to accept this gift from me.' Amir pushed Tiffany's box towards Rehana.

'This is for your girlfriend in Pakistan. I cannot accept this. Please do not embarrass me.' Rehana pushed the box back.

'Let's not make a scene here. I bought this for you, and that is the truth. I do not have a girlfriend in Pakistan or anywhere else. Let's leave my family and friends out of this. You and I have to exist in separate compartments of our own without allowing others to crowd us. Please accept it. Please!' Amir insisted.

'I am touched.' Rehana was glowing. 'Why don't you put it on me? It will stay there forever.'

'Should I? In here?'

'I would like you to. Don't worry about the people here. This is Switzerland. People mind their own business.'

Amir got up, went around the table, and put the pendant around Rehana's neck. As he bent to fasten the clasp, Rehana raised her arms suddenly and held Amir's head in her hands, pulling him towards her and kissing him on the lips.

Amir was dazed.

'Sorry, I don't know what happened to me,' she said, covering her face with her hands.

'We must go. The girls will return from school soon. I must be home when they get there. Let's go,' she said.

Amir quickly settled the bill and followed Rehana out. She was already out in the street and hailing a taxi. Before entering the taxi that stopped for her, Rehana turned to Amir, hugged him, and kissed him again on the mouth.

'Remember, I will wait for you. It is up to you. Your call will make my miserable life worth living. I am broken. Today, you have made my life worth living.' She disappeared into the taxi.

Amir stayed on the sidewalk for a few minutes and then started walking toward his hotel. This trip and Geneva had been full of surprises. His world had changed. Amir no longer seemed to be in control of his life.

Chapter 9

Singapore

While Amir was shopping in Geneva, it was 7.30 p.m. in Singapore. Special Agent Liu Chen parked his car outside the Golden Hotel. He had been following the tough-looking, tall Tajik, known to Singapore authorities as Aman, for several days. The Singapore Intelligence Bureau, alerted about the Tajik by the Indians, was keeping him under surveillance. According to the Review and Analysis Wing (RAW) of the Indian Intelligence Agency, the Tajik was a senior player in one of the Afghan Mujahideen groups fighting in Afghanistan and was on a shopping tour.

Over the last couple of days, the Tajik had met a well-known South African arms supplier and had spoken on the phone to the G&P Bank's Singapore manager, Tariq Dost Shah. Singapore suspected some of the transactions being undertaken by the G&P Bank, and therefore was keeping the bank under surveillance and had its telephone lines tapped.

Earlier, the Tajik had dialled Tariq Dost Shah's direct number and said, 'Is this Mr. Tariq?'

Tariq replied, 'Yes? Who is it?'

'This is Aman.'

Tariq was immediately alert and said, 'Salaam Alaikum. Welcome back to Singapore.' Like other G&P officials, Tariq knew how to look after the bank's premier clients, and Aman represented the Afghan Children Education Society, a front for an organisation fighting in Afghanistan.

'Waalekum Assalam. I would like to see you tonight at dinner about some business transactions I am considering. I have booked a table at 9.30 p.m. in The Sun King Restaurant at the Golden Hotel. It is on Orchard Street, next to the Hyatt. Do you think you can make it?'

'Of course, I will make it. I know the place, and I'll be there,' Tariq replied.

Chen received the recording of the conversation late in the afternoon and immediately went to The Sun King Restaurant. Since it was too early for dinner, the restaurant was empty.

Chen approached the lady at the reception, flashed his ID, and said, 'I would like to see the names of the people who have reserved tables for dinner at 9.30 tonight.'

Singaporeans have a very healthy respect for the authorities, particularly the Intelligence Bureau. The lady was very cooperative.

'So far, there are only three reservations for 9.30 p.m.,' she said, reading from a book in front of her. 'There are two Chinese families who have reserved tables for six each, and a Mr. Aman, who has reserved a table for two.'

'Could I please see the table you intend to give to Mr. Aman?' Chen asked.

'This way, please.' She led Chen to a table for two in a dark corner. 'Mr. Aman made a special request for privacy,' the lady explained.

'I thank you very much for your cooperation. I would like to be left alone at the table for a couple of minutes. I'll see you when I leave,' Chen said, moving towards the designated table.

Once at the table, he slipped a small listening device with a timer set to start at 9.30 p.m. into the flowerpot full of fresh roses.

On his way out, he met the lady at the reception and said, 'Thank you for your help. I am sure you have already forgotten this visit.'

'What visit?' The lady was on the ball.

Now, it was 9.30 p.m., Chen patiently waited in his car outside the hotel for the transmission to begin.

At exactly 9.30 p.m., a Chinese voice came through. 'I hope this table is okay for you, Mr. Aman.'

'Perfect,' A gruff, heavily accented voice replied. 'Please show my guest here when he arrives.'

Soon thereafter, 'Assalam Alaikum.'

'Waalekum Assalam. Are you well?' The Tajik replied courteously.

'I am okay, and you?'

'Still surviving,' Aman replied, not untruthfully.

'I know you live here and may know a lot more about Singapore restaurants, but I consider this to be one of the best Chinese restaurants here. I really enjoy the food and service here. This is my favourite table. I'm told that the prime minister of Singapore visits this place quite regularly,' Aman said.

'Although I live here, this is the first time I have come here. It seems to be a popular place,' Tariq replied.

For some time, they both appeared to be involved in small talk and discussed the menu. They ordered a well-selected combination of Chinese soup, dim sum, spring rolls, and several other dishes for the main course. Chen was getting a little restless, as nothing of interest was coming through.

Then Chen heard, 'Over the last few months, you should have received deposits in excess of two million US for the credit of the Afghan Children Education Society. I would like you to open a letter of credit for 980,000 US in favour of Tiny Angels Supplies (Private) Limited for a supply of children's books for our society to be shipped in the first week of January on the TIG Bright Star on a voyage to Karachi via Colombo. Here are the detailed instructions for opening the letter of credit and an invoice for the goods, together with the necessary authorisation that you need for releasing the payment. The letter of credit will be for payment of the invoiced amount upon the shipment of goods. You should release the payment when you receive the bill of lading and other necessary documents confirming the shipment. Please send all the documents by courier to the society's address in Peshawar, Pakistan. Our people in Peshawar will make arrangements for collecting the consignment in Karachi and its transfer overland to Afghanistan. The children in Afghanistan need these books urgently.'

The tape recorder in Chen's car was recording it all.

'I must tell you that a lot of deposits for the society come in cash. I am afraid that the Singapore authorities may become suspicious and start investigating these transactions.'

'Oh, come on. Charities are normally made in small cash sums. A lot of these deposits are donations from good, God-fearing believers who want to support the children of Afghanistan.

Singaporeans love money and business coming to Singapore, so there will be no problems.' The Tajik responded.

After this, the discussion returned to other matters, such as the rising property prices in Singapore and how well the Singapore government had done in managing its economy.

Around midnight, Chen noticed the tall Uzbek and a well-dressed Pakistani banker coming out of the restaurant and going their separate ways.

The next day, Chen passed the results of his surveillance in the form of a tape and a note narrating his personal actions to the head of the counterterrorism section, who immediately got a transcript of the tape made and passed on copies to the heads of the Anti-Money Laundering and Foreign Banks' Monitoring Units at the Central Bank.

Meetings of senior officials were called in at both locations, and a line of action was decided to investigate and monitor the activities of Mr. Aman and G&P Bank.

Chapter 10

Lagos, Nigeria

Abdu Ovululu worked at the G&P Bank's Lagos branch. His title at the bank was public relations officer, PRO, and he was supposed to fix any matters arising with government agencies in Nigeria. He was well-connected and seemed to know almost everyone who was worth knowing. His additional job was to fly with suitcases supposedly full of 'documents' to destinations outside Nigeria. He loved these trips, as they involved travelling first class and receiving generous bonuses.

Today, he was asked to go to Geneva. This was good. With the bonus he would get, he could afford to spend a few days in Europe during Christmas and do some shopping. He knew perfectly well that he was to carry a valuable cargo of currency and gems deposited with the bank by some very powerful people. He considered these assignments a privilege and took pride in the trust placed in him.

Abdu was flying Air France via Paris to Geneva at 10.30 p.m. Since both the bank and Murtala Mohammed International Airport were in the Ikeja suburb of Lagos, Abdu did not anticipate any difficulty reaching the airport. He left his home at 6 p.m. in his Volkswagen minivan. He would leave the van at the designated space at the airport for a friend to collect later.

Abdu reached the bank in about fifteen minutes. He was right on schedule. As was his custom when handling these special assignments, he drove straight to a special door in the back of the branch that was reserved for emergency use only. There, a security guard allowed him to enter the bank. The branch manager, Habib Jalil, was waiting for him with two very heavy suitcases.

'Good evening, Abdu.' Habib greeted him.

'Good evening, Sir'

'Ready? All your travel documents with you?'

'Of course. How many times I have done this now? I know the drill. Don't worry. Your goods will be safe in the hands of Mr. Masood in Geneva tomorrow.'

'I am relying on you. Have a safe trip.' And with that, Habib Jalil left.

Abdu stayed for a few minutes longer to load the suitcases in his van with the help of two security guards.

'These bags are so heavy. They are making a fool of you, Abdu. There are only rocks inside,' one of the guards joked.

'Don't worry, my man. Just load the damn things, and I will be out of here.' Abdu replied.

Abdu was soon racing on the Abeokuta Expressway, which linked to Murtala Mohammed International Airport. It was normally a forty-five-minute drive, but the traffic was heavy. Abdu recalled that Ikeja was a nice suburb not long ago, but with the unplanned and uncontrolled expansion, it had also become a concrete jungle and mess, not unlike other parts of Lagos. The famous electronics market housing hundreds of computer shops was a source of major population explosion and a fire hazard in the area. Loose electric wires were hanging everywhere in the streets. It was not very easy to drive through Ikeja or any part of Lagos anymore.

Approximately ten minutes from the airport, a couple of police cars blocked the road with their lights flashing. Six police officers were spread out, checking the papers of the drivers. They allowed only one car to pass at a time. Abdu knew that this was a ruse to collect Christmas beer money. The gift depended on who you were and how you handled the cops. It may be as high as a couple of thousand naira or as low as a few packs of cigarettes.

Abdu took out the carton of cigarettes he kept stashed under the front seat for these occasions. He slowed down and came to a complete stop behind a Toyota that was being looked at by a young policeman.

The policeman waved the Toyota ahead and asked Abdu to come forward. Abdu stopped near the policeman. 'Assalam Alaikum,' He greeted the policeman.

The policeman ignored the greeting and came very close to the car. Suddenly, he lifted his AK-47, pointed it at Abdu's head, and fired a burst. Abdu's head was completely blown off, and blood was splattered everywhere.

At the sound of the gunfire, all the policemen rushed to Abdu's van. They quickly opened the rear door of the van and transferred the two suitcases to one of the police cars. All the policemen then jumped in the two cars and sped away, leaving behind a scene of panic and chaos. The whole thing was over in less than a couple of minutes.

Robberies and hold-ups were not unusual in Lagos, but this was slightly different from the normal hold-ups. For the large crowd that had started to converge, this was entertainment and a story to be narrated for days to come. Some people who managed to reach the van tried opening the van's doors to see if the driver was alive. Others started looking for any valuables they could lay their hands on. Abdu's personal bag was gone in no time. The chaos was made worse by the traffic jam and the blaring horns of the drivers trying to pass.

After a few minutes, possibly in response to a telephone call by somebody, two police patrol cars and an ambulance arrived. By then, the scene of the crime was a complete mess. All the van's doors were open, and the windows were smashed. Everybody in the crowd had a different story to tell. According to one witness, he had seen the driver of the van shouting and then opening fire on the policeman, who returned the fire in self-defence and killed the driver. Another said that he had seen the policemen take out what looked like a container with a bomb inside and rush off to diffuse the bomb.

It was two in the morning when the police were finally able to establish the identity of the dead man as Abdu Ovululu, an employee of G&P Bank's Lagos branch. Further investigations indicated that the man was scheduled to travel on Air France to Paris and Geneva that night. Because of the connection with a foreign bank and the profile of the driver, who was to travel to Switzerland, the chief of the Lagos police's criminal investigations department was informed.

The chief himself had dealings with G&P Bank and knew of the bank's connections with the senior government leaders in Abuja. He called his connection at the Internal Security Bureau in Abuja and reported the event.

It was 4 in the morning when Habib Jalil's sleep was shattered by the constant ringing of the telephone on his bedside table.

'Hello.' Habib mumbled in his sleep.

'This is Colonel Ateequ N'devu from Abuja.' The caller said.

Habib sat up as if hit by 440 volts of electric current. Colonel N'devu was the head of security and was known to be a personal friend and manager of the assets of the military ruler. Habib started sweating.

'Yes, Colonel. I hope everything is okay. Your consignment left last night and must be halfway to its destination on the Air France flight to Geneva,' He blurted out.

'Everything is not okay. The courier's van was attacked on the expressway by a gang posing as policemen. The courier has been killed, and the goods have disappeared,' the voice said.

Habib started shivering uncontrollably. He could not believe what he was hearing. This could not be true. Surely this was a nightmare. He bit his hand to confirm that he was awake and that this was real.

'We have some leads and are following them. We believe that the Agoni tribe bandits were involved. There was also negligence on your part. You should have sent an escort with the courier. There was probably a leak inside your bank. My team is already on its way to interrogate your staff. I'm sure somebody was involved in providing the information to the thieves.

'The consignment was worth 80 million dollars. All of this was for my boss's personal account. We deposited it with the bank. As far as your client and all of us in Abuja are concerned, these were your assets and your losses. I hope you have insurance. We are investigating the crime and will try to retrieve the consignment, which will be returned to you after the necessary formalities, as it was your property. As far as we are concerned, your bank is responsible to us for the deposit we made with you. Just so there are no misunderstandings or rash acts, neither you nor your staff should leave Lagos until the investigation is complete. Please make sure that all your expatriate staff's passports are deposited with my department first thing tomorrow morning, otherwise, my staff will collect them forcibly. The border exits have already been notified to ensure that nobody working in or connected with your bank leaves the country.' With that said, the telephone went dead.

The receiver slipped from Habib's hand. He sat down on the floor leaning on the bed behind him.

Habib's Nigerian girlfriend, Sosu, shuffled in bed and woke up from the noise. 'What was it, darling? Some problem at the bank? Leave it 'til tomorrow. Darling, I am getting tired of you bringing your problems to our bedroom. You know that I come here to be with you to enjoy,' she moaned.

'Oh, shut up, and go back to sleep!' Habib raised his voice in frustration.

'I will not have you talk to me like that. I am your girlfriend, not a street whore. I will go now. NOW! TAKE ME HOME NOW!' Sosu screamed at him.

Habib could not afford a scene at this time and needed to concentrate. He took control of himself. 'Sorry, Sosu, darling. I have a serious problem, so I lost control. Please forgive me and sleep while I make a phone call. I will make it up to you tomorrow. We will buy a nice watch for you. Okay?'

'This is more like what I am used to.' Sosu was satisfied with the apology and calmed down. 'Make your call, but do not stay away for too long. Momma wants you in bed.'

Habib went to his library. It was a library in name only as it only had a few books and magazines, it mostly housed Habib's personal papers there. It also had an unlisted direct telephone line not connected elsewhere in the house. He walked slowly and found it difficult to keep his balance. He collapsed into the nearest chair, still in shock. His entire life, his carefully built career, both appeared to be falling apart. The Nigerian government officials were ruthless and would not hesitate to destroy the bank and imprison him if their assets were threatened. He could end up in a Nigerian prison for a long time.

Habib Jalil, son of a government clerk, joined Tijarat Bank as a cashier in their main Bunder Road Branch in Karachi in 1964 after passing his matriculation exams from a government school in a poor neighbourhood of Karachi. He had worked very hard. His books always balanced, and he was always ready to do special errands to deliver cash to important customers who were too busy to visit the bank. The manager liked him.

Habib went to an evening college and completed his Bachelor of Commerce from Karachi University. He was quickly promoted to the officer grade. His parents were happy; he earned good money and was working for a respectable bank. He soon married a distant cousin and settled into life. However, soon after his marriage, Pakistan went through political and economic turmoil. The country was dismembered in the 1971 Bangladesh war, and the whole country was depressed.

Around the same time, Sheikh Tayeb formed G&P Bank and was heavily recruiting staff for its various operations. The manager of Tijarat Bank's Bunder Road Branch, Jamil Hassan, decided to join the new bank for a posting outside Pakistan. He was appointed to work in Banjar, which was a backwater and very unpopular place for people to go and work at that time. Jamil Hassan encouraged Habib to join him.

In the gloomy days of post-Bangladesh Pakistan, hope was in short supply. Many Pakistanis were looking for work outside Pakistan, so Habib decided to join G&P Bank in Banjar. At that time, Habib had two young children, his four-year-old son, Shamim, and his two-year-old daughter, Zulekha. Shamim had just started school, and as Banjar was not a suitable destination for expatriate families, Habib decided to leave his family behind in Karachi and live a bachelor's life in Banjar.

He was miserable in Banjar. The only thing to keep him busy was work. He worked hard and late hours and visit his family in Karachi twice a year for a couple of weeks. He was treated like a prince when he was there. With the money he earned in Banjar, he could afford a small house in the upper-middle class Nazimabad area of Karachi. His children were growing up, and they started going to better-quality schools than Habib himself had attended.

Habib's hard work and flair for customer relationships was paying dividends. He was very popular with the bank's customers and was able to open accounts for the hundreds of Pakistani workers who needed reliable banking services for remitting money home. Habib used to visit the worker's dormitories on their paydays and collect funds for remittance to Pakistan. The workers did not have to waste time or money travelling to the bank.

Life in Banjar was, however, very dry. With his enhanced profile at the bank and money in his pocket, Habib eventually found other recreations. He joined a group of Pakistani bankers and middle- and upper-middle level project workers who met in the evenings for a game of cards and dinner. With the passage of time, the dinner group became larger and more adventurous. They started inviting dancing girls called *Raqquasas* to entertain them with *ghazals* (Urdu poetry) and *Mujra* (classical and semi-classical Indian dances) during the dinners. Alcohol was freely available in these *Mehfils* (gatherings). The *Raqquasas* were also available for private entertainment for clients. Habib developed his taste for ladies and liquor in Banjar. He enjoyed the company of a pretty Pakistani dancer, Shazadi, and often took her to his flat after the dinner parties.

Habib's family frequently travelled to Banjar for visits, but they did not like to stay there. The pretext for not staying was the children's schooling in Karachi, but the family was comfortable in Karachi with the remittances from Banjar. They liked independence and affluence.

Habib understood this and was initially unhappy that his family was unwilling to live with him. This feeling changed with his increased involvement in the dinner group's activities, and Habib also started to like his independence.

Life was no longer boring, and Karachi was far away. The fun was in Banjar. G&P Bank was prospering, and so was Habib. He was now a senior officer at the bank. Sheikh Tayeb rewarded loyalty and performance. With the expanding network of G&P Bank's operations, positions were available around the world. London and Geneva were reserved for the first-circle officers, but others who were not so close to upper management also got opportunities.

The taste for alcohol and ladies acquired in Banjar stayed with him. Despite this, Habib considered himself a good Muslim. He prayed on Fridays, gave alms to the poor, and fasted during the holy month of Ramadan. He even went to Makkah for the Hajj pilgrimage.

Nigeria was fertile territory for G&P Bank. It was a military dictatorship, and the senior government officials were known to be in need of the type of services G&P Bank was quite adept at providing, so it was only natural for G&P Bank to start operations there. When the decision was made to open a branch in Lagos, Habib was selected. This was five years ago. He worked very hard to build the business. This required working very long hours, recruiting and training staff, creating a solid customer base, and making connections with the ruling elite.

With perseverance and tricks that he learnt over the years, he managed to establish contact with the power brokers in Abuja. This completely changed the bank's business profile in Nigeria. Deposits started flowing in freely, and special private banking accounts were opened with the bank's Geneva branch, where hundreds of millions of dollars were deposited.

In accordance with the bank's policy, Habib received bonuses based on a percentage of deposits obtained and profit earned, as the bank's business and profits grew. He bought a large house for his family in the posh area of Defence Society in Karachi. His son Shamim was now studying to become a doctor. His daughter was enrolled in business studies at a prominent Karachi institute. With the availability of funds, Habib also purchased properties in London and New York and started living a life of wealth.

All of this was at risk now. He must speak to the headquarters.

It was approximately 9 a.m. in Karachi. Sheikh Tayeb and Azhar Alam would be at the bank. Habib dialled Azhar Alam's direct number.

'Hello.' Azhar Alam picked up the telephone on the first ring.

'Sir, Habib here. Assalam Alaikum.'

'Waalekum Assalam, Habib. Isn't it a little too early for you? You well?'

'Sir, something has happened here.' Habib immediately came to the point and briefed AA about the theft of the suitcases, the murder of the courier, and the telephone conversation with Colonel Ateequ N'devu.

AA's response was calm and measured. 'This is serious. Let me speak to the chairman, and we will call you on your direct home number in thirty minutes.'

True to his word, AA phoned Habib exactly thirty minutes later.

'The chairman and I have discussed the problem. We must act with caution. First, please tell Colonel N'devu that we will take responsibility for the loss and will give full credit for the funds and securities deposited with us. The chief should not worry about this.'
'Please tell him that the chairman would like to speak to him and set up a conference call at a time of the colonel's convenience.'

'You should immediately contact our senior Pakistani staff and brief them about the incident. Tell them to be very careful. Collect their passports, and take all the passports, including yours, to Pakistan's consul and deposit them with him. This should protect you from losing your passports and ability to travel should the Nigerian government decide to hold you. The chairman will also speak to the high commissioner in Abuja and request his cooperation.'

'First thing tomorrow morning, please remit our investment, including branch capital, retained profit, and management fee, to Geneva. Your local assets should equal your local liabilities. No more. In case of any unusual local demands arising, you should handle them through short-term inter-bank borrowings from other banks in Lagos. I repeat that, except for the bare minimum requirement to meet your normal expenses for the next few days, our investment in Nigeria should be transferred out by tomorrow morning.'

'You should also contact our lawyers, Akpaka & Joseph, and brief them about the incident and seek their advice to protect the bank and our staff.

'We will call you from time to time. You are also free to call the chairman and me any time during the day or night. We will be available at the bank or at home. You have the numbers.

'Don't worry, we will sort this out. The full resources of the bank will be used to protect you and our staff there. We are with you.'

'Thank you, Sir. I am sorry that this has happened, and I want you to know that we are proud to be working for the chairman and you. We know that you will do everything to protect us, whatever the cost.' Habib was relieved that the bank would meet its commitments and protect its staff.

'That we will do,' said AA, and hung up.

Habib was relieved after talking to AA. With the tension easing off, he started to feel guilty about his lifestyle. He stood up for the dawn prayers, and after the prayers, he sought Allah's forgiveness for his sins, promised to lead a sin-free life, and give up all his vices.

While Habib was still sitting on the prayer mat, busy seeking Allah's forgiveness, Sosu walked in. She was completely nude, her black body glistening like mahogany in the early morning light.

She had never seen Habib on a prayer mat before. She was shocked. 'What is wrong, darling? Come, baby, come. Momma will take away your troubles and make you happy.' She advanced towards Habib.

Habib looked at her as if he were stricken by the devil. He immediately cast his eyes away and recited a verse from the Quran. 'O Allah, save me from the clutches of the detested Satan.'

Sosu, believing that Habib was in distress and needed comfort, lowered herself onto Habib's lap and started kissing him. Habib pushed her away and stood up.

He said, 'Listen, Sosu, please do not take this as disrespect to you. Something terrible has happened. I don't know how the matter will develop in the coming hours or days. For your safety, it's better if you are not seen with me unless I call you. Some very senior government officials are involved. I have to do what I have to do, so please go as quickly as you can. There are two thousand dollars on the bedside table. Take them. Also, there are a few bottles of Black Label in the fridge. Take them if you want, or just drain them in the bathroom. I don't think I will need them anymore.'

'Come on, darling. Nothing can be so serious that you are turning me away and giving up your whisky. Come, give me a kiss, and everything will be okay. I am with you.'

'No, Sosu. Your life may be in danger. I am safe because they want something from me. You will be treated as what they call collateral damage. Please go.'

'Okay. I will go. Promise that you will call me, and let me know that you are fine. I am very worried. I have never seen you like this. I'll be back as soon as you are ready.' She started dressing.

After Sosu's departure, Habib phoned his four senior Pakistani officers and advised them to meet him at the Pakistan Consulate with their passports in approximately one hour. He told them that something had happened, and he would explain when they met.

Then he went through the papers in his library. He was an organised man. He knew exactly what he was looking for and where to find it. He shredded the papers he considered important under the prevailing circumstances. After he was satisfied that he had destroyed any damaging information, Habib quickly dressed. He made himself a coffee and drank it hot. He had no time for breakfast or even a leisurely cup of coffee today.

Habib picked up his briefcase and checked that his passport and chequebooks were inside. Before leaving, he looked out the window and was not surprised to see a police patrol car parked outside his apartment building. This required quick thinking. He locked his apartment and went to the service elevator that operated from the backdoor of the building. He exited the building through the tradesmen's door into a small street.

It was still very early morning, and although there were school buses in the street, the office traffic had not yet started. Habib walked through the small back streets of the city for ten minutes and came out on a major thoroughfare. There, he hailed a taxi and asked the driver to take him to the Pakistan Consulate. Fortunately, the consulate was also located in the Ikeja district and was not far away. It was only a few minutes' journey.

When he was only a couple blocks away from the consulate, Habib decided to disembark from the taxi and walk. When he entered the consulate's street, Habib was shocked to see a security checkpoint outside the consulate. Tough-looking soldiers in full battle gear were checking documents and frisking people before letting them pass.

Habib stopped and went across the street to a coffee shop. He bought a coffee and asked the salesgirl if he could use the telephone. She told him it would cost him one hundred naira for a call. Habib paid, and then called the consul's telephone number. The Pakistani Consulate security officer answered the phone immediately.

Habib identified himself and asked the reason for the heavy security outside the consulate.

'A little while back, we got a call from the Nigerian Diplomatic Security Department that they had information about a potential attack on the consulate and advised us that they would check anybody passing near the consulate or coming into the consulate. Of course, we were grateful and had no objection,' the security official replied.

Next, Habib made a call to one of his senior Pakistani colleagues and asked him not to go to the consulate and to advise other colleagues, as well. He told him that certain events had transpired and that he would explain when he meets with them at the bank.

He then took a taxi and asked the driver to take him to G&P Bank. Again, he was not surprised to find a police patrol car parked outside the bank.

'Good morning, Sir,' the security guard said, opening the door for Habib.

'Good morning, Ahmedu,' Habib replied. He was struck by the look on the guard's face. He looked as if he had seen a ghost. Habib immediately knew that something serious awaited him inside the bank.

The bank was still deserted, as only a couple of the usual early birds had arrived. They nodded to Habib as he passed them; they looked scared.

Soon, Habib found out why. A couple of tough looking gentlemen were waiting inside his office. They were wearing light safari suits – standard attire for senior Nigerian security officials when they are not donning their uniforms, national dresses, or suits.

One gentleman stood up and asked, 'Mr. Habib?' Habib nodded, acknowledging his name. The man continued, 'My name is Lieutenant David Aluto from the State Security, and with me is Sergeant Ikera Obomoso. Please sit down. We need to talk to you.'

Habib sat down. He had no strength to keep standing anyway.

'Colonel N'devu asked us to see you and ask that you listen to this.' The lieutenant took out a small Walkman-type tape recorder and handed it over to Habib. 'Please play the tape in the recorder,' he instructed.

Habib pressed the 'Play' button, and the room was filled with recordings of his telephone conversations made earlier that morning. The colour drained from his face. This explained the roadblock and security check outside the Pakistani Consulate. He knew that the Nigerian security apparatus was good, but this was too good. This proved that Abuja had a personal interest in the matter.

'First, as instructed by the colonel, please let me have your passport,' the lieutenant said. Habib opened his briefcase and handed over the passport without a word. 'Good. You should tell your expatriate staff to do the same. We need a list of the names and addresses of all the people working here. Sergeant Obomoso will take this from your HR department. A two-man team will speak to your staff individually. We will need a secure room for this purpose. Nobody will be allowed to leave until they have been spoken to by my staff. Staff that do not come to work today will be picked up from their homes and brought here. We could very easily take all your people to an interrogation centre, but we do not want to create an atmosphere of crisis and affect the bank's operations or reputation. So that no panic is created, I suggest you speak to your staff and tell them that your PR official Abdu was assassinated last night, and this enquiry is in connection to that. We will try to be as unobtrusive as possible so your business is not affected. The colonel has also requested that you call him. Here is his direct telephone number.' The lieutenant handed over a slip of paper with a telephone number on it.

Habib dialled the number given by the lieutenant. The call was answered by an authoritative voice.

'My dear Mr. Habib. Thank you for calling. I just wanted to speak to you so there are no mistakes, and you do not take any actions which may be considered unfriendly by us. We in Abuja were very happy to hear Mr. Azhar Alam's voice again and particularly pleased with his assurance that the bank will meet its commitments. We, however, did not like the other advice that he gave you.'

'Please understand that there has been a murder, probably by a group of thugs operating against the security of this nation. This needs to be investigated and dealt with. Please cooperate fully with Lieutenant Aluto. This is in your interest.

'I suggest you refrain from any unusual activity, despite Mr. Alam's instructions. There is no need for you to take these actions, particularly as they may be considered suspicious and may trigger action from our Central Bank and affect your operations in Nigeria and elsewhere in the world.'

'We would like to keep the whole matter confidential. After all, we are your friends, and we'd like to stay that way. There are, however, certain matters that need to be sorted out in person. I will make arrangements for you to meet the governor of the Central Bank soon to discuss these matters. Have a good day.' With that, Colonel N'devu closed the line.

Following the call, Habib called his senior staff and told them that Abdu was murdered by some bandits. The security agencies were investigating the murder and wanted to interview the bank's staff as a routine procedure. Nobody was being suspected, and everybody was expected to cooperate by giving any information that may be useful to the agencies. He also relayed that the officials would collect the passports of expatriate staff as a normal procedure adopted by the Nigerian police in such circumstances and return them after concluding enquiries. Habib asked his senior staff to relay the information to others in their departments accordingly.

The two visiting officers were given a room next to Habib's office. They were efficient. They quickly collected the details of the bank's employees and started interviewing them according to seniority. The senior expatriates were summoned first.

Around noon, Habib received another call. This time it was from the governor of the Central Bank, Dr. Iringa Okuwu. He wanted to see Habib in the Lagos office of the Central Bank in one hour's time.

As instructed, Habib was at the Central Bank's Lagos building at the appointed time. He was well known at the Central Bank and immediately ushered into the governor's office.

'Mr. Habib, it's good to see you. I hope you are well.' The governor welcomed Habib.

'It's nice to see you, also, Sir. I wish the circumstances of our meeting were a little better. I'd be lying if I said that I am completely well and relaxed,' Habib replied.

'These were very unfortunate events last night. This has complicated the matter between us. Our friends in Abuja are very nervous.' The governor did not beat around the bush.

'I do not know why Abuja should be nervous. I agree that assets worth a large amount of money was looted, but that was through no fault of ours. We have served our clients in this country sincerely over many years. I am sure that your security agencies, which are very efficient, will track down the perpetrators and get the assets back.' Habib took the high road.

'I am not sure if the bandits will be caught or the assets recovered. I understand they may be from the Agoni tribe who are fighting against our government and might have already disappeared with the loot.

'That is why our friends are nervous and want to ensure they do not suffer any loss. They entrusted the assets to the bank. It was up to the bank to ensure that these were handled efficiently. As far as our friends are concerned, you owe them the value of these assets.

'I'm sure you are aware that our friends have deposited approximately 800 million dollars with your bank. They want to withdraw their deposits. I have been instructed to advise you that they would like to transfer all their balances and assets from your bank to certain other banks. Full instructions for the transfer of deposits are included in this envelope.' The governor passed a sealed envelope to Habib. 'Our friends expect this will be done immediately.'

'We are fully committed to honouring our obligations. However, there are very large amounts involved, and it might take some time for our bank to liquidate the investments made against these deposits and transfer the proceeds to the designated banks,' Habib protested.

'Time is what you do not have in plenty. Considering our relationship, our friends are willing to give you up to two weeks maximum. In the meantime, you and your senior staff will not be allowed to travel outside Lagos. All of you will be required to report to the central police station in Ikeja every Monday morning. Your bank may continue to carry on normal business operations, but you will not be allowed to make any transfers of funds on your own account outside Nigeria. I hope you appreciate that this incident has affected the trust of our friends in your bank, and therefore, once the funds owed to our friends have been remitted, you will be allowed to continue without any restrictions.

'Instructions have already been issued to place you under investigation under the Anti-Money Laundering and Financial Crimes Law. This is the first step necessary to build a case against you and your bank in case a rift develops between you and my principals. Non-compliance with the instructions given to you will immediately trigger you and your senior staff's detention and prosecution under the law. I understand that the law carries a minimum penalty of fifteen years in prison for violators. Therefore, I strongly recommend that your bank transfers the assets as requested. Of course, we will do everything possible to assist you in your efforts and make your stay here pleasant.' The governor stood up and offered his hand, indicating that the meeting was over.

Habib exited the Central Bank building quickly. He was in shock. His life, as he had known it, was coming to an end.

From the Central Bank, Habib drove straight to the nearby offices of Akpaka & Joseph, the bank's lawyers. He had to wait at the reception, as he had not sought an advance appointment and the senior partner, Tarimo Akpaka, was busy with another client.

As soon as Mr. Akpaka finished with his other client, he came out of his office and greeted Habib. 'Habib, my friend. How are you? This is a busy time at the bank nearing the year-end closing. You must do a lot of work to decorate the books at this time of the year, eh?' He laughed at his own joke as he ushered Habib into his private chambers.

Tarimo Akpaka was a UK-trained barrister and was known to be one of the most effective lawyers in Nigeria. He rarely lost cases. He knew everybody of importance in Nigeria, both inside and outside the court. He had influential friends and contacts in Abuja, which also helped.

'Sorry I came without an appointment, Tarimo. I'm in trouble; the bank is in trouble. We need help.' Habib got straight to the point.

'Tell me.'

Habib narrated the whole series of events, beginning with the previous evening and continuing into the morning. He also relayed that Mr. Azhar Alam had asked him to speak to Mr. Akpaka.

'This is serious not because what happened was unusual. It's serious because of the amount of money involved and the people affected. We need to move quickly.' Tarimo was quick to grasp the situation. 'Here is what we will do. First of all, if you agree, I will speak to Colonel N'devu and tell him that I am helping you. I will request him to do the following: Withdraw the requirement for you and your colleagues to report to the police station and not treat you or your colleagues as criminals. After all, you have not committed any crime and are unlikely to do so; give you more time to remit the funds deposited with your bank; and let you continue with normal banking operations in Nigeria as if nothing has happened. Of course, they might need certain guarantees that the bank will return the lost money and remit the funds as requested by them. Do you have any plans to meet this requirement?'

'I will have to speak to Mr. Alam. Unfortunately, our telephones are tapped.'

'You may phone Azhar from here. I presume my telephones are not tapped, at least not yet. I don't think I will be able to remove a tap from your phone. Even if they say they have removed it, they will continue to listen in. To make confidential phone calls, go to a friend's house or find a public phone.'

'Will you join me on the call to Mr. Alam?'

'If you wish, sure.'

Habib dialled Azhar Alam's private telephone number, and he got a response immediately.

'Hello, Azhar here.'

'Sir, this is Habib.'

'Habib. I hope you and the others in Lagos are safe.'

'So far, we are okay, but it is getting hot. I am with Mr. Akpaka. First, I want to brief you about the events since we spoke this morning, and then Mr. Akpaka and I want to discuss the options to deal with the situation.'

'Tarimo, my friend, how are you and your family?' Azhar Alam greeted Tarimo Akpaka.

'Everybody is fine. I hope you and your family are good too. Habib has told me about the difficulties that have arisen because of the sad events that occurred last night.'

'Yes, this is a very unfortunate situation.'

Habib very quickly gave a brief of the events that had occurred, including the meeting with Dr. Okuwu and Tarimo Akpaka's suggestion for dealing with the matter.

'I am sorry to hear that you are facing this difficult situation, Habib.' Azhar Alam was full of sympathy. 'Please tell your colleagues that we are working on this matter and will do everything possible to protect you and the bank.

'I agree that Tarimo should speak to his contacts in Abuja and get these ridiculous restrictions removed. As he said, you have neither committed nor are likely to commit a crime. Your telephone should not be tapped. You are a professional banker, the head of a foreign bank legitimately operating in Nigeria, and you cannot do your business if you are not assured confidentiality.

'As to the guarantees, we are a big bank. We deal with depositors' funds. The bank issues guarantee. It does not go to others to obtain guarantees. Please tell the colonel that the bank has billions of dollars in assets, and they should not worry about their investments with us.'

'Now, I want to ask a few questions to Tarimo.

'Tarimo, what do you think of this nonsense of threats and high handedness by the authorities? There has been a crime. We have lost a staff member and a considerable sum of money. We are the victims. I don't understand this hostile attitude from the authorities. They are treating us as if we are criminals. There must be legal recourse against this. Please tell me.'

'You are dealing with the people right at the top. They seem to fear that their personal investments are at risk. Your advice to Habib to withdraw all your investments from Nigeria and contact the Pakistan High Commission might have added to their fears. We will have to work hard to remove those fears and assure them that their assets are safe. I believe that is possible.

'As to the legal recourse, this may get very messy for all the parties concerned. In order to approach the court against the officials' action, you would have to come clean and admit that your employee was carrying a very large sum of money in cash and other securities for transfer out of the country. As to the source of these funds, the depositors will flatly deny they had anything to do with it and claim that they suspect you were involved in assisting criminals in illegally transferring funds outside Nigeria. This is a crime, and therefore action was being taken against your bank as well as your staff who were involved in this matter. Under the circumstances, referring to a court in Nigeria does not sound like a good option.

'If you agree, I'll talk to my contacts in Abuja and get them to relax the hardships being imposed. You may have to pay a fee to intermediaries to achieve this.'

'How much do you think this would cost?'

'Our fee for dealing with this matter initially, without getting involved in any litigation, may amount to five hundred thousand US dollars. The intermediaries' services would cost another five hundred thousand US. Fifty percent of the combined fee, ours and the intermediaries should be deposited into our account immediately.

'Of course, you will have to assure the parties that you will make the loss good within a reasonable time. Since you are a sound bank, there is no reason for them to withdraw their balances from you, and we will request them to continue their relationship. They may not agree to this, but we'll try.'

'One million dollars, in addition to the eighty million lost, is a very big sum. The bank may not be willing to pay such a large fee and decide to take its chances with the courts. The bank also has strong contacts in the Pakistan government who might help.' Azhar was not happy with the suggestion.

'It's up to you. I consider that it is already too late, and it may not be possible to get any relief. I know that it's not always possible to dissuade the people in Abuja from changing their minds.' Tarimo replied.

'I'll call you in half an hour. Please ask Habib to stay in your offices until I call back.'

'Sure. We'll wait for your call.' With that, Tarimo Akpaka disconnected the call.

Habib sat deflated in his chair during the conversation. He had no energy left. This was a nightmare.

'By the way, why didn't you send an escort with your man to the airport?' Tarimo asked him.

'We didn't want to attract any attention to the operation. Security convoys get noticed. We'd done this many times, and it was a routine affair. Abdu used to travel every month. This had never happened before.' Habib replied.

'It is going to cost your bank a lot of money and possibly a loss of business this time, my friend.' Tarimo remarked.

Exactly thirty minutes later, Tarimo's telephone rang. It was Azhar Alam, as expected.

'Hello.'

'Hello. This is Tarimo Akpaka. I have Habib with me here.'

'It seems we have very little choice at this stage, so I request you proceed as discussed. Sheikh Tayeb has asked me to pass on his personal request to you to deal with this matter as swiftly and economically as possible. The bank is your regular client. We appreciate your services and would be grateful if the total expense is limited to five hundred thousand US dollars. As instructed, this amount will be deposited in your usual account.'

'I'll talk to my partner and reduce our fee to four hundred thousand US. I'll charge you the exact amount we will have to pay to the intermediary. This will not exceed five hundred thousand dollars. We'll try to reduce it as much as possible.' Tarimo was gracious.

'Thank you, Tarimo. Habib, I understand you are going through a difficult time. Please stay calm and focused. You are the leader of the team. We will do everything to support you from here. Please keep us informed of developments. I hope Tarimo will be able to remove the tap from your phone so we can talk freely.'

'Thank you, Sir. I'll do my best to ensure that we do not lose our nerve and stay focused. Please also pray for us, as we do not know how and when this will end,' Habib responded.

'Oh, this shall also pass. Don't worry. We will pray for you. Good luck and take care.'

'Goodbye, Sir.' the telephone call ended.

After the call ended, Tarimo said to Habib, 'You go back to the bank and behave as if nothing has happened. Stay calm. I will now get busy. Your telephone is bugged, and you'll be followed. We'll have to think of a safe method of communication.

'To start with, tonight you go to dinner at Rajmata's. It's a new Indian restaurant at the Marina, Bayo Kuku Road in Ikoyi. Arrive there at 7.30 p.m. There will be a table booked for two in the name of Mr. Tony D'Souza. When you enter the restaurant, tell the head waiter that you are expecting a guest to join you and that he might phone you before he arrives. At exactly 7.45 p.m., I'll call you and brief you about developments. We'll take it from there.'

'I have never been to Rajmata's, but I've heard good things about it and know where it is. I'll be there at 7.30 p.m.'

'Speak to you then. Hopefully, I will have some good news for you.'

'I certainly hope so. I am very frightened.' Habib was nervous.

'I agree it is not a good situation, but with the right connections, it will be sorted out,' Tarimo said, shaking Habib's hand.

Habib drove to the bank straight from the lawyers' offices. The atmosphere at the Bank was very tense. Apparently, the staff members were called in one-by-one by the investigating officers. Lieutenant Aluto asked questions, and Sergeant Obomoso made notes of the information they were getting. They were very thorough and wanted to know the full personal history of each individual, their role in the bank, their relationship with Abdu Ovululu, if they knew why Abdu travelled so much on the bank's business, and if they knew about Abdu's travel plans for the previous night, among other questions.

When Habib entered, the officers were speaking to Haseeb Serai, the senior officer in charge of the corporate clients' department. The officers wanted to know everything about Haseeb: how long he had been with the bank, his family, his friends, whether he was a friend of Abdu and aware of Abdu's travel plans on the evening of the incident. Their tone and attitude were aggressive.

Haseeb responded to the questions truthfully and told the officers that he was not involved in Abdu's activities in the bank. Abdu reported and dealt with Habib only. When Lieutenant Aluto saw Habib arrive, he released Haseeb and walked into Habib's office.

'I need to see you for a few minutes,' he said, closing the door behind him.

Habib realised this was not a request, but a demand, and closed the file he had opened in front of him to look busy.

'Sure. Please take a seat.' Habib showed the inevitable courtesy.

'We have been talking to your staff here, and we haven't found any leads so far. The people at the department are making all-out efforts to track down the culprits. We will get them.

'Somebody from within the bank leaked the information about Abdu's role and travel plans to the criminals. So far, it appears you were the only one in the bank who knew about Abdu's work and his travel plans.' He looked pointedly at Habib.

The colour drained from Habib's face. 'I do not like your insinuation, Lieutenant.' Habib was getting angry. 'Of course, I knew and directed Abdu. He worked for me. But to indicate that I might be involved in passing on the information to the criminals shows your lack of understanding of the situation. Both the bank and I stand to lose everything – the bank's international reputation, the business here, my career and probably my liberty if this matter does not get sorted out, so I suggest that you concentrate on finding the real culprits instead of harassing my staff and me.'

The lieutenant didn't appear surprised at Habib's reaction, he had anticipated it. 'I was not insinuating anything. I only mentioned the findings so far. Don't worry. We'll get the real culprits. As I said, my entire department is on this case, and the bosses have assigned their best people on this matter,' the lieutenant said, getting up from his seat.

'Please let me know how this develops and if I can do anything to assist you.'

'That we will do.' the lieutenant said as he left Habib's office.

It was difficult for Habib to concentrate on work. At exactly 5 p.m., the bank's official closing time, he left the bank and took a taxi home. Once at home, he slumped on the sofa. There was no energy left in him. He was finding it difficult to sit down or even breathe.

Rajmata's was located at Lagos Marina. The Marina was about forty-five minutes from Habib's home. He planned to leave at 6.30 p.m., so he put on the TV to distract himself. Mercifully, there was no mention of Abdu's killing or the robbery. There were a lot of murders and robberies in Lagos. The killing of an individual did not merit coverage in the daily news.

Habib showered, changed into casual attire, and left his home at exactly 6.30 p.m. This time, he did not have to worry about being followed. He knew he would be, so he took his car from the underground parking and started driving towards the Marina.

He had no difficulty finding Rajmata's with its brightly lit signboard. He arrived at exactly 7.30 p.m. The Sikh doorman, dressed like a courtier, courteously held the door open for Habib.

'I have a table reserved in the name of Mr. Tony D'Souza,' he said to the pretty Indian girl sari who approached him with a welcoming smile.

'Yes, Sir.' The lady led him to a dimly lit table in a corner.

Rajmata's, which meant *the King's Mother* in Hindi, was a new, upmarket restaurant in Lagos. There were not many guests in the restaurant. Habib thought it was perhaps because it was still too early in the evening for the high society of Lagos to go to dinner.

'I am expecting another guest. He will telephone me before coming,' he told his usher.

'Sure, Sir. We will bring the telephone to your table if anybody calls.'

Habib was served roasted *papads* (Indian crackers) with yoghurt, mint chutney, and Indian pickles as a complimentary entrée. The papads were crisp and delicious. He looked at the menu. There were vegetarian and non-vegetarian dishes. The vegetarian dishes were South-Indian, whereas all the meat dishes were North-Indian.

'I'm waiting for a guest. I'll order when he arrives,' Habib told the waiter. 'Just bring me a bottle of still water at room temperature.' This was new for Habib; he normally liked wine with dinner.

At exactly 7.45 p.m., Habib saw the hostess approaching his table with a telephone receiver in her hand. 'Your call, Sir.' She passed the receiver to Habib and quickly returned to her post.

'Tony D'Souza.' Habib spoke into the phone.

'Tony, this is Okuju. My friend, I am sorry that I cannot join you for dinner tonight, as something very urgent has come up. You know, I love Indian food and am surely missing good food and delightful company.' Tarimo sounded as if he was really going to miss a good dinner. 'Now, listen very carefully.' The tone changed to serious and business-like. 'My contact will be able to help. His fee will be four hundred thousand US dollars. I have discussed and convinced my partners to charge you only three and a half hundred thousand for our services.

'I have already told my friend to proceed. He'll get into action tomorrow morning. He will try to get the restrictions removed and work out a mutually acceptable solution for the settlement. My friend says he is confident that sometime tomorrow morning, the investigating team at the bank and all the restrictions placed on your staff, except the expatriates, will be withdrawn. There will be a newspaper announcement by the Lagos police that the culprits of the hold-up and murder of Abdu Ovululu were arrested and are in police custody, so there will be no reason for further investigation.'

'This is what you are required to do: make sure that fifty percent of the fee mentioned by me is deposited into the usual firm's designated bank account within twenty-four hours. If this does not happen, then my friend and I will cease our involvement immediately. The fifty percent balance should be paid in two weeks, during which time we hope to clear the whole mess.

'Opposite the bank, there is a supermarket called Africa. I will send messages to you through the manager of the supermarket. You should send a messenger to buy cigarettes or soft drinks at 11 a.m. and 2 p.m. every day from now on. The messenger should say hello to the manager, who will give him my message in a sealed envelope if there is one. In case you want to communicate with me, you should also go to the supermarket and tell the manager that you want to speak to Mr. Okuju. He will get you through to me.' Tarimo was being careful.

'You had said that the restrictions on the bank's staff, except expatriates, will be withdrawn. What about us expatriates?' Habib asked.

'Unfortunately, the foreigners will not be allowed to leave the country until this is sorted out. However, I have been told that there will be no telephone tapping, but I would still be very careful and not make any sensitive calls. I don't think that the other staff of the bank will merit much attention now, so you may use their telephones.'

'Thank you, Okuju. I'll speak to my boss and ensure that your request is complied with.'

'Good. But do be very careful in your communications. Enjoy your dinner, and I will speak to you soon.' Tarimo disconnected the call.

Habib called the waiter over and handed back the receiver. He was not completely happy, but he was relieved that the pressure was easing. He understood that he and the other expatriates were hostages until the clients were satisfied that their assets were secure.

'My guest is not coming. I am ready to order. What is the speciality here?'

'In non-veg, today, *achari tikkas* are special as starters. This is a very special dish from our grill, created by the chef. For the main course, you might try our *chicken jalfrezi* (spiced chicken curry) with buttered nan. The biryani is also very good.'

'Okay. Get me an achari tikka and chicken jalfrezi with buttered nan. I would like to drink a *sweet lassi* (yogurt drink).'

The waiter noted the order, repeated it for confirmation and left.

The food was delicious. It was some of the best Habib had tasted. In any other circumstance, he would have really enjoyed and relished it, but today there were many other things on his mind. After finishing the meal, Habib called the waiter over and asked if there was a place nearby where he could make an international call.

'Sure, Sir. You may use our telephone. There will be a fifty percent service charge for international calls. We have the facility for international calls for our valued customers,' the waiter responded.

It's good that Asian businessmen rarely miss an opportunity to make money. They provide valuable life-saving services when needed, Habib thought.

'Sir, give me the number. Our telephonist will dial, and when connected, she'll pass the telephone to you. There is a telephone metre with our telephonist to calculate the charge.' The waiter was eager to provide service to this wealthy-looking Asian guest who might leave a generous tip.

Habib wrote Azhar Alam's private number on a slip of paper and handed it to the waiter. Within a few minutes, he came back with the telephone receiver in hand.

'Your party is on the line, Sir.' He handed over the receiver to Habib.

'Hello, Sir, this is me.' Habib did not want to speak his name for the restaurant staff to hear.

'Yes, yes. I know and understand. How are you, and how is it going there?'

'Difficult, Sir. I hope this gets sorted out soon. It is too much pressure, not only for me but for others, as well.'

Habib then briefed his boss about the events of the day, including the results of Tarimo's efforts, using the vaguest terms and language. He was glad that Azhar was quick to grasp the details and understood everything without asking him to repeat or clarify.

'Unfortunately, this has arisen at a very bad time, as our senior team is busy dealing with the annual financial closing issues. I have briefed the chairman about the situation in Lagos. He has authorised me to do whatever is necessary. Tell your friends in Lagos that their instructions will be followed. We will also be ready to compensate the growers for the lost crop. About other matters, I'll discuss these in our security committee meeting tomorrow. Your friends should understand that at this time of the year, we like to store new products in our warehouses and not empty our stocks, particularly when our warehouses are not completely full at this time. But we will make our best efforts and find an acceptable solution. I know it's not easy, but don't worry, and leave it to me. We will sort this out,' Azhar Alam said.

'Sir, I cannot help but worry. I will try not to. We are going into Christmas and the New Year. I hope this thing does not drag on,' Habib replied.

'We'll try to move fast once we hear how your friends want to solve this. It might need some discussions, though. We might need to have some secure communication facilities,' Azhar Alam said.

'I'll ask my friends to guide us in getting those facilities and will let you know.'

'Good. I will speak to you soon.'

'*Allah Hafiz (*may Allah protect you*)*, Sir.'

'Allah Hafiz.' The call ended.

The waiter returned immediately and took the receiver away. He asked Habib if he wanted any dessert.

'No. I am fine. Just get me the bill,' Habib said.

Habib settled the bill and left a hefty tip for the waiter. He knew he might have to use the telephone facility again, and the restaurant staff would welcome him if he was generous.

It was close to 10 p.m., and Habib still had to drive home. It had been a long day. Habib felt very tired. He did not want to drive but had no choice. As soon as he entered his car and was about to put the key in the ignition, a young boy appeared at the window on his side of the car. Habib did not know where the boy came from, but he had a gun in his hands.

'Give me your wallet and your watch,' the boy said, pointing the gun at Habib's head.

Habib was shocked. He did not know how to react.

'Do it, man, or I'll blow your head off.' The boy was getting jumpy. He removed the safety of the gun.

Habib quietly gave him his wallet and Rolex. The Rolex was his favourite, given to him as a gift from Sheikh Tayeb at the completion of ten years with the bank.

The boy grabbed the wallet and watch and raced away. Habib saw him laughing and heard him shouting profanity at Habib. This was really becoming a nightmare. Habib sat in the car, dazed and paralysed. He could not move or think. Slowly it dawned on him that with his passport with the police, his identity and credit cards are gone and no money in his pocket, he was completely helpless. He felt naked.

He had to report the robbery to the police. He would need them to make a report to get his identity and credit cards. The robber was probably already spending money on his credit card. He needed Abdu Ovululu, who was good at sorting out these things for him. But Abdu was not there.

He looked at his car's petrol gauge. It showed that he was on reserve. *God, please don't let the car run out of gas*, he silently prayed. Getting gas for a car was a major problem in Lagos. There were always mile-long queues at the gas stations, and with no money, he wouldn't be able to buy the gas anyway.

Habib needed to get home. At this point, his only goal in life was to get to the relative safety of his home. Everything else appeared to be irrelevant. He was sure that he could not take any more stress. He slowly reversed the car out of the parking. He did not need a crash tonight. Not with nothing on him.

He drove very carefully and took the longer but less-crowded route and managed to reach home by 11.30 p.m.; mercifully, the car had not stopped for lack of gas. As soon as he was home, he called Tarimo and told him that he had lost his wallet and watch somewhere. He was very careful not to mention the exact place or circumstances of the loss. Tarimo was sympathetic, but not excited.

'These things happen. Tomorrow, give me the list of credit cards with their numbers and other items lost. I'll call a police friend and tell him to register the report of the loss of a wallet with money, credit and identity cards so you will get the official police report needed for obtaining the replacement. I suggest that you call your banks immediately and block the credit cards,' Tarimo advised.

After finishing the call with Tarimo, Habib called the banks and blocked his credit cards.

Chapter 11

London: Offices of Tolbert and Gibbs. Chartered Accountants

A meeting was being called to order in the wood-panelled partners' executive meeting room of Tolbert and Gibbs. Charles Ramsey, Senior Banking Partner, was in the lead chair. Also in attendance were David Finner, Banking Partner, George Hansel, Executive Manager, Banking Audits, and Danny in his capacity as the Audit Manager and the Field Audit Team Leader of G&P Bank.

The meeting was to discuss the audit issues arising out of the interim audit of G&P Bank and to plan for the final audit. The bank required the audit to be completed and the signed audit report issued on the financial statements by 20 January. As this was a tight deadline, the audit team had to be fully prepared and any outstanding issues would need to be resolved quickly.

'I have reviewed the Audit Findings Memorandum for G&P Bank,' Charles Ramsey began. 'There seem to be quite a few issues that need resolution before we are able to complete the audit and issue our report.'

'First of all, we are not sure if the loan loss reserve is adequate. There are several investments that do not appear to be fully realisable. They seem to remain inactive or do not show any recovery, and suddenly large sums of money are deposited in these accounts at periodic intervals. The worst of them are the accounts relating to Tanganyika International Group - TIG. They seem to have hundreds of companies in their group involved in inter-group transactions, transferring funds between themselves, making it very difficult to assess the age of the outstanding balances for determining whether the bank's advances to the group are secure and recoverable. David, you have discussed this matter with Mateen Saeed, the bank's controller. How does he explain this?'

David did not seem to be worried and appeared happy to accept Mateen Saeed's explanation. 'Mateen says that most of the bank's large clients are based in the Middle East or Asia. These people are very secretive and erratic in managing their banking affairs. These clients are very, very rich, so there is no financial risk. He seems to be right as last year we also had several non-performing accounts at the interim audit stage. These were subsequently cleared. A few of these were, in fact, closed by the bank because the bank's management was not happy about the way those clients operated their accounts. Also, some clients keep accounts in various countries with the bank. The bank is collating information about these accounts to ensure that the debits are set off against deposits, provided there is no contravention of banking laws. As to the Tanganyika International Group, it is the bank's oldest and biggest client. The group is owned by Ismail Soothar and his family. They are very rich and made their money in Tanzania. Ismail Soothar had large business interests there before moving to Pakistan. He is a personal friend of Sheikh Tayeb, and according to Mateen, it is unthinkable that Ismail Soothar would renege on his commitments to Sheikh Tayeb or the bank. These things simply do not happen in Pakistan or the Middle East. Business is still done on the basis of personal reputation and honour there. Your word is your bond.'

Charles listened intently, then remarked, 'Well, on 30 November, the bank was exposed to close to 1.5 billion pounds in some of these unusual accounts. I hope you and Mateen are right in that these accounts will not prove to be bad. Otherwise, the bank will have a serious problem. We'll need to follow up on these at the final audit and ensure that the exposure is considerably reduced, or we will insist on the provision against at least some of the large outstanding balances. Failing that would leave us with no option but to qualify our report. That would be a disaster for everybody, most of all the bank itself.'

'We will take this as a follow-up point for the final work.' Danny made a note.

'Are there any other major issues?' Charles enquired.

'The other issues seem to be more of an irritation rather than any real problems,' David responded as he thumbed through the file. 'Their management style seems to be quite unique. A lot of very senior people at the bank spend more time in Karachi than in

London. They make decisions there, approving millions of pounds of transactions. London executes those decisions without the proper supporting documents, which are eventually completed. We will include these matters and our recommendations for improvement in the letter to the management and insist that our recommendations are complied with as soon as possible. Does everybody agree?'

Nobody said anything.

David continued, 'The bank's operating style has to change. The way they operate may prove quite dangerous for them, as well as for us. George, Danny, please ensure that this is done.'

'I believe there are opportunities here for us. Don't you think, David?' Charles winked at David.

David was very quick on the uptake. 'Of course. I'll tell Mateen that all this mess is causing us to make extra efforts, and it increases our time cost. We should be compensated for this, if not through the audit fee, then through some other means. I believe we should be able to get at least an additional two hundred fifty thousand pounds from them. I will also offer to arrange for a review of their operating procedures for granting and monitoring loans and advances. That could be performed by our business systems group. I'm sure this will be a very intricate and specialised assignment deserving around a million pounds in fees. I believe Mateen will have no problem getting the additional fee and special assignment approved by the bank's board.'

Charles appeared to be satisfied and moved to wrap up the meeting. 'So, how is my old friend, Sheikh Tayeb? Say hello to him for me when you see him next. I hope he also lets you enjoy some of his legendary hospitality.' Charles had fond memories of his visits to G&P Bank when he was a junior partner directly handling the bank's audit during its initial years of establishment in London.

'Both, Sheikh Tayeb and Azhar Alam now spend most of their time in Karachi. I haven't seen them for a long time. But Mateen and his crowd do look after us. Their hospitality is still special. We are invited to their Christmas party at Dorchester.'

'Dorchester, eh! Typical G&P Bank. They would have nothing less,' Charles commented, and the meeting was adjourned.

Chapter 12

Hong Kong – The Offices of Tanganyika Investment Group (TIG)

It was the Monday before Christmas, and Hong Kong was festive. Buntings, huge paper lanterns, and balloons were festooned all over the city. On a normal night, the city was brightly lit by huge neon signs everywhere, but the seasonal Christmas decorations made the city shine even brighter. There was a saying that during Christmas week, Hong Kong was visible from space because of its illumination.

TIG headquarters was on the top floor of the thirty-three storey Crystal Tower on Canton Road in Kowloon. Hong Kong was a tribute to the achievements of enterprise and capitalism. The city was a mass of humanity packed like sardines in the space of a few miles. Kowloon's golden mile, where Crystal Tower was located, was perhaps the most expensive piece of real estate on Earth. Hong Kong never went to sleep. Kai Tak Airport, with its runway located right next to the harbour, was busy around the clock as huge jumbo aircraft landed and took off incessantly. Hong Kong also had the world's largest container seaport.

TIG owned Crystal Tower and occupied the top ten floors of the building. Other occupants included a prestigious law firm, the Hong Kong offices of Tolbert and Gibbs, the famous UK accounting firm, G&P Bank, and some Japanese export houses. G&P Bank also had a branch on the ground floor.

Although located on Canton Road, which was one of the major arteries of Hong Kong, Crystal Tower's main entrance was on a small backstreet because a Feng Shui expert had advised that the building was located on a very uncomfortable part of a dragon's body. The main entrance of the building, which would have heavy traffic, should be located in a way not to cause discomfort to the dragon. Otherwise, the dragon would be unhappy and harm the owners and occupants of the building.

Ismail Soothar did not believe in what he called the 'Feng Shui humbug', but he had to surrender to the Feng Shui expert's advice because no Hong Kong businessman would rent in the building unless it was considered safe and auspicious according to the standards of Feng Shui. Hong Kong residents relied heavily on Feng Shui to ensure that their accommodations and interior settings were harmonious. The senior partners of Tolbert and Gibbs had the smallest offices nearer the kitchen, based on a Feng Shui expert's advice. A junior partner was given the prestigious corner office because his role was not considered critical to the firm's success and that office had poor feng shui.

Today was the executive board meeting of TIG that would be attended by Ismail Soothar, his three sons: Yakoob, Haroon and Rafik, and their group finance director, Salim Chaliwala. Later in the day, the meeting would expand to include Alex Brun, head of Europe and Americas, Mansukh Lal, head of the Asia Pacific, and Nari Patel, head of the Middle East and Africa.

It was a very pleasant morning. Decembers were pleasant in Hong Kong.

Ismail Soothar had been in the office since seven in the morning. Yakoob, who had flown in his personal executive jet that morning, was with him. The father and son were very close. They had some papers spread before them and were involved in a serious discussion. The other two sons, Haroon and Rafik, and their group finance director, Salim Chaliwala, would join them at ten.

Ismail had given away the management control of the group to his eldest son. Although he kept an office at TIG's headquarters in Hong Kong, he was only involved in TIG matters when asked. With his advancing age, Ismail spent more time in spiritual activity. His health was not good; he knew he would not be around for long and wanted to spend time writing his memoir and doing social work.

He was told that today's meeting was important, and that TIG needed his help.

'Tell me, what is happening?' He asked Yakoob.

'Papa, we have financial and other difficulties. Salim and I believe these are temporary, but we need support.'

'What do you mean by financial and other difficulties? Are we bankrupt?'

'Not yet, and will never be if we get the support. Otherwise, it could be bad. I believe that we have suffered a loss of approximately 500 million US dollars in the currency market and on property alone. Salim will give us full details in the meeting this morning. This does not include the continuing losses we are incurring on other businesses. Our shipping business has really suffered because of the downturn in orders. We had a bit of breathing space because of the troubles in Afghanistan. In view of our connections, we have been the preferred shippers for American goods sent to Afghanistan. Unfortunately, the war between the USA and the Soviets ended with the Soviets exiting Afghanistan.

'Papa, I know you are worried. I am, as well. But we have assets. The current downturn in the shipping business is temporary. It will turn around soon. Our properties in the UK are good, and they should bring us good profits when the market improves. It's only a question of time. Our main problem is that G&P Bank is finding it difficult to continue to support us. We need their support for a short time only. Other creditors are also pressing, particularly the UK banks. I hope we will be able to develop a plan to solve this crisis in the meetings today and tomorrow.'

Yakoob found his father's attention wandering. Ismail was staring at the wall. 'You are not here today, Papa.' Yakoob remarked.

'I am thinking about where we were and what we achieved. All this from a small business in Mwanza, Tanzania, and now everything is at risk,' the father replied.

Yakoob knew the mood and understood it was better to leave the old man to his thoughts for a while.

Ismail sat quietly, recalling in his mind the history of TIG.

Ismail Soothar remembered how Tanganyika International Group, TIG, had grown from a small shipping company plying ferries on Lake Victoria between the ports of Mwanza and Bukoba in modern day Tanzania. His father, Mohammad Ali Soothar, had arrived from Jamnagar in India in the British colony of Tanganyika, now Tanzania, along with other immigrant workers brought in by the British. As his name indicated, he was a carpenter by profession and was employed as such by the British on the East African Railways project.

After working as a carpenter for a while, Mohammad Ali Soothar opened a small furniture shop in Mwanza on the shores of Lake Victoria. Taking advantage of the growing activity in Mwanza, he also opened a general store next to his furniture shop.

Lake Victoria is the largest lake in Africa and second in the world. It connects all three countries of East Africa: Tanzania, Kenya, and Uganda. On the Tanzanian side, the main cities are Mwanza and Bukoba, on the Kenyan side, Kisumu and in Uganda, Entebbe. Because of the connectivity of all three countries of the East African Community, an excellent ferry and lake transport business had developed. Although there was a bus service going around the lake to the cities located along the lake, it used to take a long time. Journeying across the lake was easier and less expensive.

Mwanza was also an important regional centre. It was the centre for the supply of cotton grown in the region and tea from the gardens in Bukoba, which was just across the lake. Ismail Soothar was born and raised in Mwanza. All three of his sons were also born there. Ismail worked hard with his father and expanded the business. Soon, the family owned the largest general merchandise shop in Mwanza, selling almost everything. Realising the opportunities provided by the lake transport business, Ismail Soothar bought a couple of boats to ferry passengers across the lake. This was the beginning of Victoria Lake Ferries Ltd, which later grew into TIG Shipping Lines.

He also started trading in cotton. He would purchase it from the local farmers and send it to the textile mills in Dar Es Salaam, Kenya, and other parts of the world. With his growing business and increased prosperity, Ismail bought a building to operate as a hotel, Lake Hotel, for the tea planters and other businessmen staying overnight or coming to shop in Mwanza. Lake Hotel was run by an English manager named David Turff.

These were the days when Dr. Williamson, the famous geologist, who discovered the Williamson Diamonds Mine, was exploring for diamonds in the area. He was convinced there was a diamond vein around Mwanza, but he was not yet successful in striking pay dirt. He was running out of funds, and the local traders were refusing to give him credit. During this time, he was staying at Lake Hotel. After failing to pay for his room for a couple of weeks, the hotel manager, David, gave Dr. Williamson notice to vacate the room.

Dr. Williamson was distressed. With no money to buy anything and no place to live, he was close to abandoning his quest for the diamonds. He went to see David, appealing to let him stay in the hotel and promising a quick settlement of dues once additional funds were received from certain investors.

David was extremely rude to the doctor. He said, 'Doctor, I have seen many adventurers like you in my time. They all go broke and die in the end, dreaming about the treasures. I am afraid that I cannot allow you to stay for even one more hour. You have exceeded your welcome here, so please leave.'

'You know, I have my wife here and some extremely valuable material kept in the room. Please give me at least a couple of days to move out. I cannot go out in the bush and pitch a tent there. My wife will die of Malaria, and all my work will be lost.'

'Get out of here, Doctor. I have no time for dreamers like you. You are a plague on the business. Either you get out of here now, or I will throw all of you out in five minutes!' David shouted.

Just then, Ismail Soothar walked in on one of his routine visits to the hotel.

'What is happening here?' He asked.

Then, seeing Dr. Williamson, he said, 'Good morning, Doctor. How is the exploration going?'

'Sir, the exploration is not going well. I'm afraid I'm coming to the end of my resources. I am expecting some more funds from certain investors, but they are taking time. In the meantime, I'm overdue in settling your bill. Your manager has very rudely asked me to get out in five minutes or he will throw out my wife and belongings in the street. Please, Sir, I need a few more days' credit in order to organise my affairs. I am sure that I will be able to pay your bill within a week,' Dr. Williamson pleaded.

'You say my manager was rude? That is not acceptable. To be rude to anybody is totally unacceptable. I can't tolerate it, particularly if the behaviour is directed toward a person in need.'

Then he looked at David Turff and said in a cold voice, 'David, is this true that you have been obnoxious to this good doctor who is going through a bit of a bad patch at the moment?'

'I had no choice. This moron will not pay the bill and keeps begging to stay on in our hotel.' David was unrepentant.

'Watch your tongue, David. Your bad manners and language are disgraceful. This is not *our* hotel. This is *my* hotel and you are now fired. Get out of my hotel this minute, or I will have you physically thrown out. You may come to my shop tomorrow to settle your dues. I believe that you have been taking loans from my sons and might have to refund money instead of getting anything from me.' Ismail was furious. He turned his attention to Dr. Williamson. 'Doctor, this is your hotel and home. Stay here as long as you wish, and pay me when you have money. I will ensure that nobody will bother you again.'

'Thank you very much, Sir. I am deeply obliged. I promise, I will pay every shilling that I owe you.'

'Call me Ismail. And don't worry about the bills. I know you will pay. Let's go in and have a drink.' Ismail took Dr. Williamson by the hand and led him to the hotel's small bar.

Thus started a lifetime friendship between Ismail Soothar and Dr. Williamson. Soon thereafter, Dr. Williamson got lucky finding diamonds at Mwadui, not far from Mwanza, near Shinyanga. As one of the first acts after discovering diamonds, he paid the debt he owed Ismail. He also sent a pouch containing several high-quality diamonds, each weighing over a carat, as a gift to Ismail.

Dr. Williamson became very rich. He routinely sent diamonds to Ismail as gifts. Because of these gifts, Ismail had amassed a small collection of very high-quality diamonds. He appreciated the diamonds for their value, but he didn't know what to do with them.

Trading or exporting diamonds from Tanganyika was prohibited unless by a government-licensed entity. DeBeers was controlling the diamond business internationally and did not want the world to be flooded with diamonds, so they took part in hunting down the illegal diamond trade.

At that time, the independence movement in several African countries was heating up. In Kenya, The Mau Mau movement, led by Jomo Kenyatta, was turning violent. African nationalism was also growing, as well as talks of action against the Europeans and Asians who were considered outsiders and robbers of African wealth. Fearing that there may be problems if the Africans came into power, Ismail Soothar, like other businessmen, considered it necessary to create a base outside of East Africa.

With that in mind, he sent all his three children to the UK, ostensibly for education. All three went to UK universities and also obtained British citizenship. With his children located in the UK, Ismail established a company named Tanganyika International Ltd., with offices in London's West End. At that stage, the purpose of the company was to support the trading activity and manage assets of the East African business. It was considered necessary to transfer as much cash as possible outside Tanganyika.

Yakoob, Ismail's eldest son, was given the responsibility to ensure that the family's assets were protected. The Soothar family bought a beautiful house in Kent. The funds received from Tanganyika were invested into real estate, shares of prominent companies, and Swiss bank accounts. The experience of handling and managing large amounts of liquid resources prepared Yakoob to handle a much larger fortune in the future.

Ismail Soothar's wealth continued to multiply. Profits from trading in general merchandise, cotton and the shipping business were good. In addition, now there was the much more lucrative business of diamonds. With the experience of disposing the diamonds gifted to him by Dr. Williamson, Ismail had established connections with the black-market diamond merchants who catered to the international demand for high-quality stones at lower than the DeBeers prices.

Ideally located in Mwanza, not far from Shinyanga and Mwadui, Ismail had local connections and knew people who smuggled diamonds out of the mines. These were given to him at extremely low prices. He now had to arrange delivery of these stones to contacts that were mostly located in Europe and Asia.

He had developed ingenious methods of smuggling the hot diamonds. They were stuffed in toothpaste tubes or stitched to travellers' belts, among other methods. With the volume increasing, he resorted to putting pouches of diamonds in the cotton bales marked for export to Europe or India. All the money earned from these sales was invested or deposited at the direction of Yakoob in London, who was acting as the family's treasurer.

Ismail was not completely happy with only the UK as a base outside East Africa. The UK was a highly regulated country and there was the danger of the UK government looking through his diamond business and penalising him for not complying with its laws. Tanganyika was a British colony, and the UK laws applied there as well. He needed a place in other countries with lax legal systems and helpful bureaucrats for his business to prosper.

It was at this time that he looked at Pakistan. Pakistan was ideal, as it had a stable, business-friendly government headed by General Ayub Khan. Pakistan's economy was growing rapidly and was considered one of the upcoming economic powers of Asia. It had all the right ingredients to be successful: a stable business-friendly government, educated manpower, a growing business class, archaic laws applied infrequently, no state controls, and very lax income tax and court systems. This was the country to go to.

With the contacts he already had and lavish gifts to government officials, Ismail opened an office on the major business thoroughfare, McLeod Road, in Karachi. For this, he bought a newly constructed five-storey building.

With funds flowing in from every direction, Ismail Soothar started making investments in the up-and-coming industries in Pakistan. Ayub Khan's government, in its zeal to industrialise Pakistan, was giving generous facilities and support for industrial projects. Of course, in Pakistan, one had to look after government officials for permits and facilities. Ismail was well versed in the techniques of looking after people in powerful positions. In Pakistan, even honest officials needed houses to live in. A clever businessman might offer to supply the building material at a wholesale price to an official to be settled later when convenient to the official – in return for a favour. It was also not unusual for the top government officials to receive gifts of new cars at the weddings of their offspring.

With the usual ways of looking after the people around him and his lavish spending, Ismail Soothar soon created a business empire in Pakistan. His Tanganyika International Group, incorporated in the Cayman Islands, was a force to be reckoned with in Pakistan.

During this period, when Pakistan appeared to be rising as an economic power in Asia, the major beneficiaries were a few business families who were building business empires with the help of the government. Pakistan also had good infrastructure and skilled manpower to support the growth. The banking sector was very strong, and it had a highly trained corps of enterprising and innovative bankers.

Ismail needed a smart banker to help him deal with all the investments and fund transfers from his group's various enterprises. At that time, Sheikh Tayeb was an ambitious and hungry banker trying to build Tijarat Bank. Tijarat Bank's head office was in the building adjacent to Ismail's.

The converging commercial interests of Sheikh Tayeb and Ismail Soothar brought them closer together and become friends. In later years, when Sheikh Tayeb was unpopular with the government, Ismail helped him in moving out of Pakistan and establishing the G&P Bank. TIG was one of the very first business groups to appoint the G&P Bank as its principal banker.

Ismail Soothar had appointed a group of reliable technocrats to assist his family in managing his growing empire. He also appointed his sons in key positions in the Group. Yakoob was selected to be CEO, with particular attention to managing finances. Haroon was made responsible for managing the shipping business as the chief executive of TIG Shipping, and Rafik looked after other business interests of the family.

With the boom in the shipping business, Haroon convinced his father to acquire a large fleet of vessels. Roll on, roll off (RORO) and large containers ships were the major new developments in the shipping trade. Ownership of ships also provided flexibility for the family to transport its own cargo with the help of customs officials to many ports around the world without attracting undue attention regarding the nature of the cargo. One such consignment was the cotton bales shipped from Tanzania, which included pouches of diamonds carefully hidden in the bales.

The family, however, suffered two serious setbacks in the late sixties. The officials in the newly independent government of Tanzania (Tanganyika had changed its name to Tanzania after federation with Zanzibar) had learnt of the unofficial diamond business undertaken by Ismail Soothar and his family. Warrants were issued to arrest him and his sons. Their properties in Tanzania were confiscated. Fortunately, none of the family members were present in Tanzania at the time. They did, however, lose all their assets there. This wasn't terribly bad, as Ismail had already established business entities and located assets in many countries outside of Tanzania.

A more serious blow came when there was a change of government in Pakistan. After the creation of Bangladesh from what was East Pakistan. Socialist Zulfiqar Ali Bhutto came into power as the head of the government in Pakistan.

Pakistan was in a state of shock at its dismemberment and loss of East Pakistan. This created a vacuum and gave Zulfiqar Ali Bhutto a free hand to do whatever he liked with all the organs of the government. He declared that approximately twenty families were sucking the blood of Pakistan and therefore arrested the heads of these business families and nationalised their key assets in Pakistan. Ismail Soothar was included in the group of people arrested. He spent three months in prison, after which he was released and allowed to travel outside Pakistan. Fortunately, most of his investments in Pakistan were made through holding companies

114

formed outside Pakistan. His ships were also registered under foreign flags of convenience. As most of these assets were protected under investment and other treaties with other sovereign governments, the government could not touch them. So, Ismail's investments in Pakistan were safe.

His friend, Sheikh Tayeb, had also gone into exile because of his troubles. Both men parked themselves in London, and their friendship was further cemented. During his stay in the UK, Ismail obtained British citizenship. Now he had three citizenships, Tanzanian, Pakistani and British.

TIG, with the able assistance of Sheikh Tayeb, the G&P Bank, and a group of loyal advisers, continued to prosper. The shipping business was growing, and the world seemed to have an insatiable need for shipping space. The Vietnam War, the economic boom in the Middle East, and the emergence of Japan as a major exporter of electronic goods and automobiles were all providing excellent opportunities to expand the business.

TIG's shipping business also found some unusual clients in several independence movements and arms dealers. At the time, several wars were going on in Africa and Latin America. The Arab-Israeli conflict seemed to be heating up. All of the parties involved in these conflicts needed arms shipped with little scrutiny or public awareness. There were also customers requiring shipping space for controversial cargo, such as ivory, teakwood, and rhino body parts. There was lucrative yet risky business involving the transport of narcotics from Colombia to US ports.

With the world economies booming, the shipping business also showed very strong growth. TIG Shipping became one of the major shipping lines, plying between ports around the world. The more lucrative business came from the customers who were operating outside or on the fringes of the legal world.

The expansion in business required the acquisition of more ships, and they did not come cheap. Each vessel cost tens of million dollars. G&P Bank was there to finance these purchases.

With funds rolling in from every direction, TIG started diversifying its business. Yakoob believed the US dollar would strengthen against other major currencies, particularly the Japanese Yen and Pounds Sterling. He entered into large transactions going short in these currencies as well as gold. Real estate looked like another investment that could never lose value. UK property values had increased significantly over the previous five years, and there seemed to be no upper limit. Yakoob went on a buying spree and acquired high-value properties financed by G&P Bank.

The Soothar family's normal frugal and religious lifestyle also changed. They started living like kings and Hollywood celebrities. All three brothers purchased private jets for their personal use. Their children were given gifts of Ferraris or their own holiday homes in France and Switzerland. On their birthdays, lavish parties were thrown on the French Riviera where Hollywood and Indian film stars were flown in chartered jets. Drugs were freely available at these parties; beautiful girls and gigolos were also brought in for the entertainment of demanding guests.

In order to meet its financial commitments, the group continued to borrow from G&P Bank, where it appeared as if there was an unlimited supply of funds. However, in order to protect itself from questions from the regulatory authorities and auditors, the group was advised to diversify its borrowing entities.

Accordingly, TIG went on creating companies, many of them without any substance or assets, just for the sake of appearing as an independent borrower. At the time of the meeting in Hong Kong, there were over five hundred companies in the group. In order to show the bank that their loans were repaid, a new company would be created. This new company, known in accounting jargon as NEWCO, would enter into a fictitious transaction of acquiring goods or services from a group company that was already a 'debtor' of the bank. NEWCO would borrow from G&P Bank to finance its business transaction, obtaining goods or services from the debtor company, and paying the funds received from the bank to the debtor company, who in turn would pay these funds to the bank in settlement of its debt. On the surface, the borrowing company appeared to be financially and commercially sound, as it was earning money from transactions with another company and repaying its debts.

For its part, G&P Bank was happy, as its debts continued to appear as sound, and it was recording interest income from these investments.

The group was, however, not doing so well financially and existed on the continuous ballooning of funds borrowed from G&P Bank and other creditors. The group had severe financial difficulties. The money coming in from Tanzanian diamonds had stopped. Pakistan's investments had gone sour because of the political troubles in the country. Because of the availability of surplus capacity, shipping companies were going bankrupt around the world. The value of ships had decreased drastically. The group was finding it difficult to continue operating ships, and many of their vessels were anchored at ports awaiting business. London's property market had crashed, and the group was struggling to service the debts obtained for their purchase. The final blow came when the Japanese Yen's value increased tenfold against the dollar. TIG had suffered a loss of over a hundred million dollars in one stroke because of the currency rate fluctuations.

Ismail was shocked when Yakoob told him that the group was facing financial difficulties and requested that he attend the meeting in Hong Kong to discuss this and work out a solution.

In the forthcoming meeting, he wanted to learn the exact situation the group was in and offer whatever help he could. His family's future was at stake. Ismail felt tired and wondered how long he could continue to take on these stresses. Since his health was not good, he felt too old and drained to have to solve the business problems created by his children. He hoped they would be able to find a solution to the problems they faced.

***

At 10 a.m. sharp, Ismail's secretary, Lin, knocked on the door.
'Sir, Haroon, Rafik and Salim are waiting for you.'
'Send them in,' Ismail replied, getting up.

Ismail's two sons, Haroon and Rafik, and the group finance director, Salim Chaliwala, filed in. Haroon and Rafik bent and kissed their father's hand and shook hands with their brother. Salim shook hands with all of them. They all sat around the small conference table. Lin quickly took refreshment orders and left.

'I hope you gentlemen had an uneventful journey coming in,' Ismail remarked.

'Rafik and I flew in from London. Salim was in Geneva talking to G&P Bank there.'

'London and Geneva must be very cold. Give me Hong Kong anytime,' Ismail said.

While the group was involved in small talk, Lin came back with a tray of tea and coffee and some light snacks.

'Lin, leave the tray here. We'll serve ourselves. Please make sure that we are not disturbed,' Ismail told his secretary. He then turned to the group. 'Today we should have a frank and open discussion about our current status and find a solution to our problems. Yakoob tells me we are in a difficult financial situation. I understand that G&P Bank is concerned about their exposure to our group. Frankly, I am surprised. I have been requested by Sheikh Tayeb to attend a meeting in London on 29 December, as the bank has to make certain decisions about their investments before the annual closing.'

Yakoob responded, 'Yes, Papa, as I was saying to you, we have suffered a very large financial loss this year, and our financial position is not ideal. I will ask Salim to give us more details. Our meeting today is divided into two parts. We will be briefed by Salim about the financial position and think about a way forward. This should take us up to lunchtime. We'll go to Hoi Choi Seafood Restaurant in Kowloon for lunch. We'll be joined by Nari Patel, Mansukh Lal and Alex Brun there. We'll continue the discussion after lunch with the expanded group. We will not give the new arrivals all the information that Salim gives us in the morning. We'll learn their views about the operations they are managing.

'We are booked for dinner at Tandoor Palace for a nice Indian barbecue. They have the best barbecued chicken I have tasted anywhere. There is live Indian music and dancing for those who want to loosen up. I hope everybody will enjoy the trip to Hong Kong, although it is under less-than-ideal circumstances. The family and Salim will meet here again tomorrow morning to agree on a final action plan. So, let's learn from Salim what the actual results for the year are.' With this, Yakoob indicated to Salim to start.

Salim Chaliwala consulted the sheaf of papers he was carrying, and started:

'Good morning. First of all, I am sorry to say that, as you have already heard from Mr. Yakoob, the financial position of our group is not good. As you may be aware, we have close to five hundred companies in our group, and we are still receiving data from our various entities around the world to compute the group's consolidated financial results for the year-to-date. On the basis of the information received so far, we have suffered a very large operating loss this year. According to my information, the loss may be in the region of three hundred fifty million US dollars. We have a brought-forward deficit of seven hundred million dollars. Our accumulated loss at the end of the year will be over a billion dollars. This is what we accountants call as *on a going concern basis*. On a *realisation basis*, the loss will be much higher.

'Kindly explain the difference between the two bases you mentioned without being too technical.' Ismail requested.

'On a going concern basis, you prepare the financial statements as if you would continue operating as normal, and therefore all your assets and liabilities are carried at book values. On a realisation basis, you assume that your business may be liquidated. In this later situation, you would have to sell off your assets at market values, which may be higher or lower than the book values. Normally, for a loss-making concern, these would invariably be lower. Also, the company may have to pay claims from suppliers and others, which might not be acceptable under normal circumstances. Also, on a realisation basis, all your liabilities for government dues, staff pensions and retirement benefits would crystallise and may have to be settled immediately,' Salim explained.

'How much of this information about the loss for the year and accumulated loss mentioned by you is already available with our bankers and other interested parties?' Ismail asked.

'Sir, we never share this information with anybody other than Mr. Yakoob. As per Mr. Yakoob's instructions, we have been keeping two sets of books for the last several years. Our consolidated financial statements to be circulated are prepared on the basis of the official books. These are presented to the auditors, regulators, bankers and other interested parties. The official books show a profit of ten million US dollars for the year,' Salim said.

'And how do you achieve this remarkable feat of converting the loss of three hundred fifty million dollars into a profit for the year?' Ismail asked.

'There are several techniques. We create transactions for the sale and purchase of goods and services between group companies. Some of the group companies do not appear in our family tree, so nobody is aware that they are related parties. These companies are registered in the names of nominee shareholders such as lawyers, accountants, and trusted employees. It would be impossible to link some of these companies to our group. In shipping, documents of freight and voyages that never occurred are produced, and income for the freight carried and voyages undertaken is recorded. Interest is charged on receivables from group companies. The interest income and expense are not offset in group consolidation, as some of these companies are not shown as the Group companies. We routinely overvalue stocks of goods appearing in our books at market prices. In reality, these goods do not exist or have no value.'

'What do the auditors say about these so-called "techniques" adopted by you?' Ismail was very uneasy.

'They do not know, and they will never know if we are able to obtain funds to turn around our business.'

'How much of our financial position is known by our bankers?'

'They know that we have difficulties, but they are not aware of the true picture and do not know about the companies hidden from the group tree. I have been telling them we have some temporary cash flow problems, which we are trying to overcome. They understand that and are happy to support us.'

'If we are showing a profit when we actually have a loss, would we not have to pay tax on this profit, which would be further damaging to us?' Ismail Soothar knew his business fundamentals.

'Our top group company is incorporated in the Cayman Islands. There is no tax there. Almost all the profit was recorded in companies located in tax havens such as Cayman Islands, Banjar and the like. We have ensured that no profit is recorded in the countries which impose tax on profits.' Salim was also very thorough.

'Let me ask you this: Is it possible for us to get out of these difficulties, and how?' Ismail Soothar asked.

Salim replied, 'We need ten million US dollars per month just to meet the ongoing operating expenses. This is in addition to whatever cash we can generate from our continuing operations, and it does not include the payments already due for the debts already incurred. In some places, we have not paid salaries for months to our employees, so the situation is getting precarious.

'Our difficulties are temporary. The shipping business has to improve. It is only a question of time. We have good properties in the UK and other places. At the moment, the property prices and rental incomes are very low. Some of these properties are owned and registered in the names of some of the group companies which are not connected with our group. We borrowed funds to buy these properties on mortgages obtained from some of the high street banks in the UK. They are threatening to foreclose and auction our properties. Again, it is a question of time as to when the property market will begin to improve.

'We still have good ongoing business in the commodities where we are making profit and generating cash. There is already a shortage of essential commodities in the world, and the prices of cotton, rice, wheat, tea and others are rising. We should be able to expand our commodities' operations to compensate for the temporary difficulties in other sectors. To get out of our temporary difficulties, we need cash quickly and at regular intervals for some time. We already owe approximately two billion dollars to G&P Bank. They have difficulty in lending further. An additional one hundred million dollars might see us through this crisis. I met with G&P's Abu Talib in Karachi. Unfortunately, some analysts at G&P Bank are making trouble for us, as they seem to sense our financial difficulties. Abu Talib asked me to go to Geneva and meet Masood Qadir there. Masood manages Geneva and is authorised to approve any investments he deems appropriate. I met with Masood. He has promised to consider our request for support. There is a meeting of the bank's senior management; they will review our position in that meeting.

'We have the option of selling off some property and ships. But this would have to be a fire sale at a heavy loss. Another option may be to invite a partner to join us. You have good contacts in the Middle East. Perhaps you may be able to interest a wealthy investor. As I mentioned before, our official balance sheet is very healthy. We should also consider liquidating some of the group companies with large accumulated losses that are not directly or apparently connected with our group. Let the creditors take the loss. The nominees would feel the heat and may try to pass the responsibility on to us, but there are no documents to prove that they are not the real owners, so they would not be able to do us any damage.' Salim gave a succinct overview of the position.

With this, the group left for lunch at Hoi Choi Seafood Restaurant on Carpenter Road in Kowloon. The restaurant was famous for its Cantonese seafood. Nari Patel, Head of Middle East and Africa, Mansukh Lal, Head of Asia Pacific and Alex Brun, Head of Europe and Americas were already at the restaurant. Ismail greeted each man warmly and enquired about their health and families.

Nobody talked business over lunch, only social talk and the inevitable Pakistani political and economic situation were the main topics. After enjoying a truly memorable lunch with dim sum, live lobsters and fish cooked to individual taste, the group returned to TIG's headquarters.

Ismail started the meeting. 'Gentlemen, with the lunch we just had, there is no desire to work. Unfortunately, we have important matters to deal with. From our discussions this morning, I have learnt that we have difficulties to handle. Salim has briefed us about the cash flow problems we face. We are considering certain actions that we may need to take.

'However, before making any decisions, I would like to hear from our business chiefs to know what is happening in their respective areas. Let us start with Nari Patel. Nari, please tell us about what is happening in the Middle East and Africa.'

Nari was a Parsi gentleman in his late forties. Parsis were a highly respected business community in India and Pakistan. They were originally from Persia, the descendants of the Zoroastrian community, which worshipped fire. They had migrated to India a few centuries earlier, when their life in Persia became difficult because of their religious beliefs.

Nari had come prepared. 'I do not have the latest financial numbers which Salim is still computing, but based on the information available to me, our business has contracted substantially in the region. We had a period of tremendous growth from the oil boom after the Arab-Israeli conflict of 1973, which changed the economies of the Middle East. At that time, we did not have an inch of space available on our ships to carry freight. This was followed by the Iran-Iraq war and conflict in Afghanistan between the Soviets and the Islamists backed by the USA. Our ships were busy all the time. In addition, we were making tremendous profit by acting as buying agents for the parties in the conflict zones. We were helping everybody. We supplied everything from chocolates and cigarettes to tanks and anti-aircraft missiles to anybody who was willing to pay the price.

'The political situation in the Middle East and subcontinent has changed. The Iran-Iraq war is over. The Soviets have been defeated in Afghanistan. There is still a fight going on there between various Mujahideen groups for power. There is still money to be made by supplying weapons to these Mujahideen groups. They have the cash. But the business is not on the same scale as before. I hope that a conflict starts in our region soon, otherwise we will continue to suffer. I wonder if our contacts could help by triggering a Pakistan-India war. That would be a real bonanza.

'A lot of conflicts in Africa have also subsided, though Africa could never be without a war. We are still making money from supplying arms, providing freight and support to various warring parties, and picking up diamonds and gold. Africa is our best business partner.

'Our commodities business is doing well, and that is covering our losses in other sectors, to a certain extent. Cotton crops are good this year, and there is high demand. We bought our requirements at low prices, so we will make a profit there. We have also obtained sufficient stocks of tea, sisal, maize and high-quality wood from our sources in Asia and Africa. All our purchases are on credit, and we need to pay our suppliers. We have been delaying payments as much as possible. We have unpaid rents to settle. We have not been able to pay salaries to our staff for months. We need cash to carry us for three months. We need at least ten million dollars to see us through.'

'I know we need cash. This is our major difficulty. Any suggestions?' Ismail asked.

'The cash generated from trading and other activities in my region is always sent to headquarters. We are not allowed to keep the funds for our own short-term requirements. I understand that we have demands for cash from other areas, and therefore we must remit what we have, but we need funds to continue our business, otherwise we will collapse. Nobody will sell us anything, and our customers, sensing that we have difficulties, will stop dealing with us. I have to request that once we are provided with some cash to tie us over the current situation, we should be allowed to keep cash for three months' requirement on a roll-forward basis.' Nari replied.

'We will have to find solutions for each region's special problems as well as for the general problems faced by the group as a whole. Let's hear from Mansukh to see what's happening in the Asia Pacific.' Ismail turned his attention to Mansukh Lal.

Mansukh Lal was from an East African Asian family like Ismail's. His father had worked for Ismail's family in Mwanza in

East Africa. He had grown up with Ismail's children and went to the same primary and high schools in Mwanza.

He shared his updates with the group. 'Our challenges in the Asia-Pacific region are not much different from those described by Nari for the Middle East and Africa. Our customer base and the type of merchandise handled are different, though.

'With the decline in oil prices, the economies of the region, which had ballooned in the mid-seventies and early eighties, are suffering. Singapore's economy has slowed. Their oil refineries are working below capacity. They are now trying to diversify to the knowledge economy, which might help them but will not be helpful to our business. Indonesia is suffering the same fate; with a large population, it is trying to cut development projects, and there are signs that there will be serious economic problems ahead. Malaysia is just holding on. Thailand's property boom is over. China is cutting its teeth, but it is still early days.

'Our commodities business is still doing well. Chinese exports are increasing, and we are able to pick up a good share of their products for resale, as well as freight for shipments. Burmese timber is still in high demand in some parts of the world, and with our connections with the junta, we are the prime marketing agents and shippers for the timber. Trade in commodities considered questionable, such as ivory and gemstones from Burma, is still providing an excellent source of profit and funding for our business.

'Our shipping business, however, is suffering. Because of the economic conditions, there is a reduction in our normal freight business. We do, however, provide a lot of assistance to various suppliers who want to ship their merchandise without being visible. The local authorities, particularly in Hong Kong and Singapore, who benefit from this transit business turn a blind eye and leave everybody to go about their business as long as there is no direct effect on them. With the departure of the Soviets from Afghanistan, the USA is not interested in funding or helping the Mujahideen groups. They are apparently at each other's throats for power and fighting with whatever they have there. There are still some groups who are purchasing arms in the international market but such transactions have slowed down. With the USA taking its hands off, the Singapore and Hong Kong governments do not want to be seen to be fuelling the conflict in Afghanistan. The shipments from these ports are coming under closer scrutiny. India is also not making life easier; they are worried all these sophisticated weapons will be used in India, they have increased their surveillance of the arms transactions and are blowing the whistle on them as and when they know about them.

'The Chinese triads continue to be in business and are getting bolder. They are expanding their business operations, which are a major remaining source of freight for our vessels. They pay good prices. However, they are demanding smaller and faster craft. We do not have such vessels in our fleet. Our 'Roll On Roll Off, RORO, and container vessels do not suit their requirements. Being aware of our constraints, some groups have started developing their own capability to transport their merchandise. There is, however, some uncertainty about the future of their operations once Hong Kong goes under Chinese control. They are certainly looking to diversify their bases and looking as far as Australia and Latin America as alternative or support bases. After all, Hong Kong was established on the drug trade and piracy. These people know how to survive.

'Our ships operate at less than half capacity. Obviously, this has created a huge cash flow problem as we have to settle port charges and local agents' expenses before we are even able to lift anchor. With the shortage of funds, we are terminating crew and limiting our voyages to only a few ports where we can still gain profitable business.

'We need to restructure our business if we want to survive. Our fleet has to be modernised in order to stay competitive and continue to get business. We need to overhaul our current fleet or junk some of them. I even thought of sinking one or two vessels and collecting the insurance, but that would be messy and may create an international scandal. We need to train our employees in order for them to operate a more modern fleet and learn efficient business techniques. Once we have our capability enhanced, we will need strong marketing support to regain our market share.

'We need quick action. We cannot survive the present conditions for very long. Already there is talk of TIG facing bankruptcy, and our customers and employees are hedging their bets. We are losing our good people. Our large competitors are getting stronger and capturing our business. I am sorry to sound so negative and depressed, but we need help. We need strong actions to prove that we are still a powerful player in the shipping market.'

'Thank you, Mansukh. I hear you and appreciate the difficulties you are facing. I am happy that I attended this meeting. I have learnt a lot. We will definitely consider all the factors and make some tough decisions. Let's hear from Alex about the European and American situation.' Ismail was now in full command of the meeting. Yakoob was taking a back seat.

Alex was a naturalised British citizen born in South Africa. He went to university with Yakoob, and they were close friends.

Alex began his explanation. 'The situation in Europe and the Americas is not much different from other regions. In Europe, the landscape is changing. There may be serious changes in the political and economic conditions of Eastern Europe. Poland and Hungary are simmering. These countries will infect others in the region. The economies and the way businesses are conducted in Europe will change considerably if there are changes in Eastern Europe and the Soviet Union. We should think ahead and prepare for these changes.

'Our commodities' business will be affected if the Eastern European markets open. They have cheap labour, agriculture products and manufacturing facilities to export to the rest of Europe. Our shipping business may also have an impact. Our shipping business is already suffering because of the excess capacity and the availability of larger and more modern facilities of our competitors. We have ships anchored in Limassol and Istanbul requiring major repairs. The shipyards are asking for money in advance before carrying out any work.

'On the American front, our normal freight business is suffering. Also, we used to provide shipping facilities for special cargo to our major customers from Colombia and Panama. The US Coast Guard has become more vigilant and we are on their radar. Our ships are normally checked on the high seas by the US Coast Guard, and we get more than the normal cursory customs examination when we dock at any of the US ports.

'We made some good investments in Latin America, particularly in Brazil and Argentina. These investments have increased significantly in value. We may be able to sell some of these investments for a profit. We will have to do this at lower than the market value to get the payment quickly.'

'How much cash can we get if we sell these investments?' Ismail asked.

'We own properties in the prime locations of Sao Paulo and Buenos Aires. We may be able to get fifty million dollars there.'

'Are these not mortgaged?' Ismail was not completely naïve.

'These are mortgaged by G&P Bank. Sheikh Tayeb may be able to help us in asking the bank to release the mortgage,' Salim replied. 'That fifty million might help us meet our short-term obligations and put our ships back into the oceans.'

'I don't know if Sheikh Tayeb will release a good security and continue to extend a clean facility to us in these difficult times. However, this is a good suggestion, and I will have a think about it,' Ismail replied.

'I have been approached by some Columbians to let us handle their cargo under an arrangement. They are willing to pay good rates and provide regular business. They are talking in tons, not kilograms. I have not yet responded to the proposal. I wanted Yakoob's approval before proceeding. This may also help us solve our difficulties.'

'You said that the American Coast Guard was taking an interest in our vessels. How are you proposing to get away with this?'

'We would have to do it in two ways: We carry the regular freight of Brazilian coffee and Argentine meat from these countries to the USA. Since we could transport the more expensive Columbian freight in the same vessel, we could offer subsidised rates for the regular cargo and expand our market. We should be able to hide the Columbian cargo with the coffee and other regular goods.

'To service the Columbian business, we will need to purchase smaller and faster vessels capable of anchoring on shallow beaches. There would also be overhead attached to this business. 'We would have to please some people in the Coast Guard and customs, and we will have to work with small boat operators to take cargo from our vessels on the high seas and hand them over on land. We have contacts and are already doing this on a smaller scale. I suggest that we go big,' Alex suggested.

'This looks like the lifesaver we are looking for, Alex. Well done. I suggest we go for it,' Ismail's son Haroon said.

Ismail glared at Haroon and said, 'I do not like to get involved in this type of business. However, today, I am only learning about the situation. We will make our final decisions tomorrow. Gentlemen, I have learnt enough about our business today. I suggest we break, and you guys enjoy the evening. Have a good dinner. Unfortunately, I am a little tired and will not be joining you. I'm sure Yakoob has, as usual, made excellent arrangements for the evening.'

Ismail Soothar stayed in his office for another hour after everybody else left. He sat there with his head in his hands, wondering how everything went so wrong and how they ended up where they were.

He knew it was partly his fault because he had left the operations of the group in his sons' hands and did not get involved for several years. He was aware of the lavish lifestyle his sons and their children led and the financial drain it must cause to the group. He was certain that the problem was deeper than what was made out by those in the meeting. He was shocked to learn of the nature of activities his people were involved in. The operations they were proposing in the meeting were a one-way street to disaster.

Ismail blamed Yakoob for not controlling the affairs of the group and getting involved in speculations. He had trusted his eldest son. His son had not been able to measure up to the trust. He did not know how to solve the situation. He hoped that Sheikh Tayeb would do him a favour and offer some help, but he was uncertain if that would be sufficient to see the group through. He had a feeling the group was going down, and him with all his family would also go down with it.

He got up and prayed to Allah to save his family from the disaster that appeared to be imminent. He left the office a depressed man with tears in his eyes.

Ismail asked his driver to take him straight to his villa at Stanley in the South Hong Kong Island. He had a beautiful house by the side of a cliff jutting out on the sea. His manservant, Aslam, was surprised to see Ismail returning home early. He had assumed that Ismail would join his sons for dinner. To be safe, however, he had prepared Ismail's favourite dish, *chicken karahi* (chicken cooked in a wok).

'Salam, Sir,' Aslam said as he rushed to take Ismail's jacket and offered him a pair of slippers.

Ismail collapsed on a sofa and said, 'Get me a glass of water, Aslam. I had a very tiring day.'

'*Abhi laya* (bringing it immediately), Sir,' Aslam replied. 'Should I also mix you a Drink, Sir?'

'No. Just water, please.'

Aslam had been with Ismail for over twenty years. He respected and treated Ismail as his own father. He had never seen Ismail so depressed.

'Is everything all right, Sir? I thought you might go to dinner with the children.' Aslam was concerned.

'Nothing is all right, Aslam. The world as we know it is coming to an end. I don't know how we will be able to come out of this quagmire,' Ismail replied.

Aslam was sensible enough not to enquire further. He bought water. 'What time would you like to eat, Sir?'

'I really do not feel like eating, Aslam. I am tired and will sleep early.'

'Sir, I have made your favourite chicken karahi. You'll enjoy it with fresh *chapattis* (thin wheat flour traditional Indian/Pakistani bread). You must eat dinner.'

'I'll let you know if I feel like eating. Don't wait up for me. Have your dinner, and go to bed if you do not hear from me. As I said, I might sleep early tonight.'

After dismissing Aslam, Ismail quickly changed and lay down. He was uncomfortable and felt like throwing up. He did not take the discomfort seriously, thinking it was because of the fatigue caused by the events of the day or something he had eaten at lunch.

***

Dinner at Tandoor Palace was as delicious and enjoyable as advertised. Yakoob had ordered some of the best wines available in the well-stocked cellar of the restaurant. There was a live orchestra with an Indian artist singing *ghazals* (poems in Urdu or Hindi). Haroon appeared to be enjoying the dinner and the show the most. He kept filling up his glass and sending small slips of paper with requests for special numbers for the artist to sing, along with US hundred-dollar bills. Other members of the party were also enjoying themselves. Nobody looked depressed or the slightest bit worried about the matters discussed earlier that day. That was business. This was fun.

The party ended at two in the morning. They all returned to their hotel, except Haroon. He had an apartment in Kowloon where his Indian film star girlfriend was waiting for him. Before going to dinner, he had sneaked away from the group saying that he needed to buy some medicine. He had gone to a jewellery store and bought a diamond necklace for his mistress. He was looking forward to enjoying the rest of the night with her. He was sure she would appreciate the present and make him happy.

***

Around the time the party was breaking up, Ismail got up badly shaken. He was drenched in sweat and felt as if a great weight had been placed on his torso. He was breathless, and there was pain in his chest. The pain transmitted from his chest to his left arm. Thinking it was due to a muscular problem, he picked the pain relief ointment from his bedside table and applied it to his chest.

With every minute, the pain was increasing. His heart seemed to beat very fast. Ismail could not move his hand to reach for the bedside table. The pain in his chest was now unbearable. He felt as if his heartbeats sounded like a drum beating.

For the first time, Ismail thought he might be suffering from something more serious than muscular pain and tried to pull himself up. He had no energy. He struggled out of bed and started calling for Aslam. He managed to walk a couple of steps before he collapsed, hitting the bedside table and the lamp.

Aslam heard Ismail calling his name and then the loud noise coming from Ismail's bedroom. He rushed in and found Ismail lying on the floor, clutching his chest.

Aslam immediately phoned for an ambulance. He also tried The Pearl, the hotel where Yakoob and Rafik were staying. The hotel operator told him that the guests were not in their rooms and took the message for the brothers to call Aslam as soon as possible.

He then called Haroon at his apartment.

'Who is it?' Haroon was surprised and annoyed. His apartment number was not available to anybody he knew. He was even more surprised to hear Aslam's voice.

'Sir, Aslam here. Come quickly. Mr. Ismail has fallen and is unconscious. I have called for an ambulance.'

'Is he badly hurt?'

'I do not know. He is not responding. The ambulance must be coming any moment.'

'I'll be there. Have you informed Yakoob and Rafik?'

'I have called their hotel, but they are not in their rooms. I left messages.'

'I'm on my way. By the way, who gave you my number?' Haroon was not happy at the breach of his privacy.

'I know your maid, Sir. She gave me the number for emergency use only.'

I will sort out the maid later, Haroon said to himself.

'Who is it, darling?' Haroon's starlet girlfriend, Angela, asked. She had received the necklace and was ready to please Haroon.

'Papa is sick. They are taking him to the hospital. I have to go.'

'Oh, darling. It seems that we cannot have even one evening together. I wanted to make you so happy tonight,' Angela said.

'I'll be back as soon as possible. It is so disappointing. I really wanted to make tonight very special. Don't worry. I'll be back as soon as possible. I must go see the old man, otherwise they will say that even after hearing the news of his illness, I did not respond. Yakoob and Rafik always try to find faults in me, you know.' Haroon was not happy to go, but he felt it necessary to do so.

***

At Ismail's house, the ambulance had arrived. The senior paramedic took one look at Ismail and knew it was too late, however, he checked the man's heartbeat. There was none. He opened Ismail's eyes and shone his torch in. There was no reaction.

'Sir, I think it is too late. We'll take him to Queen Mary Hospital, which is the nearest.' The senior paramedic said, indicating for his colleague to carry the body to the waiting ambulance.

'Please do something. Give him some medication or do something. He was okay earlier this evening.' Aslam was in tears and refusing to accept the worst.

'Sir, there is nothing we can do here. Please come with us to the hospital. The doctors might want to speak to you to learn more about this gentleman,' the ambulance attendant spoke gently to Aslam.

Aslam dutifully went into the ambulance and sat in the back with Ismail's body. However, before leaving the building, Aslam spoke to the concierge at the hotel where Yakoob and Rafik were staying and told him that Mr. Soothar had been taken ill and was being taken to Queen Mary Hospital. When any of Mr. Soothar's sons arrived, they should be informed to go to the hospital.

At the hospital, Ismail's body was rushed into the emergency room, where a team of doctors was waiting. Aslam was asked to go to the admissions counter near the reception to fill in some forms requiring information about the patient's medical history and insurance details.

The senior doctor on duty looked at Ismail and he too knew that it was too late. Mr. Ismail Soothar was no longer in this world. This would have to be reported to the police and a post-mortem would have to be conducted. There would be a lot of forms to fill in before this was over. He went to the nearby telephone and dialled the number of the hospital administrator.

'We have a DOA. Name: Ismail Soothar. Asian, non-oriental male, approximately 70-plus. Please initiate the necessary procedures for the police and forensics.' He paused for a moment, listening to the voice on the other end of the call. 'No. I do not suspect any foul play. There are no signs of any injuries or struggle. Looks like a simple case of cardiac arrest resulting from an attack of angina pectoris. His manservant called for an ambulance when he heard a crash and found him lying on the floor in his bedroom.' The doctor replied to the administrator's question, who was trying to ascertain if there was going to be a criminal investigation.

**

Haroon took a cab and asked the driver to take him to Stanley. He hoped his father would be back from the hospital by the time he reached the house. He was certain that Aslam had panicked and rushed his father to the hospital for something very minor. He would have to sort out the maid for giving his telephone number to Aslam and ask Aslam not to call him on that number ever again. He cursed the old man. Why did he have to get sick on that night of all the nights when he, Haroon, was in Hong Kong for a memorable time with his beautiful lady friend?

Despite Haroon's impatience, he had to go through the Hong Kong traffic, which, even at that hour, was heavy. The Crown colony never slept. And this was Christmas time. People were still out in the streets.

***

Yakoob, Rafik, and the others went out for a walk after dinner to see the festival lights. They had quite a few drinks and were walking with difficulty. They reached The Pearl around 3.30 a.m.

At the reception, Yakoob had a message waiting for him from the hotel operator. It read:

Mr. Aslam phoned to say that your father has been taken ill. Mr. Aslam was taking him to Queen Mary Hospital. He requested that you and Mr. Rafik go to the hospital immediately.

'What is it?' Rafik asked.

'It's a message from Aslam. Apparently, Papa has been taken ill and rushed to Queen Mary Hospital.'

'Papa was okay earlier this evening. It must be something very minor. Aslam always panics. Why don't you go have a look? Call me if there is anything serious,' Rafik said.

'Are you not coming?'

'I am too tired and would like to get some rest. Had too much to drink. Besides, I think this must be something minor, and you'll be able to deal with it. There is no need for both of us to go.'

'Okay. I'll go see what it is,' Yakoob replied.

The other members of the group also heard that Ismail was not well and that Yakoob was going to see him.

'I would like to come with you, Yakoob,' Salim said.

'Okay, if you want to,' Yakoob said, walking toward the main door of the hotel.

***

Yakoob, Salim, and Haroon reached the hospital almost at the same time. Haroon had first gone to the house, hoping his father might have already returned. He was informed by the security guard that neither Mr. Soothar nor Mr. Aslam had returned.

They found Aslam in the waiting area. He had tears in his eyes. Aslam stood up when he saw Yakoob, Haroon, and Salim. He embraced Yakoob and started crying loudly.

'*Sir jee, Yeh kiya zulum ho gaya.* (Sir, what a blow we have been dealt!)'

'Hold yourself, man. What happened?' Yakoob tried to free himself from Aslam's bear hug.

Aslam continued to wail and was unable to speak. Unable to get any sense from Aslam, Yakoob walked to the reception.

'My name is Yakoob Soothar. I am the eldest son of Mr. Ismail Soothar, who I believe was admitted here as a patient,' he said.

'One moment, Sir.' The receptionist avoided eye contact, looking at some papers in front of her. She dialled a number and said, 'Mr. Soothar's family is here.'

Shortly after she hung up the call, an immaculately dressed man in his early thirties came out. 'Mr. Soothar?'

Yakoob turned to him and said, 'I am Yakoob Soothar, the eldest son of Mr. Ismail Soothar, and this is my brother, Haroon. How is our father?'

'I am Liu Chi, Senior Patients' Families' Counsellor.'

'You are not a doctor? Please let me speak to the doctor who is treating my father.' Yakoob had serious misgivings now and feared the worst.

'I am also a qualified doctor but not involved in patients' treatment. My job is to help the patients' families who might go through emotional difficulties. I have unfortunate news for you. I am sorry, your father has passed away. We cannot say the cause of the death with certainty, but we are almost certain that he died of a heart attack. Mr. Soothar was already dead when our ambulance reached his residence.'

Yakoob turned back and heard Haroon scream. Salim was trying to hold him. Aslam was not making it easier either, by wailing and beating his chest.

Yakoob went to Haroon and embraced him, holding his brother's head close to his. 'Patience, my brother. Patience. This is all from Allah. His life in this world had finished, so he had to go.

He was a good man. Allah will look after him. Take hold of yourself. We have to deal with this and other issues that might arise.' He said all of this with tears in his eyes, but he was trying to act strong.

'Yakoob, how did it happen? He was with us this evening. How could he just leave us like that?' Haroon was hysterical.

'It's all right, my brother. This is life. Nobody knows when his time is up.' He turned to Aslam. 'Aslam, I know it is a big loss to you, as well. You were very close to him. But what could anybody do? Tell me, how did it happen?'

'Sir, Sahib came home exhausted. He asked for a glass of water only. He refused anything else. He said that he was very tired and wanted to lie down. He asked me not to wait up for him for dinner. Around 2.45 a.m., I heard him calling me, and then there was a loud noise, as if something or somebody had crashed. I rushed to his bedroom and forced myself in. I saw him lying on the floor near a table lamp. I immediately called an ambulance. I then called your hotel and Mr. Haroon. When the ambulance arrived, the attendant told me that Sahib was no longer with us and asked me to accompany him to the hospital.' Aslam narrated the entire episode.

'Salim, please call Rafik and ask him to come here immediately. Don't tell him that Papa has passed away. Rafik will find it hard to take the sudden blow. Tell him that Papa has suffered a heart attack and is in critical condition. I'll handle him when he gets here.

'We need others of the group here, too. We have to think a few things through. We have some serious matters to deal with. Ask our Hong Kong office administration manager, Shaukat, and the public relations officer, Shin Lou, to come here. We'll need them to help us make the arrangements.' Yakoob had pushed his grief back and had taken control. He returned his attention to Liu Chi, who was patiently standing to the side. 'So, what is next? What do we need to do to get the body? We'll take the body to Pakistan for the funeral.'

'Sir, because the death occurred away from a medical facility, there will have to be a post-mortem before a death certificate is issued. In addition, the coroner's office will have to be informed. He may or may not want to conduct further enquiries or examinations.

Seeing that this looks like a clear case of a cardiac arrest, I think the coroner might dispense with further formalities and sign authorisation for the release of the body. You may then take away the body. However, if you want to ship the body outside Hong Kong, you will require a certificate from the Health Ministry that the body is free from infectious disease.

'You may then arrange for the embalming of the body and its encasement in a coffin of your choice. You'll also have to make arrangements for an airline to carry the casket to your home country. Normally they require that a sealed coffin be handed over to them at least twelve hours before the flight. The airline will have to get permission from customs to transport the casket out of Hong Kong. This is normally a formality. You are a Muslim, right?' Liu Chi asked.

'Yes,' Yakoob replied.

'You might take the body to one of the two mosques in Hong Kong, Jamia Mosque on Shelly Street or Kowloon Masjid and Islamic Centre at the corner of Nathan Road and Haiphong Road. I understand that the Kowloon Islamic Centre is better equipped to complete the Muslim formalities of the last rites.' Liu Chi was very well informed about the formalities and rites to be completed in death cases.

'How long do the procedures of post-mortem, coroner's authorisation and the Ministry of Health's certification take?' Yakoob asked.

'Normally, you would be lucky if you are able to complete all the procedures within forty-eight hours, but if you have good people working for you, these things may be expedited, and you may be able to ship the remains within thirty-six hours. You might have to spend some money.' Liu Chi was candid.

'It's almost 5.30 a.m.,' Yakoob said, to Haroon and Aslam. 'Hopefully, we may be able to take away Papa's body some time tomorrow.' He turned back to Liu Chi. 'May I see my father?'

'The body is still in the emergency room. We will go there,' Liu Chi said, leading the group.

Ismail Soothar appeared to be sleeping peacefully. To Yakoob he seemed to be free from all his worries. He approached his father's body, touched and gently kissed his forehead. Yakoob again had tears in his eyes.

Haroon and Aslam started wailing again. Yakoob looked at both of them and said, 'Listen, you have to hold yourself. Papa has gone, and it is a big blow. Our crying will not bring him back. We have to give strength to others around us. Let us pray for his soul. He was a good man.

'We have to make all the arrangements for Papa's funeral and deal with the business issues, so calm down. Aslam, you go to the villa. We will be here until others arrive, and the arrangements for the release of Papa's body are in place. Then, we'll come to the villa. We have to meet to deal with certain matters quickly. The villa is as good a place as any, and perhaps more private than anywhere else.'

'Sir, if you don't mind, I would like to stay with *Sahibjee* (Respected Sir).' Aslam did not want to leave.

'Aslam, I know you are in shock and find it difficult to accept this. We are all in the same situation, but we have to go on and deal with other matters, too. We will not leave here until everything has been set in place. There will be people here to ensure that Papa's body is not disturbed. We have to deal with a few important matters. You know everything at the villa. I want you to be with us; you are one of the family. We may need to consult you,' Yakoob said gently.

Soon after, Rafik rushed in. He saw Haroon standing in a corner, crying. 'Where is Papa? What happened? How is he now?' He asked.

Yakoob went to Rafik and held him in an embrace. 'Papa has passed away. *Inna lillah e wa inna elaihe rajeoon* (We all belong to Allah and to Him we return),' Yakoob said, quoting the Quran.

'No. It is not possible. He was okay with us yesterday evening. They have probably not examined him properly.' Rafik was beside himself.

'Hold yourself, Rafik. I have seen Papa myself. He passed away before he got here.'

Rafik freed himself from Yakoob and went to Haroon. Both brothers embraced each other and started wailing. Others in the group stood quietly.

Salim took the lead and approached the brothers, embracing each and saying, 'Patience, gentlemen, patience. He who comes to this world has to leave. He was like a father to me. I have also suffered a big loss. We all will have to be strong and move forward.'

Others followed, embracing each brother, saying similar words of condolence.

The TIG Hong Kong administration manager, Shaukat, and public relations officer, Shin Lou had also arrived. They stood quietly on side after expressing their condolences.

Yakoob turned his attention to them and said 'We would like to take Papa's body to Karachi as soon as possible. I will go with Papa. I must know the time of arrival in Karachi well in advance to ensure that we are received appropriately there. Make sure you are able to complete all the formalities as soon as possible. Spend whatever is necessary. I would like both of you to come to the villa as soon as you have been able to ensure that the arrangements are in place and being taken care of.

'Haroon and Rafik will go to Karachi before us. We'll meet at the villa to discuss a few matters as soon as we can leave here. After that, they can take my plane. Tell the crew to get the plane ready for a quick departure to Karachi. You might have to ask for a few favours to get a priority slot for take-off.'

'Don't worry about anything, Sir. Everything will be taken care of. We'll ensure that all the matters are handled smoothly. I have asked my assistant, Hu Win, to come here also,' Shaukat said.

'Don't let anybody know about this without my saying so. We have to make sure this is handled properly. There is a lot at stake here,' Yakoob said.

'Sure, we will not let this news get out. What do we do with the office? Should we open the office as normal?' Shaukat asked.

'Yes, for the time being. My brothers, other executives and I will meet shortly. We will let you know about the office and the public announcement to be made after our meeting,' Yakoob replied.

Chapter 13

Ismail Soothar's Villa at Stanley, Hong Kong

The group consisting of the three brothers, other executives, and Aslam arrived at the villa around 8.30 a.m.

'Aslam, we'll meet in the main sitting room. Please arrange something to eat and refreshments for everybody. I don't feel like eating myself, but we have many things to take care of and we must conserve our energy. Falling apart won't do,' Yakoob said to Aslam.

Aslam did not like the idea of preparing food, serving it, or eating it himself. He was in deep shock. But he said nothing and went to the kitchen. He called the maid and asked her to come to the villa immediately as there was a lot of work to be done.

The sitting room was huge and tastefully furnished. The group settled down on the two sofa sets.

Yakoob started the meeting. 'Gentlemen, this is a very sad day. Our father has gone. And with his passing, the guidance, wisdom, support and goodwill we were so used to has also vanished. I'm sorry to talk business before Papa's body has been moved from the hospital. You may all think this is callous, but I am terrified by the challenges facing us. We have to move on, and move on quickly before we are completely wiped out. There is a lot at stake here, and we do not have the luxury of hiding ourselves in a prolonged period of mourning. Every minute is important, as the news will get out, and our stakeholders and competitors, will react. They will assess how Papa's death will affect them. We have to be prepared to deal with the situation, and we should have a plan.

'Everybody has to go one day. One cannot stay on and enjoy this life even for one second more than what has been ordained. So, Papa went when his time was over. We should accept this. In one way, the timing of Papa's departure could not have been better. As we discussed yesterday, we are facing serious challenges. The group is facing a financial catastrophe.

'Papa's death will generate a wave of sympathy for the family from the government, media and our creditors, which will give us time to deal with the issues. Nobody with a heart will push us to meet our financial obligations, at least for a few weeks, provided we appear in control and financially sound.

'This also means that we will have a free hand in dealing with the issues without worrying about obtaining Papa's approval. I could sense yesterday that he was not happy with some measures that were suggested. We will talk about these measures again but we may have to make some tough decisions quickly.'

All of a sudden, Haroon started sobbing and was beside himself. Nari got up and started comforting Haroon.

Yakoob addressed his brother. 'Haroon, as I said just now, we have to be strong to deal with this. Patience, my brother. If you think you cannot take this, please go to the next room and lie down.'

Haroon spoke up. 'We did nothing for Papa. He did everything for us. We are not even at the hospital with his body. I don't like this. I am going back to the hospital. I would like to be with Papa. You have my consent for whatever you decide here.' He got up and left the room.

In the sitting room, Rafik also started sobbing.

'Not you, too,' Yakoob said sternly to Rafik.

'Haroon and I are not as strong as you. I understand that what you are doing is important, but it's difficult for me to concentrate on business matters right now. I cannot accept that Papa has left us. Please go on; I will manage.' Rafik said.

Aslam and the housemaid entered the room, pushing trolleys with freshly toasted bread, croissants and pastries, juices, tea and coffee.

'Thank you, Aslam. Now please see that we are not disturbed,' Yakoob told Aslam.

Aslam left with jerky steps, indicating that he did not like the idea of a breakfast or the business meeting so soon after the boss had passed away.

'Gentlemen, let's take some food and we will continue,' Yakoob said.

The group got up and took small portions of food. Nobody seemed to have much of an appetite.

Yakoob continued. 'Well, before we were interrupted, I was saying that in a way Papa's departure has opened up some opportunities for us to handle the issues we talked about yesterday.

'First of all, we have to make the arrangements for transporting Papa's body to Karachi and for his funeral. I suggest that Haroon, Rafik, Salim, Nari, Alex, and Mansukh should leave for Karachi immediately after this meeting and make arrangements there. Please work with our media consultants to make sure that all the newspapers in Pakistan have a full front page coverage announcing Papa's death and obituaries. These should be very praiseworthy of Papa's achievements and complementary to our group's status in international business. We have to ensure that anybody who is anyone in Pakistan attends the funeral or turns up at our house in Karachi for condolences. Try to get the Pakistan Shipowners' and Shipping Agents' Association to declare a holiday for the funeral as a mark of respect to Papa.

'Salim, Haroon and Rafik are very emotional at the moment, and they will also have to be present with the family to receive condolences. Please take charge of the Pakistan side of the arrangements with Nari and Mansukh. You may take my plane for the flight. I have already instructed Shin Lou to get it ready for a quick departure.

'I will accompany Papa's body. We will come by any commercial flight that we can get on. Unfortunately, the time of our departure depends on the completion of the formalities here. Please make sure there are arrangements in place at Karachi airport for an immediate release of the body.

'I'll also use our media relations firm in Hong Kong to get a press release issued to all major news agencies announcing Papa's death. That will reiterate our prominence in the business world, particularly in shipping. Full-page advertisements announcing the death will also appear in the *South China Morning Post*, *The Wall Street Journal's* Asia edition, and *The Standard*. The UK's *Financial Times* will also publish the obituary.

'I'll speak on the phone to Sheikh Tayeb and Azhar Alam at the G&P Bank, as they are our major business partners. I'll promise to go see them to assure them that everything is being handled as efficiently as possible and there is no threat to the group's business.

'We should meet at my house in Karachi after the *soyem* (third day of mourning). That will be Friday. We'll discuss the business situation and come up with an action plan in that meeting. We also need to involve our legal adviser, Masoom Ali Pirani, as soon as possible to ensure that all the legal issues that may arise are dealt with efficiently. I will call Masoom after this meeting and ask him to be available for the Karachi meeting. Any questions or comments?'

Nobody had any.

'Okay. I'll use Papa's study to make a few calls and work on some documents. Salim, I would like you to join me to discuss a couple of matters while you are waiting for clearance for the plane's departure.'

Part II
Desperation

Chapter 14

G&P Bank's offices, Karachi

It was customary for the G&P Bank's senior executive board, which included Sheikh Tayeb, Chairman; Azhar Alam, Chief Operating Officer; Abu Talib, Senior Executive Vice President; Retired Major Shakadir Khan, Personal Assistant to the Chairman; Masood Qadir, Head of Geneva and Mateen Saeed, Chief Financial Officer, to meet several times around Christmas, before the financial year ends, to review the bank's affairs and decide on the bank's financial reporting and future strategy.

However, the meeting taking place on that Monday in the last week of December was different. There was tension in the air. All the executives attending the meeting were in their designated seats before 8 a.m., which was early for Karachi, where the banks started at nine in the morning and the trading activity did not commence until eleven.

'Good morning, gentlemen.' Sheikh Tayeb started the meeting by speaking into a microphone. 'We are meeting here under very difficult conditions. We are perhaps facing the gravest situation in the bank's history.

'Our financial position is serious, as Azhar and Mateen will also tell you. Our auditors are finding it difficult to clear our financial statements. We are being looked into by some regulatory agencies, and if that is not enough, there are certain internal threats and customers' demands.

'I understand that the draft financial statements of the bank do not look good. We have an exposure to a potential loss of four billion dollars, which may entirely wipe out our capital and reserves. Our main exposure comes from the potential loss on investments and advances, the loss on foreign exchange transactions because of the sudden plunge in the dollar's value versus the Japanese Yen and Swiss Franc, volatility in the precious metal market, the sudden fall in the value of oil and a very sharp decline in property values across the UK. Our shareholders and backers have also learnt of our difficulties and are clamouring for action.

'Let's review these issues in a little more detail and work out a strategy to deal with them. Azhar, please tell us about the current situation we are in and the steps we need to take to resolve the problems.'

Azhar Alam pulled the microphone towards him and said, 'First, let's look at the reasons for the potential loss exposure. We have advanced funds to certain clients who seem to be in financial difficulties and may not be able to fully repay their balances. Our exposure to bad advances appears to be near four billion US dollars, of which two billion US dollars are from only one client: Tanganyika Investment Group - TIG.

'Recently the chairman of TIG, Ismail Soothar, died in Hong Kong. Sheikh Tayeb and I are going to meet his eldest son and heir apparent soon. We'll try to work out a plan to reduce our exposure to this group. Initial indications are that the group has some difficulties, which seem to be temporary. The Soothars are very capable businessmen.

Because we think our investment will eventually be recovered, we have only provided five million US dollars against possible loss from TIG.

'We also have an outstanding receivable balance of eight hundred million US dollars with Caricorp. As you are aware, Caricorp is owned by the G&P Bank through nominee arrangements. Caricorp trades in currency and commodities markets. The funds available with Caricorp were also used to pay off some of our benefactors in various countries.

'In addition, there has been a sharp decline in the value of our investments, particularly in real estate. If we were to provide for potential loss on these investments, our total losses would exceed four billion US dollars. I understand the auditors might insist that these potential losses should be provided for. Let's ask Mateen Saeed about financial reporting and the threats we face there. He is very deeply involved with our auditors and the UK regulators on this issue.' Azhar turned to Mateen Saeed.

'As Azhar has mentioned, we are in a difficult financial situation. Our auditors, Tolbert and Gibbs, have been meeting with us to finalise our financial statements. I have a strong friendship with the senior banking partner, Charles Ramsey, and David Finner, the banking partner in charge of our bank's audit. They are a pretty relaxed bunch and will accept almost anything we tell them over a good lunch. I've been keeping them happy. Charles has already taken a loan of five hundred thousand pounds from our Geneva branch for some personal needs. I also treat both Charles and David to lavish lunches and send gifts on appropriate occasions. Charles Ramsey's daughter recently passed her A-levels. I sent her a Cartier watch as a gift and offered to arrange a scholarship for her university education under the Sheikh Tayeb Educational Foundation. Tolbert and Gibbs' partners are always looking for more revenue. I have advised them that the bank will be looking for a consultant to study our credit control and management procedures. I have also indicated that although there are other competitors, Tolbert and Gibbs stands a very good chance to get this assignment and that I will be recommending them.

'This seems to have silenced them for a while. However, the audit manager responsible for our bank's audit is a fellow named Danial Rafi. Danny is very clever and is giving us a hard time. He believes the investment loss provision is inadequate and should be reviewed thoroughly before clearing the financials. He insists that we show him full documentation for our major accounts, such as TIG and Caricorp, in order for him to assess whether these accounts were performing and our investments were secure. We have always avoided giving too much documentation to our auditors' junior and mid-level staff about these accounts. I normally tell them I will give the information only to their senior partners. I usually take the senior partners to lunch when they want to discuss the loan loss provision. I give them as little information as possible, and I advise them that these accounts are personally managed by Sheikh Tayeb and Azhar, who guarantee full recovery of outstanding amounts. We provide them with written assurances from Sheikh Tayeb and Azhar to satisfy them. This has always worked as the senior partners are keen not to upset us.

'This year, Danny is insisting that he would personally like to examine the files of major receivable accounts. Unfortunately, he has issued memos asking for the information. As these matters have now been put in writing, the senior partners will find it difficult to overrule him and clear the financials.'

'Danial Rafi, sounds like a Pakistani name,' Shakadir Khan, who up to now had been sitting quietly, said. He had nothing to do with banking operations or financial reporting, but he seemed to be interested whenever there was a threat to the bank.

'Yes. He is a British citizen of Pakistani parents. Very smart kid but very stubborn.'

'Could we not do anything to dissuade him from pursuing this matter further?' Shakadir did not like a threat to the bank by a Pakistani kid.

'I tried. Invited him to dinner at my home. Asked my daughter Nida to look after him. She was all over him, but the guy is very dry. He was polite with Nida but did not follow up with further contact.'

'Do we know about his family in Pakistan?' Shakadir was bent on solving this issue.

'He comes from an average middle-class family from Lahore. He told me that his father worked as a shop manager for a garment company. I could get more information if you think it might be helpful.' Mateen replied.

'Before we try to persuade Danny, let's make sure he is the only problem regarding the audit and that once he is satisfied, others will not create any difficulties.' Azhar said.

'I am satisfied that if Danny clears the audit, others will not be difficult to handle. We will have to promise and deliver a management consultancy assignment to Tolbert and Gibbs. It may cost a few hundred thousand pounds.'

'All right. Why don't you get some more information about Danny for Shakadir? Shakadir, please see what you can do about this. But please try to be subtle. I only want to ensure that this is handled with no adverse reaction and with nothing that can be traced back to us. We don't want this Danny guy to get angry and try to do more damage to us than he would have done otherwise. Mateen, you ask Charles Ramsey to dinner and invite him to give a proposal for reviewing our management information system. This should be fairly harmless. Please tell him we will be happy to sign on the engagement after the bank's accounts have been cleared. Tell him that other major accounting firms are also being considered but you will ensure that the assignment goes to Tolbert and Gibbs. Please try to keep the cost of the assignment as low as possible and definitely below four hundred thousand pounds.' Sheikh Tayeb decided and continued the meeting. 'This was about financial statements. I understand that the Bank of England is also getting active against us.' He turned to Azhar, indicating he should take the lead and explain.

Azhar elaborated, 'We have received letters from the Bank of England to give details about some of the large deposits we received from certain major customers. As you know, we never show the true names of our major customers to protect their confidentiality. Apparently, the Banking Intelligence Unit has been advised by the Americans that we receive large amounts from some parties in Mexico, Colombia and Panama who are on the US watch list. The BOE wants to know who these large depositors are and their source of money. I have replied that they are very wealthy, respectable people who have been dealing with us for a long time.

'I am afraid this might become more serious as the BOE is pressed by the Americans. Recently, there were arrests in the USA of some South Americans with large sums in cash. They told the investigators they were to meet our representatives in Miami and hand over the cash to them. Of course, our people in Miami have strongly denied any knowledge of or connection to these characters. As you know, we have placed Shaheen Shafi and Robinho Gonzalez in Miami to source funds for deposits with our bank. Although we do not know for sure, I believe that the US agencies might still be sniffing around and may take action against our people. Unfortunately, we do not have any banking licence or an official presence in the USA. Our representatives have to use other banking channels and courier services to transfer deposits received from clients there.'

'I do not want the US government agencies to go after us. Those people are like bulldogs. They don't let a thing go once they get it between their teeth. I'll have to contact Bernard Schlom to do something about this,' Sheikh Tayeb commented.

'Where does this leave our problems with BOE?' This time it was Masood Qadir who questioned.

'I know some very senior people at the BOE. I look after some of these guys by inviting them for lunches and dinners and sending Christmas gifts and such. The BOE normally moves at a snail's pace. Unless they get serious pressure from some other source, I believe that this will go on for a long time, so this is not an immediate problem but may become one,' Azhar explained.

'I asked because I am afraid that one of my staff might have been contributing to the problem. I have an Englishman named Richard Bringsen. He was recruited in London and worked in our Knightsbridge branch for a while before he was transferred to Geneva. He is a good, competent banker but a little bit of an old woman. I get reports he has been snooping into the files of our major clients and trying to follow the trail of the deposits coming into the bank. He has been photocopying some documents, which might have been taken out of the bank. He was also overheard talking on phone, telling somebody that the bank's operations were not completely legal and the bank was receiving deposits from questionable sources abroad. He promised to give the information to expose the bank. We traced the call to a senior reporter of the *Financial Times*.'

'This sounds serious. Very serious. We need to deal with this immediately,' Shakadir commented.

'I was thinking to transfer Richard to a less substantial and sensitive location and posting Amir Ramli, the kid you sent from Karachi, in his place. He seems to be a sincere team player. I have already told him he may have to work in Geneva for a few weeks more. He likes Geneva and was happy with the idea of spending some time there. I would prefer him to be transferred permanently to Geneva.'

'Transferring Amir is not a problem, but I don't like the situation with Richard Bringsen. We should not transfer him to any branch. He should not be with us, period. We have to ensure that he does not inflict any damage.' Azhar was angry.

'Oshko, our security officer, is already on to him. Every communication made by Richard, whether personally, on the phone, or in writing, is being monitored. Right now, he is away on holiday with his girlfriend. They are spending Christmas and New Year's with the girl's parents in Speyer, a small town across the border in Germany. He'll return after the new year.' Masood replied.

'I suggest that Shakadir take charge of this matter personally and ensure that this guy is not in a position to do any harm to the bank. It is better if it is done while he is on holiday, so there is no connection with the bank. We should ask Amir to return to Geneva immediately to work in a different department, so there isn't any connection with the action against Richard and Amir's transfer. Azhar, please speak to Amir and ensure that he moves to Geneva quickly. If necessary, promote him to the vice president grade.' It was Sheikh Tayeb speaking this time.

'I'll speak to you after this meeting to get full details about this guy, Richard. Please do not worry. Consider the problem solved,' Shakadir said directly to Masood.

Azhar Alam said 'I also want to brief you about the situation in Nigeria. Our courier carrying a consignment of approximately eighty million dollars was killed, and the containers with these assets were lost. The funds belonged to some very senior people in Nigeria. As a result, we are facing difficulties there. We have assured the clients that the bank will be responsible for the deposit and that they will not suffer a loss. The authorities have threatened to take away our licence and are treating our senior staff as criminals.

'The Nigerian clients have deposits aggregating eight hundred million US dollars with us. They've indicated that they want to withdraw it. We are trying to persuade them not to. In any event, we will have to pay the eighty million which were lost. This has to be done immediately. Given our current cash flow issues, this is not helpful.'

'What do you have in mind for the Nigerian situation?' asked Abu Talib, who had been quiet until then.

'In the current situation, it is not possible to pay out eighty million dollars to Nigerians, let alone their full deposit of eight hundred million. We'll have to confirm to them that their accounts have been credited with the deposit of eighty million and that these funds are being invested in the shares and other gilts as is normal. We'll then have to send them bank advices for the investments held on their account. This trail of documents will have to be created from Geneva. Thank God for the Swiss banking laws guaranteeing secrecy. We have the freedom to create any paper we want in Switzerland. However, in order to ensure that we are not exposed if an audit is undertaken, we'll have to spread the investment through other Swiss banks who are eager to acquire deposits. They do not want to know where the money is coming from.

'Of course, by doing all this, we are buying time. We have to take some very radical steps to top up our capital and cover the losses we seem to have incurred,' Azhar Alam replied.

'How much do we need to get us through so that we don't have to default on any of our commitments?' Again, it was Abu Talib who asked the question.

'In my opinion, if we can inject close to two billion dollars, we might be able to sail through the crisis and turn the situation around. We need to find a way to deal with the hole we find ourselves in. We need more investment and should restructure to avert any threat of bankruptcy.' Azhar Alam replied, turning towards Sheikh Tayeb.

Sheikh Tayeb took the cue and said, 'Our consultants have prepared a report with some suggestions to reorganise our affairs. We urgently need more funds. I will have to approach Bulund Khan to give us financial support. He is ill. I am worried about our status in Banjar. I'm receiving cryptic messages from Yousuf Ali, our manager there. Apparently, there have been quite a few changes in the power structure there. It appears that Sitara Khan has taken full control of the government as Bulund Khan's health has deteriorated. Unfortunately, Sitara Khan is not very friendly with us. He has an Indian adviser, Sajan Mala. Sajan does not like the G&P Bank's prominent position in Banjar. I have also learnt that there is a new bank there being patronised by Sajan Mala. He may be a secret partner in that bank. Yousuf Ali has not been coming out openly about the affairs there. He may be worried for his own safety. I'll have to go to Banjar as soon as possible to see if Bulund Khan is able to help us.

'I also know some very wealthy businessmen and influential people in the Middle and Far East. There are some wealthy people in Asia also. We'll have to offer them a stake in the bank. Our consultants have advised us to create another investment holding company that may hold shares in the bank. We'd hold over fifty-one percent of the new company, thus keeping control of the bank in our hands.

'I'll also approach Yakoob Soothar. He's in charge of TIG after his father's death. He is a shrewd player. I'll have to pressure him to reduce the bank's investment and repay at least five hundred million US dollars. I understand his group has not been doing well, but they had a small profit last year.

'All of this will take time – at least three months before we get some support. We'll have to somehow survive the quarter. We must ensure that our financial statements do not show any weakness. We need to control the information about our situation very tightly. Therefore, it is especially important that we are able to plug any leaks and place only those people whom we trust in important positions.'

Shakadir raised his hand. 'Please don't worry about plugging any leaks. I'll take care of that. You said it might take three months to get the support we need, but it might take longer. I have a couple of suggestions to partly remedy the situation in the short term.'

All eyes turned to Shakadir. People around the table were surprised, as Shakadir was not a banker and he rarely spoke on banking and financial matters.

'First, I have some friends in Columbia and Peru who have approximately two billion dollars. They need some investment advice. They are offering a twenty-five percent fee for helping them make legal and safe investments. They want it done now and do not want to wait. I'm not a banking specialist but I suggest if you consider it worth our while to undertake this transaction, then assign somebody who is able to deal with this transaction quickly.

'Second, I know of an arms supplier in South Africa who is sitting on a large amount of ammunition ordered by and especially manufactured for a Mujahideen group in Afghanistan who has already partly paid for the arms. The delivery of the arms will only be made upon payment of the balance due. With the exit of the Soviets, the Mujahideen group has lost interest in taking the delivery and wants to dispose of these arms at whatever prices they get. So, these arms are available at throw away prices. With several conflicts going on at the moment, there is a great demand for these goods. I have been contacted by several potential buyers in Africa who are interested in acquiring them. I believe that acting as facilitators could make us at least a couple of hundred million dollars from this transaction. All we have to do to profit is pay a small amount to the Mujahideen, pay the balance due to the supplier, and lift the cargo from a port somewhere in Africa and deliver it to a buyer in another part of Africa.'

Everybody looked at Shakadir with admiration. He was an angel who had descended from heaven to save the bank.

Sheikh Tayeb was the first to react. 'Shakadir, this is great. With these two transactions, you say that we may make almost seven hundred million dollars in a very short time. All we need to do is to make some arrangements. We certainly have people who are capable of dealing with this. What do you say, Azhar?'

'I'm sure this could be handled by our people. We'd have to organise the monetary part of the transactions through Switzerland. As for the transfer of cargo from the supplier to the buyers, I'll have to make some arrangements with the help of Shakadir. Shakadir, let's talk offline and take this further. We shouldn't let these opportunities pass. Masood, please join us, as your involvement will be essential in completing these transactions.' Azhar Alam said.

'Sure. It'll be my pleasure. I'm sure Geneva will be able to handle the funds.' Masood replied.

Sheikh Tayeb took over again. 'To summarise, gentlemen, we have some difficulties, as you have heard, but these are not insurmountable. We need to make some efforts and take some innovative steps. We also need more business. This requires us to motivate our staff further and work on our clients. We have to ensure that our financial statements look good, and we give better than last year's bonuses to our staff to encourage them to bring in more business.

'I suggest that we have two annual conferences this year instead of the usual one. The first should be a two-day conference for our senior staff only. One month later, we should have a two-day conference for our major clients and other dignitaries. At the first conference, we work with our staff to develop future strategies and plan for further growth in business. The second conference will be a lesson in showmanship. We'll look after our clients and dignitaries like they have never been looked after before.

'In order to prepare our staff to achieve the type of deposits and other business we need; we have to move quickly. I suggest that the first conference is held at the beginning of February in one of the luxury hotels in Bangkok. Our staff and their families will enjoy being there, although I suspect that since it'll be in Bangkok, many of our people will come without families. The second conference should be in London, right in the middle of the financial world with some very important people singing the praises of G&P Bank in front of a global audience.'

'I think that this is a fantastic idea.' Azhar Alam was the first to react and compliment Sheikh Tayeb's ideas.

'Let's have our first conference on Monday and Tuesday, 5 and 6 February, and the second on 4 and 5 April, which are Thursday and Friday. Our guests from outside London might want to stay on for the weekend. Of course, we'll make all the arrangements and pick up the charges for their travels and stay.' Azhar Alam suggested.

'Good. Then it's agreed. Azhar, please make sure these conferences are handled efficiently. I'll work with you to refine the programme and other arrangements. Well, gentlemen, let's stop here and keep an eye on the situation. We might have to meet regularly in the next few weeks to ensure that the matters discussed today are dealt with properly.' Sheikh Tayeb ended the meeting.

Chapter 15

England – Danial Rafi's apartment, Milton Keynes

It was a cold and dark early evening on Christmas Eve in England. Amir had taken a taxi from Heathrow to Danny's apartment. Normally he travelled on public transport when in England, but he felt rich with the bonus in his pocket. He rang the bell.

Danny opened the door. 'Hey, you made it! Your letter and telephone call had me very worried.'

'Yes, I have made it to London. During the flight to Geneva from Karachi, I had thought I might only make it to a Swiss prison. I will tell you the whole story in a bit. How are you?' Amir replied.

'I'm fine. Very busy these days due to the annual closings. You know I'm the audit manager responsible for your bank's audit. I'll have to work over the holidays. How was the flight?' Danny enquired.

'The flight was fine. It was short, but I feel tired and drained.'

'Working very hard for a change?' Danny joked.

'Not hard work, but a different type of stress. Has Samira sent you any papers?'

'Nothing. The mail gets slower around Christmas. We will have enough time to discuss all this. You freshen up first. Your usual room is ready. After that, let's have a drink.' Danny said, having carried Amir's bags up the stairs and placing them in the small bedroom.

'This looks the same as how I had left it,' Amir said as he looked into the room.

'Of course. Nobody has used it much since you left. My parents visit from Pakistan every year and stay only for a few weeks,' Danny replied.

Danny left the room to give Amir some time to freshen up. Amir quickly unpacked and changed into a polo shirt and jeans. He walked into the sitting room and found his friend sitting in front of the television, watching the news.

'What would you like to Drink? I know you like whisky. I have a Johnny Walker in the cabinet over there. Help yourself. I'll join you,' Danny said when he saw Amir walking in.

Amir went to the cabinet and took out the bottle of whisky. He poured it into two tumblers, gave one to Danny and slumped on the sofa.

'How long are you planning to stay in England?' Danny asked.

'Throwing me out already?' Amir countered.

'No. You're welcome to stay here as long as you want. Just asking.'

'I'll be here for four days, do some shopping, and go to Karachi. The bank wants me to return to Geneva in the New year.'

'Geneva is nice, much better than Karachi, I'm sure,' Danny said with a sly smile.

'Sure, Geneva is nice. Actually, it's perfect for what I want to do,' Amir said.

'How is Seemi?' Danny asked.

'She is great, enjoying the never-ending wedding season in Karachi. She dropped me at the airport. She wants me to buy her a Cartier.'

'The lady has expensive taste. Her husband will have to work hard to keep her happy. Actually, I'd like to send her a New Year's gift, so don't forget to remind me to give it to you before you leave.' Danny spoke fondly of Seemi.

'Sure. Give me whatever you want to be delivered.'

'We're going to dinner. I booked a table at Shahi Mahal in Mayfair. I believe it is the best Indian restaurant in England. They're in Berkley Square, so we'll have to take a train. You better put on a warm layer and take a coat. It is cold outside.'

'Give me a minute.' Amir said, and he went to his room to bundle up.

Soon, both friends left the apartment. It took them close to an hour to reach Green Park Underground Station, which was closest to Berkley Square. Shahi Mahal was certainly a very good restaurant. Everything was perfect: the location, the ambience, the quality of the food and service. Amir enjoyed the meal thoroughly.

As they dined, he narrated his experience at Karachi airport and in Geneva to Danny.

'I am sorry to involve you in this. On the flight, I wasn't sure if I would ever be able to walk a free man again,' Amir apologised.

'Well, now you've told me everything, and with the papers coming from Samira, I'm involved. This creates a very complicated situation for me. I'm the audit manager in charge of the bank's audit so I have to take action if this information influences the bank's financial statements. It's possible that I might have to insist on additional provisions against receivables from TIG. This might be the minimum. The bank's management does not want any further provisions, so they'll resist. I'll have to brief my senior colleagues but will have to be careful in order to protect you. Let's talk a little more about this tomorrow. In the meantime, let's deal with this lovely bottle of Bordeaux, which is waiting for us to finish it.' Danny said, pouring the wine into Amir's glass.

It was past one in the morning when they returned to Danny's apartment, and Amir was tired. He bid good night to Danny and got into bed.

***

Boxing Day is celebrated in the UK on 26 December. It is a public holiday and considered a day to spread goodwill. Very rarely do people go to work unless they are employed in certain public services. Danny, although already awake, was still in bed at 11 a.m., feeling lazy and avoiding getting up. His reverie was shaken off by a sudden ringing of the telephone.

He picked up the bedside phone. 'Hello.'

'Hi, Danny. Merry Christmas. Sorry if I woke you, but this is important.' It was David Finner, Danny's boss and the partner in charge of the G&P Bank's audit.

'Merry Christmas, David. I was awake. But what are you doing calling people at this time on Boxing Day?' Danny responded.

'Partners in accounting firms are like presidents of countries, on duty twenty-four hours, you know. Anyway, the reason I called you is that Mateen Saeed phoned me. He says the bank wants its profit figure to be cleared before the year's end. Apparently, there are a few decisions to be made by the main board of the G&P Bank, and Sheikh Tayeb wants a confirmed number before making any adjustments,' David explained.

'Before the year end? Impossible. There are only four days left. We must clear the loan loss reserve. You know we have not received the information from the bank about certain major accounts. Unless we are able to review this in detail, it's impossible to determine the exact provision required by the bank.' Danny was now wide awake and, despite the severe cold weather, sweating.

'I told him that. He assured me that all the information we require is with him, and he is available today. I know it's a holiday, and you might have other plans. I have therefore volunteered to go there myself and look at the information. He has the complete list of the major balances and has already prepared a status report on each.'

'I wanted to look at the information for the major accounts myself this year. I told him so. I can come with you.'

'Don't worry. I can handle this alone. You relax today, as the next few days will be desperate. Mateen also suggested that it might be more efficient if I directly looked at these major accounts.'

'You know the bank's biggest debtor is TIG. I may get some information from certain other sources outside the bank that could affect our position on the recoverability of the bank's balances.' Danny was upset at this turn of events.

'Let me go there today. We'll discuss this further in the office tomorrow. Don't worry, I'll take thorough notes and won't make any commitment until we're able to talk. Just relax and enjoy your day off.' With that, David was gone.

Danny was angry that he was being left out of the discussions for a very important aspect of the assignment he was working on. He got up and walked into the living room. Amir was sitting on the sofa with a cup of coffee.

'Good morning. When did you get up?' He asked Amir.

'I couldn't sleep, so I got out of bed at ten. I boiled some eggs, and I'm on my first cup of coffee,' Amir replied. 'There are a couple of boiled eggs left in the pot for you if you fancy them.'

'Thanks. I just got a call from David Finner. He's the partner responsible for G&P Bank's audit at the firm. He's going to see Mateen Saeed to discuss the bank's receivables.'

'This is being pushed. What's the urgency?'

'The bank wants the auditors' clearance on profit for the year. They would like to finalise numbers before the year end. Tolbert and Gibbs are more than happy to oblige.'

'As I told you, the balances due from TIG certainly need looking into. TIG appears to be bankrupt, and the bank is very heavily exposed. You will find a lot of information about the group's financial chicanery in my memo, which I wrote for the file before handing it over to my successor, who is a very junior person at the bank. You know that the TIG's chairman and patriarch, Ismail Soothar, died recently. The group might now be headless and lost,' Amir replied.

'Yes, I read about Ismail Soothar's sudden death in Hong Kong. I hear that his eldest son, Yakoob, has taken over the leadership of the group. Nothing I can do at the moment. Let's see what David brings in. I will ensure that the provision is made for any irrecoverable investments. What do you want to do today?' Danny replied.

'Shops are open today, aren't they? I'd like to go to the West End to do some shopping. Would you like to come?' Amir asked.

'There are boxing day sales, so the large department stores may be very busy. You will enjoy the shoppers falling over each other to buy things. I don't have any other plans, so let's go to the city and have a good lunch and talk.'

On the way to London, Amir told Danny about his suspicions about TIG's financial stability. He suspected their shipping fleet was old, not properly maintained and therefore not seaworthy. Most of the assets offered as collateral against the bank's advances were overvalued and not realisable. Amir also suspected that some of the financial information provided by TIG to the bank was inaccurate and misleading.

'First of all, I need to review the bank's documentation for advances to TIG before deciding on the need for provision. I can't refer to the information you've provided. I'm sure there will be several files, and all the information will not be in one place. We have been after Mateen and his team to provide us the information about TIG and some other major accounts, and he has been delaying this with one excuse or other. Last time, the files were with Sheikh Tayeb for review as the group's facilities were coming up for renewal. Before that, the files were scattered between London, Geneva and Karachi.' Danny was frustrated, but they had just reached Oxford Street and crowds were thick, it was no longer possible to continue the conversations.

Selfridges was one of Amir's favourite department stores, so they went there. There were a lot of customers in the store, but the jewellery and watches sections were not too busy. Amir picked up a Cartier 21 for Seemi, a pair of cuff links and a couple of neckties for his father, and a pair of studs for his mother. Remembering that he would have to give something to Samira as well, he bought a pair of pearl studs. Just when he thought he was done with gifts, on an impulse he bought a beautiful pair of earrings from Tiffany for Rehana. He had them all packed up as gifts, and asked Danny if he was hungry.

'Sure. There's a nice food court on the top floor. Let's eat there,' Danny replied.

The food court had a wide variety of international cuisine. Both friends went to the Indian food counter and ordered chicken curry with rice.

'The weather is bad. It's not possible to walk outside,' Danny said.

'Yes, terrible, isn't it? The weather is one thing I don't like about London,' Amir replied. 'It looks as if we have two choices. Either go to a movie or go home.'

'I'm feeling a little tired and we have all these shopping bags with us. Let's go home, and we will decide what to do later,' Amir said.

It was late when they reached Danny's apartment, and neither had any energy left to venture out again. They ordered a Chinese dinner from a nearby restaurant for home delivery and parked themselves in front of the television.

'I have to go to the office tomorrow. What are your plans?' Danny asked.

'I'll go to the bank. I have money to pick up from there. I also want to see a good bookshop, so I'll probably go to Waterstone's in Piccadilly. I may also do some more shopping,' Amir replied.

'You still want to shop?' Danny teased. 'G&P Bank must pay you well.'

'And probably fast tracking me to jail. Please don't remind me of my job with G&P.'

'Let's not talk shop. Enjoy yourself, and don't do anything I wouldn't do.'

Chapter 16

London – Offices of Tolbert and Gibbs

As soon as Danny entered the office, his secretary, Cathy, told him about a meeting to discuss G&P's financial statements scheduled at ten in the meeting room next to Charles Ramsey's office.

Danny quickly dug out the files and his notes of outstanding issues with the bank's audit. At the top of the list was 'Loan loss reserve and review of advances.' He had jotted down the names of a few large borrowers of the bank.

He looked at his watch. It was nearly ten. He walked up the flight of stairs to the tenth floor where senior partners had their offices and meeting rooms.

David Finner and George Hansel were already there. 'Good morning, and Merry Christmas. Did you spend long at G&P yesterday?' Danny asked, looking at David.

'Good morning. Yes, I had to spend quite a bit of time.' David replied.

Just then, Charles Ramsey entered. 'Good morning. Sorry, I was caught up on the telephone, and who do you think it was? Azhar Alam calling from Karachi. He was very pleased, David, that you could go to the bank yesterday, even though it was a holiday. He appreciates our support to the bank.'

Danny did not like the drift of the conversation but he said nothing.

'Yes, since Mateen Saeed seemed as if he were panicking, I had to go. I might be divorced for deserting my family on Boxing Day, though.'

'Wives are like that. They don't understand the things we have to do to put food on the table and send the children to school. Don't worry, she'll sulk for a day and then she'll be okay.' Charles offered his wisdom learnt from many years of marriage.

'Oh, Jenny is all right. She made a face, but she understood. I'm happy that the client appreciated our efforts,' David replied.

'Yes. Azhar was very happy. I understand you got all the information, and we are ready to make a decision on the provision for losses. I understand this is the only item that worries us. If we are happy with the provisions, then we should be able to clear the profit figure for the year. Is that true?' Charles asked, looking around the table.

'I think so. There are a few housekeeping points, but they are routine and may be cleared in the coming days. What do you think, George, Danny?' David wanted to be sure there were no dissents.

'I think that's right. I know Danny had been worried about provisions, but if you have looked at them and agreed to a number with the client, then we should be able to clear the profit number,' George Hansel replied.

'I think there are serious issues about some of the loans and advances, particularly to TIG and Caricorp.' Danny commented looking at his notes.

David was ready to deal with this. 'I looked at both accounts thoroughly when I was there yesterday. They have comprehensive information for all their major advances, including both those you mentioned: TIG and Caricorp.

'Abu Talib, SEVP and head of corporate banking, has personally carried out a review of these two accounts. He has written a detailed account of the financial position of TIG. He has concluded that TIG has more than sufficient assets to back its borrowings. The group had temporary difficulties due to the current world economic situation, but the tide is turning. TIG is now in an even better position to expand and grow with the departure of its patriarch and chairman, Ismail Soothar. Apparently, Ismail was very conservative and would not let his sons participate in some very lucrative businesses for which there were opportunities in Asia and Africa.

'As for Caricorp, it has a very sound business. Mrs. Tayeb is a major shareholder in Caricorp. Nobody in his right mind would think that Sheikh Tayeb would let his wife's business go down under.'

Danny felt compelled to speak 'According to my notes, the bank has advanced almost two billion dollars to TIG alone. I have not been able to see the financial statements and security documents for the collaterals. I asked for these but was told that it would take time to produce all of the information I required.

'Caricorp is also getting unlimited facilities from the bank. There is sketchy information on file about Caricorp's business operations and financial position. There are notes indicating that there were assets that would cover the bank's investments, but I have not seen documents to support that.' Danny was confident he had made his point.

'You are quite right. They didn't have all the information to provide you earlier. However, with the pressure coming from the top to finalise the profit number, they went into high gear and carried out a thorough study of their investments. I have seen detailed information about the assets made available to the bank as collateral by TIG and Caricorp. Actually, Mateen has this information for approximately one hundred or so high-value clients. Also, they have obtained a credit evaluation report on their major debtors from Morisco. Morisco has made detailed analyses of the creditworthiness of these debtors and confirmed they are sound and there was no risk to the bank for the amounts they had advanced. I, myself, have seen the reports issued by Morisco.' David Finner seemed quite satisfied with the information he had been provided, and he wanted to clear the number of provisions made by the bank against doubtful accounts.

'So, what do we conclude?' Charles Ramsey, who was watching the exchange between David and Danny quietly until now, wanted to make a decision.

David was the first to answer. 'I have gone through the information made available by Mateen very carefully. Of course, if we had time, we would have carried out a much more thorough examination of the information, as is being suggested by Danny. But for commercial reasons, the bank is in a hurry to get their profit number confirmed. We know the bank and the senior officials quite well. If they need help right now, we should give it, provided we are not exposed. Mateen has advised they had a provision of eighty-five million dollars against doubtful advances. They will increase it to one hundred million dollars, so everybody feels comfortable. I think the increased provision will be sufficient, and we could live with that.

'Mateen also mentioned that Sheikh Tayeb and Azhar Alam were giving their personal attention to improving the bank's operating and control systems. He indicated that since Tolbert and Gibbs knew the bank inside out, they would prefer us to carry out a study of their systems and advise on improving their procedures.' David added.

Charles seemed to agree. 'That is good news. Azhar also mentioned this to me over the phone this morning. They are pleased with our services. Provided you are completely satisfied with the level of provision being made and do not think there are any other issues, we should be able to clear the profit number. I suggest you prepare a note of the process we followed and of this meeting for the working papers.'

'To be honest, I do not feel comfortable, and I believe we should do further work before giving clearance. Once we clear the profit number, they will want us to sign our report in the first week of January.' Danny made a last-ditch attempt.

'We normally sign our report on G&P Bank's financial statements in the middle of January. I don't see any reason why it should be different this year,' David responded.

'Yes, we still have to do a lot of work after the year's end in order to ensure that all the numbers tie in. Let's speed up our work as much as possible. But the signing of our report by the middle of January appears to be reasonable,' Charles replied.

***

Danny was furious. The firm was, in Danny's opinion, clearing the results of the bank blindly. The partners were recklessly approving a set of financial statements that they knew were probably incorrect and should be looked at more closely. Danny was convinced this was being done to get special assignments from the bank to increase the firm's revenue.

At this point, he was unable to do anything further unless he acquired tangible evidence indicating that the provision against doubtful investments made by the bank was grossly inadequate. He hoped the information Amir promised would arrive in time for him to present to the partners and make them do further work before clearing the financial results of the bank.

Danny tried to concentrate on the work at hand, completing the working papers to bring them to in shape for the partner review. His heart was not in it.

At 5.30 p.m., he closed his files, picked up his jacket and umbrella, and walked out of the office. He walked to Moorgate station to take the underground to Euston from where he would take the train to Milton Keynes. He reached home tired and frustrated.

Amir was not yet home. Danny changed and sat down with a drink and the latest edition of *The Economist*. He wanted to unwind and take his mind off the G&P Bank's audit. He was flipping through *The Economist* when the telephone rang. It was his father calling from Lahore in Pakistan.

'Danny, Assalam Alaikum, Beta?' His father sounded excited and was shouting into the mouthpiece.

'Waalekum Assalam, Papa. How is everybody there?' Danny replied.

'We all are fine. I have great news to share with you.' His father replied.

'I hope that mother has not found another girl for me, Papa. I have told you; I will find my own bride.' Danny was alert to a possible threat to his independence.

'No. No. Your mother is not involved in what we are talking about. You have to listen to me without interrupting. I have a regular customer, a Mr. Amin, at the shop. Today, he came in to buy some clothes. He told me that he is the branch manager of G&P Bank on Mall Road. He said that he was very impressed by the quality of garments sold and the service he was getting at the shop and congratulated me for my efforts.

'He thought it may be possible for me to own my own shop. He said that the bank would help me and set up the whole thing for me.

He said he would come tomorrow with a proposal. He knows your name and said that you were helping the bank in London and the bank appreciated your help. According to him, because of your help to the bank, everybody admires you there. He also asked me to pass on his regards to you when I talk to you. What do you think? Should I start my own shop? To be honest, I am a little scared. What if the shop is not successful? I cannot afford to incur a large debt and leave you with liabilities.' Danny's father was a simple man.

'Don't talk about leaving us, Papa. I'll have to think about the proposal. Did this Mr. Amin tell you about the arrangements?'

'He said the bank has a small business set-up unit. They would help me find a suitable shop and give me a loan to buy the shop. The bank would also encourage the major garment suppliers to give me goods on easy credit. He said he would speak to his seniors to grant the loan on very easy terms. He was certain that because of your good services to the bank in London, he may be able to get the approval for the shop to be purchased under the Small Business Assistance Programme of the bank. This is a miracle. You know they say that Allah showers his bounties from the sky whenever He wants to. This seems like a gift sent by Allah. Your mother and sister are so happy. Your mother has cooked food and sent it to the poor.'

'Did this Mr. Amin, who was so kind, ask you to pass on any message to me?' Danny asked.

'No. He said you are helping the bank in London, and everybody at the bank knew about and appreciated it. He said that you are like family and the respect and assistance were mutual. Son, please continue to help them. They are very nice people. Wait, your mother wants to speak to you.' Danny's father handed the phone over to his wife.

'Hello, Beta, how are you? You heard from your father. Allah has sent angels to bless us. Imagine! Your father owning his own shop. We will get many good proposals for your sister now as everybody will know that we are rich.'

'Mama, I am fine. I am pleased that you all are so happy. I'm sure this is very good news.' Danny did not want to break her heart and rob his family of happiness by telling them there was a hidden agenda.

They went on to talk about other matters. Danny's mother asked him to go to the mosque and offer charity and thank Allah for His blessings. Danny was stunned. He felt as if he had been hit by a tank. His remaining energy seemed to ebb away from his body. He sat on the sofa with his head in his hands. That is how Amir found him when he entered the apartment.

Amir walked in, loaded with shopping bags. He was surprised to find Danny sitting deflated on the sofa.

'Hey, what has happened? Are you not well? Do you want to go to the doctor?'

Danny opened his eyes and looked at Amir. 'I have been bulldozed. I think my life as I know is finished.'

'This sounds pretty serious. What has happened? Have you lost your job?'

'Worse than that. I will have to leave the job and maybe my profession, not that it would be a bad thing under these circumstances.'

'Tell me what happened.'

Danny narrated the day's events to Amir, ending with a summary of the discussion with his parents during the just-finished telephone call.

'Welcome to G&P Bank. They know how to get to you. They have you by the balls now. Your partners want to approve the financial statements. To ensure that you do not throw wrenches into the works, G&P has bought your parents. I can understand why you are feeling so depressed.'

'We must think this matter through with a clear head. Where is that damned information your secretary was supposed to send?'

'It's Christmas. By the time Samira gets the letter, which was sent by normal airmail, it will be around the year's end. Even if she sends the package by courier, you won't receive it before 31 December. By then, your firm will be firmly and squarely committed to the profit number.'

'I will have to declare this transaction of my father obtaining a loan from G&P Bank to the firm,' Danny said.

'That you should do. But there is nothing unusual about this transaction. We know that G&P Bank is in the business of banking. Also, as part of their social commitment, they have programmes for helping small businesses and other weak segments of society. The only unusual thing is that your father is the borrower but you have not approached the bank, nor are you involved in any way with this transaction. I believe you are making too much out of this. I'm sure that your firm will have no problems with this transaction. If your father had not informed you of this proposal, you would not have known about it,' Amir said.

'You know why they are doing this. Mateen knows that I'm the fly in the ointment. He is neutralising me,' Danny said.

'Of course, that's what he is doing. But prima facie, there is no evidence of your involvement or of you doing any favours to G&P Bank. You are doing your job professionally and have commented on the inadequacy of the documentation in support of loans and advances. Despite of your objections, your firm is going to clear the bank's profit. You have done what was required of you by registering your comments on the issue. There are other senior members of the firm who are authorised to make these decisions. It will be their decision to approve or disapprove the bank's financial results.'

'I feel very uncomfortable with this development. I would like to tell my father not to accept the loan but hearing the happiness in my parents' voices, I can't do that,' Danny replied.

'Let's stop this shop talk What would you like to Drink?

'Get me a whisky; I need a stimulant.'

'That bad, eh?' Amir asked and went to the cabinet to take out a bottle and pour a couple of glasses.

'Now that you know that my day was a disaster, how was yours?' Danny asked, taking a tumbler from Amir.

'I bought some clothes for my father, mom, and Seemi.'

Both friends chatted for a while, ordered food from a nearby restaurant and called it a day.

***

The next day, Danny went straight to George Hansel's office and said, 'George, I have something very important to discuss with you.'

George immediately kept the files he was working on to one side of the desk and asked, 'You look very worried. Is there something wrong?'

'No. Nothing is wrong yet but I believe it may not be possible for me to work on the G&P Bank account anymore.' He told George that his father was approached with the offer of a loan. 'You see, this looks like they are trying to influence my involvement in the bank's audit here.'

'Yes, when you put it like that, it does look a little suspicious. But this could be quite innocent, as well. After all, this is in line with G&P's business, and the process is not unusual for the bank. It is possible that the local manager of the bank, who apparently is a regular customer at your father's shop, might have been impressed with your father's business attitude and was trying to help. Let's speak to David. I hope he's there.' George picked up the telephone and dialled for David Finner. When David answered the call, George said, 'David, Good morning. George here. I have Danny with me. There is an urgent matter we want to talk to you about. Yes, it's about G&P Bank. We will be with you in two minutes.' He put the phone down. 'Let's go. David is waiting for us,' he said to Danny.

David greeted them as they arrived at his office. 'Come in, gentlemen. An early morning emergency? I hope nothing earth shattering?' David was in a good mood.

'Danny thinks he may have a problem continuing to work on G&P Bank. Why don't you tell David what you told me?' George said, turning to Danny.

Danny told David about his telephone conversation with his parents the night before and his concern that his independence as auditor of G&P Bank was being compromised.

'Did you or anybody from the bank discuss anything about a loan facility being extended to your father?' David asked.

'No. It was the first time I heard about my father's dealings with G&P Bank. I understand that the manager of G&P Bank has been my father's customer for some time. He did, however, mention to my father that he knew of my involvement with G&P Bank in the UK,' Danny replied.

'Of course, everybody in G&P Bank, Pakistan or elsewhere, may know about you. How many Pakistanis enjoy the high position you are in, and how many of them get involved in the audit of G&P Bank, which I understand is the darling of every Pakistani, barring the present company?

'The fact of the matter, however, is that you were not and are not involved in any way in your father's business. What G&P Bank is doing is a part of their ordinary business. Your father might seem to be a good client for giving facility under the bank's small businesses programme. To be honest, I wouldn't worry too much about this. However, to protect yourself from any future questions, I suggest you write a note for the file. All of us, George, Charles and I, will initial, indicating that there was no problem and that you had declared your interest. We will retain this note on the bank's file as well as on your personal file for reference, in case there is a question in the future,' David replied.

'Okay, then. I'll send you the note. I still feel uncomfortable, though, about us accepting the loan loss provision proposed by the bank. I believe there is a much larger exposure on TIG and some other large advances,' Danny said, getting up to go.

'I hear your concerns, but I have looked at the details myself collated by the bank's management for evaluation of these advances. We also have the report from Morisco. I'm satisfied. We must remember the famous adage that an auditor is a watchdog and not a bloodhound. We are not detectives. We rely on the information and explanations provided by the management.' David had made up his mind.

'All right. I'll go complete the working papers to be ready for George and your review. We should be ready as soon as the bank gives the final schedules.' Danny said, and left.

'What's wrong with Danny? He is unusually tense. He seems to be seeing ghosts,' David said to George after Danny left.

'I don't know. It's possible that he resents these Pakistani executives of the bank getting so successful and rich,' George replied.

'Maybe you're right. It's very similar to jealousy between siblings. It's difficult not to get jealous when a brother or sister does much better than you. Pakistanis have more of this attitude towards each other than other mature communities. Let's finalise the audit and issue our report. We'll have to move Danny from G&P Bank's engagement if we want to keep a good relationship with the bank's senior officials. I have a feeling that Danny might be a little hostile when dealing with the bank.' David replied.

Chapter 17

Karachi – The Residence of Yakoob Soothar

The Soothar brothers and their close friends had returned from the cemetery where they had gone after the mosque where they offered special prayers for the departed soul of their father. Everybody who was anybody in the Pakistani business world was present at the mosque. Some had visited the brothers earlier to offer condolences at home. This included the ministers of commerce and shipping. Those who could not come in person had phoned and offered their condolences. Among them were Pakistan's President, the prime minister, and the speaker of the National Assembly.

Arrangements were made for a light lunch for the mourners who came to Yakoob's house. Lunch was served immediately following Friday prayers. After lunch, almost everybody except the family and TIG's senior executives left.

Yakoob asked those from TIG to join him in the sitting room. In addition to the TIG senior officials who were at the Hong Kong meeting, Masoom Ali Pirani, the head of legal for TIG, was also present.

Yakoob broke the silence. 'Gentlemen, we meet here under very sad circumstances. Unfortunately, nature has struck us a blow, but we must go on. That is what Papa would expect from us. Masoom, you should quickly look at the title deeds and other documents to ensure that the ownership of assets registered in Papa's name is transferred to us three brothers. Please be careful to ensure that the assets, which are not mortgaged or offered as collateral, are not mixed up with the charged assets. In fact, we would like the unencumbered assets to be transferred to names not connected with the family so these cannot be touched in case of attacks by creditors.

'We need to liquidate a few companies in our group. Salim will brief you about those companies. They are not directly part of the group's tree and not owned on record by the family. Efforts should be made to make a clean break from these companies. I suggest that

Salim, you and I have a separate meeting to review these matters in some detail after this meeting.'

'I will do as you direct, Yakoob,' Masoom Ali replied. 'I understand that some of these companies might have large liabilities and unpaid salaries. A number of these companies might be registered in the names of some of our trusted employees. They might face difficulties if the liabilities, particularly staff salaries, are not paid.'

'Too bad. They earned good money during the good times. I will not be sorry if they suffer a little. We are also suffering. My policies will be different from those of Papa's. Papa would go bankrupt to protect a loyal friend or employee. That era has gone. We will only look after the family and this group here. Others are outsiders.' Yakoob declared the new policy of TIG.

'Now coming to other issues, let us consider each item one-by-one.' Yakoob turned his attention to the other members of the group. 'I have a meeting scheduled with Sheikh Tayeb and Azhar Alam of G&P Bank on 29 December in London. I understand that they are getting restless, and Masood Qadir, G&P Bank's Geneva head and one of our principal contacts, cold-shouldered Salim when they met in Geneva. I am upset. Masood would normally have to call several times to meet me. Now, he refuses to even meet our group's finance director. Sheikh Tayeb was my father's friend, not mine. We will take what we can from G&P Bank. Of course, when I meet Sheikh Tayeb, I will appeal to his sympathies. I hope he will be able to give us some additional funds to keep us going. If we go down, G&P Bank will also be in trouble.'

Salim offered some helpful information. 'I had a telephone call from Azhar Alam expressing condolence but also setting out the agenda for your London meeting. I did not tell you before, but G&P Bank has asked for a credit evaluation report on TIG from Morisco. I got a call from one of the vice presidents of Morisco, who is an old college friend. I assured him of the sound financial position of the group and sent him gold Rolexes for him and his wife. He was grateful and called to say that Morisco had given a glowing report about TIG's financial health.'

'Well done, Salim. So, G&P Bank will be assured that we are all right and will not put too much pressure on us. I, however, need TIG's draft financial statements and business plan to carry with me for the meeting. So, please ensure that I have the first draft for discussion the day after tomorrow. As discussed, the financial statements should show a profit for the year.

'We need some cash urgently. We have some properties in Hong Kong and London. They are either in the name of Papa or the companies that do not appear in the group's tree. Some of these are mortgaged. I'll talk to Sheikh Tayeb to release the properties mortgaged with the G&P Bank. I understand that we never signed formal documents nor deposited the title deeds with the G&P Bank for these properties. So, we are free to benefit from them. We are not responsible if the G&P Bank did not do its work properly. For the properties mortgaged with other banks, it might be difficult. I suggest we sell whatever we can. There is no point in waiting for the improvement in real estate prices. They may be down for a long winter. Salim, Masoom, let's deal with this matter as quickly as possible. Nari, you believe that you might get by if you retain the cash generated by operations in your area. Is that right?'

'Yes, Yakoob.'

'Salim, could we allow Nari to keep the cash?' Yakoob asked.

'The funds received from Nari are necessary to keep us afloat, but if Nari's operations go down, we all go down. Nari, could you manage with fifty percent of the cash generated?' Salim asked Nari.

'I'll try. At least that would be something. At the moment, we are in dire trouble,' Nari replied.

'Done. Nari, you keep half of the cash you generate and let the head office have the other half. Now Mansukh, please tell us the short-term solution for our difficulties in your area? We'll talk about the long-term reforms later,' Yakoob said, turning to Mansukh.

'Some of our ships are junk. We may be able to sell them at throwaway prices. There is still a market for them. The proceeds can be invested in the fast-speed boat-type vessels preferred by triads. We could enter into contracts with triads for shipping their goods at lucrative prices and possibly get some advance, if we guarantee performance. You know triads act violently if the promises made to them are not kept.'

'All right. Give me a list of the ships you would like to sell, the estimated proceeds and the cost of new vessels. Are all our vessels not mortgaged to G&P Bank?' Yakoob asked, turning to Salim.

'They are, but G&P Bank has been sloppy. They did not take full documents. We have changed the names and ownership of vessels several times after obtaining funds from G&P Bank. The ships they believe are mortgaged to them do not exist on any official record. We even changed the flags of their registration. Some are now registered in Liberia and Panama, Malta and Mauritius,' Salim replied with a sly smile.

'Great. So, let's do it. We must also not lose our foothold in Burma. The junta there needs help. Mansukh, please ensure they are looked after and that their families stay in nice hotels and get five-star facilities when they travel outside Burma. Even in Burma, we should send funds and gifts to keep them on our side and help us source the commodities we are interested in.' Yakoob made a decision.

'As for the Americas, I recall you, Alex, mentioning that we have good properties in Brazil and Argentina, which may fetch up to fifty million dollars.' Yakoob turned his attention to Alex Brun.

'You are right, Yakoob, but I understand these are mortgaged to G&P Bank.'

'Are the documents for the mortgage not defective as elsewhere, Salim?' Yakoob asked.

'They are the same as everywhere else. We have been giving the bank photocopies of the title deeds and registering the mortgages in jurisdictions that have no access to the properties,' Salim replied.

'This is a battle for the survival of TIG. We do not have the luxury of worrying about G&P Bank's business. They run their business, and I run mine. Let's sell these properties quickly and we will deal with G&P Bank as and when the situation arises.' Yakoob was different than his father. He did not believe in ethics or friendships in business. 'Alex, you also mentioned the potential for doing some business for some Latin American businessmen who want to transport their cargo to the USA?' Yakoob asked Alex again.

'Yes, like triads, these people demand performance.'

'You sound confident.' Yakoob pressed on.

'I believe we can do it. The risks are high, but a dying man does not look at risks when a lifeline is thrown to him,' Alex replied.

'I suggest you go ahead and enter into a deal with these businessmen.' Yakoob did not want to refer to Cali or Cartel.

'I feel confident you are making the right decision. With these steps, we can be floating in the money again.' Alex started smiling.

'To summarise, Masoom and Salim, please take care of the legal issues and ensure that the assets in Papa's name are transferred so they are not open to seizure. You may also liquidate companies not directly connected with TIG in official records. Let's meet separately after this meeting is over.

'Nari, you will manage with fifty percent of the cash you generate. We should be able to direct more resources your way to ensure that you are able to improve your business capabilities. Mansukh, you will negotiate a deal with the triads, sell some ships and buy new vessels, and if practicable, sink one or two of the junk to get quick insurance claims. You will also look after the Burmese so that our business pipeline continues from there. Alex, you will handle the Latin businessmen and improve our performance there. You may need to restructure our tariff and business model there so that we are able to give better rates than the competition, which will enable us to carry the special cargo. I, myself, will carry a payload as soon as the situation is right.

'One matter we did not talk about was involving outside investors in TIG. Papa said that he would approach some of his business friends to put some funds into our business. Although I do not like outside interference in our business, it may not be a bad idea to milk some of the rich fat cats for a   billion or so, if they have the spare cash. That would alleviate our liquidity problems and help us deal with the issues more efficiently. There is still a wave of sympathy for Papa and us. I'll go around the world, thanking Papa's friends for their support and gently ascertain if they are willing to invest some funds. I hope to do this within the next couple of weeks.

'Salim, you agreed to prepare some information for Papa to carry to his friends. Please finalise this information and let me have it as soon as possible. We seem to have addressed all the problems. With the team we have here, the problems are not insurmountable. I feel good. As a result of the decisions made here today, TIG will again be one of the richest business groups of Asia. Let's meet in approximately four weeks' time to discuss progress. My secretary will be in touch with you to advise the time and venue for the next meeting. It is too early after Papa's death to talk about any celebrations, although today's meeting calls for some indulgence. I am afraid that we will have to delay any celebrations to avoid upsetting my kid brothers.' Yakoob had a twinkle in his eyes.

Once the meeting was adjourned, everybody left except the brothers, Salim and Masoom. They continued for another hour discussing the plan to deal with the legal issues, and Yakoob asked Salim and Masoom to take steps to protect the family's assets.

Chapter 18

London, G&P Bank's offices, Knightsbridge

It was 29 December, just two days before the year's end and the official closing of the financial year of the bank. Sheikh Tayeb and Azhar Alam had arrived the previous evening from Karachi. A lot of work still had to be done to ensure the financial results reported for the year were in line with the plan. In this regard, they were to see Yakoob Soothar at 11 a.m. and there was going to be another meeting of the senior executive board at two in the afternoon.

At eleven sharp, Sheikh Tayeb's secretary phoned to say that Mr. Yakoob Soothar had arrived and was being escorted up to see the chairman.

'Good morning. Come in.' Sheikh Tayeb got up with his arms outstretched, welcoming Yakoob Soothar, who was ushered in by Sheikh Tayeb's secretary.

The secretary served refreshments. Over tea, there was small talk of the gloomy and unbearable UK weather.

Sheikh Tayeb said, 'Thank you for coming. No offence, but I do wish that my old friend was also here. I still miss him and cannot believe that he is gone.'

'Yes. We all miss Papa. It was all so sudden. We were having a two-day meeting in Hong Kong. Papa was with us on the first day. He declined to join us for dinner that evening, saying he was tired. And then he was gone, just like that. I'm still unable to believe he is no longer with us. We are devastated. I now have to formally take over control of the group but his shoes are too big for me to walk in. I can only try,' Yakoob replied with humility.

'Yes. We all miss Ismail. Unfortunately, we must go on. The world does not stop for anybody,' Azhar said, bringing the meeting back to the present.

'Yes, I know. This is why I am here today. The business has to go on. TIG's business is too big to ignore for even a day,' Yakoob replied.

Sheikh Tayeb slid into the conversation with a more serious subject. 'You know, Yakoob, G&P Bank and TIG have been close partners for a long time. You are our biggest client, and with the relationship built over many years, both of our organisations have benefited.

'Our advances to TIG are around two billion US dollars. This is a high number and almost twenty percent of the total assets of the bank. Our auditors are querying such a high exposure to one group, and we are probably in violation of the banking regulations of most countries. If it were not for the way we are structured, we would face severe reprimand from regulatory authorities. Our auditors are, however, after us and unless we provide assurance that a large chunk of TIG's balances will be cleared soon, we may face a qualification in our audit report. That would be a disaster as we would lose our credit rating and ability to operate as a bank.

'We are, therefore, looking for an immediate reduction in TIG's balances. We hope that you will be able to release at least twenty-five percent of your current outstanding balance immediately and repay other twenty-five percent within the next three months. We must have this to continue our operations.'

Yakoob responded, 'All of us at TIG are grateful and appreciate our special relationship with G&P. TIG is a very large and successful group. I have brought this year's financial statements which show that we continue to be profitable. All of G&P Bank's advances to TIG are fully secure and we are financially sound. In view of the slump in the shipping business and economic downturn in the areas where we have large operations, we are suffering from a short-term liquidity problem. In fact, my father and I had discussed this in detail, and he wanted to meet with you and request additional facilities to tide us over.' Yakoob presented the folder containing the financial statements.

'It is impossible to advance any more funds. G&P Bank itself is fully stretched and we have to recover money from our debtors. As Sheikh Tayeb said, we have crossed every conceivable limit in advancing funds to TIG. As you know, there are companies in your group that are not doing so well financially. The auditors are looking at these companies and insist that we provide for a possible loss against the outstanding balances. In addition, they want us to take legal action to recover our balances. Yakoob, we understand that you have temporary difficulties. Believe me, we also have difficulties, which is why it is essential that you pay us at least twenty-five percent of the balance immediately – approximately five hundred million US, and other twenty-five percent within three months. I am sorry, but we have to look after the larger interests of the bank.' Azhar was upset that instead of talking about repayment, Yakoob was asking for more cash.

'Azhar, I would be lying to you if I said that we may be able to pay you any money immediately. We are facing a very severe liquidity crisis. We need more cash. We need help. You are tied to us. So let us think it through together.

'We are taking a lot of measures to improve our liquidity. I have a solution. We have some properties in the UK and elsewhere. These are mortgaged by you. I request that you let us sell these properties. We would retain the proceeds for six months and pass on the amounts to you after that. By then, our cash position will have improved.'

'This is impossible. We cannot dilute our security. As it is, the bank is heavily exposed. Our auditors will kill us if we release the securities. Actually, we are under pressure to foreclose some of the properties mortgaged with us. We will not do this as we respect TIG and do not want to do anything that would harm our relationship or affect the reputation of TIG,' AA replied.

'In that case, I have no choice but to look for outside funding for our operations. This may be by an equity investment from outsiders. I hope you will help us in finding wealthy suitors.'

'Certainly. I suggest that your team and our people work together to develop a restructuring plan for TIG. Sheikh Tayeb and I will do everything possible to help with potential investors,' Azhar Alam said.

'Okay, then. I'll have the documents prepared, inviting potential investors, and pass them over to you. I'm sorry that you cannot help us with a bridging facility. I request that, at least, you do not put any pressure on us for the next six months or so to collect any funds from us,' Yakoob said this as if he were giving a concession to G&P Bank. He was pleased with himself for having warded off any further pressure from the bank.

'We'll try to help in attracting new investors for your group. You have a very profitable and sound business, so I don't see why you should not garner interest from investors. We'll try to hold any moves to recover funds from you, but I cannot promise that; the bank is in serious need of funds. I'll also use my influence to support you,' Sheikh Tayeb replied.

'There is one matter where you might help us and earn a few dollars, as well,' Azhar Alam said. 'Shakadir knows of a party that wants to export a consignment of goods from one part of Africa to another. I don't have the full details but will ask Shakadir to talk to you. 'I am sure you will be able to help with the shipping and other logistical resources available with you.'

'Sure, we are very interested in assisting you and earning some money at the same time. Please ask Shakadir to speak to me. I'm here today and tomorrow. I am staying at The Ritz at Green Park. He may contact me there.' Yakoob replied.

***

Yakoob went straight to the hotel from G&P Bank's offices. From his room, he called Salim in Karachi and briefed him about his discussions with the bank.

'It went exactly as we thought it would. Your financial statements were good. The bank could not find any reasons to claim that we were not financially sound. Sheikh Tayeb and Azhar Alam insisted we pay five hundred million dollars immediately and another five hundred within three months. According to Sheikh Tayeb and Azhar, the bank is facing severe financial stress, and our account is under the scrutiny of its auditors and regulators. I stood my ground, saying that it was not possible for TIG to make any payments at present as we had our own liquidity problems. Instead, I asked for more funds from them, which obviously they declined.

They also refused to let us sell any of the mortgaged properties. I asked them to help us find suitable investors for investing in TIG. They said they would do that.'

'This is excellent. At least there will be no pressure on us from G&P Bank, and our facilities will be renewed,' Salim replied.

'Now, here is what we should do: Sell the UK and Latin American properties at whatever prices we get. You ask Masoom Ali to ensure that all the property documents are ready and in order. We should move fast. All the transactions for the sale of properties should be done quietly so the bank does not find out. You should also prepare an offer for the sale of shares in TIG. We'll give this to G&P Bank and also to some other parties I know of. I may also approach some investment banks to help us find investors.

'I was also advised that the bank is facilitating a transaction involving the shipment of some security cargo and we may act as transporters. Sheikh Tayeb told me that Shakadir was dealing with this matter and would be in touch with me. I hope we will be able to make a killing on the transaction.'

'It's all good news. I'll move quickly to sort out the property matters and work with our consultants to prepare an offer document for the sale of shares in TIG,' Salim assured Yakoob.

***

Meeting of G&P Bank's Senior Executive Board at the bank's London offices, Knightsbridge

All the members of the senior executive board were present when Sheikh Tayeb and Azhar Alam entered the board room. Most of them had arrived the night before. After exchanging pleasantries and enquiring about the flights, Sheikh Tayeb brought the meeting to order.

'Gentlemen, we have had a very busy week since we last met in Karachi. Today's meeting will be a short one, as we need to review developments in certain special areas only. First, let's talk about the bank's financial statements. Mateen, please brief us about the status of where we are in this matter.' He turned to Mateen Saeed.

Mateen gave his update: 'After considerable thought, I decided to deal with our auditors according to plan. I called audit partner David Finner at home on Boxing Day morning and requested that the bank wanted audit clearance of its profit for the year almost immediately. No Englishman is sober enough to make a reasonable judgement or deny a request on Boxing Day. As anticipated, he agreed to come to the bank personally, bypassing our friend Danny, to discuss the financial results.

'I presented him with the income statement showing a profit of one hundred fifty million US dollars and satisfied him about the fairness of our profit figure. I reluctantly agreed to increase the provision for doubtful advances by fifteen million dollars. David had a personal request. He needed a loan of five hundred thousand pounds to buy a house in Surrey. I immediately agreed to it and asked him to present the necessary papers to me personally. He requested we keep this transaction confidential. I told him that G&P Bank was like a tomb. We keep secrets. To further satisfy him, I told him the title of his account with us would be in a different name than his, which only he and I would know. I also told David that the bank would almost certainly award a consultancy assignment, which would be very lucrative. After a positive meeting and an even better lunch, David agreed on the profit number and advised me to go ahead.' Mateen concluded his report.

'Mateen called and briefed me about his meeting with David. I then called David and thanked him for his support. He was happy that I called. I hope Danny will not create any difficulties,' Azhar added.

'He won't.' This was Shakadir. 'Our branch manager in Lahore visited his father's shop and offered him a loan at very soft terms to help him set up his own business. The Rafi family is very excited with this offer and I am certain by now Danny knows his father will be our debtor at the most favourable terms.'

'Very good. So, our auditors are neutralised,' Sheikh Tayeb remarked. 'Now, TIG. Azhar and I had a meeting with Yakoob Soothar this morning. Yakoob brought with him the draft financial statements of TIG, which show a profit. From our own credit evaluation undertaken by Morisco, the group appears to be financially healthy. They, however, have severe liquidity problems.'

'Who doesn't these days?' commented Masood Qadir.

'Yes, who doesn't?' Sheikh Tayeb responded and moved on. 'Yakoob has some ideas to come out of this problem. One such idea was for us to release our security on some properties and allow them to sell. We flatly refused. He also wanted to bring in outside investors as shareholders in TIG. He asked for our help in finding potential investors. We agreed to help. Of course, we will charge a fee for facilitating any transactions. We also mentioned to him that Shakadir might have a special consignment for shipment to be handled by TIG. Shakadir, please talk to Yakoob. He is staying at the Ritz until tomorrow.'

'Additionally, we are proceeding with Amir's promotion and transfer to Geneva as soon as possible in the New Year. He will be helpful to you in Geneva,' Azhar Alam said with a meaningful look at Masood.

Masood nodded in agreement.

'Since we do not have any other matters to discuss at the moment, let us adjourn. We will meet again in a few days. Azhar will call you and advise programme for the next meeting.' Sheikh Tayeb concluded the meeting.

Chapter 19

Speyer, Geneva and Karachi

'We must be going if we want to reach Geneva before the evening. It's a long journey. Thank you very much for having me here. I had a wonderful new year with you,' Richard Bringsen said to Otto and Else Huber, Ursula's parents.

After an early breakfast, they had settled for coffee in the living room.

Richard and Ursula had arrived in Speyer just before Christmas and had a great time there. Speyer had a population of fifty thousand, and it had a long history. The town existed before the arrival of Romans in 50 B.C., and the Romans built a fort and an infantry base there in 10 B.C. The most important landmark in town was the cathedral built in 1111. It was the biggest church in that part of Europe when it was built, and it became the burial place of eight German emperors and kings. This trip was the first time Richard visited Speyer. He thoroughly enjoyed visiting the historic sites and monuments in town.

'Thank you for visiting us. We enjoyed having you here,' Otto replied. 'Please do be very careful when you drive. It is a long journey and the roads are slippery. You know the German autobahns do not have speed limits, so the drivers go crazy.'

'Don't worry. I'll drive carefully. This is a powerful and steady car, German technology at its best. We should be in Geneva by early evening,' Richard replied as he loaded his and Ursula's bags into his Mercedes S320.

Shortly thereafter, Richard and Ursula were on their way out of the town. It was still early, and there was little traffic on the road. They were on the outskirts of the town and about to connect to the autobahn, which would take them into Switzerland. Their plan was to stop for lunch on the way and then continue to Geneva.

They were driving on a dual carriage road with frequent turns and blind curves. Richard was driving carefully but still maintaining a reasonable speed in order not to lose too much time. He noticed that another Mercedes was tailing him closely, as if asking for space to overtake him. Instinctively, Richard moved to the edge of the road to give way. His car shuddered as the other car passed him at a very high speed, almost pushing him off the road.

'Crazy Driver! He almost pushed us off the road,' he said to Ursula, turning his head toward her.

'Watch out!' Ursula screamed. They had gone into a blind curve, and a lorry was reversing toward them at high speed.

Before Richard could react, his car hit the lorry and went completely under it. Immediately, the lorry stopped as the Driver quickly changed his gears from reverse to neutral and then park. The lorry driver climbed out of his cab, cursing the car behind him.

Richard and Ursula died immediately upon impact. Their car was completely destroyed.

Soon, other cars stopped, and their drivers came out to help. There was nothing they could do. The bodies of Richard and Ursula were badly mutilated and trapped in the badly crushed car.

'This guy was crazy. He was driving at a very high speed, probably drinking early in the morning. As I was driving on a curve, I slowed down a little, and the next thing I know, I was shaken by a severe jolt as this car rammed into the back of my lorry. My neck is also hurt. I should see the doctor, but we must get the police first.' The lorry driver stated his defence to the assembled drivers, who would be interrogated by police as witnesses.

'Yes. I saw the whole accident. This guy overtook me at 160 miles per hour and went into the curve without slowing down. I don't think he cared where he was going,' Another Driver said.

'I saw that, too. This Driver was very fast and careless. He overtook me also,' another Driver in an old Volkswagen said.

By now, people from the houses by the side of the road had come out. One of them went back into his house and called the police to notify them of the accident.

A police patrol car soon arrived, followed by an ambulance. The ambulance attendant took one look at the car and knew there was nothing they could do except transfer the bodies to the morgue. But they would have to wait until the police gave them clearance. Police would require special equipment to get the bodies out as they were badly trapped in the crushed car.

One police officer took out a camera and started taking pictures of the scene of the accident. Another spoke to the Driver of the lorry.

'Is this your lorry?'

'Yes, Sir. I was going to Mannheim at a moderate speed, as I was on a bend and my lorry was fully laden. All of a sudden, I felt a jolt and heard the loud crash as this car had driven into the back of my lorry. Although I had a bad shock and pain in my neck, I got out of the lorry and rushed to see if anybody was hurt. I found them as they are. It looks like this guy was driving very fast and did not care for his or others' safety.' The Driver told his story carefully and clearly.

'Give me your driving licence, lorry registration papers and the manifest of the goods you are carrying,' the officer said.

The Driver quietly handed over the papers. His name was Ahmet Gulay, a Turkish citizen residing in Germany. The lorry's registration papers showed it was owned by a freight forwarding company in Mannheim.

'Anybody see the accident?' The officer asked

'I did.' The driver who first claimed to have seen the accident came forward. 'My name is Rudy Stern. Here is my driving licence. I was close behind this car. Actually, I was ahead first, but the driver overtook me at high speed and went straight into the back of the lorry.' Rudy was a very competent witness.

'Anybody else?' The officer looked at the other people who were there.

'I saw it too.' Another driver who had spoken earlier came forward. 'My name is Klaus Bose. I live near here. This car came very fast from behind, and as the road was narrow and turning, the driver had no choice but to squeeze in front of my car, almost causing an accident. He was very impatient and soon got out again and overtook this other car in front of him at a very high speed and went straight into the back of the lorry.'

The officer wrote each statement patiently. He asked each driver to sign their statement and took the details of their telephone numbers, addresses, ID cards and licence numbers. He told the two witnesses that they were free to go, but they should be available when contacted for further questions which might arise.

The officer called for the equipment to extricate the bodies from the crashed car and then move the car to the police yard. He also carried out a perfunctory inspection of the lorry and told the lorry driver that he would have to go to the police station for further paperwork. His lorry would be detained for forensic examination by the police experts.

It was just before noon when both vehicles were moved and the bodies were taken to the morgue. In the initial report, the police concluded that the accident had happened due to reckless driving by Richard, and there was no fault of the lorry driver, Ahmet Gulay.

Ahmet was allowed to leave without the truck, which was retained for examination by the police specialists. He was asked not to leave his usual place of work or residence, as he would be required for further information when more formal documents for the accident were drawn. From the papers recovered in the car, the police were able to establish the identity of Richard and Ursula. Ursula's parents, being in Speyer, were informed first. They could not believe that this had happened and that Ursula had died. Ursula's mother collapsed when she heard the news and had to be taken to a hospital. The police found Richard's G&P Bank ID card in his wallet. They contacted the bank, informed them of the accident and asked for the details of Richard's next of kin, who were promptly informed.

Masood Qadir also spoke to Richard's father in Kent and expressed his condolence and promised to contact him shortly with further details about Richard's state of affairs in Geneva. After speaking to Richard's father, Masood called Oshko, the bank's security officer, and informed him of the sad event. Oshko had a strange shine in his eyes when he heard the news and advised that he would get busy ensuring that the bank's property and interests were protected.

Masood next called the senior officers and department heads of the bank and told them about the accident in Speyer. Everybody was shocked and deeply saddened. A staff meeting was called where all the bank's employees were informed of the death of Richard Bringsen. Everybody observed a two-minutes silence as a mark of respect for Richard, and then they all went back to work.

Masood then called Sheikh Tayeb in Karachi and informed him about the death of one of their officers. Sheikh Tayeb was deeply saddened at the sudden death of a young and promising officer of the bank and promised to speak to Richard's father. He also sent a fax for distribution to the employees of the Geneva branch expressing his sympathies on the sudden death of their colleague. A general staff note was sent to all employees of the bank around the world announcing Richard's death and praising him as a loyal and dedicated rising star.

Since it was past the normal business hours on 2 January, the Karachi branch staff learnt of Richard's death when they arrived at work on 3 January.

***

Adana, Turkey

It was long past the evening prayer time when a motorcyclist dressed in black came to Ahmet Gulay's parents' house in a shabby neighbourhood of Adana, Turkey, and rang the bell. Aysu, Ahmet's sister, opened the door. After enquiring that the address was correct and he was dealing with the right party, the messenger handed over an envelope.

'This contains ten thousand dollars, sent by Ahmet from Germany. Please count the money and sign the receipt,' the messenger said.

Aysu was overjoyed. Her hands started shaking with excitement. This was a great deal of money and would help her family live very comfortably for quite some time. She prayed that Allah blessed more families with sons like Ahmet.

Chapter 20

Karachi, G&P Bank's offices

Amir arrived at the bank before 8.30 a.m., as was his habit. It was the second day of his return to Karachi.

He had come home with a plethora of gifts for his family and friends. Everybody was happy to see him return, and there were numerous invitations for lunches and dinners. Amir's mother, who kept a watchful eye on Amir's progress at the bank, had spread the word that he was due for a promotion at the bank, and that she was looking for a bride for him.

He was also welcomed warmly at the bank. Azhar Alam's secretary, Samira, came down from her office and congratulated him on his very successful trip and advised that she had sent the information to Danny by courier. She had retained a copy for Amir.

Amir gave her the pearl studs he had bought for her. She was thrilled and wanted Amir to take her out for dinner and present the gift there. Amir requested her to keep the gift and promised to go for dinner soon.

Then Amir looked at his in-tray. On the top of the pile was the note from the chairman's office announcing the death of Richard Bringsen from the Geneva branch in Speyer, Germany. Amir was stunned and started shaking uncontrollably. No, it was not possible. There must be a mistake. Richard had promised Amir that he would share some information with him when they next met. Now he was gone.

Amir could not shake the suspicion that the bank was somehow involved in the tragic event. But how? The accident had occurred in Germany. It was not easy to organise such a thing in countries like Germany. There must be witnesses. The German police were very professional and thorough. They would certainly get to the truth.

For a long time, he sat with his head in his hands.

'Did you meet this guy, Richard, when you were in Geneva?' It was Saima, who had taken over TIG's account from Amir.

'Yes, I saw him in Geneva, but I knew him from London. We joined the bank together in the Knightsbridge branch. I cannot believe this has happened.'

'It's very tragic, but there was nothing anyone could do,' Saima replied philosophically. 'I don't want to disturb you, but when you have time, I have a few matters to discuss with you about TIG.'

'Let me go through my in-tray and I'll sit down with you to discuss TIG,' Amir replied.

After looking through his in-tray to see if there was anything urgent, Amir went to Saima's office. 'Hello, Saima. What do you want to discuss?' He said when he met her.

'I have looked at your memorandum and the information in the file for advances to TIG. We have a two-billion-dollar exposure to this group. I consider that eighty percent of it is unsecured and a large amount may be irrecoverable. Although we have a positive credit review report on file from Morisco, I hear from other sources that the group might have financial difficulties. You know their chairman died recently. His funeral was a big show in Karachi,' Saima said, looking through her notes.

'You are not just a pretty face, are you? You have reached the same conclusion as I have.'

'This is what I don't understand. I received a note this morning from Azhar Alam not to spend any more time on TIG, as the board has already extended the facilities for another year.' Saima showed the note from Azhar Alam.

'They must have got assurances from TIG and other sources that there are no serious risks in extending the facilities. As the decision has already been made by people more senior than us, let's not waste any more time on this,' Amir said. He did not want to express his suspicions or tell Saima about his plans.

'This has been frustrating, but a good learning experience, I suppose,' Saima said, getting up.

'Let me have the files. I might want to make some notes for future reference,' Amir requested.

As soon as Amir reached his office, the telephone started ringing.

'Hi. The boss wants to see you.' It was Samira.

'I'm on my way,' Amir said, picking up his jacket.

'Go straight in. He's waiting,' Samira said when Amir reached Azhar Alam's office.

'Come in.' Azhar Alam stood up from his chair. 'Welcome back. I hope all is well with you and your family. I hear you did an excellent job in Switzerland. Masood is very pleased.'

'Everything is fine, Sir. Actually, I didn't do any work there. If anything, I might have wasted people's time. Masood Sahib is very kind. Thank you very much for giving me the opportunity.' Amir was making the right noises, although he was seething inside for what he was exposed to. He felt used.

'I'm glad that you enjoyed the trip.' Azhar Alam was oblivious to Amir's sentiments and believed that people liked international travelling, extra cash and would do anything to please him, the boss.

'I understand that TIG's facilities have been renewed for another year,' Amir said to keep the conversation going.

'Yes. We had a careful review of the group's operations, their asset base and the potential of further business for G&P. We also got them checked by Morisco, and we met the new chairman, Yakoob Soothar, in London. Following the review and meetings, we decided to extend the facilities for a year. Thank you very much for the good work you and Saima did on this account,' Azhar Alam replied. 'I actually called you to give you some good news in person. Masood has requested that you be transferred permanently to Geneva to work directly with him. There will be a promotion for you, as well.' Azhar Alam stated the real purpose of the meeting.

'I am honoured, Sir, and grateful to you and Masood Sahib for the confidence in me. I, however, need to discuss this with my parents. So, please allow me a few days to reply to you,' Amir replied.

'Sure. Talk to your parents. I believe this is a tremendous opportunity. I would jump to grab such an opportunity if it came my way. I suggest you advise your response by the weekend. We will have to organise your Swiss work and residence permits. Both permits are issued by different authorities. Talk about bureaucracy.

You will get what the Swiss call Permit B, which is normally issued for a period of up to five years. Masood should have no difficulty getting these permits but it might take a few days.' Azhar Alam emphasised the need for a quick decision by Amir.

'I'll let you know of my decision within the next couple of days. I am sure that my parents will be pleased but it is appropriate that I should speak to them first.'

On his way out of Azhar Alam's office, Samira seemed to be waiting for him. She looked at Amir and smiled. 'Are some guys lucky? I don't know what you did to impress the boss and Masood but your star is ascending. Congratulations!'

'So, you know,' Amir said.

'Of course, I know. I am the confidential secretary of the boss. So, are you going to take me with you to Geneva?' Samira was incredibly direct.

'Not so fast. First, I have not yet decided to go. I'll consult my parents and consider the offer carefully,' Amir said.

'You men! I suppose Swiss girls are prettier than Pakistani. I can wait. But you will have to take me out on a date.' Samira said.

'I'll take you out for dinner. Sure,' Amir said evasively.

Amir's head was spinning. Events were moving too fast. First, the news of Richard's death. Now, the offer of his promotion and transfer to Geneva. He felt he was no longer in control. He liked the idea of going to Geneva. In fact, he had made the request to that effect to Masood Qadir. But he had not asked for a permanent transfer. He had hoped he would go there for a few months, complete his mission, and get out. The news of Richard's death had shaken him. On the other hand, he was elated at the possibility of his promotion, which probably depended on his accepting the offer to go to Geneva.

His mind drifted to Rehana. He was very attracted to her. Although Rehana was married and had kids, there was a flare, a sophistication and a warmth without any expectation, which made her different from, girls like Samira. Samira was targeting Amir to get married and settle down. Rehana had no agenda except that she was thirsty for him.

Amir returned to his office, but he could not concentrate. He sat for a long time, staring at the wall. His life was on a roller coaster. Somehow, he managed to busy himself for the rest of the day.

***

'What's wrong? You look depressed.' It was Seemi who noticed that Amir was not his usual cheerful self at the dinner table.

'Nothing. Some issues at the bank.'

'What issues?' asked Amir's father.

'There are several. Let's talk after dinner,' Amir said.

After dinner, they all sat down in the living area, eager to hear Amir share his worries.

'Azhar Alam called me today. I don't know if you have heard that one of the bank's middle-level officers in Geneva was killed in an accident in Germany. Apparently, there is a vacancy in Geneva, and they want me to transfer there. Azhar Alam said that the management was very happy with my performance, and that there would be a promotion for me.' Amir outlined the issue quite succinctly.

Amir's mother's face lit up. She got up and kissed him on the forehead. 'This is great news! I heard that the bank's management was very pleased with you. I was so proud when Shakila told me about you. She told me that Swiss girls were all over you when you were there. We can now make the arrangements for your engagement, so you can go to Geneva with your wife.'

'Yes. Where is the problem? I don't understand,' Amir's father said.

'There are several. The bank is not financially sound. I believe it will face serious financial difficulties soon. In order to avoid a financial collapse, the management is involved in a lot of trickery. Geneva is in the thick of this. Also, it is a permanent transfer to Geneva. I don't mind going there on a short-term basis, but I'd like to stay here with you guys.'

'I have never seen somebody more cynical and ungrateful than you. Please excuse me for saying this. The bank is very sound and prospering. I was talking to Sheikh Tayeb the other day and he shared some of his plans for further growing the bank. G&P Bank is the shining pearl of every middle-level businessman's eyes. It is our bank. The enemies spread rumours and try to harm it. But nothing is going to happen. The bank will keep growing and may become one of the biggest banks in the world.

'I sympathise with you for not wishing to live away from family and friends in Pakistan and want to find excuses to reject this fantastic offer. You should realise that there are no real career prospects in Pakistan. Geneva gives you international experience and entry into the world of finance. Grab it. Don't let anybody at the bank even feel that you are not happy with the offer. If I, were you, I would be celebrating?

'Your mother is right. Please tell us if you have a girl in mind here. We will send the proposal and make the necessary arrangements. Otherwise, your mom knows of several beautiful young ladies from very prominent families and should have no difficulty finding a suitable match for you, so you will have a home life in Geneva.' Amir's father was unhappy that Amir was even thinking of rejecting this great opportunity.

'All right. I will think a little more about it. I mean about the transfer to Geneva. Not about the marriage. I do not want to marry or even get engaged at this stage.'

'Go to Geneva. We will wait for your signal to find a bride for you.' Amir's father did not want to push the subject of marriage if Amir was ready to go to Geneva.

Amir was tired. He excused himself and went to bed early.

Chapter 21

Singapore

It was nearing the scheduled departure time for the bulk carrier, the TIG Bright Star, at Pier 9 of the Singapore port. The 11,000-deadweight tons Panamanian-registered ship was on its return voyage from Shanghai to Karachi via Singapore and Colombo. All the cargo was loaded except one consignment, which was still awaited. The ship was ready to lift the anchor once the final consignment was received and properly stowed away. The captain of the ship looked at his watch. They were cutting it fine, he thought. Earlier, he had received a message from the head office that a special consignment would be brought on board just before the departure time. This consignment was sensitive and needed special handling. There would be a bonus for the captain and the first officer if this was handled with care and discretion. At no stage was the cargo to be opened, and it should be stored in the special compartment designated for fragile and sensitive goods. The shipping agent was also asked to handle this consignment with special care and not let the packaging be disturbed. There was going to be a special fee for the agent as well.

A few hours earlier, the shipping company's agents had submitted papers to the port's bonded warehouse officer to release a consignment of children's books stored there for re-export to Afghanistan via Pakistan.

All the papers were in order, and the consignment was released upon payment of the necessary fee. The truck collecting the consignment went directly to the berth where the TIG Bright Star was anchored. The customs officer briefly looked at the papers and barely glanced at the truck, which was loaded with boxes clearly showing that these were children's books originally shipped from South Africa and stored in the bonded warehouse for re-export. He was previously alerted to keep an eye on the movement of goods to and from the TIG Bright Star.

The ship's first officer was also aware of the sensitive nature of the consignment. He only looked at the documents, which included the necessary commercial invoice, customs clearance documents, bill of lading, packing list of the goods, insurance papers and certificate of origin, attested by the Durban Chamber of Commerce, showing that the goods were of South African origin. Since everything was in order, the papers were presented to the captain, who signed them.

The consignment was taken to the special hold under the main deck, where fragile and sensitive items were located. As all the consignments were now on board and supplies and fuel for the journey were already taken, the ship was ready to lift its anchor.

Special Agent Liu Chen was looking at the TIG Bright Star from a distance through his field glasses. Ten agents were waiting nearby for his instructions.

'The ship has received the goods. You may go into action. We are moving in.' He spoke into his wireless phone. 'Let's go,' he said to the agents, and they all jumped into the three vehicles standing ready nearby.

Their destination was the TIG Bright Star. Once shipside, Liu took out his megaphone and said, 'This is Special Agent Liu Chen of Singapore Intelligence Bureau. I need to speak to the captain.'

Soon the ship's captain appeared on the deck. 'What is it, Officer?'

'We are here on an important mission. I request permission to come aboard, Sir.' Liu said.

'Permission granted. Please come aboard,' replied the captain. He was a little surprised, as it was not usual for the Singapore Intelligence Bureau to visit ships. A crew might be suspected of being involved in some illegal activity and might need to be questioned by the officers, the captain thought.

Soon, the whole group led by Liu walked up the gangway to the deck.

'Sorry to bother you, Captain. We have information that this ship is a part of an international arms smuggling chain and has a large quantity of arms on board.' Liu said.

'Nonsense. We are not part of any chain or gang. We're a merchant ship carrying legitimate cargo with proper documents.' The captain was indignant.

'I have to apologise, Captain, but I have orders to search the ship.' Liu was polite but firm.

'You cannot do that. This is my ship and you have no right to search it.' The captain refused permission.

'Wrong, Captain. You are in Singapore waters. Actually, you are at the Singapore port. Singapore government has jurisdiction over your ship for any crimes which might have been committed on Singapore soil in which the ship might be involved. I have a search warrant issued by a Singapore court with me. We will not take long if everything is in order,' Liu said, producing an official search warrant issued by a Singapore judge earlier in the day. 'Okay, boys, let's carry out our inspection. Please be careful not to disturb anything, as far as possible,' he said to the assembled team.

The team was divided into pairs of two and went to work systematically, opening various crates and bulk packages. The captain and the ship's crew stood around, sullenly looking at the agents' working.

'Sir, we have something here,' The agent who opened a crate marked *Books for Children* in the compartment for fragile and sensitive goods called out.

'Shall we go see what this agent has found, Captain?' Liu asked the captain.

'Sure. I am certain there is something very innocent and totally legal there,' the captain said, walking with Liu toward the agent who was beckoning them.

A large crate had been pried open. It was full of neatly stacked AK-47 sub-machine guns.

'Can I see the documents for this consignment, please?' Liu asked, turning to the captain.

The captain, who had gone white, motioned for his first officer to give the papers to the agent.

'The bill of lading states that these are books for children of Afghanistan. These may be for Afghanistan, but they are certainly not books, and not for the children there,' Liu said.

'I know nothing of this. My first officer accepted the consignment based on the shipping documents prepared by the exporter. We rely on these documents and do not normally open the crates to inspect the cargo,' the captain replied.

'I accept that this might have been snuck upon you, but you are responsible for the cargo on your ship. Anyway, now we have to inspect everything. First, let's open all the crates containing these children's books. We will also have to examine all the other cargo very carefully,' Liu said.

All the crates marked *Books for Children exported by Tiny Angels Supplies (Pvt) Limited* were opened by the agents. Every crate contained a large number of weapons, including sub-machine guns, rocket launchers, missile launchers, grenades, and ammunition belts for machine guns.

Liu Chen spoke into his wireless telephone, reporting his findings to the headquarters. After he finished his call to headquarters, he turned back to the captain.

'Well, Captain, we have some very unusual children's books here. I'm afraid we will have to ask you and your crew to stay in Singapore with your ship until the investigation is complete. You will receive written instructions from the Singapore Port Authority shortly.'

'We are innocent and are not a party to any crime here. It is totally unjustified to detain us. I must lodge a protest and will challenge this high handedness in court. I have no problem if you want to seize the offending cargo for your investigation, but my crew and I are not involved. We should, therefore, be allowed to leave with our ship as scheduled,' the captain replied.

'Captain, this matter is no longer within my powers. Further action is being taken against various parties as we speak. The Singapore government's highest security officials are now involved. Our government does not tolerate arms smuggling. You are entitled to take whatever legal action you consider necessary.

'Please give us your passport and all the sailors' merchant navy cards. These will be returned to you when you are given permission to travel outside Singapore. We have also arrested some staff at the ship's agents, Sunshine Shipping Agency in Singapore. 'We believe some of their people might be involved. I'm sure their representative will contact you soon and extend whatever assistance you may require.

'We are taking away these crates of so-called children's books. I'll give you a receipt. In fact, both of us should sign the list of contents in these crates. I'm sorry for your troubles but I have no choice.'

It took a few more hours to complete the paperwork and remove the consignment. The ship's crew was stunned and disappointed that they were not allowed to leave. They were also worried.

***

At the same time as the ship was raided, raids were also conducted at various other places in Singapore.

Tiny Angels Supplies (Pvt) Ltd.'s warehouse near the port was raided, resulting in the discovery of another huge cache of arms. These were confiscated, and the staff working there were taken into custody. The owner of the company, a South African by the name of Willem Haar, was also arrested.

The intelligence agents also visited Docks Hotel, where Aman was staying and arrested him on charges of involvement in terrorism and arms smuggling. It was difficult to establish Aman's real identity as he had several passports with different names, in addition to more than two hundred and fifty thousand dollars in cash in his possession.

Two agents visited the apartment of Tariq Dost Shah of the G&P Bank and asked him to accompany them to the Bureau's offices to answer some questions. He was nervous and wanted to call a lawyer to accompany him. He was told by the agents that there were no charges against him, and the involvement of a lawyer might complicate the situation. It was best that he went alone. They promised that Tariq would be free to go after answering a few questions.

At the Bureau's offices, he was asked about his relationship with Aman. Tariq advised that Aman represented the Afghan Children Education Society, a client of the bank, and he knew Aman in that context only. Tariq was told that Aman was under investigation for money laundering and smuggling arms, and the Bureau believed that G&P Bank might have been used to support these activities. The Bureau requested cooperation from the bank and asked for details of all the transactions that had been handled in all accounts where Aman was involved. He was asked to provide this information by noon on the next day.

Tariq promised full cooperation and agreed to provide the information. He was cautioned not to disclose the information about this matter to anybody, including the bank's head office, and not to leave Singapore without obtaining permission from the Bureau, as he might be required for further information in connection with the case.

'Am I to assume that my movements are restricted?' Tariq asked the senior intelligence agent dealing with him.

'At this stage, we are asking for your voluntary cooperation only. But if you feel this is not possible, then we will have to take a more formal approach, which might cause more stress to you,' The agent politely replied.

Tariq returned home at around two in the morning. He was shaken. The Singapore Intelligence Bureau (SIB) was known to be one of the toughest in the world. He feared this was the start of a major disaster unfolding.

Although he was cautioned against speaking to anybody, Tariq thought he had to inform the bank's head office of this development. He called Azhar Alam's direct number.

Azhar Alam responded on the second ring. 'Hello.'

'Sir, this is Tariq from Singapore.'

'Hello, Tariq, how are you? Everything okay, I hope?'

'Sir, sorry to bother you at this late hour, but this is important. I was taken for questioning by the Singapore Intelligence Bureau tonight. Apparently, one of the bank's clients, the Afghan Children Education Society, is being investigated for arms smuggling and money laundering. Their representative, Aman, has been arrested. The Bureau officials wanted to know about the bank's involvement with Aman and have cautioned me to cooperate with the investigation. I have told them that our relationship with this client was above board and we will fully cooperate.'

'Good. Afghan Children Education Society is a client who I understand imports and distributes educational material for Afghan children. You did the right thing. I suggest you give the Bureau whatever information they need. We have nothing to worry about.'

'I will do as you say, Sir. But it is not a pleasant experience to face the officials of Singapore Intelligence Bureau.'

'I'm sure it is not, but it comes with the territory. Keep me informed of developments.' Azhar said.

***

Around the same time as Tariq was speaking to Azhar Alam, Haroon Soothar received a call from Chen Hua, Manager, Sunshine Shipping Agency, TIG's Singapore agent.

'Mr. Soothar, This is Chen Hua from Singapore. Sorry if I am disturbing you at the wrong time.' Chen said.

'Hello, Mr. Hua. It's all right. I'm used to late calls, but isn't it very late in Singapore? How are you?'

'I could be better, Sir. I have some bad news. One of your ships, The TIG Bright Star, has been impounded by the Singapore authorities. They have detained the captain and crew of the ship. They have also detained two of my staff.'

'What? What happened?'

'Sir, we are told that the ship was carrying a cargo of arms destined for Afghanistan via Karachi. The Singapore government has also arrested the owner and staff of the company that shipped the cargo.'

'But what is our role in this? We must have accepted the consignment in good faith. I'm sure the bill of lading did not state that arms were being shipped.'

'No, it did not, Sir. The bill of lading and other documents showed a consignment of books for Afghan children. To be honest, we were told by your assistant, Mr. Younus, to treat the cargo with sensitivity and not to carry out the routine inspection that we do before issuing the bill of lading. Therefore, we issued the bill of lading without carrying out any checks and based on the documents presented to us only. Apparently, SIB has been after this supplier for quite some time. They claim that the supplier, TIG and our company all are involved in the illegal business of arms smuggling.

'I have been talking to SIB through my contacts. They have promised to release my staff and the crew shortly, except the captain and the first officer. The ship has been moved to another berth and is held under police guard. SIB says the captain and the first officer will be produced in a Singapore court tomorrow morning to obtain a remand of a few days for further investigation. In the meantime, the ship will remain in the custody of the Singapore Port Authority and none of the crew will be allowed to leave Singapore.'

'Oh, my God! This is bad news. What should we do?' Haroon, never a strong man, was falling apart.

'We need to hire a lawyer to represent TIG and the ship's captain immediately. The lawyer should attend tomorrow morning's hearing and ask for their release. They should at least be released on bail while the investigation is being carried on.'

'You must know a good lawyer who is reputed and can deal with this type of case. Please go ahead and hire one.' Haroon was anxious to pass the buck.

'We will also need to look after the crew, house them and feed them while this matter goes on.'

'I'd appreciate it if you could take care of that, as well.'

'Sir, we will do our best, but we'll need some money immediately. So please send us one hundred thousand American dollars. I'd like the money to be here no later than tomorrow afternoon, as we have already started incurring expenses. I also suggest you or somebody you trust should come to Singapore as soon as possible to see this matter through.' Chen Hua suggested.

'I'm not sure if the money can get to you that quickly, but I'll try.' Haroon knew his limitations.

'Sir, if the money is not received here by tomorrow afternoon, then we'll have no choice but to disengage ourselves from this matter. I'm sure with the vast resources that TIG has, it should be possible.'

'I will do my best. I am not sure if I or anybody from here will be able to come to Singapore so quickly, so you will have to handle this for us.' Haroon was not prepared to go to Singapore to face the authorities there.

'As I said, we will do our best. I'll call you again tomorrow, late morning your time, afternoon ours and let you know what happens in court,' Chen said.

As soon as the call ended, Haroon dialled Salim Chaliwala's telephone number. 'Salim, I have just finished a call from our agent in Singapore. We have bad news. Our ship, the TIG Bright Star, has been detained by Singapore authorities together with the crew. Apparently, the Singapore Intelligence Bureau is involved. Acting upon a tip, they raided the ship and found a cache of arms brought aboard for shipment to Afghanistan via Karachi. The consignment was for one of our Afghan customers.'

'Oh, no. This is all we need right now. You should talk to Mansukh in Hong Kong to sort this out for us.'

'That I will do. The Singapore agents require one hundred thousand US dollars before their lunchtime tomorrow in Singapore for the expenses to deal with the situation there.'

'You know we are extremely tight for cash, and I am not sure if we can arrange for the cash to be available in Singapore by tomorrow morning our time. They will have to wait. Don't panic. These things happen and the agents try to blackmail us into paying large sums at short notice. Once you pay them, you never see the money again.'

'Salim, this is serious. Our ship is stuck there. I don't know how many penalties and other charges will be imposed by Singapore. I hope they don't convict our captain and the first officer. It will be a shame if a TIG captain is convicted of arms smuggling.'

'I understand what you're saying. I suggest you speak to Yakoob. He is still in the office, working late.'

'Salim, I thought I wouldn't have to go to Yakoob for a hundred thousand dollars. But, if you cannot help, then I don't have any other option but to talk to Yakoob.' Haroon put down the telephone angrily.

He quickly got into his car and drove to the office. He found Yakoob poring over some documents. 'Working late?' he asked.

'Yes. I'm working on the investment proposal for potential investors. What are you doing here at this hour?' Yakoob asked.

'I went home but had to return because of the situation in Singapore. I got a call from our agents there. One of our ships, the TIG Bright Star, has been raided by the Singapore authorities and the captain and crew are being held. The ship has also been detained. The authorities found a cache of arms on the ship. The consignment was for our Afghan friends and we got very special rates for the shipment.'

'This is bad. What's next?'

'The agent has asked for remittance of one hundred thousand US dollars immediately to meet the expenses of dealing with the situation. He actually needs the funds by lunch tomorrow, Singapore time, which is about 10 a.m. our time. I have already spoken to Salim but he says that we're tight for cash, and in any event, it cannot be done so urgently and asked me not to panic. I think that the situation there is desperate.'

'Salim is right. We are extremely short of cash. And if we were able to manage the cash, how do you propose we'd accomplish the transfer so quickly?'

'If Salim or you speak to somebody in G&P Bank, it may be done.'

'You know that G&P Bank is extremely reluctant to advance any more funds to us. What would happen if we're not able to send the cash by lunchtime tomorrow?'

'The agent has threatened to withdraw from dealing with this matter and let us be at the mercy of Singapore authorities with no legal assistance. Yakoob, our people are in jail. We had close to eighty people on that ship. Soon, we will have a very difficult situation with the crew's families here in Pakistan.' Haroon was angry.

'Haroon, you are fully aware of our problems. We are trying our best to manage under the circumstances. Do you realise that to help the shipping business, we are now dealing with triads and drug barons? What more do you expect from us?' Yakoob held his hands up in frustration. 'When you came in, I was working on a proposal for investment by potential investors. It won't be easy. Our people are trying to sell some of our properties as we speak. But unfortunately, the market is not good.

'They are crying for cash everywhere. We are scraping the bottom of our cash box. I have resorted to cutting my own expenses. Yesterday, I had to refuse to buy an Aston Martin for my son, Sabir. You know how difficult it is for me to refuse anything to my family and tell them not to buy something. By the way, have you talked to Mansukh about this?'

'No. Mansukh does not know anything about this. I personally authorised the loading of this consignment and the special freight was paid directly to our special account in Geneva. I spoke to the captain and Singapore agents to accept the consignment without any examination. I thought we'd be able to solve this without involving outsiders.'

'Outsiders? Mansukh is not an outsider. He is a member of the board and the head of our Asia Pacific division. He has forgotten more about dealing with authorities in Asia than you and I will ever learn. I suggest you speak to Mansukh. It's late in Hong Kong, but you have no choice.' Yakoob was angry.

'Okay, I'll speak to Mansukh. Thanks for the help,' Haroon said and walked out.

Once in his office, Haroon dialled Mansukh Lal's number in Hong Kong. He was told by the maid that Mansukh and his wife had gone out for dinner. She did not know where they had gone and promised to give them a message.

Haroon was frustrated. He waited for an hour for Mansukh's call and then left.

He was already in bed when Mansukh finally called. 'Hello, Haroon? I got the message that you wanted to speak to me urgently. Sorry, I was out for a late dinner.'

'Thank you for returning my call. We have a desperate situation in Singapore and I hope you can help,' Haroon said.

'Tell me what has happened.'

Haroon described the situation in Singapore and asked Mansukh to help with the situation.

'I'll speak to Chen Hua. He is a blackmailer and con artist. I don't know if the situation is as desperate as he wants us to think. Unfortunately, we don't have any cash to spare in Hong Kong and we might need some funds in Singapore. I'll try to speak to Tariq Dost Shah of G&P Bank to see if he can help. Yakoob may be able to get some cash quickly if he speaks to somebody at G&P Bank in Karachi.'

'Both Yakoob and Salim seem reluctant to do anything. They asked me to speak to you.'

'Well, I'll speak to Chen Hua first thing tomorrow morning and let you know the status,' Mansukh replied.

Haroon went to bed, but he could not sleep. He was in the office early the next day, waiting for the call from Hong Kong. It was 11 a.m. Karachi time, 2 p.m. Hong Kong time when the call finally came.

'Hello, this is Mansukh.'

'Mansukh, I've been waiting for your call since seven this morning. What is the news?'

'I've been trying to get a handle on the situation before calling you. I just finished a call with Chen Hua in Singapore. They have just finished the court hearing there. Unfortunately, it's not good news. Apparently, the action against our ship was initiated at the instigation of the CIA and RAW jointly. Both the USA and India have been putting pressure on Singapore authorities to curb arms

211

smuggling to Afghanistan via Singapore. The TIG Bright Star has been caught red-handed and is being made an example of.

'At the initial court hearing this morning, the court set bail at two million Singapore dollars each for the captain and first officer and instructed them not to leave Singapore. The crew is to be released without any charges. They'll have to be repatriated by air because of international interference, I am afraid this matter may turn very ugly. Our company and staff may suffer greatly. It is possible that our captain and the first officer may be jailed and fined and our ship confiscated. We need a good lawyer in Singapore to help us with this matter.

'Good lawyers cost money. I've already paid fifty thousand US dollars to Chen to keep him happy. We need more funds for legal fees and to post bail for the captain and first officer. We also need funds to repatriate the crew. They cost money while they are in Singapore. Apparently, Chen's staff who were picked up by police last night have been released. Chen has good contacts in Singapore.'

Haroon's mouth went dry. He had feared there would be difficulties in Singapore, but he did not anticipate they would be this big.

'I'll talk to Yakoob and see what we can do from here.' Haroon was barely able to speak.

'Okay, let me know what he says. We need the money quickly to take action to salvage the situation, otherwise, the matter may get more complicated,' Mansukh said and hung up the telephone.

After finishing the call, Haroon walked over to Yakoob's office. He was told that Yakoob was in a meeting with Salim and Masoom Ali, the legal adviser, and had asked not to be disturbed.

Haroon was feeling desperate. He did not know what to do. Whenever he was nervous or scared, it was Haroon's habit to seek refuge in the arms of a girl and a bottle of whisky. He maintained a suite in the Rock & Sea Hotel near Karachi's seaport permanently and had a list of ladies available to please him. Finding that Yakoob was not available, he returned to his office and dialled a number from his direct line, which bypassed the switchboard.

'It must be my good fortune that my *jan* (darling) is remembering me today,' a sweet voice said, lifting the telephone at the other end.

'Yes, I need you today, darling. Come to the usual place.'

'I'll be there in thirty minutes,' the lady responded.

Haroon quickly cleared his desk, threw some papers in his briefcase, and walked out of his office.

'Tell my driver that I will not need him today. I will drive myself,' He told his secretary.

Chapter 22

Karachi, G&P Bank's offices

Amir got up early, he hadn't slept well. He had agonised for two days over his transfer to Geneva. He had carefully analysed his situation.

He liked Geneva. He had a mission to complete, and that made his going to Geneva a necessity. Matters were getting complicated as Danny appeared to have been neutralised and Richard Bringsen was killed. Amir was certain that Richard's death was no accident. He must get the dossier Richard prepared if he wanted to succeed in his mission.

He had accepted his transfer but he was unsure if he wanted to be transferred permanently. Also, there was a great risk for him and his family if he pursued his plans. Richard's death was indicative of the way those people operated.

Do I have a choice? He asked himself. Clearly, if he declined the offer, his career would be ruined. Besides, he had a debt to settle with the bank.

After a careful and painstaking analysis of his position, Amir decided he had no choice but to say yes. He would try to avoid involvement in any illegal or wrong activities, as he was certain there would be investigations and retribution once the bank's real activities were revealed. He was also afraid he would be asked to carry a further consignment of the bank's 'papers' to Geneva. He would have to find a way to avoid that.

With these thoughts in mind, Amir arrived early at the bank and called Samira to ask if Azhar Alam was in and was told that he was in his office. Amir asked Samira to check if Azhar Alam could spare a few minutes for Amir. She called back within five minutes and advised that Azhar Alam would be happy to see him.

'Good morning, Sir,' Amir said, knocking at the door of Azhar Alam's office.

'Good morning. Come in,' Azhar Alam replied.

'Sit down. Do you want a coffee?' Azhar Alam asked.

'No, Sir. I only want a few minutes of your time. Actually, I came to tell you that I feel privileged by the offer of transfer to Geneva and have decided to accept it. You and Masood Sahib have been very kind. I will do my best to meet your expectations,' Amir said with feigned humility.

'This is great. I was sure that you'd accept, and I'm certain that you will do extremely well there. Geneva is our most important centre and we only send extremely competent and loyal people there. Masood will be delighted.

'Actually, Masood is eagerly waiting for you to join him. To avoid losing time, he has already applied for your Permit B. We hope to receive the approval soon, and the actual permit should be received by courier a few days after. You'll have to take the permit with your passport to the Swiss Consulate in Karachi to have it stamped on your passport. I understand that it's a simple process, and that the Swiss are very efficient.

'Masood and I also recommended to the chairman that you should be promoted to the rank of a full vice president. The chairman kindly approved our request. Here is the letter advising you of the good news. There will be a substantial increase in your salary and other benefits. You should attend the bank's executive conference in Bangkok, Thailand, on 5 and 6 February. We'll congregate there to develop the plans for the bank.' Azhar Alam handed Amir a sealed envelope.

'Thank you very much, Sir. I am indebted to both you and Masood. I hope he won't be disappointed in me,' Amir said as he accepted the envelope.

'Masood and I normally do not make mistakes in recognising a good person when we see one. You are a good person and an asset to the bank. We look after our good people,' Azhar Alam said pompously. 'We'd like you to leave for Geneva a few days after Thailand. Please let me and Samira know when you plan to leave. Samira will make all the arrangements.'

'Sir, I would like to take a week's holiday. I have some personal business in London. If possible, I'd like to go next week. As for

Geneva, I'd like to stop over in Turkey on the way to Geneva. I have always wished to see the Topkapi Museum in Istanbul. So, if you allow, I'll make my own travel arrangements. I'll advise you and Masood of my expected arrival date in Geneva.' Amir cleverly denied Azhar Alam any opportunity to ask him to carry any 'papers' to Geneva.

'Sure. Take whatever time you require. Istanbul is a great city, and Turkey is a great country. You are right, the Topkapi Museum is a must-see.' Azhar Alam was in good mood.

'Thank you, Sir. I'll let Samira know of my travel plans,' Amir said, getting up.

Outside Azhar Alam's office, Samira was waiting for him. She got up from her desk and rushed to him. She hugged Amir and kissed him on the cheek. Amir was dazed. He had never known of such an open expression of affection in Pakistan.

'Congratulations. You deserve it. I am so happy, Mr. Vice President,' She said.

'Thank you, Samira. I am obliged for all you do for me.'

'Well, there is a fee for everything. I'll wait to collect mine.' Samira said, unabashedly.

Amir went back to his desk and opened the envelope Azhar Alam gave him. It was from the chairman, congratulating him on his promotion to the position of vice president, effective immediately. He was also informed that he would be advised of his new salary and benefits by the human resources department separately. He phoned his mother and father in quick succession and told them about his acceptance of transfer to Geneva and promotion to vice president. They were delighted. He also phoned his sister and gave her the good news.

After making the calls, Amir tried to busy himself with the papers in front of him. They were credit reports and facilities approval requests for certain smaller clients. He could not bring himself to look at those papers. His thoughts went to Samira. She was all for him. Amir, however, did not have the same feelings for her as he had for Rehana. Still, Samira was a great friend and good company so he must take her out for lunch or dinner.

Thinking of lunch, Amir started feeling hungry. He picked up the phone and dialled Samira. 'Hey there, busy?'

'Since when have I ever been busy for you?' Samira replied.

'Join me for lunch?'

'How can I say no? Where are we going?'

'Let's go to Marriot. They have a nice Chinese restaurant, Suzie Wong there,' Amir said.

'I love Suzie Wong. It's so good. Let me tell Boss. I'll meet you in the banking hall in five minutes,' she said.

True to her word, Samira was in the banking hall in less than five minutes. Amir asked the attendant to bring his car to the main door of the bank.

'I told Boss you're taking me out for a rare lunch. He was delighted and asked me to go and enjoy it. He is the nicest boss anyone could work for.' Samira was happy.

'Yes. He is nice,' Amir said.

'Let's leave Azhar Alam and the bank. Tell me, how will you celebrate your promotion and the transfer?' Samira asked.

'I'm sure my mom will arrange a party. I'll make sure you are invited.'

'Who wants to attend a party with all those old snobs?' Samira made a face. 'You must celebrate with the younger crowd. I'll organise a party for you. You'll meet some of the most beautiful girls of Karachi at my party but promise me that you won't flirt with anyone.'

'Me, flirt with girls? You know that never happens. A party would be a good change. I haven't gone out to party for quite some time.'

'That's settled then. We will have a party at my place before you go. Next Saturday?'

'I think next Saturday should be okay,' Amir said.

'Good. Then it's done. I'll start working on the invitations.'

Chapter 23

Danial Rafi's apartment – Milton Keynes, England

Amir was resting in the spare bedroom of Danny's apartment after a nine-hour flight from Karachi.

After accepting the offer to move to Geneva, Amir had lightened his workload. He transferred most of his work to Saima, who was very keen to take on as much work as was available. She believed that by working harder and longer, she would be nominated for a quick promotion.

Amir had also been invited to endless parties and dinners. For his family and family's friends, his promotion and transfer to Geneva was the equivalent of hitting the jackpot, calling for non-stop celebrations.

Amir had a hard time convincing his parents that he needed to go to London to take care of some unfinished business. He was cagey and did not reveal the exact nature of his work in London. He did, however, let them know he would be staying with Danny. Amir's mother actually suggested that maybe Seemi should go with Amir, as she had not been to London for some years and it might be a good break for her. Amir politely told them that he and Danny had some serious business matters to deal with, and Seemi would get bored if she was not properly looked after.

Amir opened his eyes and checked his watch. It was nearly 5.30 p.m. Danny should arrive home soon. He had met Danny briefly that morning as he was leaving for the office and was looking forward to seeing him shortly. There was a lot to discuss.

Amir heard footsteps and the turning of the key and pulled himself out of bed, freshening up before he went into the living room. Danny was there, standing in the middle of the room with his coat still on, staring at a newspaper. He looked as if he had been struck by lightning.

'Hello. Why are you standing like this? Is something the matter?' Amir asked.

Danny handed Amir the Financial Times without a word.

'Has the stock exchange folded or something?' Amir still could not comprehend why Danny looked so shocked.

'Look at the right-hand side, at the bottom of the first page,' Danny said.

Amir opened the newspaper and saw the item Danny wanted him to read. It was an advertisement by G&P Bank announcing, with pleasure, that according to the audited financial statements for the year, the bank had recorded a profit of one hundred fifty million US dollars. This was a great achievement for the bank as the profit had increased over the previous year despite the financial turmoil prevailing in the world. The bank's management thanked its clients for their support and recorded their gratitude to the staff for their untiring efforts in looking after the bank's clients and achieving excellent financial results. The management also thanked the bank's shareholders and stakeholders for their support.

'Shit. Have you guys issued the audit report already?' Amir asked.

'Don't ask me. Ask those idiots Charles Ramsey and David Finner. They were in a hurry to sign the report so they could get the management consultancy contract offered by the bank.'

'You must have received the package sent to you by Samira. It clearly shows that the bank does not have securities for the funds advanced to TIG and, in many cases, there is no proof that some of the collateralised assets even exist. TIG is in deep financial trouble,' Amir said.

'You know that. I know that. The idiots at Tolbert and Gibbs do not want to know that. They believe TIG is sound and the bank is in excellent financial health. They believe the bank is making a profit,' Danny lamented.

'Anyway, you can do nothing about this, so relax. Actually, I'm here on a mission. I've been promoted as vice president to be permanently located in Geneva?' Amir asked.

'Have you? Congratulations. So, you are a part of the gang now?' Danny was very angry.

'No. I am not a part of the gang. This position gives me an excellent opening for what I have in mind. I've already told you that I'm deeply hurt by what they did to me. I might have told you that there was a fellow by the name of Richard Bringsen in Geneva who was also unhappy with the bank's operating style and was putting together a dossier of the bank's illegal activities conducted out of Geneva.'

'What use are these dossiers, anyway? Who is going to listen to us? We need to have documents and details of transactions to prove that the bank was involved in unlawful activities. Extension of facilities to TIG may be risky, but it's not illegal,' Danny said.

'True. This fellow Richard communicated with me when I was about to leave Geneva. He said that he was preparing a detailed dossier of such activities by the bank. He was afraid the bank might have found out he was snooping and therefore was going to leave the material he had gathered with his girlfriend's father in Speyer, Germany. He was going to spend Christmas and New Year's with his girlfriend's family and return to Geneva immediately after the New Year.'

'I don't understand where this is going. Mr. Bringsen might have prepared a dossier. So what?'

'Richard Bringsen and his girlfriend died in an apparent auto accident just outside Speyer when he was on his way back to Geneva. I think he might have been killed.'

'You are crazy. An auto accident in Germany at the precise time Richard was leaving his girlfriend's place would not be the easiest matter to arrange, even for G&P Bank. How would anybody at the bank know what time he was leaving? And don't tell me that the bank has a bunch of professional assassins on its payroll available to bump off anybody the bank dislikes.'

'He might have told somebody the exact time or date when he would be returning to Geneva, and they might've been lying in wait for him to come out. It would not need a rocket scientist to guess that somebody trying to reach Geneva before evening from Speyer might have to start early in the morning. You'd be surprised how resourceful the bank is in dirty tricks. I've had first-hand experience of the bank's resourcefulness. So have you. Has your father bought the new shop?' Amir asked, rubbing salt in Danny's wounds.

'Don't remind me of that. At least I have reported the matter in writing to my superiors.'

'Yes, you have. Anyway, I plan to visit Richard's family and his girlfriend, Ursula's, family to offer my condolences. I'll tell them I was a colleague of Richard's. I hope Ursula's father will give me the dossier left behind by Richard. I'll also look around in Speyer to see if there are any clues as to what actually happened there,' Amir replied.

'You are obsessed. My friend, these matters are not for you. You just got a promotion and posting to a plum location. Enjoy it. Make sure that you do not get personally involved in any of the bank's undesirable activities,' Danny said.

'You are older, wiser, and calmer than me, so you don't want a confrontation. I am different. I am spoiling for a fight. Don't forget that I almost went to jail. Had the contact in Karachi not worked, I would be sitting in a dirty cell in a Pakistani jail serving a ten- to fifteen-year sentence. I need to teach those bastards that they cannot play with people's lives.

'I'm not going to tell anybody of my visit to Richard's and Ursula's families. I'll go to Mannheim by train and take a taxi to Speyer. I'll pay all expenses in cash, so there won't be any record of my visit there.' Amir explained.

'You seem to have figured everything out. When are you planning to go?'

'I'd like to visit Richard's family first. I'll call them first thing tomorrow morning to see if they are around. If Richard's father is there and willing to receive me, then I'll take a train and go to Tunbridge Wells in Kent to see the family. It'll be painful to meet the grieving parents, but I must do it. That will strengthen my resolve to deal with the matter at hand.

'I have booked a seat on the train to Frankfurt am Main and then to Mannheim for the day after tomorrow. The train leaves Waterloo at 6.30 in the morning and reaches Frankfurt am Main at 6.30 in the evening. I'll get a connecting train to Mannheim and a taxi from there. I should be in Speyer at 10 p.m., and I'll stay at Hotel Barn Hoff near the station and visit the family on the following day in the morning. I'll call them from a public telephone booth before visiting.'

***

Tunbridge Wells, Kent, England

As expected, Amir's visit to Richard's parents was sad. They were both in their seventies and lived in a nice Victorian house in the centre of the town. They received Amir with obvious efforts to avoid showing their grief.

'Thank you for coming.' Richard's father, David, said.

'Thank you for allowing me to come. I was in Karachi when I heard the news. I know it is not easy for you to receive visitors when you have suffered so much. I had to come. Richard was a friend and colleague. We both joined G&P Bank in London at almost the same time. He was very bright and knew what he was doing. On the other hand, I didn't have a clue about banking. He helped me learn the ropes. I will always remember him with fondness,' Amir said.

'The sadness will stay with us for the rest of our lives. Susan is finding it very difficult to carry on. She takes heavy tranquillisers to be able to stay calm. We are still in shock. Richard was such a sweet boy. He told us that he and Ursula would get engaged in a few months. Although Richard had met Ursula's parents before, she wanted him to spend some time with them and let them know that she and Richard would be engaged to be married soon. Now, it's all finished.' Richard's father said.

'I still remember Richard when he was young. He was different from other boys his age. He always wanted to read when others played. He was interested in finance and said that he wanted to be a top banker. He was extremely happy when he got the job at G&P Bank and got transferred to Geneva. He loved Geneva.' Richard's mother recalled; she was clearly still in shock.

'Did you bury him near here?' Amir asked.

'No. We decided that Richard and Ursula should be together forever. On getting the tragic news, Susan and I went to Speyer and met Ursula's parents. After the bodies were released, we had a private funeral and cremated them at a crematorium in Mannheim.

'An official from the bank by the name of Oshko also came. After offering condolences, he promised the bank would send Richard's dues to us as soon as his affairs at the bank were sorted out. He enquired whether Richard had left any documents or other items relating to the bank with us. We told him that Richard didn't live with us and only visited us occasionally. All we have left of Richard were the personal items given to us by the German police and some photographs in our family album.

'This Mr. Oshko wanted us to sign a letter authorising him access to Richard's flat in Geneva for collecting Richard's personal belongings so he could send them to us. He said the rent was paid only until the end of January, so quick action was required.

'You know, Ursula was living with Richard. To protect the couple's privacy and to make sure that their personal effects were handled properly, after discussions with Ursula's parents, we agreed that Ursula's father and I would go to Geneva and sort these matters ourselves. Mr. Oshko was not happy with this and said that we would require court papers to access the flat. We have already started the process with the Swiss to get the appropriate authorisation to do that.'

After spending about an hour with the family, Amir left and returned to London. He was convinced that Richard's accident was a set-up, and the bank was responsible. He also believed that Oshko was fishing for the information Richard might have left behind. He was sure Oshko had approached Ursula's parents also; Amir hoped that they had not handed over the information prepared by Richard to him.

Chapter 24

Speyer, Germany

Amir's arrival in Speyer was uneventful. It was a tiring journey, but the German railway system, like everything else in Germany, worked perfectly. The twenty-five-kilometre car journey from Mannheim to Speyer was also comfortable.

He reached Hotel Barn Hoff at five minutes past ten. He was exhausted, so immediately after registering at the front desk and being shown his room, Amir got into bed and promptly fell asleep.

He got up early the next morning; it was still dark outside. He checked his watch; it was six thirty. The piece of paper on the desk advised that breakfast was served from 7 a.m. to 9 a.m.

After a shave and a quick shower, Amir walked downstairs to the breakfast room, where a few business people were having breakfast. Amir looked for a newspaper in English, but all of them were in Deutsch.

It was very cold outside, with an overcast sky and a slight drizzle. After finishing breakfast, Amir went back to his room, put on his coat, and went for a walk. Speyer was a lovely town with nicely laid down streets and neat houses. He walked up to the cathedral. It was difficult to imagine that this beautiful structure was built almost nine hundred years ago and was the burial place for several kings and emperors. After spending some time at the cathedral and walking around other monuments such as the Old Speyer City Gate *Altportel,* Amir returned to the hotel.

Back in his room at the hotel, he consulted the telephone directory and was able to find the entry for Otto Huber, with the telephone number and address at 51 Lindenstrasse.

It was 9.30 a.m., not too early nor too late to make the call. He dialled the telephone number he had found in the directory.

'Guten morgen.' He heard a guttural German voice from the other end.

'Good morning, Sir. Do you speak English?'

'Yes. Who is speaking?'

'Sir, my name is Amir Ramli. Am I speaking to Herr Otto Huber, please?'

'Yes, you are,' replied Mr. Huber.

'I am a friend of Mr. Richard Bringsen. I was very sorry to hear of the sad accident which resulted in the loss of Ursula and Richard's life. I have already visited Richard's family in England and I am coming from there. I would like to visit you to express my condolences in person if it is not intruding upon your privacy.'

'Oh, okay. Come over. We normally do not receive any visitors as it upsets my wife, Else, but since you have come from far and are a friend of Richard's, we will welcome you. Where are you staying?' Herr Huber was very direct and precise.

'Thank you, Sir. I am at Barn Hoff,' Amir said.

'We are at 51 Lindenstrasse. It's not far from Barn Hoff. You may be able to walk here in fifteen minutes.' Herr Huber said.

'I'll be there within half an hour.' Amir said.

Amir quickly changed in a black suit, white shirt, and black tie. He knew the Germans were very formal people and he wanted to dress properly according to the circumstances. He walked in the direction given by the hotel concierge and was ringing the bell of a one-storey house marked with number 51 on Lindenstrasse in less than thirty minutes.

A tall old man wearing a cardigan over green shirt and beige corduroy trousers opened the door.

'Guten morgen. Herr Huber?' Amir asked, extending his hand.

'Guten morgen, or should I say good morning?' Herr Huber said, taking Amir's hand. 'Come in.' He stepped aside to make room for Amir to enter. Behind him, an old lady looking very fragile was standing quietly. She tried to give a welcoming smile but found it difficult to do so.

'This is Else, Ursula's mother.' Herr Huber said.

'Willkommen,' the lady said, extending her hand.

'She speaks very little English.' Herr Huber explained.

'It is very kind of you to come to pay your respects to Ursula and your friend, Richard. They were so happy in life together and they died together.'

'I am sorry for your loss. I feel the pain myself. Richard wrote to me before coming here for the holidays. We were to meet after his return.'

'One could never overcome such a loss. Else is taking it very hard. She sits by herself with tears in her eyes, does not speak to anybody. She has forgotten how to smile.' Herr Huber too was beside himself with grief. Tears were welling up in his eyes.

'Sir, I did not mean to disturb you or cause you more pain. I just had to come. Richard and I joined G&P Bank almost at the same time in London. He was much more intelligent and knowledgeable than me. He helped me a lot. I saw him at the bank in Geneva before he travelled to come here.' Amir said.

'He was a nice young man. Although they said he was driving rashly, I find it difficult to believe. He was always so careful in everything he did. He also promised me that he would drive carefully when he was leaving.' Herr Huber said.

'I am surprised, too. Richard did not appear to be the reckless type.'

'The police said it was a clear case of an accident resulting from rash driving. There were witnesses. Apparently, the police are still keeping the file open to see if any further evidence turns up, otherwise they will close the case and release the other driver from any obligations.' Herr Huber opened the side table and pulled out a photo album. 'We took some photographs of Ursula and Richard while they were here.'

Amir looked at the photographs. Ursula was a beautiful girl. She and Richard were obviously very happy together.

'Richard's father told me that you cremated them in Mannheim.' Amir said.

'Yes. We thought it best that they should stay together. We mixed their ashes and spread them over the Rhine. It was a small private ceremony. A Mr. Oshko was here from the bank.'

'Mr. Oshko is the security officer at the bank.'

'I am surprised the bank sent a security officer to the funeral instead of somebody who directly worked with him. Mr. Oshko was interested to find out whether Richard left anything behind. He was also interested in accessing Richard and Ursula's apartment for collecting their personal belongings and sending them to us. Richard's father and I decided that we'll do it ourselves and we have started the necessary process to be able to do that.

'Richard left a file with me for safekeeping. I do not know why, but I didn't give it to Mr. Oshko. Somehow, I did not trust that gentleman. I have the file here. I wonder if you'd be able to take it and deal with it appropriately.' Herr Huber went to a drawer, took out a thick folder and handed it to Amir.

'Sure, I'll see what's in it and deal with it as necessary.' Amir said, accepting the folder.

Amir wanted to run away with the file and read it as soon as possible, but he spent some more time with the Huber family before he left.

He quickly returned to the hotel after leaving the Huber family so he could check out and take a taxi to Mannheim. From there, he booked the most convenient connection to Frankfurt am Main and London, Waterloo. He was back in Milton Keynes the next morning.

Chapter 25

Milton Keynes England
Richard Bringsen's Folder

Danny had already left for work when Amir reached the apartment.

After a quick shower and breakfast, Amir sat down with the folder. He had resisted the temptation to open and read it during the train journey for fear that he might drop some papers or damage the contents of the folder.

It was a thick folder with several pages neatly written in longhand by Richard. There were copies of various documents to support the information in the memo.

In the memo, Richard introduced himself as a vice president and a direct assistant to Masood Qadir, head of the Geneva branch of G&P Bank. Richard stated that along with Masood Qadir, he was responsible for looking after certain major clients' accounts.

He mentioned that after working for a few months, he realised the bank was involved in massive bank fraud, money laundering and illegal transactions. He felt disgusted as he had come to the bank to make a career as an honest professional banker. He decided to gather as much evidence as possible to expose the bank and its coterie of senior management, who did not appear to have any moral or legal constraints and were driven by greed.

He also stated that during his efforts to gather the evidence, he suspected the bank's security team had taken an interest in his activities. He was afraid that he might be in serious personal danger and therefore he was taking precautions to protect himself and his findings. He requested the reader should pass on the contents of the file to the appropriate authorities and the press in the event that he, Richard, was dead when the file was being read. He had already spoken to David Randel of the *Financial Times* and indicated that he might have some information about the bank that he would like to make public. David Randel was interested but hadn't yet committed to putting anything in print and asked Richard to send the information to him without obligation on the part of the newspaper. David had emphasised that the *Financial Times* was a serious newspaper and would not be interested in publishing sensational reports unless they were backed by solid evidence. He further advised that if Richard was interested in creating sensational news, he should approach a tabloid instead of a serious financial paper such as the *Financial Times*. Richard planned to communicate with David Randel again when he was satisfied that he had all the information to nail the bank.

Next, Richard explained the layout of the folder, explaining that it was divided into the following sections:

- o Secret Accounts
- o Illegal transfer of money and money laundering
- o Falsification of records to show incorrect financial and liquidity position to the regulatory authorities
- o Bribes and illegal payments by the bank

Secret accounts

In this section, Richard had covered the bank's procedures for setting up secret accounts for high-net-worth customers to handle transactions without disclosing their identity or the source of funds being invested.

Richard accepted that the Swiss banking system was founded on secrecy and customers' confidentiality was sacrosanct. He, however, believed that the bank had no qualms in dealing with corrupt government officials and criminals who routinely indulged in illegal activities and needed the bank's services to remain anonymous and enjoy the fruits of their ill-gotten wealth.

He explained the elaborate system the bank had created to keep the details of such client's secret. According to Richard, the bank had many high-profile politicians, drug barons, civil servants, arms merchants and smugglers as their valued clients. Each client was given a secret number known only to the top five executives of the bank: Sheikh Tayeb, Azhar Alam, Mateen Saeed, Masood Qadir and Rehmallah. The assignment of numbers to the individual depositors was controlled jointly by Masood Qadir and Rehmallah, who kept a black book to record this information. Identical black books were kept by each of the aforementioned officials.

The number assigned by Masood Qadir was then assigned a fictitious name. For example, there was an active account in the name of Rabindranath Tagore, the famous Bengali writer, playwright, and winner of the Nobel Prize for Literature who died in 1941. Once a name was assigned, the account opening forms and other information were completed for the bank's top secret special accounts, which were handled by a special department in Geneva of which Richard was a member.

The account holder desiring to carry out a transaction would be referred to the special department where an official would first identify the customer by obtaining only a part of the secret account number and confirming certain information. The account holder would then have the full facility to operate the account and carry out any transaction he wanted in complete secrecy. At the end of each day, a list of transactions executed for these special accounts would be passed on to Masood Qadir, who kept a separate ledger for these accounts and personally updated the ledger accounts for these special customers. A copy of the ledger was also kept by Rehmallah. Only the five designated executives knew the details of the account holders and their balances with the bank.

Richard further wrote that he had come to know of the system during his various discussions with Masood Qadir and Rehmallah. Apparently, Masood was grooming Richard to take a role in managing the special accounts and was familiarising him with the procedures of these accounts. Masood had, however, not shown him the black book or the confidential ledger for the special accounts. Two copies of this information were made. One was kept by Masood Qadir, and the other was with Rehmallah. Masood had a heavy safe with a digital combination lock in his office where he kept this information. Rehmallah kept the information at his home.

Richard also mentioned that at a grave personal risk he had tried to get the secret information. One day, when Masood was away, Richard went to Masood's office and tried to fiddle with the digital combination lock, but was unsuccessful. He then tried to open

Masood's drawers. The bottom drawer was not locked. In it, he found the accounting papers for Client No. 075196101. The papers indicated the account holder's real name was Rafael Dorado, with an address in Panama. The bank's assigned name for the client was Rabindranath Tagore, with the address Jorasanko Mansion, Calcutta, India. For the bank's official records, Account No. 075196101 was of Mr. Tagore. Richard quickly made a note of the details of Account No. 075196101 on a plain sheet of paper and hastened to return the documents to the correct drawer. He had just put the documents in the drawer and was straightening up when Masood walked in. Richard explained that he had come to put some documents on Masood's desk and Masood seemed to be preoccupied and did not say anything.

Richard then followed up on the details of Account No. 075196101 in the bank's official ledger. The ledger showed a balance of thirty-seven million dollars in the account, which was invested in certificates of gold holdings issued by Credit Suisse and term deposits with the bank. There was a remark that the bank statements should be retained with the bank and not sent to the account holder. Richard filed the paper with the details of Account No. 075196101 in his folder.

According to Richard, sometimes more than one account was opened for a special customer. All these accounts were in different names created by Masood Qadir. Rehmallah assisted Masood Qadir and also kept with him the consolidated real account details of these special clients.

Illegal transfer of money and money laundering

Richard wrote that the bank was deeply involved in laundering money for its clients.

According to Richard, as an example, the holder of Account No. 075196101 was clearly involved in illegal activities and was facilitated by the bank in handling the proceeds of these activities.

Richard had been able to follow the build-up of the balance from the credit advices and other intimations in the account file for Account No. 075196101. The principal was involved in the trading of goods. He periodically visited the bank's Panama branch and handed over boxes full of US dollar bills. The last deposit was for ten million US dollars. The bank transferred these amounts, along with other similar deposits, by the bank's special staff travelling between Panama and Geneva.

To avoid any enquiry, it avoided showing large cash deposits in an account. When the funds were received in cash, the bank credited only one-tenth of the amount to the customer's account initially, keeping the other nine-tenth in liquid assets in the bank's vault. The bank then bought high-value items such as paintings, postage stamps, antique collection items, et cetera, paying for these items in cash and by cheque in proportion to the credit available in the customer's account.

The asset thus purchased was sold to the same dealer after a few weeks. This time, the sale proceeds were received by cheque, which was then officially credited into the customer's account. The deposit was now legitimate, and the customer was free to use the funds in any way he or she liked. The bank charged hefty fees for carrying out these transactions for the special customers.

Again, Richard was able to copy the documents of transactions involving the purchase and sale of assets on behalf of Account No. 075196101 and he identified the names, addresses and telephone numbers of the merchants who participated in the transactions. All the transactions were fully documented with invoices and receipts and agreements of sale and purchase. The appropriate amount of Swiss government tax was paid on these transactions.

He also described the extensive use of the bank's staff around the world to act as couriers for carrying money and assets. Amir was shocked when he found his name as one of the bank's staff who was involved in the transfer of money and other assets out of Pakistan. Being fair, Richard stated that Amir was not personally involved and was duped into carrying the money and had difficulty at Karachi airport, which was sorted out by the octopus-like contacts of G&P Bank.

It also stated the problem in Nigeria, where the bank's courier was ambushed and the bank had lost a lot of money.

TIG also featured prominently in the section for illegal transfer of money and money laundering. According to Richard, a TIG company (say, Company A) would buy a junk vessel in Cyprus or Panama at a very low price. The bank would finance the purchase. The ship would then be repainted and its name and the registration flag would be changed. This reborn ship would then be sold to a 'third-party conduit' for a heavy profit to the seller. Another TIG company (say, Company B) would then buy the same vessel from the conduit by paying a fraction of a percent more than the purchase price paid by the conduit.

By structuring the transaction in this manner, Company A would record a heavy profit on the purchase and sale of the ship, which was paid as dividends to its shareholders, the Soothars.

The bank acted as the financier and facilitator for the transaction.

Everybody involved in the transaction was happy, as the TIG's owners made a lot of money on the acquisition of a junk vessel, the conduit made money and the bank acting as financier made a killing in fees and charges for the transaction. The bank's officers involved normally earned a special bonus for earning large fees on structured deals. In addition, the TIG companies appeared to be liquid since they borrowed funds and repaid the outstanding dues to the bank by purchasing and selling ships.

As the bank was aware of the actual worth of the ship, they normally structured such transactions by syndicating their loans. For this purpose, G&P Bank would approach other banks, asking them to join in financing the purchase of the ship at very high interest rates. The banks would join the syndicate eagerly, as apparently there was a very small risk (the loan would be fully secured by a mortgage on a newly purchased vessel, and TIG had a good credit rating) and good money to be made.

In support of his case, Richard mentioned the transaction involving the purchase of a bulk carrier, *Tangerine 3,* by Tangerine Shipping Lines of Curacao, who in turn had purchased it from another dealer. This dealer purchased the ship from a company titled Travel and Transport Inc. of Cayman Islands, who had bought the ship from TIG, refurbished it, and changed its name and flag. At each turn, the value of the ship increased by several million dollars. The transaction was financed by a syndicate of several banks led by G&P Bank at five basis points above LIBOR (London Interest Rate for Overnight Borrowings). G&P Bank made a hefty sum in interest, both in commission and fees. TIG skimmed a tidy profit by selling one of its own ships and buying it back with a different name and flag.

There were copies of memos written by Azhar Alam, Abu Talib, and Masood Qadir in connection with the transaction.

Falsification of records to show incorrect financial and liquidity position to the regulatory authorities

Here again, Richard was thorough and scathing. He restated the culture of secret bank accounts, which enabled the bank to cover up the non-performing accounts with deposits from unrelated borrowers, thus showing a lesser need for provision against doubtful balances than actual.

Richard again referred to the funds received in suitcases from abroad. These funds were credited to whatever accounts Masood Qadir instructed, and sometimes they were transferred between different accounts when management considered it appropriate. These transactions for the transfer of funds between accounts had no written instructions from clients, therefore, it would be difficult for an independent person who was not part of the select group to establish how much balance belonged to each client.

There were strict banking regulations in Switzerland and the UK requiring banks to restrict lending to one group or client. The lending should not exceed a percentage of the bank's deposits to avoid any run on the bank. The banks were also required to maintain certain prescribed financial and liquidity ratios to stay liquid and financially sound. G&P Bank was able to circumvent these requirements by moving funds between accounts and parties with impunity and with no regard to the banking regulations or sound practices.

Richard stated that a lot of loans and advances given by the bank were irrecoverable and were camouflaged by false entries and credits to one customer's account against another customer's deposit. There were copies of memos in the dossier that clearly supported his argument. Richard attached copies of several statements of accounts showing inter-transfer of large balances between the accounts with no apparent connection.

Bribes and illegal payments by the bank

Richard wrote that Masood Qadir and Rehmallah kept large sums of cash in various currencies in their offices. They used these funds liberally to buy gifts for visiting VIPs or make cash handouts to government officials and staff of the bank for favours or illegal work.

Richard quoted the example of the bank buying a large diamond necklace worth two hundred thousand US dollars for one of the several wives of a central African ex-president when she was visiting Geneva. He attached the receipt from the Geneva Boutique of Humboldt & Tolini, the famous French jewellers. There was a note in Masood's handwriting that the necklace was presented to the ex-president's wife at the instructions of Sheikh Tayeb.

Visiting government officials and VIPs from several countries were routinely provided with luxury accommodations and first-class airline tickets for travel around the world. In one case, a yacht was chartered for the birthday party of a British politician who had to resign later when his habit of accepting favours was exposed and became an embarrassment to the ruling party.

As a part of the web of corruption and bribery, Richard wrote that even the auditors were not spared. He quoted the example of a low interest rate loan of two hundred thousand UK pounds to Charles Ramsey, Senior Banking Partner, Tolbert and Gibbs. For security reasons, Charles Ramsey had been given a secret account number and officially the balance was shown to be due from Clarke Gable, the famous Hollywood actor who had died a long time ago.

He also stated that the bank was paranoid about security and would not hesitate in using threats of violence, blackmail, and getting involved in criminal acts if they perceived a threat. The bank's security officer, Oshko, a STASI (German State Security) colonel in his earlier life, was responsible for ensuring the bank's interests were not harmed and was authorised to take whatever action he deemed necessary. Oshko had an unlimited budget and was quite ruthless. Richard believed Oshko was on his scent and his life may be in danger.

Amir looked at the photocopies of all the documents attached. They were clearly referenced with the narrative and proved Richard's information beyond any reasonable doubt.

***

Amir looked at his watch. It was nearly noon. He had been engrossed in the folder and did not notice how the time passed. He felt tired and drained. He thought he should have a plan to go forward. He was now certain that he was dealing with some extremely dangerous people and that he and his family were in danger. He must move cautiously.

He needed a lawyer to protect his interests and help him investigate further. The folder had excellent information, but Amir needed more evidence to completely nail the bank's management. He needed the evidence of their direct and personal complicity in commissioning and aiding and abetting the criminal acts. He wanted the top echelons of the bank in jail. He remembered one of his friends at Polytechnic, a fellow named John Delon. John had gone on to do law and had joined his father's law practice as a junior partner. Their firm was called Delon, Delon and Tomsky. Amir had joked with him that his firm's initials were DDT, a pesticide, probably very appropriate for a law firm. Amir last saw John when Amir was with the bank in London and John was canvassing for work. Amir decided to contact John Delon and explore whether his firm may be able to help him.

First things first, he said to himself. He must ensure that the folder is safe. Amir locked the folder in his briefcase and walked down to the Milton Keynes Central Railway Station. He had noticed that a WH Smith outlet there had a photocopying machine for public use.

He went there and made two copies of the contents of the folder. He also bought some envelopes and a permanent marker. From there, Amir went to the Milton Keynes Shopping Centre, and after enquiring at a couple of places, he found Milton Keynes Long- & Short-Term Storage. There, he rented a safety locker in his own name. He paid a year's rent in advance and got the key. He put the original folder in the locker and locked it. He carefully noted the locker number in his personal diary and left.

He went to the nearby McDonald's and ordered a Big Mac and coffee. He was hungry. After eating his burger and drinking his coffee, he went to the storage house again. The attendant who dealt with him earlier was apparently out to lunch. There was a different girl on the counter this time.

Amir said he wanted to rent a locker. He completed the form, this time giving his name as Danial Rafi of 16 Half Moon Drive, Milton Keynes. This time he placed one of the copied folders in the locker and again carefully noted the locker number in his diary and stated that it was rented in Danny's name. He was careful not to write the name of the locker company in his diary. He also marked the key with the marker he had purchased, indicating that it was for the locker rented in the name of Danial Rafi and should not be mixed up with the other, which was in his name.

He placed both keys in separate envelopes, marking one envelope with the initial A, indicating that the key belonged to the locker in the name of Amir, and the other envelope with D. Satisfied that the folders were now secure, he returned to Danny's apartment. He still had one copy of the dossier in his briefcase, which he had to safeguard.

When safely in the apartment, Amir phoned the Directory Enquiry and obtained the telephone number of Delon, Delon and Tomsky. He was told that the firm was located at 35B South Audley Street, London. Amir thought they must be doing well; South Audley Street was in Mayfair, one of the most expensive areas of London.

He dialled the number he obtained from the Directory Enquiry.

'Delon, Delon and Tomsky. Good afternoon,' said a modulated voice, almost on the first ring.

'May I speak to Mr. John Delon, please? My name is Amir Ramli and I am a friend of Mr. Delon.' Amir said.

'Hold on, Sir. I'll see if he's in,' said the telephonist.

Almost immediately, a very enthusiastic voice came on the line. 'Amir! What a pleasant surprise. How are you? I heard that you had moved to Pakistan. Are you in London now?'

'I'm fine, John. And you? I'm in London for a short visit and thought to say hello to you. I didn't get around to saying goodbye to you before leaving the last time.'

'I'm fine. The practice is doing well. We now have twelve lawyers and deal with almost all branches of the law. I am specialising in financial law and have most of my clients in the city. Tell me, how long are you here for and will you have time for a meal?' John asked.

'I'm here for the next couple of days. Actually, I wanted to see you on a professional matter and wondered if you might have some time tomorrow morning.' Amir said.

'Professional matter, you say? Music to my ears. G&P Bank has finally decided to pass some work our way, have they? We must be moving up in life. Last I knew, they only dealt with the magic circle firms.' John Delon said.

'It is not for the bank, although it is related to the bank. I'll explain when I see you. So, tell me, when can I see you?' Amir asked.

'If you come at say, 11.30 tomorrow morning, we can discuss business for an hour or so and go out for lunch at a nearby restaurant. There is a very nice Iranian restaurant in South Audley Street called Shehrzad. You don't mind Iranian, do you?'

'I love Iranian food.' Amir replied.

'Okay then. I'll see you tomorrow morning. You know South Audley Street? We are about a hundred metres from the American Embassy if you are coming from Selfridges. There's a newsagent next to our office building.' John said.

'I know South Audley Street. Don't worry, I'll find your offices and see you at 11.30 tomorrow morning.' Amir said, and hung up.

He looked at his watch. It was nearly 3.30 p.m. There was still time before Danny returned. Amir sat down in the sitting room, and while watching TV to kill time, he dozed off. He was tired.

Amir thought he heard somebody saying, 'Hey there, why don't you go to your bedroom and sleep?' He opened his eyes and saw Danny taking off his coat.

'I am tired but don't want to sleep. How was your day?' Amir asked.

'Routine. I have lost interest since the G&P Bank audit fiasco. What is the point of carrying out an audit if the auditors are to accept whatever the client says?' Danny was still angry. 'How was your trip to Germany?'

'Tiring, but very fruitful. It was miserable to see Ursula's parents grieving. They are really suffering. It was fruitful in that Ursula's father gave me the dossier I was looking for.'

'What? You got the dossier? I am sure you have gone through it. Anything interesting?' Danny's curiosity was now piqued.

'Very. You change and we'll sit down and talk about it.' Amir said.

'Give me ten minutes. Why don't you make some tea?' Danny said.

'You'll require something stronger once we are finished but tea is fine to start with. I'll put on the kettle.' Amir said, getting up.

Danny was back a few minutes later. He had changed into the traditional Pakistani dress of *shalwar kameez* (baggy trousers and long loose shirt). He looked relaxed.

'Tell me, what did you find?'

'I'm now almost certain that Richard and Ursula were murdered and the accident was a set-up. You'll agree if you read this.' Amir handed over the folder to Danny.

'It will take time to read. Why don't you give me the gist of what's in it?' After a long day, Danny wanted to avoid reading anything technical.

'There's ironclad evidence to indict G&P Bank's management for criminal activity. It's difficult for me to summarise. I suggest you read it quickly. Don't go through all the supporting documents. Take my word. These are good and will stand up in court. Reading Richard's notes won't take you more than thirty minutes. I'll watch the news while you do that. We need to talk after that.' Amir replied.

Danny was too tired to argue. He took the folder and started reading. Before long, he was engrossed in the file.

'Your tea is getting cold.' Amir said.

'This is dynamite,' Danny said, taking a sip from the cup. He was able to finish reading Richard's narrative within thirty minutes. Even though he didn't go through the attachments and supporting documents, he said, 'This could get people killed.'

'Exactly. This could and did. Remember, the author of this treatise is dead.' Amir replied.

'And Tolbert and Gibbs have just given them a clean bill of health.' Danny lamented.

'Now we know why. We know at least two senior people at Tolbert and Gibbs involved in the audit have been bought.' Amir replied.

'Don't rub it in. You know I was not involved. The Bank went directly to my family.'

'Yes. That's how they play. They find out where you are most vulnerable and attack at your weakest point. Yours was your family. I don't know about Charles Ramsey. And we don't know if these are the only people at Tolbert and Gibbs who have enjoyed the bank's favours. There might be others Richard did not know about.' Amir said.

'Obviously, you've been thinking about this. Where do you want to go from here?' Danny asked.

'Where do I want to go from here? I am alone in this, am I? I had thought you would say let's go after the bastards. We now have evidence in our hands.' Amir was scathing.

'You misunderstand me. I wanted to hear what you have in mind. Of course, I am with you, but everything has to be thought out very carefully.' Danny tried to mollify Amir.

'That we have to do. What do you suggest we should do?' Amir deflected the question back to Danny.

'It won't be easy to take on G&P Bank. They have all the resources, legal and illegal, at their disposal. You and I are very small guys. There might be severe legal implications if we accuse them of wrongdoings that may prove to be incorrect and malicious. They'll fight any allegations we make. In addition, we, we, and our families might be in danger. We are from Pakistan and our families are located there. Don't forget that they have the ability to do almost anything there. You already have experience of their power.

'Personally, I am scared. Believe me, I feel in danger by simply having this folder in our possession. G&P Bank is a rogue bank. So are many others. We cannot go after the whole world. I appreciate that you have a vendetta against them and wouldn't mind risking everything to get them. I suggest that neither you nor I come out in the open to attack them. Perhaps, like Richard had planned, we should pass this information to the press anonymously and let them deal with the bank.' Danny replied.

'Despite his precautions and playing safe, Richard is dead. Killed. Here is what I believe we should do. We should consult a lawyer to advise us how to use this information discreetly and legally to expose the G&P Bank.' Amir replied. 'We need somebody to let us know the exact circumstances of Richard's death. Again, we should speak to a lawyer to see how this may be achieved.

'I've already spoken to a lawyer friend of mine. You might know him. His name is John Delon; he used to be at the Poly with me. He went on to read law and qualified as a lawyer. He's a junior partner with his father and another lawyer in a West End firm. I'm going to see him tomorrow. You are welcome to join, if you wish.' Amir was not happy with Danny's attitude, but he did not show it.

'I'm afraid I can't. You're planning to act against a client of my firm. I'm a senior member of the team working on that engagement. I'd like to help, but I can't be a party to any meetings or overt acts against G&P Bank. I suggest that you also should be very careful. Don't forget that you are working for them.' Danny replied.

'I understand. Let me see this lawyer tomorrow, and we'll work out a strategy for going forward after that.' Amir was not prepared to write off Danny so quickly.

'Please be very careful. What are you going to do with this folder?' Danny asked.

'I'll take it with me tomorrow to the lawyer. We'll see what we can do with it after that.' Amir didn't mention that the original and a copy of the folder were safely locked away.

'I hope nobody has seen you with the folder. These are very dangerous people. You shouldn't expose yourself by going around with it.' Danny was clearly scared.

'Oh, don't worry. Don't forget I brought the folder back from Germany. They don't suspect me at the bank. At least not yet.' Amir assured Danny.

The discussion about the bank ended, and both friends changed the subject to talk about politics and their plans for dinner.

Chapter 26

Meetings in London

Amir knew the UK trains were not among the most punctual in the world, so he started early, keeping a margin for the delays. He reached Euston around 10.30. From there, he took the underground to Bond Street Station and walked to South Audley Street.

He was familiar with South Audley Street since he used to take a train to Green Park and walk from there via South Audley Street to Bond and Oxford Streets for shopping when he was working in London. Amir noted that there was considerably more security around the US embassy, and people with their visa applications were asked to queue outside.

35B South Audley Street was a nineteenth-century house converted into an office building. The building had a shiny brass sign, 'Delon, Delon and Tomsky.' Amir rang the bell at precisely 11.25 a.m. The receptionist inside released the buzzer after taking a good look at Amir from the security camera mounted near the main door.

'Hello. I am here to see Mr. John Delon.' Amir said to the smartly dressed lady at the reception. She was wearing a name tag indicating that her name was Suzy.

'Mr. Amir Ramli?' Suzy asked.

'Yes, that is me.'

'Please, have a seat. Mr. Delon is expecting you. He'll be here in a moment.' She said, pressing some buttons on the console.

A few minutes later, John Delon walked down the stairs.

'Hey, it's nice to see you after such a long time. It's been ages since we met last. Two years?' John shook Amir's hand warmly.

'Yes, it must be. Time flies. How are you doing?'

'Can't complain. The business is good. We're now dealing in almost all the branches of law. I have more or less settled down. I got married last year. The wife works for Barclays Bank in the city. That keeps her busy. And how are you doing?

'I am well and still single. I've recently been promoted by G&P Bank to the vice president's post and asked to go to Geneva.' Amir took off his coat and muffler and placed them on the stand across from the receptionist.

'Well, come on in.' John said, leading Amir to a small meeting room.

After coffee and a little more chat about each other's personal life, Amir came to the point.

'John, I have a serious matter to discuss.'

'I'm all ears. We have an hour and more if we want. Tell me what's bothering you.'

Amir narrated the story, beginning with his problems at Karachi airport to his desire to expose G&P Bank and the findings of the bank's illegal activities. He also told John about the folder Richard Bringsen put together and his suspicion that Richard was killed because of his enquiries into the bank.

John sat through the narrative without making any comment.

Amir handed over Richard's letter and the copy of the folder, which he was carrying in his briefcase. 'This is a copy of the folder put together by Richard Bringsen. The original has been left in a secure place. I would appreciate it if you could only read Richard's memo while I wait. You may look at the copies of the documents Richard has accumulated later. Let me assure you, they are very thorough.'

John Delon took the folder from Amir and engrossed himself in it. While John read, Amir browsed through a copy of the *Financial Times*.

'Interesting. Very Interesting,' John said, closing the folder.

'Is that all you have to say? I'd think that the evidence there is pretty damning.' Amir said.

'Depends on who is looking at this folder and for what purpose. If you want to prosecute G&P Bank, then you require more than what is here. If you want to damage the bank by starting a media campaign against them, there is plenty here. Let's leave your emotions aside and look at the situation objectively.'

'First, your incident at Karachi airport. There is no proof except your word that this happened. And don't forget that you did not immediately blow the whistle. In fact, you continued to cooperate with the bank and were rewarded with a cash bonus and promotion for your efforts, both of which you accepted.

'Next, the accusations made by Richard. Let's start with the secret accounts. Everybody knows that the Swiss have numbered private accounts and they bend over backward to protect the details of their customers. The Swiss law is designed to provide maximum secrecy to the banks' clients in Switzerland. We all know that there are a lot of ill-gotten funds lying with Swiss banks. There are funds deposited by the Nazis still kept there safely, and we are talking about the major Swiss banks. The only place you might accuse the bank of wrongdoings in connection with the management of secret accounts is in the Swiss courts. You'd have to prove that the bank was violating the Swiss banking laws. I think it would probably be impossible to win against G&P Bank in Switzerland. In fact, I suspect the whole banking industry in Switzerland will be up in arms to defend the secrecy procedures allowed to banks in Switzerland.

'Let's talk now about the money laundering operations undertaken by the bank. It's done cleverly. They ensure there are transactions of purchase and sale of high-value items and the Swiss taxes are paid properly. It will be very difficult to prove that the money for the original purchase came in through couriers, and let's face it, a lot of funds fly around the world in suitcases.

'As for the transactions for the purchase of ships by this company, TIG, I suspect transactions like this take place every day. However, these are very difficult to prove because the paper trail is usually impeccable in these transactions.

'In all the transactions narrated by Richard, it'll be very difficult to prove that any Swiss laws were violated. Laws of certain other countries might have been violated, but the bank is probably powerful in those countries and nobody may be interested in taking any action against the bank. Countries like Panama and Nigeria are very capable of taking action when they want to.

'We also know that politicians and government officials in a lot of countries enjoy gifts and accept gratuities. Nothing new in that. As far as the loan to a partner of Tolbert and Gibbs is concerned, it's probably in violation of UK laws and the ethical standards set out by the Institute of Chartered Accountants. It would, however, appear that it is Mr. Ramsey who is guilty in accepting a loan from a client. If there was a complaint in the UK, the UK Institute of Chartered Accountants would probably act against him and Tolbert and Gibbs. I'm not sure if the bank would face any serious consequences except maybe some embarrassment. The bank might get into outright trouble with several authorities if it were proven that they were involved in falsifying the records and wrong financial reporting. You would, however, require more information and evidence for taking this further.'

Amir was crestfallen. He believed there was sufficient material in the folder to nail the bank and its management. John said that most of the accusations were difficult to prove and more evidence was required.

'So, there is no case against the bank.' Amir said.

'I didn't say that. Let's decide which countries' laws the bank may have violated. You should concentrate on the Western countries only, as other countries may not be interested in pursuing the bank's wrongdoings unless there is political capital to be earned by the current rulers in those countries. Once you know which countries' laws have been violated, you gather enough evidence so a case may be made against the bank in the courts in those countries.

'I think you have a lot of material here but you need to be more systematic about this and get more information. You always have the option to go to the media with this information. They might publish it or they might not. You can never be sure of the outcome of media mud-slinging as people tend to discard stories of commercial scandals unless they are personally affected.'

'What about the murder of Richard Bringsen?' Amir asked.

'You don't know for sure that he was murdered. The German police are investigating the matter, and there are pretty good professionals out there. You may, however, initiate enquiries of your own if you wish to do so. It may cost money, though.'

'How?'

'I know a private investigator who might make enquiries beyond the routine police procedures. He could get a background check on the Driver of the lorry and the witnesses. If you wish, I can speak to him to see what he can do and ask for an estimate of his fee.'

'I'd like to do that. How else can you help me? I know G&P Bank is a rogue institution playing with the lives of people working with them and the assets of their customers. I have personally suffered. I want to stop them.'

'You want some free advice? Give up this madness. It may cost you a lot, both personally and financially. As you yourself said, they won't stop at anything. Yours and your family's lives may be at risk. If you don't like them, leave them, and let the government agencies responsible for dealing with bank fraud tackle them. However, if you cannot let it pass then you should handle this matter in a different way.

'You should analyse how the bank has violated the laws and business norms of each of the countries in which they are operating in and how seriously those violations would be perceived in the respective countries. For this purpose, as I said earlier, you should concentrate on the Western countries.

'For example, the UK environment is like the proverbial ostrich. They keep their heads in the sand until the problem becomes a public scandal. For the British public, fiduciary trust and fairness are the cornerstones of a bank's business. They cannot abide cheating. If you were to prove that the bank was cheating its depositors, involved in bribery of government officials, or knowingly violating banking laws, then it may get action. In any case, the wheels of the British bureaucracy move very slowly.

'Swiss are another matter. If you were to prove that G&P Bank was involved in illegal and improper dealings that could harm the reputation and credibility of the Swiss banking system, they would be ruthless in dealing with the bank.

'It's a pity the bank doesn't have operations or involvement in any illegal dealings in the USA, although I believe, given your description of the bank's activities, they'll definitely have dealings with the US government agencies like the CIA. The CIA is known to use these unsavoury organisations for its clandestine activities. I'm sure at some point, the bank has been used by the CIA. One established pattern of the CIA's behaviour is that they will go to bed with anybody who may be useful to them, and then destroy that individual or entity once their objective has been achieved. They do it as part of their house cleaning to avoid any comebacks.

'If possible, you should find out if G&P Bank has violated any US laws or been involved with any of the US clandestine agencies. In both cases, G&P Bank's demise would almost be a certainty.' For a young lawyer, John had a lot of depth and showed a considerable grasp of the matter at hand.

'You've seen the folder, and you obviously believe it is not good enough for us to proceed against the bank.' Amir replied.

'I'm not saying that. I suggest you analyse the information in the folder to see which country's laws have been violated and then decide whether the information you have there would be sufficient for a court of law in that country to take action against the bank or its management.

'As a lawyer in the UK, I'd say there is not sufficient information in the folder for a UK court to take action against the bank in the UK. Indeed, the information would create a stink if it were published in a newspaper, but that might not achieve much. The newspapers would also be wary of publishing anything they could not defend in court; in case they are charged with defamation. You'd need to get more on the operations conducted out of the UK to prove the bank is operating improperly within the UK.

'I am not a Swiss law expert, but I expect some Swiss laws may have been violated. You may need to consult a Swiss lawyer to determine if you need to go to the Swiss authorities with this information. I can give you a contact in a law firm in Geneva. Swiss lawyers are expensive. You'll have to watch where you are going.

'You said that you are being transferred to Geneva. Your friend Richard Bringsen was in Geneva, and you believe his death was arranged by the bank's Geneva branch. I am concerned about your safety, especially if the bank catches you snooping for information.'

Amir was firm in his position. 'As of now, I have only one goal: to hit G&P Bank. I'll be careful. I have hidden the original folder in a safe place. I'd like to leave this copy with you and you can do whatever you consider appropriate if you hear that I have died an unnatural death. Can you keep this folder in a safe place for me?'

'Sure, I can. I'll store it with client documents. You'll have to sign an engagement contract with us and give me a fee in order to be listed as our client. I'll also need instructions in writing from you detailing how to deal with the papers you leave with us. I can organise the paperwork very quickly. My secretary can prepare everything while we go have lunch.' John said, getting up.

*****

Shehrzad was an authentic Iranian restaurant. Amir ordered chelo kebab with saffron rice. John ordered the same. Both asked for the traditional yoghurt Drink. As was the custom, the waiter brought them complimentary uncut salad and vegetable soup called shorba and freshly baked Iranian bread. The kebab and rice were delicious.

After lunch, they walked back to John's office. His secretary was waiting with the papers for Amir to sign. They included a letter of engagement laying down the terms of appointment of Delon, Delon and Tomsky as the lawyers of Amir Ramli, powers of attorney to the partners of the firm to represent Amir in any matter that required them to attend to protect Amir's interest with any government agency or courts in the UK or elsewhere in the world. There was a letter from Amir giving complete protection and immunity from damages to the law firm in dealing with any matters on his behalf.

'My God, you guys know how to protect yourselves. I suppose there is no other choice.' Amir remarked.

'These are the usual forms. Don't worry about the immunity. It's only a form. A UK court would probably hang us if you suffered a grievous injury because of our failure to act on your behalf in a proper manner. I need these papers in order to enlist you as a client of the firm.' John explained.

Amir signed the papers.

'You must give me an advance of, say, five hundred pounds just to indicate that this is a serious fee-paying engagement and not pro bono work. Again, this is in accordance with the norms here.' John said.

Amir handed over ten fifty-pound notes to John. John handed the money and signed papers to his secretary, who quickly returned with a receipt and copies of the documents signed by Amir.

John then asked his secretary to bring a thick manila envelope. He took the folder from Amir and placed it in the envelope. On impulse, Amir took the key for the locker obtained in Danny's name and put it in the envelope. John saw him do this, but he didn't say anything.

Once Amir was finished, John sealed the envelope with the firm's official stamp. He attached a memo on the top that stated the envelope was to be opened only by Amir, or if instructed in writing by Amir, or if anything were to happen to Amir. He went to a large safe in his father's office and together with his father, he placed the envelope in the safe.

'Well, the documents you gave me have now been safely stored. Thinking further, I believe it may be possible for me to do something. The Securities and Investments Board, commonly known as SIB, attached to the Bank of England, would be the first agency to investigate if there were any indication of a bank's involvement in improper operations. They are generally slow but very diligent.

'In case of a crime, Scotland Yard would have to be involved. In case of frauds and crimes involving financial wrongdoings, the Serious Fraud Office investigates potential wrongdoings. The Serious Fraud Office would file charges and initiate action in case of bank fraud and similar crimes.

'A very senior official at the Securities and Investments Board attached to the Bank of England, a fellow by the name of David

Ringbutton, is a good friend of Dad. If you want, I could meet him and sound him out to see what he advises.'

'That would be very useful but we don't want the cat out of the bag prematurely.'

'No. I would tell Ringbutton that I heard rumours that there were problems at G&P Bank and that the bank might be involved in financial fraud. Of course, he might not tell me anything, but on the other hand, he might know something himself and point us in the right direction.'

'I don't see any harm in it as long is Mr. Ringbutton is not in the bank's pay.' Amir said.

'I don't think he is the type. He's one of those civil servants who likes a quiet life and spends time with his wife, tending his garden in Surrey.'

'Please go ahead. How will you let me know what he says?'

'That's another question I wanted to ask you. How do you suggest we stay in touch?'

'I'll give you the contact number and address of my friend, Danial Rafi, Danny. He'll be able to pass the message to me. I'll make the necessary arrangements for direct communication between us, once I get to Switzerland. Let me give you Danny's contact details.' Amir wrote down Danny's name, address and telephone number.

'You still want to find out about the accident in Germany?'

'Yes, please.'

'Okay, I'll speak to this private investigator friend of mine. His name is Ian Softsol. He is anything but soft. I'll authorise a fee of five hundred pounds for his efforts. You'd better give me another five hundred if you have it on you. The firm doesn't give credit to clients.'

'The accident happened at Speyer, a small town in Germany, near the Swiss border on 2 January. The name of the lorry driver is Ahmet Gulay. He's Turkish,' Amir said as he handed another ten notes of fifty over to John. This time, the receipt indicated that the payment was for the clients' monies account. 'I have taken a lot of your time. I should get going. I'll try to get as much information as possible as suggested by you and contact you when I'm ready. In the meantime, please do whatever you can.' Amir stood up.

'I'll follow up on this thing with David Ringbutton and Ian Softsol, and I'll pass on messages to you through your friend, Danny. You'd better take my home number and my dad's direct number. These will come in handy in case you need to urgently contact me and are not able to get through.' John wrote the telephone numbers on a piece of paper.

Amir pocketed the paper, shook hands with John, and walked out to the street. He felt calm and soothed. He had taken steps to further his quest against G&P Bank and had engaged a very competent lawyer to help him. He had now a clear direction for proceeding further. He'd need a plan to get the information required without getting caught.

Amir walked through South Audley Street at a leisurely pace, as he had time on his hands. He went into the bookshop opposite Selfridges on Oxford Street. There, he browsed through the new arrivals section and purchased a couple of thrillers. After he left the bookshop, he took the underground from Bond Street to Euston. At Euston, he found out that the train for Milton Keynes was almost ready to leave. He was at Danny's apartment in Milton Keynes around five-thirty.

Back in the apartment, Amir changed and brewed himself a cup of tea. He was just making himself comfortable in front of the television when Danny walked in.

'Hi.' Danny said.

'Hi. I won't ask how your day was. Routine, right?'

'Right. Bloody boring these days. You seem relaxed. Had a good day?'

'Yes. I went and met this chap, John Delon. He's good. Very good. He carefully reviewed the information and gave me some useful suggestions.'

'Didn't he advise you to drop it?' Danny asked.

'He did, but I was not to be dissuaded. He has taken me as his client and told me what to do to succeed. I've also asked him to make some enquiries for me. He'll send you the information; we both agreed that sending the information to Geneva wouldn't be wise.'

'So, I'm involved now. Well, I suppose I should get involved seeing how these people operate.' Danny said.

'I'm delighted to hear it. The information you might be able to provide will be invaluable.' Amir said, and then he briefed Danny about his discussion with John.

'He's right. We must proceed systematically per the laws of evidence and sensitivities in each country. I'll try to see what's available in the audit files, which could help us in presenting a case to the authorities in the UK.' Danny looked excited.

'It'll be very useful. I think I'll have to visit London regularly if we want to take this matter in the right direction. I don't want you to come to Geneva and be exposed to the bank's thugs there.' Amir replied.

'What are your plans now?'

'I'll return to Karachi by PIA tomorrow and wait for my Swiss work permit there. I'll also have to go to Bangkok at the beginning of February to attend the bank's senior staff conference. That'll be the first time for me. I'll be very interested to hear the bullshit propaganda fed to everyone there by the top management.' Amir said.

'Bangkok will be nice in February.'

'I hope so. I've never been there. I understand it's a very nice and friendly town.' Amir shifted back to explaining his plan. 'I have given your name to John Delon. I suggest you speak to him to establish contact. I'll work out a system to stay in touch with you once I'm in Geneva. It would be tremendous if you could get information against the bank that would be considered actionable by the UK authorities.' Amir said.

Danny was feeling angry toward his employers, just like Amir was angry with his. 'I would like Tolbert and Gibbs to go down with them for their reckless attitude in issuing audit clearance to G&P Bank. I'm sure that G&P Bank is not alone. There are surely other clients getting similar favourable treatment by our great firm, but let's concentrate on their relationship with G&P Bank.'

'Good. Let us pray that we succeed in unmasking this bunch of crooks.' Amir replied.

Chapter 27

Lagos, Nigeria

Habib came to the bank at eight in the morning, as was his custom. It has been almost two weeks since the murder of Abdu Ovululu. The pressure had eased on the bank since the bank's clients were assured that their assets were safe and the bank would carry out their instructions for reimbursing the loss.

Habib and his team of senior staff were, however, still very nervous. Their passports were still with the authorities and the staff did not speak freely over the telephone. They had developed codes for normal communication among themselves. Nothing was routine anymore.

The only thing making life bearable for Habib in this situation was his relationship with Sosu, even though he had previously decided his troubles were because of his relationship with her, he could not stay away. She looked after him in every possible way. She was a mother, wife, whore and barmaid, all rolled up into one. She knew how to make Habib happy, in and out of bed. Habib had also returned to drinking, despite his vow never to touch the stuff. He believed he would go mad if he did not have Sosu and the bottle.

The bank had paid fifty percent of the agreed fee to Tarimo Akpaka on time. Tarimo was happy and was working hard to resolve the problem. The bank had yet to confirm that the missing eighty million US dollars were deposited, as instructed by the Nigerian clients. Habib had made several calls to Azhar Alam, beseeching him to expedite the deposit, but after the initial show of support, there was very little action from the bank's management.

Habib was at his desk, trying to keep busy. He had read the major newspapers and the mail brought in by the bank's messenger. He was now looking at the branch's financial summary for the previous day, this was produced by the staff at the close of every day.

He was shaken out of his feigned interest in the balance sheet by the telephone's ringing. It was too early for a bank customer to call. A call at this early hour was ominous.

'Yes?' Habib picked up the phone.

'This is Tarimo. How are you?'

'I am okay. Bearing up. And you?'

'I wish I could say the same. I'm calling you on this number because I do not have time. Your people have not delivered to both, us and the clients. I understand there will now be action against you and the bank. I'm trying very hard to stave off the action for at least a few more days, but the client is adamant that either your side keeps its word or you all face the music. In view of the urgency, I tried to call your superiors, but the boss does not appear interested in talking to me. You'd better speak to them and let me know within an hour,' Tarimo said and put the phone down.

Despite the air conditioning, Habib started sweating heavily. Beads of perspiration were forming on his forehead. He had to talk to Azhar Alam.

As a matter of precaution, Habib never called Karachi from his official telephone but today he decided that, under the circumstances, he did not have the luxury of going out and finding another telephone. He dialled Azhar's direct number.

Samira picked up the phone. 'Hello, Azhar Alam's office.'

'This is Habib Jalil from Lagos. I have a crisis here. I need to speak to the boss immediately.' Habib sounded panic-stricken.

'Mr. Alam is in London. It's too early for a call to London. Should I give him a message that you called?' Samira, ever protective of her boss, asked.

'No, I don't care whether it is day or night in London. I must speak to Azhar Alam now. Please understand that this is a grave emergency.' Habib was screaming into the phone.

'Okay, Sir. I'll give you his hotel contact number in London. I hope he won't get upset with me for waking him up early.' Samira said, and gave a number to Habib.

'Hello,' a groggy voice, obviously that of Azhar Alam, still in bed, said at the other end when Habib called the London number.

'Sir, this is Habib from Lagos. I am sorry to wake you but this is an emergency.'

'You know it is still very early here in London. I hope you have a good reason for calling me here at this hour.' Azhar was not happy about being woken up.

'Sir, I just got a call from our adviser, who said that we have not kept our side of the bargain, and therefore an action by the client was imminent.' Habib tried to be as circumspect as possible.

Azhar was now fully awake and alert. 'We released the initial consignment. There were some difficulties that caused a delay. Tell your clients that we will try to complete the transaction as soon as possible.'

'Sir, I have been asked to report within one hour. I believe the client will not buy the "as soon as possible" assurance.' Habib had a very sick feeling in his stomach.

'Okay. Tell them we will take action in the next twenty-four hours and at least make the initial fee and loss good. And don't panic. These things happen. We are doing our best to sort out the matters.' Azhar sounded as if he were chastising Habib for not being able to handle the situation without bothering him.

After putting the phone down, Habib felt very angry. Here he was, facing some of the most vicious individuals who had the power to make him disappear from this planet, and Mr. Azhar Alam was annoyed at being woken up early while on a junket in London.

'To hell with the bank and Mr. Azhar Alam and Sheikh Tayeb. I'll be out of this brothel as soon as this matter is sorted out.' Habib muttered to himself.

He called Tarimo Akpaka. 'Tarimo, I spoke to the boss. Your request will be acceded to within the next forty-eight hours. The boss apologised for the delay due to his absence from the centre. He is in London at present.'

'Look, you came to me with a problem. I agreed to help. You must now keep your side of the bargain. My reputation and my contact's reputation are at stake here. I will try to talk the clients out of taking immediate action but forty-eight hours is the absolute maximum time you will get. Don't blame me if this does not work.' Tarimo said, and hung up.

Habib was shaken. He was angry at the bank management's callous attitude toward the problem. They knew the situation was precarious and you do not renege on your word to Nigerian customers. These people were serious.

He picked up his jacket and left the office.

Chapter 28

Bangkok, Thailand

Amir arrived in Bangkok on Saturday morning before the start of the conference on Monday. He had heard so much about Thailand and its capital city that he wanted to see a little of the country.

The Royal Thai Airways flight from Karachi landed at 8.30 a.m. at Don Mueang International Airport, located thirty kilometres from the city. Being a business class passenger, Amir was cleared quickly. He was impressed with the number of people inside the terminal; it was busier than a railway station in some of the European or Asian cities. Amir had learnt that it was probably one of the oldest airports in the world, the second busiest in Asia and the eighteenth busiest in the world. Large jumbo jets were landing every few minutes, disgorging passengers from everywhere. And this was not the normal tourist season in Thailand for European tourists. Amir could imagine why the airport was not sufficient to cope with the traffic during the busy season. He knew a huge new state-of-the-art airport to be called Suvarnabhumi International Airport was being built. It was expected to take a few years before it would be ready.

Bangkok is notorious for its traffic jams. Amir saw why. Coming out of the terminal, he got into a waiting taxi and asked the Driver to take him to Bangkok Grande Hotel on Charoemakoru Road. He was told that this luxury hotel was by the riverside and within the shopping district of Bangkok.

The taxi made slow progress toward the city centre. The only road connecting the city with the airport was completely clogged. This same road served other outer districts also and was a nightmare during rush hour traffic. The taxi driver was friendly. Very friendly.

'Why are you staying at Grande? I can suggest some very good hotels at a much lower price.' He offered.

'I like Grande.' Amir replied curtly.

'Grande is good. You will like it there.' The Driver immediately changed his tactic.

After going a few metres further, he produced a photo album and handed it over to Amir. 'Nice Thai girls. Ready for massage, companionship and fun. You select, Boss. Not expensive. Don't want too much money. Make you happy.'

'No, thanks. I have friends of my own here.' Amir handed back the album without opening it.

'You want to see Bangkok, Boss? I will take you around. Show you all the places. Take you out for shopping. Take you to good shops with reasonable prices. Also, take you to nice restaurants. Good food. Cheap. I do not charge much.' The taxi Driver was persistent and did not want to lose a business opportunity.

'No, thank you. I told you; I have friends here.' Amir replied.

Amir was tired from the overnight flight and was in no mood to respond to the overtures of the taxi driver. He shut his eyes. The driver got the hint and drove the rest of the way in silence. It took almost two hours to get to the hotel. It was an imposing thirty-three storey building. The reception area was large with several counters for checking in. The hotel was bustling with guests. Apparently, many tourists from nearby Asian countries, like Malaysia and Indonesia, visited Thailand at this time of the year.

Amir's check-in details were ready, all organised by the efficient events management agency. Bangkok was geared to look after visitors. Their hospitality was phenomenal. Others talked about their traditional hospitality, but real hospitality was found in Thailand.

Amir was quickly escorted to his room by a beautiful Thai hostess dressed in a traditional Thai dress. He had a room on the club floor with a fantastic view of the Chao Phraya River and the shopping district. There were several tourist boats plying on the river. It was a tribute to the enterprise of the Thai people that Bangkok was ranked as the world's seventeenth tallest city with almost one thousand skyscrapers. The city hummed with activity.

Amir had read that Bangkok had another old name that was not even remembered by the residents of Bangkok. Its short Thai name was *Krung Thep Mahanakhon,* which meant *The City of Angels.* It became the capital of Siam (The original name of Thailand) in the eighteenth century following the destruction of Ayutthaya

Once in his room, Amir quickly changed and lay down. He snoozed for a couple of hours and got up fresh and ready to explore Bangkok. It was lunchtime, but he was not hungry. It was still too early for lunch according to Karachi time.

To overcome his jet lag, Amir decided to eat something and then go out. He went down to the coffee shop and ordered a sandwich. After his light lunch, he went to the concierge and asked about the places he should visit in Bangkok.

He was offered packaged tours leaving from the hotel every hour. Amir declined and asked if there were any places he could visit on his own. He was told that the Grand Palace was not far and should be visited. In the Grand Palace, there were several temples called *Wat* in the Thai language. Wat Phra Kaew temple was also known as the Temple of The Emerald Buddha, carved out of dark green jade. The Emerald Buddha was revered by Buddhists and there were always people visiting Wat Phra Kaew.

He was also told that he may take a cruise on the canal, which would take him to Wat Arun, known as The Temple of Dawn. People climbed to the top of this conical shaped temple. On his way back, he may visit Wat Pho, which housed The Reclining Buddha.

Amir left the hotel and hailed a taxi. He went to the Grand Palace. It was an impressive structure. He bought the entrance ticket at the higher price for foreigners, got an English guide for the palace, and went in. There were several temples within the grounds, including Wat Phra Kaew and Wat Traimit. Wat Traimit housed a three-meter-high statue of Buddha made of 5.5 tons of pure gold. Amir also visited other buildings used by the king for various ceremonies. Then, he visited the historical arms and jewellery museums, which housed the arms and jewellery historically used over the centuries in Thailand.

After spending a couple of hours in the Grand Palace, Amir went out to the pier and hired a boat for a cruise on the canal. The boat stopped at Wat Arun, a complex of ancient temples. The most important of those was the Dawn Temple. It is a temple built like a conical tower with stairs to the top. Amir tried to climb to the top but he returned after climbing only three-fourths of the way.

His cruise ended at Wat Pho, which housed a huge statue of reclining Buddha in gold. Amir was impressed with the minute details in the sculpture. He was told that the statues of Buddha showed different body shapes depending upon where they were made. Those made in Thailand were slim and had intricate hair patterns. The statues from China and Korea showed a more rounded Buddha without hair.

After completing his visit to Wat Pho, Amir found an auto-rickshaw called *tuk-tuk* to take him to the hotel. He negotiated hard for the fare. The tuk-tuk was stuck in Bangkok traffic, and it took him over an hour to reach the hotel. The gatekeeper at the hotel was impressed. 'You travelled by Bangkok Ferrari.' He spoke.

'Yes. They are fun to ride in.' Amir replied. Appreciating the frustration of driving in Bangkok, he gave a good tip to the tuk-tuk Driver.

After a full day of sightseeing, Amir was tired. He returned to his room and slumped in the bed.

It was 9.30 p.m. Bangkok time when Amir finally opened his eyes. He was hungry. He quickly got up, showered, changed, and went downstairs to find something to eat. In the cafeteria, he ordered a light Thai meal of tom yum soup, boiled catfish and thick rice. He loved Thai food; it was so tasty.

After the meal, Amir wandered outside the hotel. The street was full of people. About half a kilometre from the hotel, there was a small shrine by the roadside with a statue of Buddha. Hearing some music, Amir walked into the area around the statue. There, a troupe of eight dancers and musicians were singing hymns to the Buddha. There was a price list indicating the amount charged for the length of the hymns sung. People came in and booked the time at a special counter and joined the troupe when their turn to sing the hymn came around. Amir was very impressed with this cultural activity blended with religion.

Amir returned to the hotel around 11.30 p.m. and ran into Rehmallah, who was coming from the opposite direction, holding the hand of a young, scantily dressed Thai girl. She looked hardly sixteen. 'Assalam Alaikum.' Rehmallah said with a grin when he saw Amir.

'Waalekum Assalam. How are you?' Amir said politely.

'As you see, I could not be better. I'm enjoying myself. Bangkok is a fun city. Rehana wanted to come with me, but I said no. I told her I would be busy in meetings. Only a fool would bring his wife with him here. And, how are you? I hope you are also enjoying yourself.' Rehmallah was obviously drunk.

'Yes, I'm enjoying Bangkok. It's a lovely city. I've been out the whole day; I'm tired now and will go to my room and sleep.' Amir replied.

'Sleep? Sleep in Bangkok at 11.30? You must be crazy. It's time to wake up. Meet Chhaya. She is lovely. Gives you a very good massage and knows how to please you in other ways as well. She's going to keep me up the whole night. Won't you, Chhaya?' He said, turning to the girl.

'Yes. Of course. I will make you very happy tonight.' Chhaya replied.

'Chhaya may ask one of her friends to look after you. Enjoy, young man. You won't get these opportunities often.' Rehmallah said.

'Thank you for the offer, but I am really tired. I have no energy left. Enjoy yourself.' Amir turned away in disgust.

'Good night, then. Chhaya and I should also be going to my room soon.' Rehmallah said, rubbing his cheek against that of the Thai girl.

Amir went to the elevator. He was surprised to find several other people from G&P Bank waiting there, hand-in-hand with young Thai girls. They all appeared to be heavily drunk, except one or two, who smiled at Amir sheepishly; the others ignored him.

Amir now understood what Rehana meant when she complained about Rehmallah's hypocrisy. He wanted his family to behave in the normal life and isolated from the world while he did whatever he liked.

Amir slept like a baby and got up around nine the next morning. He got ready and went down for breakfast. The variety of food available impressed him. There were at least a dozen types of fruits and every type of food one could dream of. Amir enjoyed his breakfast; he did not see any of the people he had met the previous night. They were probably still in bed with their companions.

After breakfast, Amir went to the concierge and asked for suggestions for going out for the day. The concierge advised that if Amir had time, he might visit the floating market at Damnernsaduak Rajburi. At the floating market, people sell goods loaded on boats, and customers buy merchandise while sitting in boats. The concierge also suggested that on his way back, Amir might also see the rose garden, a lovely spot where an elephant show was presented. The trip would, however, take five to six hours.

Amir decided he would be too tired if he were to go out again for several hours in the heat. The temperature in Bangkok was around thirty degrees Celsius that day.

The concierge then suggested that Amir might walk around and visit several shopping malls, called plazas, in the area, all selling a variety of merchandise. There were nice restaurants in these shopping plazas that catered to all tastes. In the afternoon, Amir might want to visit the famous Chatuchak weekend market, the concierge added.

Amir decided to take this second suggestion and walked out in the direction of a shopping plaza, as directed by the concierge. He found that the shops in the plaza were in no way inferior in variety of brands available or décor and facilities to any of the big shopping malls and departmental stores in the West. After moving around a bit and picking up a few items on impulse, Amir went into a Chinese restaurant and ordered a hot and sour soup, Szechuan shrimps and egg fried rice. The food was delicious. He noted the prices were also very reasonable, almost one-fourth of what he would pay in London for a much inferior meal.

That afternoon, Amir hailed a taxi and went to Chatuchak weekend market. It was an amazing sight. Thousands and thousands of small stalls were spread over an area of several kilometres. Every type of merchandise one could think of was available. There were several hundred stalls selling handicrafts, textile, shoes, household items and even furniture. Many stalls carried fakes of international brands, including shoes, dresses, bags and watches. Amir noted many tourists happily buying copy Cartier and Rolex watches and wearing them proudly. He bought a couple of handicraft items. The market was full of people. Many of them were just walking about and buying food items and snacks. There were several Buddhist groups singing hymns and asking for alms. Amir also found a very young girl dressed in traditional Thai attire and dancing to the music played by a boy not much older than her, probably her brother. Amir gave them a few hundred baht.

After spending almost three hours in the market, Amir was tired and decided to return to the hotel. He did not want to confront the crowd he met yesterday. He was embarrassed seeing them drunk with very young girls. He entered the hotel from the side door and took the elevator directly to the guest floors.

Amir found a large folder lying on his bed. It contained the conference programme. According to the agenda, the conference would start at 9 a.m. and continue until 5.30 p.m. In the evening, there was dinner with traditional Thai entertainment, which Amir thought could be classic Thai dances or nude Thai girls gyrating at the beat of Western music. The second day was going to be relatively lighter, starting at 9.30 a.m. and finishing at 1 p.m. The dress code throughout the conference was smart casual.

The folder also contained the list of delegates. There were nearly two hundred delegates from G&P Bank's branches all over the world.

Chapter 29

Bangkok, Thailand: G&P Bank Conference

Amir had an early breakfast and headed to the royal ballroom reserved for the conference half an hour before the start time. There were already many people mingling with cups of coffee in the foyer. Amir went to the registration desk, where he was given a name tag that read Vice President, Geneva.

He went into the ballroom and put his stuff on a chair nearer the exit and returned to the foyer to meet other people. He grabbed an Americano coffee and went around saying hello to the assembled colleagues. Most of them did not know him, and Amir had to introduce himself. Some of the people he said hello to were those waiting outside the elevator with young companions the previous evening. The conversation mostly revolved around three topics: how nice and joyful Bangkok was, the pride in the success of G&P Bank, and how G&P Bank was beating the high street Western banks at their own game.

At five minutes before nine, a hotel boy went around with a bell, urging everybody to go into the ballroom. At 9 a.m. sharp, all the lights in the ballroom, except those marking exits, were switched off. Suddenly, a beam of light illuminated the centre of the stage, where Sheikh Tayeb was standing with his head bowed down and his hands clasped in the Thai-style greeting. The whole room stood up and clapped and cheered.

After staying in that posture for a minute or so, Sheikh Tayeb straightened up and said, 'I bowed to say thank you for making the G&P Bank what it is today. G&P Bank is the world's greatest bank.'

A thunder of claps roared from the audience.

'Before I say more, let us thank Allah for making this success possible. I ask Qari Amjad Wani to recite verses from the Holy Quran to offer our thanks to Allah.' Sheikh stepped down from the stage, and the *maulana* (religious scholar) stepped onto the stage where a chair and microphone were placed for him.

The maulana recited from the first chapter of the Holy Quran, which praises Allah for His kindnesses and blessings, confirms allegiance to Him and seeks His help to tread on the straight path and not on the ways of those who went astray. After the recitation, the maulana left the stage, and again, the room went dark.

All of a sudden, the stage turned pink from the coloured lights and turned hazy with smoke. The side door of the stage opened, and two people dressed in traditional Indian attire entered with bugles. They were followed by six strong barefooted men dressed in loose flowing baggy pants and headgear carrying a paladin. On the paladin sat Sheikh Tayeb in a golden robe and golden turban studded with colourful beads. He was holding the stem of a red rose in his hands. Four other men walked behind the paladin with a golden throne, which was set in the centre of the stage.

The paladin was set down by the side of the throne. Two young girls in traditional Thai dress rushed to lead Sheikh Tayeb to the throne. The paladin bearers quickly exited with the paladin. The girls went behind the throne and stood there with their hands clasped. Sheikh Tayeb waved at the assembly and the ballroom exploded with clapping.

Sheikh Tayeb waved everybody down and started speaking. 'I am again privileged to welcome you today. This attire and atmosphere are to emphasise our origins and glory.

The room still roared with clapping.

Sheikh Tayeb continued. 'As every economist would tell you, money is not the means in itself. It is a tool to achieve certain objectives. Every society in the world is against the hoarding of money. Money is to be circulated and invested for the economic betterment of people. If money is hoarded, it will serve no purpose at all.

'We are fortunate. We are fortunate that we have succeeded in creating G&P Bank to channel the money sitting idle in the coffers of rich people. We are trusted by the wealthy of this world who still have a conscious because they accept that we are a bank with a conscious. Ours is a noble mission.

'As you should already be aware, your bank has achieved very good financial results. This means rewards for all of you. You could not ask for more in life. You are being rewarded with huge financial and social benefits for doing a noble job. The job for which there will also be a reward hereafter. You are involved in bettering the economic life of millions of people who are benefiting from the financial services provided by you, which bring economic benefits to the businesses who would otherwise not get any financial support because of the rules created by the greedy, bloodsucking financiers serving their greedy masters and themselves.

'What we have achieved to date is good but not sufficient to make us world leaders. Our aim is to be the largest bank in the world... bigger than all of them. This can only happen with your hard work and dedication. Please promise that you all will work harder and get us to the summit of the banking world.' He asked the audience.

'Yes! We will!' The whole room boomed in unison.

'Then I promise that G&P Bank will be the world's largest bank in three years' time. I promise!' Sheikh Tayeb bellowed.

The whole room again erupted in thunderous clapping.

'It is not going to be easy. The reason we are congregating here today is not to sit on our laurels but to plan for the future. To plan for G&P Bank to grow to be the biggest bank in the world in every respect: by deposits, capital and reserves, profit, customer base, and the number of branches; by every key performance indicator applied to measure a modern bank.

'The path to get there will be difficult. We will have to be daring and innovative. But, the ideas to get there will come from you, as you know your business more than anybody else.

'We will spend today in groups and come out with a plan to achieve our objective. We will divide into five groups, as shown on the screens.' Immediately, the screens around the stage illuminated to show the following groups:

1. Growing Our Deposit Base
    a. Attract new clients

      b. New products to increase our business from existing clients

      c. Improve our relationship with key business leaders

2. Interest-Free Banking
3. New Markets: Development of Strategies to Enter the Following Markets:
      a. China
      b. India
      c. Brazil
      d. South Korea
      e. Thailand
      f. Vietnam
4. Planning to Deal with The Increasing Regulatory Constraints In:
      a. Switzerland
      b. USA
      c. UK
      d. European Community
5. Preparing Against the Political and Sovereign Risks in Some of The Countries We Operate
      a. Political environment
      b. Attitude of the key players
      c. Possible financial and other costs to the bank

'Each of the above groups will be led by a senior executive vice president and member of the board. We have assigned people for each of the groups mentioned above according to their specialisation and affiliation. The groups will divide into sub-groups as appropriate. A considerable amount of background material has already been prepared, which will be handed over to each group at the beginning of their session.

'We will now break for coffee for thirty minutes. After the coffee break, all five groups will go into their assigned rooms and deliberate on the topics given to them.

'Lunch will be at the main dining hall at 1 p.m. Today's session will officially end at 5.30 p.m., but individual groups might find it necessary to stay on for longer.

'At the end of the day's session, each group will prepare a presentation for the plenary session, to be presented by the group leaders tomorrow.

'We have booked Siam Yacht Club for dinner and after-dinner entertainment. Buses will leave from the hotel at 7.30 p.m. There will be a Thai food dinner followed by a cultural show by Thai artists.'

Slowly, people started getting up and walking out of the ballroom. Amir also walked out with everybody to the foyer, where coffee was served.

In the foyer, Amir talked to a few people. All were full of praise for the morning session and the vision shown by Sheikh Tayeb. They were all fired up.

They seriously believed that they could beat the world's major banks and achieve the position of the world's biggest bank. Amir felt sorry for their naiveté. He knew the bank was not very healthy and there were issues that might, very seriously, affect the bank's existence. Achieving the position of the world's largest bank was nothing more than a pipe dream and was misleading.

He also found the morning session a little amusing. The pomp and regal presentation with which Sheikh Tayeb was ushered in was over the top. The G&P Bank was full of contradictions. Did the bank have any direction, or was it being run according to the whims of a showman? Amir thought the whole charade was probably because Sheikh wanted to become even richer and more powerful than he was today.

From the handout given to him, Amir found out he was in the group assigned to deliberate for increasing the deposits base, which was unsurprisingly led by Masood Qadir. The group was to meet in Jade Hall.

After finishing his coffee, Amir went to go find the rest of his group in the Jade Hall, where large round tables were set with chairs for people to sit in half-moon circles. People were already standing around these tables, chatting informally with each other. Amir found a vacant chair next to Rehmallah.

He walked over to the table and said, 'Assalam Alaikum. Mind if I sit down here?'

'Waalekum Assalam. Please have a seat.' Rehmallah replied, waving his hand at the vacant chair.

'Interesting morning.' Amir said.

'Inspiring and awesome. This is the only way to describe what the chief said and did this morning.' Rehmallah said.

Amir glanced around the table. Besides Rehmallah and himself, there were people from London, Karachi, Singapore, Nairobi, Beirut and Bogotá at the table.

Amir quickly went around and introduced himself to everyone around the table.

At exactly 11 a.m., Masood went to a table set out in the front and said, 'Ladies and Gentlemen. Please be seated.'

Everybody sat down, and the room became quiet. Masood took the microphone in hand and said, 'Today we have been entrusted with the task of identifying the means to improve the deposits for our bank. We have, among us here, are people from all of the major branches and offices of the bank The management has taken great pains in developing background information and parameters for consideration by our group. These are included in the folders, which are being passed on to you now.'

Several young ladies came around and passed on the folders to the delegates.

'The folder with you includes the results of the research done under the following headings: A. Attract new clients; B. New products to increase our business from existing clients; and C. Improve our relationship with key business leaders.

'The bank's research department has studied the approach taken by various banks and financial houses around the world in all of the above areas. For example, to attract new clients and improve its deposits, Safe Bet Bank in Miami has launched a banking unit to specifically deal with the personal needs of their high-net-worth retired clients residing in the Miami area. They look after the healthcare, recreation, entertainment, settlement of bills, arranging the domestic staff, provide concierge services and even arranging the regular supply of groceries to the homes of the target clients. Of course, they charge for these services and require a healthy deposit from them to be entitled to the privilege of getting these services. We understand they are hugely successful and have almost monopolised the banking services to the retired community in Miami. You may see that this initiative covers all three requirements stated in the brief. New clients are attracted, new products to increase business from existing customers and improve the relationship with the key business leaders.

'We should all discuss new ideas and come up with suggestions. There are forty-eight people here. Each table has eight people. I suggest each table should act as one group and jot down the ideas until three in the afternoon. After that, each table will present the ideas that it comes up with. I will jot down these ideas on the flip chart here. We will debate these ideas and at the end of the day, we will have a list for presentation in the plenary session tomorrow. Please let me know if anybody has a suggestion to do this differently.' Nobody said anything. 'Okay, so this is agreed. Let us begin.' Masood sat down.

Rehmallah, believing himself to be the natural leader for the table, took over. 'Well, gentlemen, I believe ours is the most important and challenging session of the whole conference. In these days of the tightening money market, we have to think up ideas to get more deposits for the bank.

'I suggest that each one of us take a turn and give one idea. I request that Amir, you act as the secretary and take notes. We should discuss each idea and once we all agree that it is suitable for forwarding, Amir should note it down on a separate sheet with comments about the merits of the idea and how it may be implemented in practice. At the end of the assigned time, one of us will present the final agreed-upon ideas to Masood. Agreed?'

Nobody said anything, apparently accepting Rehmallah as the leader of the table; they began going around the table and one-by-one, giving suggestions.

'I believe the bank should introduce international bearer prize bonds.' The suggestion came from the smartly dressed, gold-

Rolexed delegate from Bogotá. 'I know for sure that people in Latin America love lotteries. So, we divide the interest on the bond into two parts. A portion of the interest should be distributed as a prize to the bondholders. The other part of the interest would be retained and paid when the bond is redeemed, say at the end of five years. This scheme has the advantage of complete confidentiality and anonymity for the investor, as the bonds are bearer and may be encashed over the counter. No information is required to be provided by the investor when buying or redeeming the bond or collecting the prize.'

'This is an excellent suggestion.' The not-too-smartly dressed delegate from Karachi chipped in. 'You'll recall that there was a similar scheme in Pakistan introduced in the days of Ayub Khan; it is enormously popular, particularly among low-income citizens and businessmen who do not want to declare their wealth to the government.'

The chap from London, who lived in a more regulated banking environment than his colleagues from Bogotá or Karachi, chimed in. 'I'm afraid there would be regulatory barriers in many countries for a private entity offering such bonds. I'm sure the UK will not allow the launching of such bonds there. The US anti-money laundering laws will also not allow funds to be deposited in bearer instruments without any information about the investors or the recipients of the funds.'

'The US and certain European countries may prohibit such a scheme, but the US and Europe are not our markets. Our market is Latin America, Asia and Africa. That is where the hidden wealth is waiting to be grabbed,' Bogotá insisted.

'We have very capable legal resources available. The lawyers may look into this scheme to see where it may be initially launched. I'm sure they'll find that with the government's blessing in several countries, the bank should be able to funnel in tons of money through this scheme.' Karachi was very supportive of Bogotá.

'Okay, let's note this down as an idea. We'll discuss this again before passing it on to Masood.' Rehmallah said.

'Our bank has not floated any investment funds. Why don't we create special purpose vehicles and float funds? There are several stock market indices funds and other products in the market. We could be innovative in ours. One such fund, which I'm sure would attract a lot of interest, could be a dollar-based fund indexed to the Chinese stock market incorporated into a tax haven and investment-friendly jurisdiction. The Chinese market is growing very quickly, and there may be interest in investing in such a fund. We missed the opportunity of cashing in on the Singapore boom.' This suggestion was from Singapore.

'How does an investment fund help in increasing our deposits?' London sounded very sceptical.

'Simple. First, we get a subscription from clients. These are deposited with the bank and withdrawn when the investment is made, which may be within three months of the date of receipt of the subscription. Secondly, we earn commission on the purchase and sale of investments. Third, we make money on the management of funds. Any unused and surplus cash is retained in the bank.' Singapore appeared to know what he was talking about.

Nairobi said, 'Most countries have very strict regulations for launching and managing investment funds. Normally, there are considerable legal hurdles. Also, the mutual funds require continuous attention to ensure they are in compliance with legal and financial requirements.' Apparently, the Kenyan government did not encourage investment funds, particularly those requiring investments outside the country and had very severe regulatory requirements.

'There are also countries with very lax regulations for investment funds. Many funds are incorporated in the Cayman Islands, Luxembourg, Bahamas and such places where the local governments welcome brass plate companies with no operations there. All a fund needs are a bunch of suave marketing people to go around and sell it. That's how a lot of blue-chip fund managers do their business.' Singapore had done his homework.

'I believe that this is a good idea and should be jotted down,' Rehmallah said. 'Let's see if we have anything on improving our relationship with key business leaders.'

'We should launch a Business Leader of the Year Award. It should be at three levels. Level one should be for the countries where we operate. The next level should be for each continent, such as The Asian Business Leader of the Year, and at the third level, it should be for The World Business Leader. Each award ceremony would require involvement for several days, if not weeks, with candidates by the bank's designated officials, who should be specially trained to look after the VIPs. The award ceremonies should go on for several days at locations such as Monte Carlo, Dubai, Bali, Cannes, Lausanne, et cetera, in the full glare of the world media.

'We should dedicate a complete team for this project if we decide to launch it, as in my experience, planning for and execution of such a project will require meticulous teamwork.' Beirut, true to Lebanese tradition, was in full marketing mode.

'Excellent. The best idea I've heard in a long time. Let's note this down. I don't think this requires any further discussion.' Rehmallah gave his verdict.

The group wanted to come out with as many ideas as possible, so they decided to have a quick lunch and return to their discussions. They continued coming up with more ideas, though some of the more farfetched ones were not noted down.

At three in the afternoon, Masood got up and took the microphone. 'Ladies and gentlemen, I could see that there were some very lively discussions at the tables. I understand that you have come up with some excellent ideas for presentation at the plenary session. Let's hear them. As agreed, I'll jot down these ideas on a flip chart, and the finally agreed-upon ideas will be presented to the plenary session tomorrow. Let's start from the first table on the left.' He pointed to the table.

'My name is Samir Razai from the Teheran office. I have been asked by my colleagues at this table to present the ideas we discussed.' A tall Iranian shared. 'Our first idea is to work with the OPEC member countries and convince them to increase deposits with our bank. We have excellent contacts with these governments. For example, I personally know that the bank is highly respected by the Iranian government and they give us a lot of business. In return for the increased deposits, we may use our contacts in America, Europe and Asia to market our clients' products in territories where we have influence.'

Amir could not help but laugh at the simplicity of the people he was sitting with. Several ideas were presented. Some were ridiculous. Others were good. The delegate from Kinshasa, Zaire suggested the bank should work with the rulers of the countries to keep their entire foreign currency reserves with the bank. For this, the bank should pay a commission to the ruler. The delegate from Venezuela suggested the bank should act as an intermediary for the distribution of drugs from Latin American countries. This would not only provide huge deposits but also a steady stream of income for the bank. Compared to these, the ideas discussed at Amir's table appeared to be reasonable and plausible.

After a considerable amount of debate, five ideas were selected for presentation at the plenary session. It was agreed that the other ideas would be noted and forwarded separately to the management. Of these, the idea of the Businessman of the Year Award was at the top. The group discussion ended at 6.15 p.m., forty-five minutes later than scheduled. Amir went to his room straight away and, after a little rest, he got ready for dinner.

***

He was in the hotel's lobby a few minutes before 7.30 p.m. It was full of G&P Bank delegates. They were excitedly talking to each other about the events of the day, sharing the ideas discussed in their groups during the day's session.

Five coaches were parked outside the hotel entrance. Amir went into one and found a seat next to a chap in his mid to late forties.

'Hi. I'm Amir. I am from Karachi but being transferred to Geneva.' Amir introduced himself.

'Shamim. Banjar.'

'I was in the group discussing ideas for growing our deposits base. Very interesting.' Amir said to start the conversation.

'Yes, the topic is the most relevant in the current economic environment. We need to improve our deposits base to be stronger. I was in the group discussing the political environment and risks. Very timely, too. There's a lot happening around the globe.' Shamim replied.

'Some very interesting ideas were presented in our session. How was yours?' Amir asked.

'You know, many countries where we operate are going through political and other changes. For example, in Banjar, there is a change of guards as the Khan is very sick and the Crown prince has assumed the day-to-day running of the government. Obviously, the Crown prince's thinking is different from his father's. In addition, there are other factions within the ruling family vying for more power. A political tug of war is also going on in Nigeria, Zaire, and many other countries. We have very large investments in all of these countries. This conference is at the right time to discuss these matters.'

'This is my first conference. Are the religious overtures a normal feature in these conferences?' Amir asked.

'Our chairman is a deeply religious person. He considers this bank as a part of his religious mission to provide equality to mankind. We have to realise that we have been given a great opportunity by the Almighty to correct the economic ills in this world. Ours is a religious job, and we should try to perform it with a religious passion. Sheikh Tayeb never lets us forget this and in all the conferences, this is a ritual.' Shamim replied.

Amir was impressed with the conviction by which Shamim believed in the bank and its management, and accepted everything blindly.

Soon, the coaches arrived at Siam Yacht Club. It was a sprawling complex of banquet halls and gardens full of lotus flowers and orchids along the bank of the Chao Phraya River. The delegates were guided to a very large banquet hall. In one corner, there was a stage where several young people were singing Thai folk songs. Beautiful Thai hostesses were moving around with trays laden with drinks, both alcoholic and soft. Waiters with trays of finger food were also going around.

Amir separated from Shamim and sat down at an empty table, wondering who his luck would bring to him this time. The table was soon filled with delegates from several countries.

Suddenly, the lights in the hall started flickering and then dimmed. The stage was illuminated. On the stage was a completely nude, beautiful Thai girl, who looked barely seventeen, standing with the microphone in her hand. Everybody clapped and some even whistled.

'Ladies and gentlemen, welcome to the beautiful Siam Yacht Club in the wonderful city of Bangkok,' the girl said. 'Soon, you will be served very delicious Thai food on your tables. To incite your taste buds and for you to enjoy the evening, there will be a Thai cultural show at the same time. I have been told that all of you are very serious business executives and need to loosen up a bit. My friends and I will make sure that tonight you forget all the business and live in a different world. I promise that tonight you will find yourself in heaven. This will be the most memorable night for you in a long time. So, enjoy.'

Several musicians came onto the stage and started playing their instruments. Soon, a group of young girls wearing only the scantiest of briefs came on the stage performing some sort of Thai semi-classical dance. They were joined by a group of young boys who touched the girls all over their bodies and danced with them, rubbing and kissing their bodies.

'Most of the artists, even those who are dressed as girls, are, in fact, boys. They cultivate their bodies to look like girls.' Amir's neighbour commented.

'Are they? Well, they all look like very pretty young girls to me.' Amir replied and turned his face.

The food was being served at the same time as the show was in progress. Amir noted that almost all the delegates on his table were having liqueur and appeared to be getting drunk already. Only Amir asked for Perrier with fresh lime, and he looked bored with the proceedings.

Soon all the food was served. They began with starters such as spring rolls, satay, and puffed rice cakes. These were accompanied by Thai salads. Then came the *Tom yum kung nam khon* (prawn tom yum with coconut milk), followed by servings of *Kai phat khing* – chicken stir-fried with sliced ginger, *Kaeng khiao wan* – called 'green curry' and *Kai yang* – marinated, grilled chicken. The food was mildly spicy and delicious. All of this was followed by two desserts, *Chaokuai* (grass jelly served with shaved ice and brown sugar) and *Khao niao mamuang* (Thai mango with glutinous rice). Amir enjoyed the food thoroughly and almost decided to find work in Thailand so he could eat the lovely food every day.

In the meantime, the show continued. On the stage, a group of Thai girls clad in traditional Thai Ruean Ton were performing a classical dance, apparently, a supplication to please the Lord Buddha. The show went on until midnight, with a variety of items with nude dancers gyrating and shaking their breasts, acrobatic acts, magic numbers and traditional Thai dances. At midnight, the hostess came on the stage, still not wearing anything, and thanked the group for giving them the opportunity to show them Thai culture.

The group filed back to the waiting coaches and returned to their hotel. Amir felt exhausted. He could not help wonder how the people in the group were able to reconcile their religious beliefs and conversations in the morning session with the vulgar show they all seemed to have enjoyed in the evening. He thought again of how the G&P Bank was full of contradictions.

***

Amir woke up early the next day and went down for breakfast around seven; nobody from G&P Bank was in the breakfast room. He had a table for himself by the window. Breakfast included a variety of juices, fruits, bread, cereals and hot and cold food with hot beverages. Amir had a good breakfast. As he ate, he glanced through the morning newspaper. It was full of news of the usual turmoil going on in several parts of the world.

After breakfast, Amir went to his room, freshened up, picked up his belongings for the day and reached the foyer of the royal ballroom a little before the scheduled 9.30 a.m. start for the conference. The usual crowd was going around with coffee and pastries. Amir said hello to a few delegates, poured a black coffee, and went into the ballroom.

A couple of minutes before 9.30 a.m., the hotel bellboys went around ringing bells, asking the delegates to take their seats in the ballroom. At 9.30, the lights in the room were slightly dimmed and the stage was illuminated as it was the previous day. On the stage sat Sheikh Tayeb with his group of senior executive vice presidents.

'Assalam Alaikum, good morning.' Sheikh Tayeb got up from his seat and, with the microphone attached to his lapel, he said, 'I hope you all enjoyed the party last night. I, myself, enjoyed it very much. Quite a show.

'As agreed, we will now ask each group leader to present the ideas agreed by their respective groups. This is an open session, and everybody is welcome to make any comments or give suggestions. Feel free to give your view on any of the ideas presented.

'We will note down these ideas and make a business plan for making our bank even stronger to achieve the number one position in the international banking world. To start with, I will ask Masood Qadir, who led the group for suggesting ideas for growing our deposits, to tell us what his group has come up with.'

Masood stood and went to the rostrum. 'Good morning, ladies and gentlemen. Our group was very interactive and came out with a lot of great ideas. Of these, I have selected only five to be presented for this session. I have, however, noted down a few more ideas, which I will forward to the board for consideration.'

He presented the ideas discussed the previous day, starting with the programme for the Businessman of the Year Award. The ideas presented were received without much discussion. Sheikh Tayeb commented that the Businessman of the Year Award was an excellent suggestion and should be adopted immediately.

After Masood, other vice presidents presented ideas and suggestions from their groups. Amir thought some of the ideas suggested were very weird and lacked maturity. For example, there was a suggestion from the group discussing political developments to create an organisation like the CIA within the bank to influence and manage political developments in the countries where the bank operated.

There was a lot of discussion and appreciation of the ideas for interest free banking. Everybody felt the time for interest free banking had come. The suggestions, however, revolved around the efforts to camouflage the interest element by naming it mark-up or commission and creating paperwork to support the renaming of the products instead of making a real effort to change the nature of the banking as was required by Islam. The session covering the suggestions for the future ended around noon.

'I am very encouraged by the ideas and suggestions I have heard today. This shows that there are real brains amongst us who will make the bank stronger and a leader in the banking world, but who will also create an organisation with the true spirit of serving the interests of our stakeholders.

'The management will consider all the suggestions received today and may carry out further studies by experts to be able to apply these suggestions in practice. Of course, a lot of work will be required before any of the ideas are given practical shape but it is for our future, and we will do everything in our power to achieve the goals we have set for ourselves.

'As you have already heard, on 4 and 5 April, we will have our annual conference in London for our major customers and the world at large. This will be a showcase event, and we are trying to get a prime minister-level official to be the chief guest. Through this conference, we will make a statement that we are the leaders in the world of banking.

'You will soon receive the agenda and other background materials for the London conference. Please ensure that you all play the role assigned to you. You will be required to ensure that your major clients attend this conference. Of course, the bank will pay for all the travel and other expenses for our guests' attendance at the conference.

'The success of this bank is in your hands. Please make sure that you continue to exert the maximum efforts within your capabilities. I am sure none of us will do less.'

'I thank you all again. I wish you safe return journeys. May Allah be with you. Good luck and goodbye.' With that, Sheikh Tayeb and the group left the stage.

People started leaving the ballroom. Amir also got up from his seat. He was amazed at the way the conference was conducted. As he was walking toward the exit, Masood appeared at his side.

'How did you find the conference?' Masood asked.

'Truly amazing. Very impressive. I have learnt a lot and am fully charged up. Tremendous performance by the chairman,' Amir replied.

'We certainly hope the people got the message that the bank is serious in aiming for the number one position in the banking world and a lot is expected from our executives. When are you moving to Geneva?'

'I'll go to Karachi from here and after a week or so, leave for Geneva. I have some personal business in London, so I will come via there.'

'Let me know the exact dates, as I will need to organise your initial accommodations and office facilities. I now need you in Geneva as soon as possible. You heard about the sad passing of Richard. That's left a gap. Also, we need to work very hard to ensure Geneva's customers attend and are looked after during the London conference.' Masood said.

'I'll let you know as soon as I arrive in Karachi, and I'll try to be in Geneva within the next ten days,' Amir said.

***

'It was excellent. Congratulations on such a motivational presentation.' Azhar Alam was the first to congratulate Sheikh Tayeb. The inner board had gathered in Sheikh Tayeb's presidential suite for a meeting.

'Do you think it went well?' Sheikh Tayeb was being modest.

'It went extremely well, Sir. I have spoken to several people. They are all in a trance. Everybody I have talked to is singing your praises.' Masood said.

'I have also spoken to several delegates. Everybody is ready to go out there and achieve the goals set out by you.' Abu Talib also joined in.

After the round of congratulations, Sheikh Tayeb said, 'Well, let's hope we get more from our people. We have received some excellent suggestions. Azhar, please collate all the ideas and develop an action plan to execute some of the better and more practical ones. I liked the idea of starting the Businessman of the Year Award. That should massage a few egos and bring us more business. It'll require us to do a lot of work, though.'

'I'll get all the ideas, evaluate them and present them in the next meeting,' Azhar replied.

'We have a few matters from previous meetings that need to be discussed,' Sheikh Tayeb said. 'First, you did an excellent job getting the audited financial statements from Tolbert and Gibbs, Mateen.' He complimented Mateen.

'Thank you. I had to use a few tricks and dangle a few carrots. The auditors, regulators and lawyers are all the same. They all fall for the prohibited fruit.' Mateen was very pleased that Sheikh Tayeb had praised him in front of others.

'We still have the problem with TIG. What do you think of the situation there, Abu Talib?' Sheikh Tayeb turned to Abu Talib.

'I believe the group is insolvent and overextended. Unless something is done quickly, I fear TIG might create difficulties for us. We certainly need more funds for other needs, but I also do not trust Yakoob Soothar. He is a very clever operator and does not have the same ethics as his father. He turned the tables on us by asking for more funds instead of offering to reduce his outstanding dues.'

'I agree. Let's watch this account carefully and keep the pressure up. We should call Yakoob in a couple of weeks and see how they are doing. He also promised to provide us with the documents to invite outside investors. Theirs is a profitable business, so it might be possible to get some new partners. I know a couple of potential investors who might be interested.'

'There was a report in *The Straits Times* that one of TIG's ships had been impounded in Singapore and the crew arrested for involvement in arms smuggling. We are also facing difficulty with the Singapore authorities for our dealings with one of our Afghan customers.' Abu Talib reported.

'We all know that TIG's ships get involved in carrying contraband cargo. It's their problem, and I hope there are no implications for us there.' Sheikh Tayeb replied.

'So far, we do not seem to have faced any difficulties in connection with TIG in Singapore, except that there was a request for us to advance some more funds to help them with the legal issues in Singapore, which I have turned down.

'The Singapore authorities are after the Afghans, and they have asked us for a lot of information about their accounts. We are cooperating. At this stage, there is no indication of allegations of any wrongdoings by us.' Abu Talib replied.

'Let's keep this under review, and please keep me apprised of any developments.' Sheikh Tayeb said.

He turned to Shakadir and asked, 'What is happening on the projects you were dealing with, Shakadir?'

'The problem of the leak in Geneva was solved with the unfortunate accidental death of the person there.'

'Yes. That was unfortunate that the young man lost his life in an accident. Masood, please ensure that we do everything for the family of the deceased.' Sheikh Tayeb did not want to know any details.

Shakadir continued with his report. 'I am working with the two leads we discussed. Masood and I have discussed the movement of funds, which I understand will not be very difficult. We still have to arrange for the transportation of the goods. I'm awaiting Yakoob Soothar to let me know if he can carry the consignment from its present location and have it delivered to the destination of the buyers' choice.'

'Please follow up on it with Yakoob. We need to push this as fast as possible. There is a lot of money involved.'

'I will.' Shakadir replied.

'Our London conference should be a showcase. Azhar, please ensure that everything is organised down to the finest detail.'

'Everything is going according to plan. I'll pass the programme to you in a day or so. We have hired an events management company to make all the arrangements. We have also appointed a public relations agency to get the maximum publicity and coverage. You have to tell us who you want to be the conference chairman.'

'I was thinking of asking Sitara Khan. This brings me to our next important topic. We need to go to Banjar as soon as possible. Azhar, you, Mateen, Shakadir and I will go. Please make arrangements for our visit there. We need to engage with him quickly. I have to invite him to be the chairman of the London conference, and we need additional funds extremely urgently. Also, we hear there have been a few changes in the way things are done there. We'll see when we are there. Hopefully, even Sitara Khan will be impressed with our performance and plans. I cannot see how he could resist further investment in our bank after the results we have achieved.'

'We'll work on this. Let's plan to be in Banjar Monday of next week as we need time to prepare for our London conference as well.' Azhar replied.

'Well, gentlemen, if we don't have any further matters to discuss, let's go. All of you have worked extremely hard for this conference, and you have a lot to do going forward. God bless you.' With that, the meeting was closed and everybody left Sheikh Tayeb's suite.

Chapter 30

Banjar City, State of Banjar

G&P Bank's Challenger 605 aircraft landed without incident at Bulund Khan International Airport in Banjar City.

As soon as the engines of the aircraft were switched off, the stairs were lowered, and Sheikh Tayeb stepped out. His wife, Shakila, was close behind. They were followed by Azhar Alam, Mateen Saeed, and Shakadir Khan. There were three other officers of G&P Bank in dark suits, carrying packages of gifts for the hosts. In addition, one man was carrying a falcon perched on a leather band on his hand. The falcon's head was wrapped in the special leather covering used for falcons so as not to cause them stress when travelling.

Sheikh Tayeb was shocked when he stepped out of the plane. Nobody was waiting to meet and greet them. Normally, G&P Bank's chairman was accorded a full VVIP reception when he arrived at Banjar Airport. The chief of protocol of the Khan's Court would normally await them with a fleet of cars to take the guests to the state guest house. Today, they were herded in a rickety bus for transfer to the arrivals hall. There, they had to queue up for stamping their passports.

Outside the arrivals hall, Yousuf Ali, G&P Bank's manager was waiting with his family. His children were carrying bouquets of flowers for Mrs. Tayeb. Yousuf looked very nervous and embarrassed.

'Sorry, Sir. For security reasons, the Banjar government has banned all outsiders from the arrival hall or airside. Despite my best efforts, we did not get the pass to come in. The bank's public relations officer, who has very good contacts, was also not allowed in today. We have rented a fleet of Mercedes cars to take you to The Empire Hotel. We have booked the royal suite for you there.' Yousuf Ali said.

Sheikh Tayeb was finding it difficult to control himself. 'I hope the Khans knew that we were coming to see them.'

'Yes, I personally advised the Khan's court and set up the appointments. The court has advised me that although His Majesty is not well, he will be pleased to give you and Mrs. Tayeb a fifteen-minute audience at 4.30 p.m. today. Unfortunately, the Crown prince is tied up today and will only be able to see you tomorrow at 9 a.m. in his office. His financial adviser, Mr. Sajan Mala, and some others will also be present. I don't know who or how many. The meeting is open-ended. There is no set agenda.' Yousuf was clearly very worried.

'I don't understand. I had hoped that we would get the proper protocol and accommodations in the state guest house, as before.' Sheikh Tayeb said.

'I tried with the Khan's court and the Crown prince's office for a more appropriate reception and accommodation, but I was cold-shouldered. Mr. Sajan Mala was most unhelpful. I'll brief you about the environment here when we sit down for a few minutes. Let's go, Sir, the cars have arrived.' Sheikh Tayeb and his wife went in the first car.

The bank had made suitable arrangements at The Empire Hotel. The general manager was waiting to welcome Sheikh Tayeb. He and his wife were whisked away to the waiting elevator.

'Azhar, Shakadir, Yousuf, why don't you come with us. I need to speak to you,' Sheikh Tayeb said, looking at his loyal friends. They were accompanied by the hotel manager.

Once in the royal suite, Sheikh Tayeb thanked the manager, who left quickly. Mrs. Tayeb retired to the master bedroom. Sheikh Tayeb looked at Shakadir meaningfully, who immediately opened his briefcase and took out some electronic gadgets. He started going through the suite systematically to see if there were any microphones planted in the room.

He found several hidden in the telephones, lamps in the sitting room and bedside table, washroom, and the plant. He took them to the washroom and threw them in the commode.

'The room is clear from bugs, but they will be replaced. I suggest we take a walk in the open if we wish to talk.' Shakadir said.

'Okay. I suggest you also check the other rooms assigned to us. Please tell all the people with us to be careful of what they say in the rooms. You're right. We should go out for a walk if we want to talk,' Sheikh Tayeb said and continued, 'I don't believe this. We created a major city and a proper country out of this barren piece of land. Now, they're treating us as if we are beggars. We have come here in goodwill and for the continuation of our relationship. After all, we are the biggest bank here. Something is seriously wrong. I knew that Bulund Khan was ill but there is something more serious here than the Khan's health.'

'You're right, Sir.' Yousuf said. 'The Crown prince has taken over running the country. The senior Khan is almost a prisoner. His favourite wife, our friend, Farah Naz, is not allowed to leave the palace or communicate with outsiders. We are no longer the biggest bank here. All the state transactions and favours are now directed to Banjar Commercial Bank. It is incorporated in Banjar and owned by His Highness, the Crown prince, and members of the royal family, along with Sajan Mala and some of his friends. Sajan Mala has appointed some more of his friends to manage the bank. I sent you memos giving an update on the situation here but I had to be careful. As you have seen, nothing is confidential here anymore.'

'I knew that we were no longer the favourites here. But I expected them to extend the usual courtesies and protocol we are used to. How could they forget what this place was and would have been without us?' Sheikh Tayeb was still very irritated.

'The reality is we have a situation here which we have to deal with.' Azhar intervened. 'Let's agree that since we did not receive a grand reception on arrival, we are not highly regarded here. A fifteen-minute audience with His Majesty indicates a formality only. I don't think you will be able to talk business in this meeting. We'll face tough questioning in tomorrow's meeting with the Crown prince and his advisers. We should prepare for that. I don't think we will get any support. On the contrary, I believe we will come under pressure to reduce our operations here and repay the amounts invested by the royal family in the G&P Bank.'

'What investment?' Sheikh Tayeb replied angrily. 'Most of the shares held by Bulund Khan and Sitara Khan were given to them as gift by me.'

'Well, they are considered their investment now and they would like to give these shares back to us at a premium. After all, on paper, the bank has made a healthy profit.' Azhar was very perceptive.

'I should also advise you of another development that might affect our financial position here.' Yousuf said. 'Banjar had an old tax law going back thirty years when Bulund Khan issued a decree for all the local Banjari businesses to pay him equivalent to one hundred Banjari rupees as tax each year. For non-Banjari businesses, the law provided for a forty percent tax on their profits. This law was never applied in practice until now. The Banjar government has now issued notices to companies formed outside Banjar or owned by foreigners to pay taxes from the date they started the business here.

'We also received a notice the day before yesterday asking us to file tax declarations and pay taxes due with delay penalties, which are fixed at two percent of the assessed tax per month of the default for the period we have been operating in Banjar. I have already consulted a tax specialist here and have been advised that our potential liability would exceed one hundred fifty million US dollars.'

'They cannot be serious. No business will pay the tax. Everybody will leave. They have gone mad. Just ignore the notices.' Sheikh was now visibly angry.

'We'll talk about the tax separately. It's not an immediate problem. We should think of our meeting tomorrow.' Again, Azhar brought the focus back to the immediate problem of dealing with the Crown prince and his advisers.

'You're right. Let's talk about the meeting tomorrow. We'll present the financial statements and information we brought with us. These will show the bank has earned a good profit this year. The presentation also shows that due to various economic constraints in the world today, the bank's liquidity was slightly stretched and therefore, the bank was not able to capture the opportunities available at present. We'll see the client's reaction and ascertain whether there is any interest in investing further funds in the bank. If so, we can offer redeemable preference shares with guaranteed dividends above the present-day LIBOR (*Interest rate applied by the UK banks for overnight borrowings from other banks*). I'll also invite Sitara Khan to be the chairman of our London conference. I hope he accepts that.' Sheikh Tayeb said.

'Sounds good. I suggest that only you and I go to the meeting tomorrow, so if Khan wants to discuss anything informally, we may do so.' Azhar replied. 'It is now almost 1 p.m. If you feel like it, let's order some sandwiches and then you and Mrs. Tayeb may want to get ready for the meeting with His Majesty.'

'Good idea. Let's order something to eat. Shakadir, please see what everybody wants and order from room service.' Sheikh Tayeb said.

'I'd like to go make arrangements for the afternoon, Sir. I have arranged for two cars for you at 3.30 p.m. this afternoon. For security purposes, you should be at the main gate no later than 4 p.m. You and Mrs. Tayeb will go in the first car. The staff bearing the gifts for presentation to His Majesty will travel in the second car. The staff in the second car will have to hand over the gifts to security at the main gate, who will send them in the car taking you to see the Khan. You'll also be transferred to another car driven by the palace security, which will take you to the audience chamber.' Yousuf said, getting up. 'If you are available, I'd like to invite you, Mrs. Tayeb, and the other guests to a dinner at my place. It will only be for the guests and two of my senior assistants with their families.

'For tomorrow, a car will be waiting for you outside the hotel at 8.15 a.m. It will take you to the Crown prince's office. I have arranged for you to come to the bank after your meeting with him. If you finish with him early, you may meet the bank's staff and we can lunch at Banjar Boat Club with the officers of the bank. If you're late, we'll order some food to be brought in and lunch at the bank. The conference room will be secure and available for your use.

'Mrs. Tayeb will be collected from the hotel by my wife at a time to be agreed between them for a shopping and sightseeing tour of Banjar, not that there is much to see here. There have been some developments and fancy buildings constructed. They have also built a museum that shows that Banjar was always very prosperous and cultured, and one of the prominent ports in this region for several hundred years.'

'Money can also buy history nowadays.' Sheikh Tayeb chuckled.

***

Palace of Bulund Khan, the Khan of Banjar
Sheikh Tayeb's convoy of two cars arrived at the main gate of the palace precisely at 4 p.m. Security at the palace was tight. They carefully checked Sheikh Tayeb and Mrs. Tayeb's passports and compared the names in a register with them. The security staff checked the cars and requested Sheikh Tayeb and Mrs. Tayeb step outside for a physical scanning. They even put the gifts they had brought through a scanner. The security personnel were delighted when they saw the falcon. It was one of the prized breeds coveted by the Banjari.

After the security check, Sheikh Tayeb and Mrs. Tayeb were issued visitors' passes and requested to go into another waiting car, which was chauffeured by a tall Banjari Baloch in Army uniform. The presents were transferred to yet another car, which was to follow the car with Sheikh Tayeb and Mrs. Tayeb. The falcon was transferred to a Banjari soldier who followed in another car. The cars that brought Sheikh Tayeb and Mrs. Tayeb were asked to park outside the security parameter.

It was a two-kilometre distance between the main gate and the palace. The family had blocked approximately thirty kilometres of land facing the sea and built palaces. The most beautiful of which belonged to Bulund Khan; it was made from white Italian marble. Navy gunboats were patrolling the sea in front of the palace.

Sheikh Tayeb and Mrs. Tayeb were taken into the audience chamber and asked to wait. At exactly 4.30 p.m., His Majesty, the Khan of Banjar, Bulund Khan was brought in a wheelchair pushed by a servant. His wife, Farah Naz, walked behind him. Sheikh Tayeb was shocked to see his friend, who was only a skeleton of his previous self. Bulund Khan's eyes still shone, but he appeared to be very sick.

'Assalam Alaikum, Your Majesty,'' Sheikh Tayeb said, advancing towards Bulund Khan.

'Waalekum Assalam,' Bulund Khan replied in a faint voice.

Sheikh Tayeb bent and kissed the khan's hand. The khan took Sheikh Tayeb's hand and held it with warmth in both of his hands. He had a smile of happiness on his face at seeing his old friend.

Sheikh Tayeb turned to Farah and said, 'Are you well, Your Highness?'

Farah smiled at Sheikh Tayeb and gave him her hand. She kissed her own hand to show her affection for Sheikh Tayeb, then she went to Shakila, who was waiting on the side.

'I am so happy to see you again, Mrs. Tayeb.' She hugged Shakila and kissed her on the cheek.

Shakila returned the compliment. 'I am also very happy to see you again, Your Highness. His Majesty seems to have taken ill since we met him last.'

'His Majesty is suffering from heart and kidney problems. He has grown very weak and can hardly do anything for himself.' Farah said. 'Sit down. Tell me, how have you been?' Farah asked as the servants entered with trays filled generously with traditional sweets, pastries, and fruits.

'Thank you, Your Highness. Shakila and I have brought some presents for His Majesty and Your Highness. If you could kindly ask the security people to bring them in, I would be honoured to present them to you.' Sheikh Tayeb said.

Farah spoke in Farsi to one of the attendants, and two men in uniform came in with the boxes and the falcon. A smile of great pleasure lighted Bulund Khan's face when he saw the falcon. It was taken to him and he stroked the falcon's head gently.

'Thank you for this beautiful gift. It is a Sakr. Sakr falcons are one of the most prized breeds of falcons. They are not easily available. Unfortunately, I cannot handle falcons anymore, but I will let my staff train the bird and fly it when I go out in the desert sometime.' Khan said faintly.

Shakila presented a Cartier box to Farah. 'This is for you, Your Highness.' She said.

Farah Naz took the box in two hands and quickly opened it. Inside was a beautiful diamond necklace. 'This is magnificent. Wonderful. Thank you.' She was almost overcome with emotions at the sight of the beautiful necklace.

'We have brought some antique ceramics and items of handicraft.' Sheikh Tayeb said, presenting other boxes.

'Thank you. You embarrass us; we were unable to do anything for you.' Farah said.

'You have done more than enough for us. Our friendship goes beyond exchanging favours and gifts. Please accept these as a mark of our humble respect to His Majesty and Your Highness.' Sheikh Tayeb said.

They sat down, chatting about families, health, and the weather. Bulund Khan sat through the discussion with a smile on his face but barely said a word. After a few minutes, Farah made a gesture to the servant hovering outside the audience chamber. Immediately, a jewellery box was brought in.

Farah opened the case and presented it to Shakila. Inside was a beautiful choker made of lustrous Banjari natural pearls. 'I hope you like this. It is from His Majesty and me.'

'This is magnificent. Thank you, Your Majesty, Your Highness.' Shakila accepted the present with a bow.

They sat down and talked about the beauty of the pearls. After a few minutes, Sheikh Tayeb stood up and said, 'Thank you again for seeing us, Your Majesty, Your Highness, and thank you very much for this wonderful gift. We have taken a lot of your time and should be leaving. I hope that we'll be able to welcome you again outside Banjar. I'll pray for your health, Your Majesty.' He turned to Farah.

'Thank you for receiving us, Your Highness. I pray you will also visit us with His Majesty.'

Farah went to the door of the audience chamber to see them off. Sheikh Tayeb noted that, although she was smiling, there was a look of sadness and helplessness in her eyes. He made a note to do something for her, if he could.

***

Meeting with Sitara Khan, the Crown prince and de facto Ruler of Banjar

Sheikh Tayeb and Azhar Alam were ushered into the conference room assigned for the meeting with the Crown prince and his advisers. The office building was a palace and looked like one of the wonders of the modern world, with fountains and plants all over the place. Pieces of art and antiques adorned the walls of the building. The entire floor was covered with beautiful Persian carpets.

Sheikh Tayeb and Azhar had to go through the necessary security procedures before being allowed in the building. Anticipating this, they had arrived fifteen minutes earlier. They were seated in the big conference room five minutes prior to the scheduled meeting.

There were already six people there: one Indian, two Englishmen and three Banjari. Sajan Mala, dressed impeccably in a black pinstripe suit, got up with a smile and introduced himself to Sheikh Tayeb and Azhar. He introduced the others present, too. They were Hamid Kastoor, Governor of the Central Bank; Abdul Rahman Jamazi, Head of Banjar Investment Authority; Dr. Mustafa Ateek, Head of the Khan's Personal Investments; David Stromer, Partner in the famous English law firm Roger Pyke; and Gordon Jobs, Head of the Finance Advisory Group: Troy, Ball and Gardner.

A secretary asked them if they wanted tea or coffee. Both men asked for an Americano coffee without milk or sugar. Platters full of pastries, biscuits, and dates were spread across the conference table. At 9 a.m. sharp, His Highness the Crown prince Sitara Khan strode into the room. Sheikh Tayeb was impressed with the authority with which the Crown prince carried himself. He was confident and obviously used to be obeyed. Sheikh Tayeb noted that Sitara Khan had gained weight and sported a substantial sharply pointed moustache since he had seen him last. Sitara Khan was dressed in the traditional Baloch attire of a long white flowing shirt, wide baggy pants known as Shalwar, a black turban with two strands, and the handcrafted triangle topped leather sandals. He also had a silver belt around his waist with a silver dagger inserted in the front, as was customary for senior Banjari Balochis.

Everybody stood up. The Crown prince walked to Sheikh Tayeb with open arms and embraced and kissed him on the cheek. Sheikh Tayeb returned the compliment. Sitara Khan then did the same to Azhar.

'Welcome, gentlemen. It is so nice to see you back in your home, Banjar.' he said to Sheikh Tayeb.

'I am thrilled to be home. I hope Your Royal Highness and the family are in good health.' Sheikh Tayeb said. He noted that there was no mention of the absence of a proper reception at the airport when the G&P Bank delegation arrived the day before.

'I am fit with Allah's blessings. I am very busy, though. There is so much to be done. The family is all in good health except for father. You met His Majesty yesterday, so you know. I had to assume the burden of dealing with the affairs here. Fortunately, my father trained me well. We are doing everything we can to put Banjar in the twenty-first century and with the help of friends like you, we shall soon achieve it.' Sitara said.

Sheikh Tayeb recalled that Sitara Khan had a Master's degree in Economics from the London School of Economics. He hoped the Crown prince would be as kind and polite in action as he appeared when greeting him.

'Thank you for receiving us.' Sheikh Tayeb began. 'As Your Highness has rightly said, Banjar is the home to both Azhar and myself. We have worked with Your Highness's family for a long time and are proud of our humble contribution to developing this great country and its people. We supported, but all the credit goes to His Majesty, your father, and you. Today, Banjar is a leading and prosperous member of the international community, with all the modern facilities of a developed country. Banjar enjoys certain facilities and qualities of life, which are better than many Western countries. I congratulate you and your family for such a grand achievement.

'G&P Bank has been in this country for over fifteen years. Banjar was the first place we opened for business after incorporation. Your family very kindly opened doors for us and gave us all the facilities. Today, G&P Bank is one of the largest non-Western banks in the world. G&P Bank is your bank, and I am proud to present to you the audited financial statements of your bank for this past year.' Sheikh Tayeb took out several copies of the financial statements and passed them around the table.

'The audited financial statements show that this year we have recorded a profit of one hundred fifty million US dollars. We have total assets of ten billion US, and our owners' equity has now swollen to four billion US dollars. We believe that G&P Bank has the opportunity to expand further and become the largest bank in the world. We have ambitious plans to reach the summit and we hope that, like in the past, the state of Banjar will make further investments so that G&P Bank can continue to be a shining star in the crown of the Khan of Banjar,' Sheikh Tayeb said.

Sitara Khan nodded politely and said, 'Actually, we are also re-examining our strategy for investments by Banjar. Over the last few weeks, we have reviewed our portfolios and developed a plan. As a part of this plan, we have decided to dispose of our investment in G&P Bank. We are grateful for giving such excellent results over the years but new circumstances require that we should invest differently. As we do not want to adversely affect G&P Bank's profile, we would like you to arrange for G&P Bank's other shareholders to buy out the shares owned by our family.'

'I do not understand.' Sheikh Tayeb replied. He wanted to learn more about what Sitara Khan had in mind.

'I'm not a financial man. All I know is that according to the information I have, Banjar's royal family owns thirty percent of the equity. We would like to dispose of our holding. Instead of offering these shares to outsiders, we believe it best if you or other existing shareholders were to acquire these shares at an agreed value. You may work out the numbers and other details with my financial team.

'You should also know that the state of Banjar is introducing banking reforms. According to these reforms, only banks incorporated in Banjar with a majority Banjari ownership will be allowed to have full-scale operations here. Foreign banks will be allowed only limited operations with one branch each. Since G&P Bank is technically a foreign bank, it will be affected. Of course, we will pay reasonable compensation to banks for their assets acquired by us.'

'This comes as a complete surprise. I'll have to discuss this with G&P Bank's executive board and report back to you. We need time to digest this information and respond appropriately.' Sheikh Tayeb said.

'Fine. You agree on the time and further process with my team. I'd like to finalise the whole transaction soon, as we have plans to embark on the banking reforms quickly. Sajan and the other members of the team here are fully authorised to negotiate any deals with you. I have another meeting,' Prince Sitara Khan said, and stood up.

Everybody else stood up as a mark of respect. Sitara Khan went to Sheikh Tayeb and Azhar and shook their hands warmly and left.

The atmosphere in the room changed immediately as the Banjar team seemed to relax. Sheikh Tayeb noticed a smirk on Sajan's face. He was enjoying Sheikh Tayeb's discomfort.

Sajan looked at Sheikh Tayeb and said, 'As you heard from His Highness, Sheikh Tayeb, the government wants to carry out major banking reforms here. This will involve the banks incorporated outside Banjar; they will only be allowed one branch with limited operations. Banks incorporated in Banjar with the majority Banjari ownership will only be licensed to carry on full banking operations here. For historical reasons, G&P Bank had complete freedom of operating here. The bank has approximately fifteen branches in Banjar. This will change. We are at your service to discuss how to take this further.'

Sheikh Tayeb replied, 'As you know, we came here with a completely different agenda. This is a surprise to me. I need to discuss this with my senior colleagues and the bank's executive board before we can enter into further discussions.'

'You will appreciate that I have to look after the interests of the government here.' Sajan reminded Sheikh Tayeb. 'My colleagues and I will do everything possible to complete this transaction as promptly and smoothly as possible.

'You must also know that effective immediately, all transactions involving remittance in excess of ten thousand US dollars will require advance notification to the Central Bank's Exchange Monitoring Unit. A circular was issued to this effect this morning. G&P Bank must have received this by now.' Sajan was smug.

'What happens if we refuse to buy the shares?' Sheikh Tayeb asked.

'I urge that you do not even consider that possibility. It may become a little unpleasant for everybody. As I said, we will try to get you the best possible terms for the deal. We understand it might not be possible for you to make an immediate settlement of whatever terms we agree. That can also be worked out. Let me assure you that the royal family of Banjar is serious about disposing of its shares in G&P Bank.' Sajan's reply was said as an implicit threat.

'I must go now. We'll contact you to make arrangements for further discussions on this subject. We might have to meet in London or some other place.' Sheikh Tayeb said, getting up.

'We'll wait for your communication. Please do it as soon as possible. We would be happy to meet with you anywhere you like, except in Pakistan. I am afraid I won't get visas to go to Pakistan.' Sajan replied.

He walked over to Sheikh Tayeb and extended his hand. Sheikh Tayeb turned away without shaking hands and strode out of the room with Azhar in tow.

'Sheikh Tayeb is a little rattled today. He thought we were all fools here and would fall for his shenanigans. It's time he learnt that he cannot fool all the people all the time.' Sajan remarked when Sheikh Tayeb and Azhar were out of earshot.

'What do you think he will do?' Gordon Jobs asked.

'He would have tried to strip the Banjar operations of G&P Bank of all the assets, created liabilities, and remitted all the funds outside. Thank God we pre-empted that by imposing exchange monitoring procedures. Sheikh Tayeb and his gang are trapped. They have given us a set of financial statements that show a highly inflated financial position of the bank. Any settlement discussions will have to be around the position shown in the latest audited financial statements. We know and they know that these financial statements are false, and the auditors must have been tricked somehow into accepting the numbers. They can't admit that, so we will win.' Sajan closed the meeting.

***

Sheikh Tayeb and Azhar did not utter a word in the car from the Crown prince's office to the bank. Azhar knew the score and did not want to face the wrath of Sheikh Tayeb by speaking to him when he was not ready. Besides, there was the Driver of the car who should not hear anything.

As soon as they arrived at the bank's Banjar head office, Sheikh Tayeb and Azhar went straight to the conference room on the top floor. Mateen, Shakadir, Yousuf and two other senior officers from the bank's Banjar branch were there, chatting amongst themselves. Sheikh Tayeb opened the door without knocking. One look at his face was sufficient to indicate the meeting had not gone well. Everybody stopped talking and looked at Sheikh Tayeb anxiously.

He looked at the two branch officers. They took the hint and quickly left without even exchanging pleasantries with the chairman.

'We are leaving Banjar now. Yousuf, you are coming with us. Please tell the pilot that he should prepare for a flight to London. I would like to leave within the next two to three hours, if possible. If we leave within three hours, we should be able to land at Heathrow before the restrictions for night landing take effect,' Sheikh Tayeb said.

Without a word, Yousuf got up and dialled the number of the hotel room where the pilot of the airplane was staying. 'This is Yousuf Ali from the bank. The chairman is here with me. He wants to leave for London as soon as possible, preferably within the next two to three hours. Kindly get all the necessary formalities and procedures completed to fly out.' He said as soon as the connection was made.

'I don't know if it will be possible to get permission from the control tower and get the aircraft ready to leave within two to three hours but I will try. I'll assemble my crew and leave for the airport immediately. I will call you from there.' the pilot replied. Sheikh Tayeb looked after his airplane's pilot and crew well and at times required them to fly at very short notice.

'I'll order some sandwiches. Mrs. Tayeb is out in the town with my wife. I'll send a Driver to look for them at the usual places and take them to the hotel. I'll also make arrangements for your personal belongings to be packed up so you are ready to leave as soon as we get a word from the airport. If you will excuse me, I'll go pack a few clothes and get my passport.' Yousuf Ali started organising the affairs immediately.

Sheikh Tayeb had sunk into a chair. Yousuf asked one of the secretaries to get coffee for the chairman and Mr. Alam and organise some sandwiches. Within ten minutes, the telephone rang. It was Mrs. Tayeb; she wanted to speak to Sheikh Tayeb.

'I have been brought back to the hotel and hear that we have to leave immediately. Is everything okay?' She asked.

'No, everything is not okay. I'll explain when we meet. Please pack up for flying out immediately. We are going to London,' Sheikh Tayeb said.

Shakila assumed that the meeting did not go well and some difficulties had arisen. 'I'll be ready to leave very quickly,' she said and put the telephone down.

A delectable selection of sandwiches and salads arrived from Banjar Grande. However, nobody was interested in the food and it remained practically untouched. They sat around the table, looking at the newspapers and passing the time with small talk. There was no mention of the meeting with the Crown prince or the bank's business. Outside, the bank's staff was waiting to meet the chairman. They were told he was busy and may not be able to see them this time.

'There is no point in waiting here. Let's go to the hotel. At least we can pack up and wait there.' Sheikh Tayeb said to the group.

Immediately, two cars were arranged and the group left for the hotel. It was 2.30 p.m. Banjar time, which was five hours ahead of GMT. At the hotel, they were given the news that the aircraft was cleared for take-off at 5p.m. Sheikh Tayeb and the party were requested to reach the airport by 4.30 p.m. at the latest.

Shakila was busy putting her clothes and other belongings in the suitcases. She looked harassed. She looked quizzically at Sheikh Tayeb when he entered the royal suite but said nothing. The trained secretary that she was, she knew exactly when not to speak or disturb him.

Yousuf arrived soon after with a suitcase and soon the party was at the airport. There was a Banjar government official waiting for them there. He led them through immigration control and to the aircraft. Near the aircraft, a Cadillac with the Banjar government coat of arms was waiting. Two young girls came out holding bouquets of flowers and presented them to Sheikh Tayeb.

He was confused. He kissed the children and walked to the stairs to the aircraft. This was totally different than the treatment they were met with that morning. Sheikh Tayeb and Shakila quickly went up the stairs to the aircraft. At the entrance, another officer was waiting for them. He handed over two gift-wrapped boxes, one marked 'Sheikh Tayeb' and the other 'Mrs. Shakila Tayeb' along with an envelope with the Crown prince's seal embossed on it. The officer quickly left and the stairs were withdrawn.

Once in his seat, Sheikh Tayeb opened the envelope. It contained a letter on the Crown prince's personal stationery that read:

Dear Sheikh Tayeb,

I am sorry you and your wife were not extended the usual VVIP protocol upon arrival this time. This was due to the revised airport security procedures in place now. I wish, however, to assure you that you are and will always remain a very dear friend of our family.

I am sure you will understand that the meeting this morning was business. We have to take certain actions to protect the interests of the state of Banjar. What we are compelled to do may not be pleasant or helpful to you and the bank but we have to do what we have to do for our country. Please understand.

I look forward to you finalising the subject we discussed this morning. I hope this will be done quickly, as we have to take certain other actions, which are being held off until this matter is sorted out.

Please give my very best regards to Mrs. Tayeb.

With best wishes,

Sitara Khan

Crown prince, state of Banjar.'

Shakila opened the two gift boxes. Each box contained a diamond-encrusted gold Chopard watch. The coat of arms of Banjar was embossed on the dial of each one. They were beautiful and looked very expensive. Shakila knew Sheikh Tayeb's mood, so she showed him the watches without comment. He looked at them nonchalantly. Normally, he would have been very pleased to have received such a gift from a very important source.

Soon the aircraft was cleared for take-off and they were airborne. As soon as the pilot switched off the seat belts sign, Sheikh Tayeb asked the group to join him at the small conference table at the back of the plane. He also asked Shakila to join.

Once everybody was assembled, he told them about the discussions at the meeting. Everybody was shocked.

'I knew that we were no longer favourites but this was an ambush. Sajan Mala and his team were planning this for quite some time. The circular issued this morning to monitor remittance out of the country was specifically to hurt us. This will not do much good to Banjar's reputation in the financial world.' Yousuf was the first to react. He felt responsible for not anticipating or briefing his boss about the ambush.

'Banjar is rich and they will overcome any threat to their reputation by passing on large deposits of the state funds to the financial institutions abroad. The reaction will be muted. The Crown prince and his team are clearly keen to push G&P Bank out of Banjar and blackmail us into buying their shares. This will be a huge blow to our plans, as you all know. We were, in fact, hoping for some more investment from Banjar and not the reverse. This is a fundamental change in our position and will we need major changes in our plans.' Sheikh Tayeb replied.

'The behaviour of the prince and his team was insulting in today's meeting. He wants to buy the shares held by his family at book value. Sajan Mala has done his homework.'

'It's clear that they are planning to take over our Banjar assets. We'll be allowed to operate a small branch with a limited number of employees. In addition, they expect to receive a large sum of money for their shares in G&P Bank. Let's not forget that for the world at large, Prince Sitara Khan and the royal family of Banjar are the principal patrons of the bank. To lose their patronage would be a disaster for the bank. This is really one of the worst existential threats the bank has faced since its incorporation,' Azhar said.

'What are our options?' Sheikh Tayeb looked around the table.

'We have to buy time to start with.' Again, it was Azhar who spoke up. 'We should also scout for potential buyers for Banjar's shares. It will take time and we may not find a suitable investor with such a large amount to spare. Let's not forget that we also need further investments in the bank for our own needs. Is it possible to talk to the father and seek his help?' Azhar looked at Sheikh Tayeb.

'Bulund Khan is wheelchair-bound and suffering from several ailments He clearly has no control over anything anymore'

'As I said, we need time. I am sure that Sajan will pester us for a quick resolution of this matter, so we'll have to present some ideas. Obviously, they do not expect us to come up with a billion dollars in cash without notice to buy them out. They'll also expect us to share a plan. Mateen and I will work on some buy-out options just to keep the ball rolling. That should give us time to formulate our own plan to deal with this matter.' Azhar said.

With that, the conference ended, and everybody returned to his or her seat. Immediately after the meeting, Shakadir handed Sheikh Tayeb a note.

Sheikh Tayeb opened the folded paper. It read:

Maybe we should use an unconventional and non-banking approach to solve the Banjar matter. I know that Prince Taj Khan, the second son, is not happy at Sitara Khan grabbing power. As you know, Sitara Khan and Taj Khan are from different mothers. Sitara is from a Balochi mother from Pakistani Balochistan, while Taj's mother is from Iran. Taj hates Sitara and would not be averse to any plans to rectify the situation in his favour. With the changing of guards in Banjar, our problems may disappear. If you approve, I could pursue this idea and see what can be done.

Sheikh Tayeb responded to Shakadir, also writing his response rather than speaking it aloud:

Please explore the possibilities but do not do anything. I want a complete briefing before you take any action.

He looked at Shakadir, who immediately came and collected the piece of paper. He read it and put it in the shredder. The aircraft had all the equipment required for an office.

Chapter 31

London

Amir came out of Heathrow Terminal One around 12.30 in the afternoon. He had arrived on an Emirates flight from Dubai and was tired. He first had to travel from Karachi to Dubai for an onward connection to London after a wait of four hours at Dubai airport.

He waited patiently in the queue for a taxi outside the airport. Once his turn came, he asked the cabbie to take him to Milton Keynes and arrived at Danny's apartment just before four in the afternoon.

Amir had the key to the apartment. He let himself in and made himself comfortable. He then called John Delon on his direct number.

'John Delon.'

'John, Amir here. I am in the UK.'

'Oh, hello. Good that you are here. I have a lot of news for you. When can we meet?'

'I am available any time tomorrow.' Amir said.

'We have a partners' meeting first thing tomorrow morning. That should be finished by 10.30. So let us meet then.'

'I'll be there.' Amir said and hung up.

Around 6.30 p.m., Danny arrived. 'Oh, hello. When did you get in?'

'I reached here around four p.m. I didn't want to disturb you so I came here directly from Heathrow. I'm on my way to Switzerland.'

'Good. The weather there must be improving.' Danny said.

'For you chaps in England, the weather is the most important thing in life. There are more important things than a sunny day in the park.' Amir commented.

'Are there? If you suffered three hundred plus days out of a year in gloomy, dark, rainy weather, you may not say so. Anyway, so are you are moving there permanently?'

'I hope temporarily. With my plans for the bank, I don't think there is any degree of permanence for G&P Bank.' Amir said.

'You sound pretty confident as if you have all the cards to crush the bank.' Danny commented.

'I have just spoken to John Delon. He has some information for me and wants to discuss it as soon as possible. I'm going there tomorrow. Do you want to join?'

'No. I can't. I still work for Tolbert and Gibbs, you know. John called me once when you were in Pakistan. I told him that it might be better to wait unless it's very urgent. He said there was nothing critical.'

'I suggest you also start looking for another job. Tolbert and Gibbs might also be affected if this thing blows up.'

'It won't be that easy to bring down G&P Bank. And Tolbert and Gibbs have a long illustrious history in the accounting profession in the UK. They won't go down that easily either.'

'We'll see. I attended the bank's senior staff conference in Bangkok. A real experience.'

'Was it? They are pretty organised, are they?'

'The conference was an exercise in contrasts and humbug. It was a mixture of religious fervour and Thai entertainment, with a lot of hot air presented in between as ideas for strengthening the business. These guys live in their own world. They believe there are no laws or regulations to be taken into account when doing business. For example, in order to attract more deposits, one delegate suggested they should bribe heads of states to keep their countries' foreign exchange reserves with the bank.'

'That's a new one. And bold, very bold,' Danny replied.

'Well, I'm hungry, so be a good host and arrange something in the food department.' Amir said.

Danny ordered home delivery from Pizza Hut. Both friends talked for a while and then went to bed early.

***

Amir arrived at the offices of Delon, Delon and Tomsky at exactly 10.30. The receptionist advised him to make himself comfortable in the meeting room and that John would join him shortly.

'Would you like to drink something, Mr. Ramli?' The receptionist asked.

'A coffee would be nice. Black, no sugar, please.' Amir said.

The coffee arrived quickly. Soon after, John walked in, as well.

'Good morning. How are you?' John asked, extending his hand to Amir.

'I am fine, and you?' Amir shook John's hand.

'Busy. Can't complain. Being busy is nice. How was the flight?'

'I took Emirates via Dubai. Very comfortable, I must say,' Amir replied.

'Yes, unfortunately, the standard of service of European carriers is not the best these days. The Middle East airlines seem to be leading the way.' John replied. 'Now, to our earlier discussions. First, Germany. You are in luck. Ian Softsol has been busy doing some serious detective work. He has been able to ascertain that there was a contract on Richard Bringsen given to the Mehwar group. Mehwars are the most lethal of the Turkish gangs operating in Germany. They have their fingers in every crime. There must have been a substantial fee, as Richard was tracked all the time he was in Germany, and they knew his travel itinerary. The truck driver, Ahmet Gulay, is a gang member and has taken part in many gang fights, some resulting in deaths.'

'This is good news for us. How can we take it further?'

'Ian tells me there is no way anybody would get any cooperation from Mehwars. So, that is a dead end. You may go to the German police and tell them you suspect he was killed because he was investigating the G&P Bank and point out that the driver involved in the accident had a history of gang-related violence. They might listen to you and lean on the Driver and make other enquiries, which may or may not result in connecting Richard's death to the bank. Once the German police are approached, you may leak the information to a local newspaper that the German police are investigating a possible connection between the death of the British banker and his employers. That should generate heat and may get the investigation going by the police.'

'You realise that if I go to the German police, I would be more dead than last year's stale fish.'

'Yes. The bank will go after you and bump you off.'

'So, it is a non-starter.'

'Not really. Ian Softsol has pretty good contacts in the police forces in Europe. He may take this matter to the German police on your behalf for a fee, but you would have to give much more information than what we have given him so far. And he does not come cheap.'

'I think it's worth doing. Would it be possible for you to continue to deal with Ian without me coming into contact with him? That way, you are acting on behalf of a client who wants to remain anonymous.' Amir said.

'I could do that but you are getting involved in something that is far more dangerous and complicated than you might imagine. I just want you to be sure that you really want to do this.' John replied.

'Listen, John, my life was almost ruined by these guys. I am certain that the G&P Bank was involved in Richard Bringsen's death. I don't know how many others have met their fate in the same manner as him. The G&P Bank's people do not have any regard to anybody's life or property. A lot of people trust them with their savings, and they do not know that their savings have evaporated. I know the bank is insolvent. There are no limits for the bank. For them, everybody is dispensable and should be used. It's about time somebody did something to stop them. I find myself in a position to be able to do something and I don't want to stop now.'

'Well, if you feel that strongly, then there is nothing else to be said. Now, about my meeting with David Ringbutton at the SIB. We seem to be in luck again. According to David, a full investigation is in progress against G&P Bank. The SIB has been receiving complaints, particularly from the US government agencies about G&P Bank's involvement in illegal activities, including money laundering and shielding of drug lords and smugglers in the USA.

Apparently, funds from suspicious parties are remitted to G&P Bank in the UK and invested in high-end properties here. They say that the very recent boom in the London property market is being fuelled by dirty money coming from outside.' John said.

Amir felt hopeful. 'I am happy the world is finally waking up to the acts of these criminals. So, where do we go from here? Should we pass on some information to the SIB?'

'From what I have read in Richard's folder, there doesn't appear to be enough material about illegal activities involving G&P Bank in the UK. They have certainly window-dressed their financial information and may have contravened the banking regulations here by not giving true information and making provisions against doubtful assets. You, however, need more information about any serious illegal acts committed by the bank in the UK in order to provoke the authorities to act. I suggest we leave Mr Ringbutton and his colleagues to do their job. I anticipate that the US agencies will force the officials here into action.

'Your best bet is Switzerland. Apparently, there may be documents in Geneva which might nail the Bank. As you are now heading there, you may personally follow this up. Please see what you can unearth there. Once in possession of further information, let me know and we can decide our approach towards the Swiss. It may be better to appoint a lawyer there to help you. Please remember that Swiss lawyers are even more expensive than UK ones.' John was very thorough. 'I'll ask Ian Softsol to speak to his contacts in Germany and see if he can get the German police to resume their interest in Mr. Bringsen's demise. Would you be willing to share Richard's folder with the police?'

Amir hesitated. 'I don't know if we should do that. I wouldn't like the information in the folder to become public prematurely as it might lose its significance and give the bank an opportunity to take protective measures. What I may be able to do is share the letter Richard wrote to me where he indicated that he was preparing a dossier with respect to the G&P Bank's activities and he sensed danger to himself. The letter is in the papers I left with you. You may make a copy and give it to Ian to pass on to the Germans in confidence.'

'That might be a good starting point. The police would, of course, interview Ursula's father and ask him if he is holding any information. Mr. Otto Huber would no doubt say that the information is with you, which would lead the German police to your doorstep.' John replied.

'Once they start the investigation, then we should be able to give them the folder with a request to keep it confidential until there is a need to use it to indict the bank's officials. It is possible they might never need to share the folder with the bank's officials as they might be able to establish a link between the Mehwars and the bank and between the Mehwars and Ahmet Gulay,' Amir said.

'All right, let's do that. I'll ask Ian to move as discussed. He might need more money. I would say a further thousand pounds. I've been spending some time on this matter also and would appreciate it if you could let me have a further advance of three thousand pounds.'

'I'll be bankrupt before this thing is over, but this is of my own choosing. I don't expect you or Ian to work for free. I'll give you a cheque for four thousand,' Amir replied, taking out his chequebook.

'Thank you.' John said, accepting the cheque. 'I will issue you a receipt. Of this, one thousand pounds will be put in the clients' monies account and three thousand will go on account of our fees.'

'Once in Geneva, I'll rent a post box where you may send me letters. I'll also see if I can hire a secretarial service to take and relay messages as well as receive and send faxes. That'll give us the flexibility to communicate. In the meantime, if something urgent comes up, please leave a message with Danny. I'll be in touch with Danny and contact you immediately in case of a need.' Amir said, getting up.

'I'll do that. Be careful, my friend. You are treading dangerous waters.' John got up and shook hands with Amir.

'I will. Let's hope we succeed in what we are doing.'

'I hope we do,' John replied.

With that, Amir left.

***

In the street, Amir noted that it had turned out to be a lovely afternoon, with the sun shining brilliantly. He thought this was not a day to be wasted and deserved a walk in the park.

Amir recalled his last few days in Karachi. He was the toast of the town. His peers envied him for getting a posting with the bank in Geneva. Girls fell over each other to be with him. He was the most eligible bachelor around.

Samira had made it known that she was Amir's girlfriend, and they were in a serious relationship. She turned up at every party Amir was invited to and stayed glued to him. She told him she would love to live in Geneva and looked forward to being able to do so soon.

Samira had invited Amir for dinner at her place, where only her family was present. Her mother kept saying that Samira and Amir would make a perfect couple. She even asked Amir to bring over his family so both families could get to know each other.

All this upset Amir, as he did not love Samira nor did he have any plans to marry her. As far as Amir was concerned, Samira was only a good friend. He hoped that this infatuation of Samira's would end once he was in Geneva and there was some distance between them.

Thinking of Geneva, his thoughts went to Rehana. He really missed her and looked forward to being with her again. Amir had not communicated with her since their meeting in Geneva. He glanced at his watch. It was 12.30 p.m. in London; that meant 1.30 p.m. in Geneva. Soon her children would be home from school. He could imagine Rehana at home, alone in the kitchen, cooking a meal for her family.

On an impulse, he walked into the lobby of The Grosvenor House and asked the receptionist for a telephone. She directed him to a corner of the lobby where a bank of telephones was located. He selected an instrument that accepted coins. He pressed several one-pound coins into the slot and dialled the number Rehana had given him.

'Hello.' He heard Rehana's melodious voice.

'Assalam Alaikum,' Amir said, his heart thumping. He was not sure if Rehana would speak to him after such a long time, and he wondered whether he was doing the right thing by calling her like this.

'Waalekum Assalam. Who is it?'

'Amir. You have forgotten my voice.'

'Is that really you, Amir? I thought it was you, but I didn't want to take any chances. It is so wonderful to hear your voice again. I am angry with you for not calling earlier. You promised.' Rehana's voice was breaking with emotions.

'I've been thinking of you every minute, but I wasn't sure if I should intrude. I thought you might not welcome me calling you like this.'

'Why would I do that? I asked you to call. I have been waiting every day for your call. Tell me, how are you? And where are you calling from?'

'I'm fine and in London. How are you and the family?'

'Same as before. Living in a gilded cage. You were a breath of fresh air which came into my life for a day and disappeared. I live in the memory of the few minutes we spent together. The children are fine and should be back from school soon. Rehmallah is busy at the bank. He was in Thailand recently for the bank's conference. Were you also there?'

'Yes, I was. I met Rehmallah there.'

'He never mentioned that to me. So, what are you doing in London?'

'I am here on some business and will be in Geneva tomorrow.'

'What? Are you coming to Geneva? This is wonderful news. How long are you coming for this time?'

'Actually, I missed you so much that I asked for a transfer to Geneva. My request was granted and now I will be based in Geneva. I'll be in your hair every day.'

'Oh, God. I will die of happiness. This is unbelievable. My prayers seem to have been answered. You have been in my heart and will always be there. I will make your life heaven when you are here. Where are you going to stay?'

'The bank has rented a one-bedroom furnished apartment in Diplomat Apartments on Rue de Lausanne for one month. I will try to find something suitable once I am there.'

'Rue de Lausanne is not far from our apartment. I'll help you find a suitable place for us.' Rehana was excited.

Amir noted that she said 'for us' and did not say anything.

'I wonder why Rehmallah didn't mention that you are moving to Geneva. Maybe he is jealous of the dinner I gave you when you were here. Anyway, we are hardly on talking terms. I'll tell you all about the troubles with Rehmallah when you are in Geneva. When are you going to be here?'

'I am flying BA tomorrow afternoon from Heathrow. Should be in Geneva around 5 p.m. I'll call you the day after tomorrow in the morning. I won't call you in the evening when everybody is home.'

'I'll wait for your call like the farmers back home waiting for the monsoons. Call me as soon as you can and find time to see me.'

'I will. I promise,' Amir said.

'Well, my darling, goodbye for now.'

'Goodbye,' Amir said and hung up, feeling exhilarated. He was really looking forward to seeing Rehana again.

After finishing his call, Amir changed his mind about walking in Hyde Park and wandered around the Oxford Street for a short while, taking in the sights and sounds.

A short while after, he looked at his watch, it was a little past 2 p.m. and Amir was hungry. He thought that it would be nice if Danny were to have lunch with him. Then, he could brief him about the meeting with John Delon. Amir stepped inside Selfridges and went to the telephone near the Oxford Street entrance and called Danny.

'Hey, busy?' he asked.

'Not too much. Trying to complete a memo for my boss. It shouldn't take long. Where are you?'

'At Selfridges, where else?' He said jokingly. 'I finished my meeting with John and had time, so I came here to look at the shops and have a meal at the restaurant here. I wondered if you would be able to join me for lunch.'

'I just had my sandwiches. If you want, we could go to a movie. They are showing *Home Alone* at Odeon in Leicester Square. Everybody who has seen it says it's a fantastic comedy. The afternoon show starts at 4 p.m. We can watch the movie and have a Chinese dinner in Piccadilly afterward.'

'Done. I'll buy the tickets and wait for you in the foyer of Odeon,' Amir replied.

After finishing his call with Danny, Amir took the escalators to the top-floor restaurant and dining area. He selected a chicken *shawarma* (beef or chicken rolled in Arabic bread) and a fruit juice. After his meal, Amir left Selfridges and walked towards Regent Street, heading to Piccadilly.

He was outside Odeon twenty minutes before showtime. He bought two tickets and a small portion of popcorn. To pass the time, he looked at the display windows of the cinema where photographs of *Home Alone* and other programmes were shown. Danny walked in five minutes before the start.

'Do you want some popcorn?'

'Yes. Let's do it properly!' Danny said.

Both friends went into the hall. The theatre had already started showing trailers of the upcoming attractions.

After the movie, Danny said, 'That was very good.'

'An excellent story. An eight-year-old with ingenuity and nerve is able to beat a couple of tough burglars. It was great! I enjoyed it.' Amir replied.

'There's a good Chinese restaurant called Chengdu not far from here. It's named after the capital city of Sichuan province of China. Sichuan is famous for hot and spicy food. I have heard great things about this place. We can walk there. I have already booked us a table.' Danny said.

'Yes, it's a very nice day. Let's walk.' Amir replied.

'How was your meeting with John?' Danny asked.

'Excellent. We're getting somewhere. The private investigator has discovered that the Driver of the lorry involved in the accident in Speyer is actually a member of a Turkish criminal gang operating in Germany. He believes there was a contract on Richard Bringsen's life. I've provided John the letter Richard wrote to me in which he expressed fear for his life. John will pass this letter on to the private investigator who will present it to the German police with a request to investigate the matter further because it might be murder.

'I have also learnt that Bank of England is investigating G&P Bank's activities here. They suspect G&P Bank to be involved in money laundering and assisting the underworld operators. I'll be in Geneva from tomorrow and I'll try to get more evidence of the bank's activities there. Once I have some tangible evidence, I'll hire a lawyer in Geneva and try to present the evidence to the Swiss. I really do hope G&P Bank officials will be held accountable for their crimes.' Amir explained.

'I've also been thinking hard about this matter. I think that the time has come for me to do my duty, as well. I'd like to speak to John and give evidence against Tolbert and Gibbs and G&P Bank to the Bank of England and the Institute of Chartered Accountants. I have a lot of information in the working papers, which would prove conclusively that the bank's financial statements were false and the bank was insolvent.' Danny was now charged.

'Why would you do that? You have a career with Tolbert and Gibbs. In fact, what you propose to do would completely destroy your future. Nobody in your profession or the financial world will even look at you if you are known to have blown the whistle on your employers and released privileged information.' Amir said.

'There comes a time when one must choose between doing the right thing and doing the easy thing. It's time I did the right thing, just like you are doing.' Danny seemed to have made up his mind.

'My situation is different. G&P Bank put my life and future in danger. I could have been arrested and be languishing in jail somewhere. I'm burning with the desire to take revenge. My future vision is limited to getting even with those bastards. You have not suffered any damage personally. Besides, you should think of getting married and settling down in life. You don't need to destroy your future. I'm sorry that I have involved you in this.' Amir replied.

'I'll try to work out a deal with the Bank of England and the Institute to keep my identity confidential. I may give them information that cannot be tracked back to me. It's for this reason that I want to involve John. In any event, I've decided to leave Tolbert and Gibbs. I have already sent my resume to other big accounting firms, industries and banks, and I've received a couple of interview calls. Hopefully, things will work out. I don't want to embarrass you, but I would like to marry Seemi. I hope she will accept my proposal.'

'You devil.' Amir was delighted. His parents' dream was finally coming true. 'Have you spoken to her? I am sure she will be delighted.'

'Not yet. I'm going to Karachi this weekend and will propose to her then. Please keep this to yourself. I don't want to be embarrassed or upset anybody in case she does not accept me.' Danny was shy.

'I will not say a word to anybody. Please let me know as soon as you have spoken to her. But I have to insist that you should not do anything to jeopardise your career or endanger your life.' Amir said.

'Thank you, my friend. I feel aggrieved by the way my seniors at Tolbert and Gibbs hijacked G&P Bank audit from me and cooked up the financial statements. G&P Bank has even lured my father with an offer of financing to pressure me. Don't worry. I won't expose myself. I'll play this very carefully. I'll talk to John after I return from Pakistan. As for you, I suggest you should be very careful, as at the slightest suspicion, they will go after you and your life won't be an insurable risk after that. I still suggest that you leave them alone and if you are not happy working there, find another job. I am sure there will be plenty of opportunities for you.' Danny said.

'I don't know about you, but I feel as though I am being pushed into this by a hidden hand. I am in it without fear of any consequences. Maybe this will cost me my life, but what is life if you cannot live by your values?' Amir sounded suicidal.

'Exactly. We both are in this for the right reasons and if there is any justice in this world, we will come through this.' Danny sounded equally philosophical.

They had arrived at the restaurant.

Chengdu restaurant was decorated in bright red with a golden roof and dragons at the entrance. They were shown to a table in a corner. Soon a waitress appeared with jasmine-scented hot towels and a kettle of green tea with small porcelain cups. From the menu, they selected hot and sour soup and hot chicken and beef dishes with egg-fried rice. The food was delicious. Both friends thoroughly enjoyed the meal. There was no further discussion of the G&P Bank or its problems. After the meal, they took a cab to Euston station and returned to Danny's flat.

'It was a lovely evening. Thanks,' Amir said.

'I enjoyed it very much. Thank you. You're travelling tomorrow. I hope you'll return soon.'

'I'll come to London frequently. I have to finish this business with John. I'll also try to establish secure lines to communicate with you and him. Please try to come to Geneva if you find time. Anyway, give me a call from Karachi and let me know the outcome there.'

'I will. I'll see you before you leave tomorrow. Have a good night, my friend.'

'Good night.'

Chapter 32

Geneva

Amir's flight touched down at Geneva Airport just before 5 p.m. This time, he was completely relaxed. His papers were in order and there was no fear of anything in his baggage being challenged.

Julia, Masood Qadir's secretary, was waiting for Amir outside the airport.

'Hi, welcome back. Masood was tied up in a meeting so he sent his apologies and asked me to meet you to make sure you were comfortable. Did you have a good flight?'

'It was only a short flight from London. No problems this time.'

'Excellent. As you might know, we have booked you into Diplomat Apartments on Rue de Lausanne. It's only a five-minute walk from our offices.' She led Amir to the parking building where her Mercedes was parked.

They arrived at the apartment block in less than twenty minutes. On the way, Julia made polite conversation, enquiring about Amir's health and family. She dropped him at the apartment entrance and gave him directions to the bank. She apologised for not staying with Amir as she had another engagement that evening.

The receptionist at the apartment building took a copy of Amir's passport for registration and handed over the key to a one-bedroom apartment on the second floor. Amir didn't think the apartment was bad; It had a small balcony with a view of the lake.

Amir quickly unpacked and went downstairs. The weather was chilly but there was no rain. He walked by the lake for an hour or so, and he felt refreshed. While walking, he thought of calling Rehana but decided against it as it was after business hours and Rehmallah and the children would be home.

Once back in his apartment, Amir found the Yellow Pages and opened the section for 'Secretarial Help.' He found names, addresses and telephone numbers of various establishments offering complete office facilities and secretarial support services. Several provided twenty-four-hour service. Amir noted the names and telephone numbers of three providing round-the-clock service nearer to Rue de Lausanne.

He called the first one, Bonjour Secretarial Bureau, located on Rue du Mole, which was only one block away from his apartment.

'Hello,' His call was answered on the first ring. *Very efficient,* Amir thought.

'Hello. My name is Amir Ramli. I am an international banker looking for secretarial support. I would like to come and make arrangements with you. Up to what time are you open?' Amir asked.

'We are open twenty-four hours, seven days a week. The manager, however, leaves around 9 p.m. You may come now if you wish.' replied the lady at the other end.

'I'll be there in fifteen minutes.' Amir said and hung up.

The offices for Bonjour Secretarial Bureau were on the fifth floor of a nice office block on Rue du Mole. Amir had to press a bell for the receptionist to release the door lock to enter the building.

'Good evening.' said the professionally dressed lady at the reception. 'You must be Mr. Ramli.'

'Yes. I am.'

'The manager, Ms. Catherine Brandt, is waiting to see you.' The receptionist led Amir to a meeting room.

Soon a very well-dressed middle-aged lady walked in. 'Hello. I am Catherine Brandt.'

'Hi, my name is Amir Ramli. I'm an international banker on an assignment here. I am also working on another confidential assignment for the headquarters, which is quite separate from the offices here. I would like to make arrangements for secretarial support services to be able to send and receive telephone messages, mail, and other secretarial assistance.'

'I understand. We will be pleased to provide you what we call the Flexi-office package. This entitles you to get a desk here for a maximum of five hours a week and you may make use of our conference rooms, telephone services, messaging, and mail services. You would have to enter into a six-month contract. We charge one thousand five hundred Swiss francs per month, plus out-of-pocket expenses, such as the cost of telephones, telexes, faxes, courier services, et cetera. You would have to give us a deposit of five thousand Swiss francs and the monthly charge at the beginning of each month. The deposit will be returned to you when the contract expires.

'As a part of the package, we will also provide you with a safety box which can only be opened by two keys. One key would be with you, and the other, a master key, remains with me or my assistant. We appreciate the needs of the international businessman and provide round-the-clock service, seven days a week. There is always somebody here to attend calls and assist our clients.'

'The package suits me. I have one other need. Because I do some work for my bank's headquarters that should not be disclosed to the local officials, I have to keep it completely confidential. I might also give you some messages to pass on to another party. How could you help me there?' Amir asked.

'We Swiss are proud of our ability to keep confidences. When registering with us, we require a copy of your passport and complete details of your local and permanent addresses. We then assign you an operational name of your choosing. For all practical purposes, this name will be used when we refer to you in our records. Your actual name and your personal details are kept in a confidential file located in my personal security cabinet. This information is known by only you and myself. We will never reveal your information to anybody outside this office unless there is a court order. To assure you of our seriousness, we provide a written undertaking of confidentiality.

'We will give you an ID card to present when you come in here to use our facilities. As to the transmission of messages given by you over the phone, we assign a security password to identify yourself before acting on your telephonic instructions.'

'This is fine. Could I assign another person to communicate with you, who could use your services on my behalf?' Amir asked. He had Rehana in mind.

'Assigning another person to have full access to the information belonging to you would complicate matters a little. What we do in these circumstances is open a sub-account for an additional five hundred Swiss francs per month. This entitles the other person to leave messages for you and get the information authorised by you. This other person is also given a special contact name, ID card and facility of a locker and other secretarial services.'

'Good, this is fine. I haven't got the money on me at the moment. I'll come tomorrow and pay the deposit and the first month's charge. I would like to pay cash.'

'Excellent. We love cash. I suggest you complete the personal information form now so we may keep the agreement ready for you when you come tomorrow.' Ms Brandt said, giving Amir a portfolio containing the information about the Bureau, the personal information form and details of services provided with the tariff of charges.

Amir quickly completed the form and gave it back to her. She also took Amir's passport and made a copy for her record.

The form-filling exercise completed, Amir got up, shook hand with the lady and left with a promise to come at the same time the next day. On his return journey, he found a McDonald's on a side street and bought a Big Mac meal. He sat down at a corner table with the tray and ate.

He was happy there was some progress; he had the facility to receive and relay confidential messages outside of his work environment, and now he was sorely missing Rehana and finding it difficult to wait to meet her again. However, he realised that his contacts with Rehana would have to be managed cautiously, so she was not exposed and did not get into more trouble with Rehmallah than she probably was already in.

After finishing his meal, Amir returned to the apartment, switched on the television to view the days' news on CNN, and then called it a day.

Chapter 33

Karachi, offices of TIG

Yakoob Soothar had called an emergency meeting of his brothers and advisers. He was angry. Very angry.

'How could they do this to us?' He looked around. 'According to Mansukh, the Singaporean court has given a two-year prison sentence to both the captain and first officer of our ship and fined them two million Singaporean dollars each for arms smuggling. They have also impounded the ship and fined the company twenty-five million Singaporean dollars. None of our ships will be allowed to berth in Singapore. This is ridiculous. I have never heard of such punishment before.'

'I tried to tell you, Yakoob, that there was a serious problem in Singapore. But you did not have time for me. We didn't have the money to hire a decent lawyer in Singapore. We were represented by a low-grade Indian lawyer who seemed to be working more for the prosecution than for us. Mansukh told me that the Singapore government's action was instigated by the CIA and RAW. Therefore, there was always a high risk of tough action by the Singaporeans.' Haroon said.

'Oh, shut up! This is happening because of your mismanagement of the whole shipping business. You should have done more to deal with this situation instead of letting matters take their own course. Now, our group's name is tarnished and our reputation is down the drain. The news of the court verdict will appear in the international press.

'Why didn't you talk to G&P Bank in Singapore directly if you considered that the need of money was acute?'

'I did. But the manager, Tariq Dost Shah, would not even take my call. Mansukh said he couldn't do anything if there was no money. I tried to talk to you and Salim. Nobody paid any attention to me.'

'You are responsible for the shipping business. You should have found a way.'

'I am not going to sit here and listen to this nonsense! I did everything that was possible within my authority. Sorry, I'm off.' Haroon was now angry.

'Where are you going? Sit down!' Yakoob tried to exercise his authority as the boss of the group.

'Sorry, I have better things to do than listen to your nonsense. Instead of finding a solution, you want a scapegoat.' Haroon retorted and left the room.

Once in his office, he dialled the number of his lady friend. 'Hi. Be there within thirty minutes. I really need you today,' he said.

He picked up his briefcase and walked out of the office. He didn't tell his secretary that he was leaving for the day. He went straight to the parking lot and drove off in the direction of Karachi's harbour, where at Rock & Sea Hotel, his beautiful friend would be waiting to relax him.

Back in the conference room, Yakoob was now even angrier.

'Haroon is not really up to it. We will have to do some reorganisation after this is over. What is the way out of this mess?' He looked at Salim and Masoom.

'Well, to start with, we should appeal the Singapore court's decision. We'll need a talented lawyer to deal with this matter. If you wish, I'm prepared to go to Singapore and organise matters there, but we'll need funds. I think we should have at least five hundred thousand US dollars available there to pay legal fees and other charges.'

'We do not have half a million US dollars to spare,' Salim said.

'Nothing happens without money. I'm afraid if funds are not available, then we will not be able to do anything to protect our people and assets,' Masoom said.

'We have to find funds for this, Salim,' Yakoob said. 'We simply need more cash.'

'How far down the road are we to transfer my father's assets in our name? We'd like to dispose of them as soon as possible.'

'We have discovered several properties and stocks in your father's name. The most valuable of these is the villa in Hong Kong and an apartment block in Knightsbridge. The block has ten apartments and a penthouse. Except for the penthouse, which Mr. Haroon was using, all of the apartments are rented out. Mr. Soothar received approximately three hundred thousand pounds in rent from these apartments. He also owned large chunks of shares in several blue-chip companies. Unfortunately, Mr. Soothar had not prepared a will before he died. As you are aware, he held three nationalities. For his UK and Hong Kong assets, his British nationality will be considered relevant, and British law will apply. This has estate duty implications. I have already initiated procedures to obtain the necessary certificates from the courts declaring you three brothers as Mr. Soothar's legal heirs, so that his assets may be transferred in your name. The wheels of bureaucracy move slowly and these matters take time.' Masoom explained.

'We have to sell these assets as soon as possible. Please move as quickly as you can.' Yakoob was unhappy that the matters, such as the absence of his father's will, were now a problem. Yakoob turned to Salim. 'Salim, have we been able to strip the companies that are not formally part of our group? Some of these companies had substantial assets. We may be able to take out the assets and leave the liabilities there.'

'You are correct. There are about ten million dollars waiting to be picked up in these companies. I am trying, but progress is slow. I have to move carefully, as we do not want to alert these companies' shareholders. These companies have net liabilities positioned in their balance sheets, as they have borrowed heavily and transferred the funds to TIG. One of the main nominee shareholders of these companies, Majeed Lakda, is a UK lawyer and understands the rules and may create difficulties. I have asked our lawyers to move on this matter quickly. I have already lined up buyers for the assets that will become available when the release papers are signed by the shareholders.' Salim replied.

'Who is this Majeed Lakda? I don't seem to have met him.' Yakoob asked.

'He is a senior man in our corporate legal department. He was trusted by Mr. Ismail. He is a pain in the neck and always creates difficulties.' Masoom replied.

'Deal with him in any way you consider appropriate. Get rid of this problem and let's get our ten million dollars as soon as possible.' Yakoob said to both Salim and Masoom.

'There is some good news, as well.' Salim, sensing the desperation, played for the effect. 'As you know, we have properties in Hong Kong and London which are informally mortgaged to G&P Bank. I say informally because G&P Bank does not have the legal papers for the mortgage. I have been in contact with some people who are interested in buying these properties. We should get approximately fifty million dollars for them. The only difficulty is that it might take up to four weeks to complete the deal.'

'If it's only four weeks, then we should go to the local secondary market to borrow. We're desperate.' Yakoob said.

'The local money lenders are criminals. They charge two percent interest per month compound and they want their interest paid promptly. They behave extremely violently if one cannot meet their obligations on schedule.' Salim replied.

'What choice do we have?' Yakoob asked. 'One of our ships has been impounded in Singapore. Our people around the world are crying for short-term funds. The banks are not lending to us. We have a lot of funds in the pipeline but for several reasons, it's taking time to get hold of them. You just said that within the next four weeks we should be able to get approximately fifty million dollars. I suggest you contact our sources and try to get a good deal. After all, we aren't just anybody, we are TIG, one of the largest companies in the region. We should be able to get preferred rates for our borrowings. I suggest you borrow twenty million dollars to take care of our immediate needs.'

'Okay, I'll move on that, but I still don't like it.' Salim was still not convinced.

'Please, not a word about this to our brothers. They do not understand business. The three of us have to carry this burden.' Yakoob stressed the need for confidentiality.

'I provided you with the list of ships we could sell. You have not replied.' Salim then moved to the next issue.

'I was surprised to see that we are only able to get forty million dollars for four ships. There's also a risk that G&P Bank might become aware of the sale and take action. We have to be extremely careful when we sell these ships.' Yakoob replied

'We will be. Some of these ships are on high waters. We'll let the agents with whom we normally deal with know that we're in the market to sell. We'll have to pay off the crew, also.' Salim said.

'Keep Mansukh involved in these. I don't think Haroon will be any help. His brain is in his balls. He'll sign any document you want him to sign. He's not capable of dealing with serious issues and would rather spend his time and money on his girlfriends. Let him be happy with his life. I don't want to start a war in the family at this time.' Yakoob said. 'What happened to the business G&P Bank was passing our way?'

'The shipment was for arms. Our insurance policy doesn't allow us to carry these types of goods. We won't be able to tell the insurers or any other party the true nature of the goods. It'll have to be a clandestine voyage. We'd have to take this on board at our own risk. I asked them for a freight charge of ten million dollars to be paid in advance as nobody would want to know us if things go wrong.' Salim replied.

'Good thinking. They accepted; I presume?' Yakoob asked.

'They're still thinking about it. Shakadir at the bank wasn't happy with my insistence on receiving the freight in advance.' Salim replied.

'I agree with you. We shouldn't agree to do anything unless we're paid in advance. We'll have to be bold.' Yakoob said.

'We will.' Both Salim and Masoom said in unison.

As there was nothing further to discuss, the meeting was adjourned and Salim and Masoom left. Within five minutes, Salim knocked on the door of Yakoob's office.

'That was quick,' Yakoob said, looking up.

'I wanted to speak to you privately about a possible opportunity. First, you must promise that you will not be angry with me because what I am proposing is illegal and dangerous.' Salim said.

'This sounds interesting. Tell me.' Yakoob's curiosity was now piqued.

'I've been contacted by an associate of Fazlullah Khan.' Salim said and awaited Salim's reaction.

'Fazlullah Khan? The notorious Drug baron?'

'Yes, the same. They know that we have the logistical capabilities, network, and facility to dispose of their product. They are willing to sell us one hundred kilos of pure cocaine at a very reasonable price.' Salim replied.

'Are they going out of business or what? Why are they offering this to us?'

'If anything, they are expanding their business. Their network is operating at maximum capacity. The supply from Afghanistan has been very good this year. Apparently, all the turmoil has contributed to more people growing poppy and producing the powder. Apparently, Fazlullah's organisation is stretched to the limit. They handle a metric ton of the product every month. In view of the insecurity in Afghanistan and increasingly aggressive attitude of the anti-narcotics agencies around the world, they don't want to keep too much stock with them.' Salim explained.

'What's in it for us? And how do you propose we get involved?' Yakoob asked.

'Fazlullah Khan is willing to give us one hundred kilos of the product at fifteen thousand dollars per kilo. The street value of this product in Europe is approximately two hundred thousand dollars per kilo. Fazlullah will give us the names of dealers in Europe and the Middle East. I understand we should be able to sell it at a minimum of one hundred thousand dollars per kilo. Fazlullah would deliver the product in Bara, near Peshawar. It would be our responsibility to transport the product from Bara to the appropriate destinations and sell it at our own risk.' Salim explained.

'And how do we dispose of this product and get our money?'

'Fazlullah will advise the dealer network that we are his associates. We would have to contact these people directly or through certain trusted intermediaries. Once the product gets there, the buyers will pick up the consignment. They'd pay us cash on delivery.'

'Sounds as if we have to learn a new trade, and how do we do that so quickly?'

'The associate of Fazlullah, who's been talking to me, is willing to join us with the blessings of Fazlullah. He knows the business inside out. He'll provide us with all the contacts and complete the transactions on our behalf. He suggested that since we have a shipping line and an aircraft at our disposal, the shipment of goods should be easy.'

'What does this man want in return?' Yakoob was still not convinced.

'He wants to be a partner in this business with a salary of two hundred fifty thousand dollars per year, plus five percent of the price of the product we pay to Fazlullah Khan. This would have to be paid when the product is sold and we collect cash.'

'That sounds like a lot. Also, the business is very risky.'

'It's no riskier than what we are doing already. We're shipping goods for triads and planning to provide services to customers in Latin America. We're already providing transport services to Afghan warring factions. We're doing all this for peanuts and at no less risk to us. One of our ships has been impounded in Singapore.

'This new opportunity opens doors for us to do business for ourselves instead of for others, with substantial profits. We could make a cool hundred million dollars if we're able to move a ton of product. Afghanistan is awash with the product and there are several suppliers in addition to Fazlullah. We're starving for cash. Desperate times require desperate measures.' Salim was very keen to get rid of the stress of operating without cash.

'Okay. I hear what you're saying, but how do we justify this to the family and other directors and the community at large?' Yakoob asked.

'We don't have to justify this to anybody. Nobody should know except the two of us. Nobody in the family has to know anything about this. We have no fear from the associate or Fazlullah, as these people know how to keep their mouths shut. And if this matter gets out by any misfortune, then what? Nothing. Several very senior businessmen are known to have been involved in this business.'

'How do we take this further?' Yakoob was now interested.

'You should meet this associate first. He is actually one of Fazlullah's nephews. His name is Barsat Khan. He's in Karachi at the moment and ready to meet you any time you want. You'll have to meet Fazlullah, as well. You might have to go to Peshawar for a day and meet him there. Once we reach an understanding, we'll have to arrange for cash to pay upon delivery of the product and then transport it. Cash, we will borrow from the secondary market. That shouldn't be a problem as we should be able to repay it very quickly. For transport of the product, your personal jet would be very useful in this, at least in the beginning. Nobody dares touch a private jet in Pakistan. Once we have moved a couple of consignments, we're in business and out of the woods from the current crisis.' Salim said.

'Are you crazy? You want to use my personal jet for this?'

'That's the easiest and the least risky option available. We won't have to involve anybody else and we can complete the initial transactions smoothly,' Salim said.

'All right. I believe we don't have a choice in the matter. Please see what needs to be done and keep me posted. I'll be available to fly to Peshawar whenever required. I wish we could sell our properties and get cash rather than getting involved in narcotics.' Yakoob was trying to convince himself that his involvement in narcotics was forced upon him by circumstances rather than choice.

***

Salim quickly arranged for Yakoob to meet Barsat Khan. The meeting took place in a suite at the Sheraton hotel booked under a fictitious name.

'Assalam Alaikum,' Yakoob said to Barsat, who was already in the room with Salim.

'Waalekum Assalam,' Barsat replied, getting up and embracing Yakoob.

After a brief chat about the conditions in Pakistan, events in Afghanistan, and the weather, Yakoob said, 'Salim has discussed the possibility of you working with us in this new business.'

'I will be very happy to. Salim has agreed to certain terms with me, which I believe have been discussed with you. We Pathans require nothing in writing. Our word is our bond, and we expect the same from the people we deal with.'

'We also operate similarly.' Yakoob lied.

'I want nothing until you are happy that I deliver. I have talked to my uncle, and he is ready to give us two hundred kilos of the product instead of one hundred kilos, as discussed before. He has even agreed to take the money for one hundred kilos up front and the other half once the product is sold. This is a rare exception only for me. My uncle and his associates never do business on credit.'

'That's good news. We are ready to do business.'

'My uncle wants to meet with you. You'll have to go to Peshawar. My uncle rarely steps out of Peshawar. He has large landholdings in northern Pakistan. The product will be available for pickup in Bara a couple weeks after you meet my uncle. The best form of transport might be your personal plane, which may bring the goods to Karachi and then fly out to the intended destinations.

'I consider that Amsterdam would be the ideal place for delivering our first consignment. I've been personally involved in dealing with the network there. I plan to go to the Netherlands immediately after your meeting with my uncle. I'll get the organisation ready to clear the goods from Schiphol Airport and have it delivered to the network. The network will pay in Dutch guilders. It will be your job to get the funds out of the Netherlands. I'll give you a complete account of the expenses incurred in travelling, clearance of goods, and other incidental expenses.' Barsat explained the modus operandi.

'This sounds very professional. I'm glad to have met you, Barsat. We will be partners for a long time and prosper together. Please arrange a time for the meeting with your uncle and all of the other details with Salim. I have another meeting, so I will leave.' Yakoob said, getting up.

Barsat and Salim also got up. 'Allah Hafiz.' Barsat said, extending his hand.

'Allah Hafiz.' Yakoob said, gripping Barsat's hand warmly.

Yakoob quickly exited the suite. He took the elevator, going up instead of down. Once he was on an upper floor, he waited for a couple of minutes and then entered the elevator going down, so anybody watching from the ground floor might see him coming from a different floor than the floor where he had met Barsat Khan.

Chapter 34

London, Knightsbridge: G&P Bank's offices

Immediately after arriving in London, Sheikh Tayeb convened an emergency meeting of the bank's senior executive board to discuss the situation in Banjar. Being the head of Banjar operations, Yousuf Ali was also invited to attend.

At the outset, Sheikh Tayeb briefed the members of the senior executive board who had not travelled to Banjar about the events that occurred during the trip.

'Gentlemen, as you all are now aware, we have a very serious situation in Banjar. We need to take urgent and decisive action.' Sheikh Tayeb started the meeting.

'It looks as though Sajan Mala and his cronies are bent on stealing our business there.' Azhar said.

'That is clear. We were hoping that Banjar would invest more funds in our bank. Instead, they want to acquire our business in Banjar without any compensation to us and sell their shares in the bank to us. They have already started putting restrictions on banking business in Banjar to force us to accept their position.' Sheikh Tayeb replied.

Yousuf gave an update of the situation developing in Banjar. 'I hear that Sajan Mala will not give us more than a few weeks before taking action. From our sources in Banjar, I hear that unless a suitable offer comes soon, the government will issue a decree nationalising our branches in Banjar and merge it with Banjar Commercial Bank. They'll take over all the assets and liabilities after an audit by an international firm of accountants. Their aim will be to accept all liquid assets at face value and discount other assets on the pretext that they were overvalued. In addition, the liabilities will be inflated. It's possible that they might come out with a net receivable amount from G&P Bank instead of paying anything for the branches in Banjar.'

'There is no way we can buy their shares at this stage. If anything, we need new investments. We may try to find parties interested in Banjar's shares but that will take time and open us to scrutiny by outsiders. It'd be a disaster if the government in Banjar were to announce nationalisation of our branches there. In order to justify and protect their reputation, they might accuse us of wrongdoings and mismanagement. This will be very messy and can only harm us. So, what should we do?' Sheikh Tayeb asked.

Mateen shared his idea. 'We need to bid for time. Let's start negotiations with Sajan Mala and his team to work out the details for acquiring the Banjar government's shares in the bank. We should offer to discuss the financial terms after an independent valuation of the bank by Tolbert and Gibbs. Tolbert and Gibbs may take several months to complete their report. As they have already reported on the financial statements, it would not be possible for them to state that our balance sheet did not present the financial position fairly. With our contacts, we can also influence Tolbert and Gibbs to go slowly.

'In our negotiations with the Banjar delegation, we should demand that any action against our branches in Banjar should be held in abeyance while the negotiations are progressing, and there should be a package deal for the sale of Banjar shares and the status of our branches there.

'In the meantime, we should try to find an investor willing to buy Banjar shares and we should also launch the various initiatives that we have decided on to improve the bank's financial health.'

'Sounds like a good idea. If the Banjar delegation goes with our suggestion, we'll have at least six months to sort this out.' Azhar agreed.

'I hope they agree. Do you want me to do anything in this matter?' Yousuf asked.

'I suggest you return to Banjar and advise Sajan that we would be pleased to meet him and his team in London in the middle of March. That's approximately three weeks from now. Let's see what he says. I want a critical evaluation of assets and liabilities located in Banjar. In the meantime, you try to clean our books as much as possible. We would like you to convert our receivables and investments into liquid cash and remit as much cash as possible. I know there are restrictions on the remittance of funds but I'm sure that banks help each other. You should also explore the money changers' route for sending money. If everything fails, there is hawala, and I'm sure there are plenty of parties still providing this service. For the books, all the remittances you make may be recorded in the books as advances to parties with local names. I'm sure the chairman and everybody in this room will agree to my suggestion.' Azhar said.

'I think this is a good approach.' Sheikh Tayeb said, endorsing Azhar's plan.

'I'll do my best. However, I'm scared that even if a whiff of what we are trying to do reaches Sajan, he will go berserk and incite all sorts of action against us. We'll have to manage this carefully. I cannot trust many of our staff in this matter.' Yousuf was clearly scared of the potential risk.

'I'm sure you will manage this nicely. We trust you and will support you in anything you need. There will be a more senior position in the bank for you.' Azhar said.

'Well, this is now decided. Yousuf will return to Banjar and convey our message to Sajan for a meeting in mid-March. We'll plan carefully for the meeting. Yousuf will also try to manage the affairs in a way that we have the bare minimum investment left in Banjar.' Sheikh Tayeb said.

As everyone started to leave the room, Sheikh Tayeb asked Azhar and Shakadir to stay.

Once everybody else had left and the doors of the conference room were firmly shut, Sheikh Tayeb said, 'What we discussed is fine, but I am not optimistic. I believe Sajan will not give us the time we need and he will go in for a quick kill. He is completely trusted by Sitara Khan. We might have to do something more drastic to protect our interests in Banjar. After all, we made Banjar what it is today. We have a right to do business and be in the front line there.'

'What drastic action do you have in mind?' Azhar asked.

'Shakadir had a suggestion.' Sheikh Tayeb turned to Shakadir. 'Why don't you explain your thoughts for turning the situation in our favour in Banjar?'

Shakadir explained, 'As we know, His Royal Highness, Bulund Khan is very sick and Sitara Khan has assumed power. This has not gone down well in the ruling circles in Banjar. There are other family members who were aspiring to be the next khan. Sitara's half-brother, Taj Khan, wants to be the next khan of Banjar. Apparently, Bulund liked him more than Sitara. He is also backed by Iran. Sitara is no longer our friend. He is hostile to us now thanks to Sajan Mala and his cronies.

'Some senior family members and officers in Banjar's armed forces back Taj Khan. It is believed that should Taj manage to be in the position of claiming the crown, Bulund may endorse it. I understand that there are moves afoot to mount an action to place Taj as the khan of Banjar.

'Taj is holidaying at present in Switzerland. One of his trusted friends and supporters, the deputy commander of Banjar's Army, Colonel Hamza Hassan, is in London. I know him well. I phoned him yesterday and asked him to join me for lunch tomorrow. If you agree, we may send a message through Hamza Hassan to Taj that we would like to meet him to discuss certain important matters.'

'It is a bold move, and like every bold move, there are risks.' Azhar said.

'Of course, there are risks. But we are in a corner. We are about to lose everything. There might be two possible outcomes of our strategy in Banjar. One: the party we favour might accede to the throne and our future is secure. This is the best outcome. Two: There is turmoil in Banjar. In that case, the players are involved amongst themselves and we are left alone. In this situation we also win as we escape an attack on our bank.' Sheikh Tayeb said.

'There is a third possible outcome, as well.' Azhar added. 'If the action fails without much turmoil and Sitara manages to keep his position and if he finds out that we supported his enemy, then he will go after us.'

'How will he find out we were involved? All the major players will probably be dead if this action fails. And if it does fail, Sitara will be preoccupied for some time before paying any attention to us. That would give us enough time to act to save our position.' Sheikh Tayeb replied.

'You seem in favour of supporting an action.'

'First, I believe there might be some action there, with or without us. Our choice is to back the party that might be our friend against a party already hostile to us and has put us on notice. Second, we do not have any option other than doing something bold and drastic to protect our position. I'm suggesting that we let Shakadir go through his contacts and explore what is possible.'

'Okay, let's explore but I suggest we do not get involved without considering the situation again in more detail.' Azhar was a cautious man.

'Agreed. Shakadir, you meet this good colonel and see what's cooking. Azhar and I will stay in London until we can decide what further action to take.' Sheikh Tayeb said.

***

The next day, Shakadir reported that Colonel Hamza Hassan had confirmed that there were plans to mount an operation in Banjar intending to unseat Sitara Khan and install Taj Khan as the Crown prince and heir apparent. Colonel Hassan indicated that his people would be most grateful for any support from G&P Bank. He also seemed to indicate that once Taj Khan became the khan of Banjar, G&P Bank would be the major bank of Banjar again, and Sheikh Tayeb may even be appointed as the governor of the Central Bank of Banjar.

Sheikh Tayeb responded by saying the G&P Bank would support Prince Taj Khan and requested that Shakadir arrange a meeting between Prince Taj Khan and himself as soon as possible to firm up the understanding for a future relationship.

Chapter 35

Geneva

Amir arrived at the bank just after eight in the morning. He wanted to have an early start and settle into his job as quickly as possible.

The receptionist was aware that Amir was joining the bank and had his security badge and access key ready. As Amir was familiar with the bank's premises, he did not need directions. He went directly to the top floor office of Masood Qadir.

Although none of his secretaries had arrived, Masood was already in his office, busy reading some papers.

Amir knocked. 'Assalam Alaikum.'

'Waalekum Assalam.' Masood Qadir looked up from the papers in front of him. 'Welcome to Geneva. I hope everything was okay with the flight and at the airport this time.'

'Yes, everything was fine. Thank you for sending Julia to receive me.' Amir replied.

'Sorry, I had a meeting yesterday so I could not come myself and had to ask Julia to meet you. I hope the apartment is comfortable.'

'Yes, it is fine. I understand that it's booked for one month. In the meantime, I'll be looking for a suitable place to live.' Amir replied.

'According to the rules here, we pay for the initial month's rent, then you are on your own. You should be able to find some very nice furnished apartments near the bank. Your new package is based on Geneva's cost of living, which you will find quite adequate to meet all the living and other expenses. Being a bachelor, you should be able to save a tidy sum unless you are the casino type and blow your money there. I'll ask human resources to help you find a good place.'

'I'd appreciate that. I might have to take a little time off in the beginning to organise my affairs. I also need a little cash advance. I hope that won't be a problem.' Amir pushed the envelope.

'Not at all. Feel free to organise your work schedule as you consider appropriate. Please ask Rehmallah for any cash you need. We look for performance here and are not interested in policing our staff.' Masood replied. Amir knew that was not true. The bank certainly spied on its people, particularly those whom they suspected. 'Speaking of your work arrangements, I'd like you to work with me and Rehmallah on certain major accounts that we handle jointly. Rehmallah is completely familiar and involved with these accounts so I suggest you work with him initially for the next few weeks, and once you are familiar with the accounts assigned to you, you can take over the primary responsibility for them with guidance from Rehmallah, overseen by myself. Rehmallah has arranged an office for you nearer to his.

'You will find working on these special accounts to be interesting as they involve certain unusual transactions that are normally not a part of the bank's regular business. We provide support to our clients, which goes beyond our duty as normal bankers and that is the reason these clients trust us with the management of their entire wealth. Some of these clients are very powerful and demand complete attention. From what I have heard of you from Karachi and London, you are perfectly suited for this position.'

'People in Karachi and London have been very kind. I hope I will be able to meet your expectations.' Amir replied modestly.

'Oh, you will. I am sure of that. By the way, Azhar was telling me that his secretary, Samira, and you are engaged and will marry soon? 'Congratulations. Samira is looking forward to living in Geneva. She has already asked Azhar if she can be transferred here.'

'Samira and I are good friends. She is a great person. But I am not yet ready to get married. I'd like to build my career first without the complications of married life. I would like to spend all my available time and energy on my job. I will think of marriage once I am firmly in the saddle here.' Amir was annoyed at the pressure Samira was mounting.

'Oh, well. I'm happy to hear of your commitment to your job and career. I will certainly help you there.' Masood replied without further referring to the subject of Samira.

'I'll go see Rehmallah and start organising myself.' Amir said, getting up.

'Sure. Please come straight to me if you need anything,' Masood stood up from his desk and walked Amir to the door of his office.

Outside, all three secretaries had arrived and were busy on their workstations.

'Morning,' Amir said to all.

'Good morning,' they all replied.

'Is the apartment comfortable?' Julia asked.

'It's very nice. I'll soon be looking for a more permanent place.' Amir replied.

'We know quite a few real estate agents who will be able to find you a suitable place within your budget. If you want, I'm happy to call them and set up appointments for you. *The Herald Tribune* also contains a lot of advertisements for properties available for rent. I'll try to help you find something.'

'That would be very kind. Let me settle down for a day or two, and then we'll seriously start house hunting.' Amir said.

'Fine. You let me know when you're ready to deal with this, and I will make the arrangements.' Julia said.

'Thank you very much, I will get back to you soon.' Amir said.

'I understand that you are going to be working with Rehmallah. His secretary, Pat, was getting an office ready for you yesterday. I believe everything is organised. Please let me know if I can be of any help,' Julia said.

Amir said goodbye to Julia and walked down one flight of stairs to Rehmallah's office in the corporate banking department. Rehmallah was outside his office, talking to his secretary.

'Welcome back,' Rehmallah said, extending his hand to Amir.

Amir took his hand and said, 'Thank you. It's nice to return to Geneva and see you again.'

'It's our pleasure. I hope your flight was pleasant, and the arrangements for your accommodation are satisfactory. Masood told me that Julia was organising these things.'

'Yes, Julia met me at the airport and took me to the apartment. I'm at Diplomat Apartments on Rue de Lausanne. It's a nice flat but only for a month. I'll be looking to move somewhere more permanent.' Amir said, walking with Rehmallah to his office.

'There may be some nice apartments available for rent in Eaux-Vives, where I live. If you don't mind being my neighbour, I'll ask Pat to contact the estate agents to let us know what is available and arrange viewings.' Rehmallah replied.

This was music to Amir's ears. An apartment in Eaux-Vives near Rehana was a dream. He tried to hide his excitement and said, 'I have been to your apartment. It's a nice area. I hope I can find something there.'

'Good.' Rehmallah pressed the button on his telephone that connected directly to his secretary.

'Yes, Mr. Rehmallah,' Pat responded immediately.

'Pat, Amir is looking for an apartment in Eaux-Vives, near where I live. One-bedroom apartment, I believe, would be fine. Please contact the estate agents in the area and arrange viewings.'

'I will do it immediately, Mr. Rehmallah,' Pat replied. Amir noted the use of the title *Mister*. The atmosphere was not entirely informal in Rehmallah's department.

'I spoke to Masood Qadir regarding a cash advance. I need fifteen thousand Swiss francs to take care of certain commitments. I understand it will be taken from my pay.' Amir said.

'No problem. Ask Pat to prepare a payment voucher and sign it. I'll approve the advance. She'll bring the cash to you. We've already opened an account for you here at the bank. Pat will give you the application form, which contains the details such as your next of kin, et cetera. This is required under Swiss law. I suggest you don't carry too much cash on you. The bank will issue you a chequebook and a credit card with whatever limit you require.' Rehmallah explained.

'Thank you. I'll get the form from Pat. But this time, I need cash,' Amir said.

'Sure. I was only telling you about the general procedure here,' Rehmallah said.

'I understand,' Amir replied.

'Now, on to business. As you might know, like most Swiss banks, we provide the facility of secret accounts and safety boxes to our clients to ensure complete confidentiality.

'For certain very important clients, who we call the VVIP, we have a special department under Masood where a relationship manager is assigned to each account. To protect the identity of the client we assign an alias to these clients. The relationship manager knows only the alias and the account number. The actual identity of these clients is known by only Sheikh Tayeb, Azhar Alam, Masood and myself. We keep a separate confidential book that contains the true identity and personal details together with the alias and account number.

'Some of these VVIP clients are very powerful people. They are also very wealthy. I guess being powerful and wealthy are synonymous. Some of these clients have balances with us in excess of several hundred million dollars. Don't ask me where the money came from. It's not our job to act as vicar for these people or to ask questions. Our job is to handle their banking needs.

'These are what we call gold accounts and require attention at the senior-most level in our bank. We are responsible for complete wealth management for these gold account holders. Due to the sensitivity and need for high priority, only Masood and I handle these accounts. Either he or I act as the relationship manager and ensure that the client's affairs are managed in the most efficient and profitable manner, both for the client and for us.

'Obviously, Masood and I cannot handle everything. To assist us, we need a highly trusted and capable team of only a couple of senior people. That's where you come in. We trust you and would like you to be a part of our team handling these gold accounts. Julia also assists us in these matters. What do you say?' Rehmallah asked.

'I don't know how to thank you for the privilege. I would be honoured to assist you and Masood in this very important business.' Amir said.

'Good. I'm happy to hear that you are willing to accept the responsibility. I hope you realise that, because of the nature of these accounts, we have to be available twenty-four hours a day, seven days a week for our clients. These clients demand service at odd hours and at short notice.'

'I'll do my best to meet your expectations. I promise that none of the clients assigned to me will find cause to complain.' Amir reassured.

'In addition to some of the gold clients, we are planning to assign to you the responsibility for TIG. You've already been working on this account in Karachi and you know that TIG is the bank's largest client. The account is handled by Azhar, Abu Talib, Masood and myself. There is a junior officer by the name of Saima who assists Azhar and Abu Talib on TIG in Karachi. She is only a junior analyst. We're planning to shift the management of the TIG account here to Geneva and make you responsible for it.'

Amir could not believe his luck. TIG, his prime target to expose the bank's aggressive and illegal practices, was being handed to him.

'I know TIG well. I will be happy to handle it here.'

'I suggest you review the files of the clients whose secret numbers are noted on the attached slip. The files will show only their aliases. You'll be given the real identities of these accounts when approved by the committee, which will be after some time.' Rehmallah passed Amir a small slip of paper with some numbers on it.

'You may also take the files for TIG. Your office is next door. There are two filing cabinets with secure locks. Only you and I will have the keys to these cabinets. Don't worry about the security of the papers you keep there. My secretary, Pat, will assist you initially with any secretarial assistance. We'll find another secretary for you in the next few days. I've already put in a request to HR.' Rehmallah said. He did not mention that every office in the building was covered by secret cameras that recorded everything and that these were viewed by the security team headed by Oshko.

'Thank you. I'll get busy.'

'Lunch is at noon. You are welcome to join us in the cafeteria.'

'Since I'm feeling a little unsettled, I would like to skip lunch today. I might go out for a stroll.'

'Sure. Whatever you are comfortable with.'

Amir completed the cash advance voucher and asked Pat to get him cash. He also asked her to get him the TIG files. Pat returned within ten minutes with cash in her hand. She said the TIG files were being retrieved and would be available shortly.

Amir pocketed the cash and told Pat he had to go out for a short while, so she should look after the files when they were delivered. Then, he quickly walked out of the bank and started walking towards his apartment, all the while checking if he was being followed. He was not. So far, he did not seem to be a suspect but he still wanted to be careful and take extra precautions.

After walking for a couple hundred metres, Amir spotted a public telephone booth. He went in and dialled Rehana's telephone number. She was at home and excited to hear Amir's voice. She desperately wanted to see him. He told her he would be at her apartment in ten minutes.

Rehana opened the door to her apartment as soon as Amir rang the bell; he thought she had probably been waiting by the door. When the door opened, he saw a different Rehana. She looked completely different from the night he had met her with Rehmallah and even from the day they had met shopping at Globus-Grand Passage. Today, Amir saw the most beautiful lady dressed in a tight-fitting dress at the door.

She rushed into Amir's arms and started kissing him passionately. She quickly pulled Amir towards the sofa.

'Oh, Amir, how have I waited for you. This must be a dream. Please tell me that this is not a dream. And I am with you in your arms.'

'You are with me, darling. This is the most wonderful moment of my life.' Amir murmured and lightly bit on Rehana's neck. 'Oh. Oh. I cannot bear this any longer.' She said, tearing off Amir's shirt.

They continued clawing and groping each other and tearing off their clothes. Soon, they collapsed on the sofa. They were like two animals merging into each other. Despite the cold weather, their bodies were glistening with sweat. Amir pushed Rehana under him and entered her with a roar. They kept swinging and holding each other until they reached the crescendo. Amir made a sound from his throat like an animal and shouted, 'Oh, my God. I'm coming. I'm coming.'

'Faster, deeper, my darling. I'm coming, too. Oh, this is a blessing. I'm coming, I'm coming.' Rehana responded.

Amir stayed on top of Rehana for some time. Then, he slid away and went to the washroom and cleaned himself.

Coming out of the washroom, he found Rehana on the bed. 'Come, my darling. Come here.' She said.

As soon as Amir went to bed, Rehana wrapped him in her arms and started kissing him passionately again. He could not hold himself back and found himself aroused again. They again started caressing and groping each other. This time, they were slowly exploring each other. Soon they were passionately swinging again, this time with Rehana on top, until they both reached their climax.

'That was lovely. Thank you, darling.' Rehana said.

'It was the most wonderful experience of my life. Thank you.' Amir kissed Rehana again.

They stayed entwined in each other's arms for some time.

'Want tea?' Rehana asked.

'Yes, tea will be nice. I need to discuss an important matter with you.'

'What could be more important than you and me together? I'll bring tea.' She quickly returned with two cups of tea and some biscuits on a tray.

Amir opened his handbag and took out the jewellery box. 'I bought this for you in London.' he said, handing a jewellery box to Rehana.

'It's magnificent! It's lovely, but I'm sorry, I cannot accept this. It's too much. You are going overboard with these gifts,' Rehana said, pushing the box back to Amir.

'I bought it for you, and it's for you only. You should wear it whenever we are together.' Amir said.

'No, Amir. This is very expensive. I'll wear it when I am with you but you should keep it and give it to me to wear when we are together.'

'Don't be silly. This is for you, and you should keep it.' Amir insisted.

'All right, then please place it around my neck.'

Amir took the pendant and leaned in to put it around Rehana's neck. As he was doing the clasp, Rehana took his head in her hands, kissed him on the mouth and wrapped him in her arms. He returned the kiss, pulled himself back, and placed the pendant around Rehana's neck.

Rehana got up and looked at herself in the mirror. 'Amir, this is the most beautiful thing I have ever possessed. Thank you. I will always keep it with me.'

'I'm happy you like it,' Amir said. 'I still can't believe we are here together in Geneva. Rehana, I worry, though, that I'm messing up your life.'

'My life is already messed up. Rehmallah is having an affair with Poonam. This is no secret. They don't even try to hide it anymore. Poonam is the wife of Jagdish in the Indian section at the bank. Jagdish knows about his wife's infatuation with Rehmallah, they already live separately and have filed for divorce. Rehmallah is waiting for the divorce to go through so he can divorce me and marry her. H has already told me so. Rehmallah and I hardly talk to each other these days.' Rehana said.

Amir was shocked. He knew that Rehmallah was straying, he had seen him in Bangkok, but he did not realise he had an ongoing relationship with another woman.

'Oh, I am very sorry to hear that.' Amir said.

'I'm not. I have never loved Rehmallah. He's a domineering bastard interested in himself only. For him, I have always been a chattel, a bonded slave available for satisfying his sexual needs, a cook-cum-maid and nanny for his children and a trophy to take to the bank's parties. Like a servant, I'm told what to wear, how to behave, and what to cook. I'm required to behave like a pious lady in front of his friends and guests. In return, I'm provided with food, clothes, accommodations to live in and a stringent budget to run the household. God has blessed us with two lovely daughters, but Rehmallah does not appreciate this and has never enjoyed them. The children have never known a loving father. They only know him as a reserved bank officer coming home to eat and sleep.

'I'm not telling you all this to gain your sympathy. My feelings for you are genuine and have nothing to do with my relationship with him. I don't want anything from you in return. Your being here is a great blessing for me. I believe you will marry a girl from your own circle and settle down with her. When that happens, or whenever you want, I will disappear from your life and will never contact you. I'm telling you all of this to assure you that my life is already a mess and cannot get worse.'

'What would happen to you and the children if Rehmallah goes ahead with the divorce?' Amir asked.

'I don't want to go back to Pakistan. A divorcee has no life there. A divorced woman is ostracised and condemned to suffer there. I'd like to continue to live in Switzerland. My daughters have to complete their education here before they go off to universities. I've already been offered a job at the International School in Geneva. I plan to start there from the next academic year. The pay will be sufficient for my daughters and me to carry on. Rehmallah can go to hell as far as I am concerned.'

'My life is a little complicated, as well. I have a mission which might cost me my life.'

'Please don't say this. I cannot bear you talking about your life like that. Tell me what you want to do and I will work with you.'

Amir told her about his experience on the flight from Karachi to Geneva, his findings about G&P Bank and his vow to destroy G&P Bank.

'I have the same feeling as you toward G&P Bank and its people. From today, we are a team. I am with you in this. As I told you, my life is complicated and not worth anything anymore. This will give me a purpose to settle the score with Rehmallah and his cronies.' Rehana said after hearing Amir's story.

'I don't want you to be involved. This may be dangerous.'

'I love danger. My life was dull before you turned up. Don't you think that it's dangerous for me to be with you alone in this apartment? Rehmallah would kill both of us if he found out that we were meeting like this. Don't forget he is a Pathan and for him, honour is everything. It won't be possible for him to bear the shame of his wife with another man.'

'Rehana, your children might suffer because of your involvement with me in this matter.'

'My children will be looked after by Allah. I won't be able to protect them if it's ordained that they have to suffer. They have to be out of Rehmallah's clutches. They are ashamed because of Rehmallah's affair with Poonam. The girls' friends at the school know about it too. The children also know that Rehmallah and I may be divorced, and they have accepted the reality. They should be on their way to universities soon, anyway.'

'One of my key targets for the information is Rehmallah, who I understand keeps the information about secret accounts.' Amir said.

'He keeps a filing cabinet in our bedroom locked with a combination lock. I know the combination because he sometimes calls me and asks me to open the cabinet to give him information over the phone. He thinks I am stupid and don't know what's going on. For him, I'm a stupid housewife who doesn't understand anything. Until now, I never bothered to look into the filing cabinet unless he asked me to. It was none of my business. Now it is.

'As I said, we are a team now. Rehmallah has plans to go to the UK on Friday evening. He says that he has to go deal with certain matters for the bank. Nobody works during the weekend unless there is an emergency. I know Rehmallah is, in fact, going to Inverness for a quiet weekend with his girlfriend. I heard him making the flight and hotel reservations. He makes these types of reservations from home instead of from the office.

'Please come here around eight in the evening on Friday and we will have dinner together. Rehmallah's flight is at 6 p.m., so he will be away. Then, we can look into the filing cabinet and get the information you need. I'll send the children to stay with their friends for the weekend, so there won't be anybody else here.'

'What if Rehmallah turns up while I'm here?' Amir asked.

'Oh, don't worry. The concierge lady is my friend. I give her good tips and send her Pakistani food. I'll request that she gives me a buzz if Rehmallah turns up. If that happens, then you can leave down the stairs. He never takes the stairs; he always uses the elevator.' Rehana had worked all this out.

'Okay. As long as you're sure that it is no danger to you and the children.'

'I'll wait for you. In fact, I'd like to see you every day before Friday, so please let me know how and when we may meet, and I'll try to make it.' Rehana said.

'I will. I have to look for a place to live. Rehmallah has suggested that there may be some nice apartments in Eaux-Vives. I might be in your neighbourhood looking for apartments soon.'

'That would be lovely. I'll also look around and arrange viewings for you.'

'I'm arranging a secure communications facility and I'll give you access. You can also leave messages for me and get my messages from there. That will save us from communicating through the bank's system. I've also been given a direct line at the bank so I don't have to go through the switchboard when I call out or receive calls. You can call me at that number for a brief conversation, but please don't call from home. I am sure the bank's security scans all the communications to and from the bank. You may also call me at my apartment but again, please be discreet.' Amir gave her a slip of paper with the telephone numbers for the bank and apartment on it.

'That'll be lovely. At least we'll be able to communicate without the fear of being spied upon.'

Amir looked at his watch. 'It's already past lunchtime. I must leave. Masood and Rehmallah will start wondering where I've been.'

'Yes. You must go. They are a suspicious lot. They have so much to hide. You'll be followed and spied upon if they suspect you of anything. Also, the children will be here soon.' Rehana said.

Amir went straight to Bonjour Secretarial Bureau from Rehana's apartment and paid the initial deposit. He also registered a sub-account holder under the name Helen Girard. Fortunately, the Bureau did not require any identification or residence address for a sub-account holder. Amir was advised that his registered name for use at the Bureau would be Alan Tipps. He selected his mother's name, Raana, as his security password for identification.

He phoned Rehana and told her about the account at Bonjour Secretarial Bureau, explaining to her that she may leave and collect messages by using the name Helen Girard. He gave the full address, telephone numbers and names of people at the Bureau.

It was almost three in the afternoon when Amir returned to the bank. He went straight to Pat and asked her if the files for TIG had arrived.

The files were neatly piled behind Pat's desk. There were twenty of them. Amir carried them to his office and started going through them. He was happy to note that the TIG files contained much more detailed information about the group's businesses, organisation, group companies, and their shareholdings than those in Karachi. He estimated it would take him several days to go through all the information.

Soon after 5 p.m., he closed the files and placed them in the filing cabinet in his office, carefully locked the cabinet and put the key in his pocket. He noted that most of the bank's staff had left, except for a few people who still seemed to be busy. Although Rehmallah's office door was closed, the lights were still on and Amir could hear Rehmallah talking with somebody, probably on the phone.

Amir quietly walked out of the bank. He turned right at the first intersection, then right and right again, returning to the front of the bank, checking in the storefronts all the time to see if he was being followed. Nobody at all seemed to be interested in him. He walked into a small supermarket and walked out of the store's back door into the street. He asked a passer-by for directions to Rue du Mole. He was soon at the offices of Bonjour Secretarial Bureau.

He identified himself as Mr. Alan Tipps and asked to use the telephone. He was directed to a small conference room near the reception. There was a telephone instrument there and notepads and pencils.

Amir asked the operator to get him John Delon's number in London. It was not yet closing time in London.

'John Delon.'

'John, this is Amir in Geneva.'

'Amir. How are you? It's good to hear from you.'

'Listen, I am using the services of a secretarial bureau in Geneva, and my name here is Alan Tipps.' Amir explained the arrangements he had with Bonjour Secretarial Bureau and advised John to use this arrangement to contact him.

'It's good, Alan. We certainly needed a facility to communicate.' John was on the ball. 'I have some good news for you. Ian has been successful, very successful, in his efforts. He's been able to interest the German police in further investigating the death of Richard Bringsen, particularly the connection between Ahmet Gulay, the truck driver, the Mehwar gang, and the bank. He's been assured they will enquire into this matter and find if there was a link. They've already lifted Ahmet Gulay's passport and told him the matter is not yet closed. We should hear some results within a week.'

'That's great, John! We are making progress. Here in Geneva, I've also struck pay dirt. I found a contact who has access to the secret documents of the bank, including the links between the aliases and the real names of the account holders. We may have to go to the Swiss authorities once we have sufficient information.' Amir said.

'This is good. Please be sure, if possible, that you obtain copies of the documents so we can provide them to the authorities. You'll also need a lawyer in Switzerland. I will arrange that for you.

'I also received a call from your friend, Danny. He wants to give the information about the inaccuracies in the financial statements of G&P Bank and sign an affidavit claiming that the partners of Tolbert and Gibbs knowingly, wilfully, and wrongly signed the clean audit report. According to your friend, G&P Bank is financially insolvent, and the financial statements are inaccurate.'

'This is excellent, but I'm afraid for Danny. He doesn't know what he's getting into. I don't want him to be harmed.'

'I'll talk to my contact at the SIB and see how we may be able to handle this. Don't worry, I'll do my best to protect Danny and keep his identity a secret. Give me a call once you have further information. I'll also call and leave a message for you at the bureau.' John said.

Amir then called Danny who was just about to leave the office for the day.

'Hey, how's the super banker in Geneva?' Danny was delighted to hear from Amir.

'I'm fine. It's only my second day here, but so far, so good. In fact, I have made much more progress than I dreamt of within these two days. I've made arrangements to be able to make confidential communication without involving the bank.' Amir then explained the arrangements with the bureau and asked Danny to leave messages there using Amir's pseudonym. 'I've also come across somebody who has access to confidential information and hates the people at the bank. I hope to get the information about the secret numbered accounts from this party. I'll let you know when that happens. We should be ready to strike once we have all this information.

'I also hear from John that you are going to provide the information about Tolbert and Gibbs's handling of the bank's audit. While this is good news as far as the project is concerned, I'm worried about you. You will not only destroy your career but you may be exposed to personal danger, as well.'

'Don't worry. I've already started looking for another job. I have an interview with a major multinational corporation for a CFO position. They don't care if I sneeze on Tolbert and Gibbs. In fact, with their public profile of the ethical standards they have to adhere to, they should appreciate my actions. John has promised that he'll try to keep my identity confidential, but that might fail, as Tolbert and Gibbs and the bank will know who was supplying the information.' Danny replied.

'Please back off as soon as you sense danger.'

'I will. Don't worry. I don't want to be a martyr.' Danny assured him.

With that, Amir said goodbye to Danny and went to the receptionist. He asked her if it was possible to photocopy documents late at night. He was assured that the bureau was open around the clock and he would be welcome to use its services, including photocopying, at any time he desired.

Chapter 36

London, Bank of England

An emergency meeting of the senior officials of the SIB attached to the Bank of England was underway at the bank's offices at Threadneedle Street. The bank was affectionately known as the Old Lady of Threadneedle Street, or simply the Old Lady.

The job of the SIB was to regulate and monitor affairs of the financial services industry in the United Kingdom. In addition to its own army of officials and staff, representatives of other divisions and government agencies, such as the Serious Fraud Office, Inland Revenue and MI5 and MI6, routinely participated in the SIB's operations and attended their meetings.

Today, there was only one item on the agenda: to consider the reports received about G&P Bank and decide on the action to be taken to protect the banking system in the UK. In chair was the SIB's head, Sir Richard Lobs. Also attending were the heads of various divisions within the SIB that were created to deal with certain specialist sectors. The participants from within the SIB included David Ringbutton, Jamie Lifton, and Clare Rocke from the regulatory, international, and legal divisions, respectively. In addition, various other support staff and assistants were there.

Sir Richard Lobs started the meeting. 'Good morning, ladies and gentlemen. Thank you for attending this meeting on such a short notice. Today, we have only one item on the agenda: G&P Bank. Unfortunately, reports coming from various sources about the bank's operations are not positive. We are also getting pressure for action against the bank from several quarters, including the Americans. The Americans seem to have a strong case against the bank and its officials for illegal banking operations and money laundering. They want concerted action against the bank. In the folder in front of you, there are documents indicating the bank's illegal and unethical activities in several countries. Last night, the governor of the Bank of England received a call from a very senior

US official asking him for cooperation. I have to report our views and recommendations to the governor to decide our role in dealing with this matter.'

Jamie Lifton, from the international division, added, 'As far as I am aware, the bank has no operations in the USA. What is the American's gripe in this matter?'

'The bank has marketing and liaison representatives in the USA who apparently help the undesirables in laundering money and make remittances around the world.' Sir Richard replied.

'Then it's easy. They should be able to arrest these guys, indict them for any illegal acts they have committed in the US, and deal with the problem there instead of involving us. I don't see any cross-border connection with us in this matter.' Jamie was insistent.

'You are right. There is more to it than meets the eye here. I understand the bank has been involved with the CIA in certain clandestine operations in Afghanistan and Latin America. The bank and its officials might now be considered excess baggage by the US. We work very closely with the US in everything, from national security to banking and sanctions enforcement. If they demand action from us, then we have to cooperate unless there are solid legal reasons not to.' Sir Richard explained.

'I don't see how we can help the Americans and others if we don't have concrete evidence of G&P Bank violating the UK laws.' Clare Rocke said. Clare was known to be a ferocious but fair lawyer.

'Oh, they have violated UK laws all right. Just consider the property boom in the UK. A lot of funds fuelling this boom came from overseas through various channels. A lot of the investors in the property are characters that you and I do not want to know nor wish to be associated with. G&P Bank is one of the major players channelling money in the UK property market. We know that a lot of G&P Bank's customers are shady politicians, dictators, and suspect businessmen.' Sir Richard seemed to have already made up his mind to indict G&P Bank.

'We knew all along who the investors were and the colour of the money pouring into the UK. We all turned a blind eye to this because it was helping the British economy and many of the investors were our political friends. G&P Bank might be one of the major players, but others, including some very prominent high street banks, were not immune from making a quick buck by facilitating these transactions and have been deeply involved. How can we now turn against only one bank and say that only that particular bank was guilty, and that the others do not deserve any attention? I would appreciate it if somebody could enlighten me about this.' Clare was the devil's advocate in the meeting.

Nobody was willing to argue against her very valid points. The room was silent.

Finally breaking the silence, David Ringbutton said, 'Recently, a lawyer I know contacted me saying that he has a client who has evidence about G&P Bank but wants to remain anonymous. According to this lawyer, G&P Bank was insolvent, its financial statements were cooked up, and the bank falsified its records to hide the real identity of its depositors. The lawyer wanted assurance from us that at no stage the identity of the lawyer or the informant would be revealed, and if, upon investigation, it was confirmed that the information was credible, then action will be taken against the bank. I told him that I would have to discuss this matter with my colleagues before reverting to him.'

'Ah, this is different. I'm all for taking action if they have violated any of our laws or cheated us. I will not be happy to act as the Americans' stooge and create problems for us here.' Clare said.

'This is good, David. I suggest we pursue this matter to see what G&P Bank has been up to. I suggest that you and Clare meet this lawyer and tell him we are interested.' Sir Richard said.

'Are we prepared to sign a confidentiality and identity protection agreement with the informant and his lawyer? Without this type of guarantee, they might not be interested. The informant is scared and believes that it is not beyond G&P Bank to harm him or his family.' David Ringbutton raised his concern

'Can we give such a guarantee, Clare?' Sir Richard asked.

'We could, provided the evidence given to us would stand up in a court without the need for producing the informant as a witness. What this means is, if the documentary evidence is not sufficient, then we might have to decide to drop this line of action, as the informant won't be willing to come forward to give evidence in court.' Clare answered.

'David, I suggest you talk to the whistle-blower's lawyer and assess the quality of information offered. Then, arrange a meeting between the lawyer, Clare, and yourself to go into further details for completing the arrangements for us to obtain the information. Once we agree on the arrangements and complete the legal formalities, we might want to meet and talk to the whistle-blower directly.' Sir Richard said.

'Okay. I'll work on this and let you know how it develops,' David said.

'Once we have some evidence in our hands, we may need to act in concert with other agencies against G&P Bank from all directions. This will probably mean the bank may collapse completely. This might be a disaster for depositors in the bank. We'll have to be prepared to deal with the fall out of this catastrophe.' Sir Richard said.

Part III
Disaster

Chapter 37

London: Century House, Headquarters of MI6

A rare joint meeting involving very senior officers of the two prime government intelligence agencies, MI5 and MI6, was in progress at the headquarters of MI6 at Century House, 100 Westminster Bridge Road and Lambeth. The roles of both these agencies were different, and their staff only met formally when their interests overlapped. Apparently, this was such an event.

MI5 is the acronym for Military Intelligence Section 5 and is primarily responsible for the internal security within the United Kingdom. MI5 does, however, have an overseas role in support of its mission to protect the British government and people.

The security service comes under the authority of the Home Secretary within the cabinet. The service is headed by a director general at the grade of a permanent secretary of the British Civil Service who is directly supported by an internal security organisation, secretariat, legal advisory branch and information services branch. The deputy director general (DDG) is responsible for the operational activity of the service, being responsible for four branches: international counterterrorism, National Security Advice Centre (counter proliferation and counter espionage), Irish and domestic counterterrorism and technical and surveillance operations.

The service is directed by the Joint Intelligence Committee for Intelligence Operational Priorities and liaises with the SIS, GCHQ, DIS and other bodies within the British government and industrial base.

MI6, on the other hand, is the name given to the Secret Intelligence Service (SIS) and is responsible for supplying the British government with foreign intelligence. They normally report to the Secretary of State for Foreign & Commonwealth Affairs, as it involves the UK government's relations with other countries.

Both agencies rely heavily on a wide network of field agents, intelligence agencies of friendly countries, and highly sophisticated listening devices located at General Communications Headquarters, known as GCHQ, in Cheltenham – for signals intelligence, known as SigInt in the intelligence community. Both have a large staff to analyse intelligence input and make sense out of the data by connecting the dots.

Today's meeting was taking place at the initiative of the DDG of MI5, David Gollard, who, upon receiving disturbing reports about the actions of certain people in the UK in connection with the distant oil-producing state of Banjar, contacted his counterpart at MI6 and enquired if MI6 was also receiving information that something was afoot in Banjar. When he learnt that MI6 also had information coming through, David suggested there should be a meeting of the concerned people in both organisations to patch together a comprehensive picture of the situation in Banjar. Jeremy Wilson of MI6 had readily agreed and asked Edwin Robinson, head of the Middle East and Indian Subcontinent, to work with MI5 to arrange for a meeting.

There were six people around the conference table, three from each service. The MI6 delegation was led by Edwin Robinson. He was supported by Joanna Fairbrand, who was in charge of Iran and Banjar, and Jeremy Snow, the specialist for analysing signals and messages received from GCHQ for information relating to the Middle East and Indian subcontinent.

MI5 was represented by David McClough, head of surveillance operations, Ian Sutton, who was in charge of keeping tabs on groups and organisations of interest, and Robyn Dell, who was responsible for watching foreign missions, visiting dignitaries and other persons of interest in the UK.

'Thank you for coming to Century House.' Edwin Robinson got the ball rolling. 'David, you start first as your people have picked up the information about possible events in Banjar which directly connect with what we are hearing at MI6.'

David McClough said, 'Recently, we have picked up a marked increase in visits at the Iranian Embassy in London by certain important people from Banjar. One of the frequent visitors there has been Colonel Hamza Hassan. He has been camping in London for some time now. We know that Colonel Hamza Hassan, a Shia Moslem of Iranian origin, is the deputy commander of the Banjar Armed Forces. He is known to be a supporter of Prince Taj Khan, the second son of the Khan of Banjar and a claimant to the throne. We understand that Khan of Banjar is ill, which has resulted in a tussle for succession between the Crown Prince Sitara Khan and Prince Taj Khan. We also know that Prince Taj Khan is encouraged and supported by the Iranians in his bid for power in Banjar. He is also supported by Farah Naz, the youngest wife of the ruler, Bulund Khan. Farah Naz is also an Iranian national and was working as a secretary to Sheikh Tayeb, the founder and chairman of G&P Bank before marrying Bulund Khan.

'From telephone conversations and other chatter and discussions we have picked up, it appears that there is a plan to install Prince Taj Khan as the new Khan of Banjar. This was further confirmed in a conversation overheard by our agent keeping an eye on Hamza Hassan recently. We spotted Hassan lunching with Shakadir Khan, Chief of Security at G&P Bank and personal assistant to Sheikh Tayeb. Hassan informed him that there would soon be action in Banjar to unseat the current heir apparent and de facto ruler, Sitara Khan. Shakadir Khan offered to support the action in return for facilities for G&P Bank to continue operating in Banjar.'

'This also seems to directly connect with the information we have received from our sources in Switzerland. Knowing that there was a tussle for power in Banjar, we kept an eye on Prince Taj Khan and his entourage in Lausanne, where His Royal Highness was holidaying. Our agents in Switzerland have reported that Prince Taj Khan seemed to be meeting some very dubious characters, including officers from the Iranian Revolutionary Guard, Pasdaran. He also had a meeting with Sheikh Tayeb of G&P Bank at his chateau. Our agent reported that Sheikh Tayeb was seen leaving the chateau in an extremely happy mood.' Joanna Fairbrand said.

'Through our contacts, we have also learnt that a ship carrying a cargo of arms was anchored at sea just outside Banjar. Its consignment was unloaded in boats and barges sent from Banjar's Sonami Beach, located outside the city. The ship's cargo was carried to and stored in warehouses all over the city. GCHQ has also picked up chatter indicating that some sort of action is imminent in Banjar. All the suspected players involved in a possible plot, like Prince Taj Khan, Colonel Hamza Hassan, et cetera, have already reached Banjar.' Joanna Fairbrand continued.

'I agree with you that something very foul is cooking there. The military attaché at the Iranian Embassy in London was seen boarding a flight to Banjar two days ago.' Robyn Dell confirmed Joanna Fairbrand's fears.

Edwin Robinson said, 'It is not our role to take sides in a family conflict for succession of a ruler. Ours is to analyse the information and pass it up the chain. I know our superiors will be concerned with the possibility of instability in Banjar, and its tilt towards Iran. The current de facto Khan of Banjar is our friend. Prince Taj Khan seems to be in Iran's pocket. Not helpful to our interests at all. Banjar is a very wealthy country and a strategic trading partner for us. It would not be wise for us to let it come under the influence of Iran. That would seriously complicate the balance of power in the region.

'It would be useful if we prepare a memorandum summarising our findings and send it to our respective masters.' Edwin Robinson urged the group. 'I suspect that time is of the essence here. We need to move quickly. I suggest we give you our findings now, and you assign somebody to incorporate your information and prepare a memo and pass it on to Whitehall this afternoon. We will also share the information with our DDG and DG for submission to the Joint Intelligence Committee.'

***

A memo giving the comprehensive findings of both MI5 and MI6 was delivered to the Secretary of State for Foreign & Commonwealth Affairs, Peter Hare, just after lunch that afternoon. The same memo was delivered simultaneously to the Chairman of the Joint Intelligence Committee.

Appreciating the urgency and gravity of the situation, a meeting of the security cabinet was called by the prime minister. In that meeting, it was decided that considering the strategic importance of Banjar both economically and geographically, the UK could not afford for Banjar to become an Iranian satellite and the UK should move immediately to protect the current ruling group of Banjar.

The prime minister then called the US president and briefed him about the potential situation developing in Banjar. The CIA had also received disturbing information about the State, and the American government was considering its options under various scenarios. The American president was greatly relieved to learn that the UK was getting directly involved and made an offer to assign the American assets in the region to assist the UK should a situation arise.

The prime minister then called the Crown prince and de facto Khan of Banjar, His Royal Highness, Prince Sitara Khan and informed him of the threat to him and his family in Banjar. He briefly shared the intelligence reports he had received and offered the UK government's assistance to protect the security of Banjar.

Prince Sitara Khan, initially stunned, was beyond himself with anger. He wanted to take swift action and wipe out the people involved with their families. He was not sure about the level of infiltration in his armed forces and the loyalty of his security agencies. He welcomed the prime minister's offer of assistance and requested, if possible, for a contingent of British troops to be made available immediately to guard him, his family, and his palace. The British could also take over the security of the important installations and, if needed, help the forces loyal to Prince Sitara Khan in dealing with the traitors. He asked for the names of the principal perpetrators of the plot and requested that the prime minister share the information gathered by the British intelligence agencies with him. The prime minister gave him the names of the key players and agreed to send a detailed dossier with the commander of the British contingent.

That afternoon, orders were received at the SAS headquarters at Hereford to airlift a battalion of five hundred troops for active combat duty in Banjar. Within an hour, under the command of Colonel Ronny Stevens, the selected commandos were aboard two

C130K Hercules aircraft on their way to Banjar. They were due to arrive at the military airbase outside Banjar City at five the following morning, just in time to save the day there.

The two RAF aircraft with five hundred SAS crack troops landed on schedule at the military airbase. They were met there by General Rustom Jamal, Chief of Banjar Armed Forces, and Sir Robert Crawford, the British Ambassador to Banjar, who had received a telephone call from the prime minister explaining the developing situation in Banjar and the role Britain had agreed to play in the crisis.

While the troops were taken to the airbase mess, where arrangements were made for refreshments and facilities to freshen up, General Rustom Jamal, Colonel Stevens and Sir Robert Crowford went to a conference room adjacent to the chief's office to discuss the plan of action to tackle the situation and make arrangements for the deployment of forces.

General Jamal had done his homework and was ready with a detailed plan for the deployment of the British troops, which he shared with Colonel Stevens. The British troops were to be located for the defence of important installations and sensitive places. The assault and arrest operations would be carried out by the Banjari forces, and the British would not get involved, as they did not want to be a witness or party to any excesses that might be committed.

The largest contingent of one hundred British soldiers was to be located at Prince Sitara Khan's palace. This contingent was to be headed by Captain William Groves. Colonel Stevens was to be based at the Ministry of Defence, with all the communication and support facilities to command and communicate with the troops under his command. He was assigned a villa for personal use within the Ministry of Defence compound.

A group of Banjari Army officers was then introduced to the British troops. A Banjari officer was assigned to each group to coordinate and liaise with the Banjar Armed Forces.

Once all the details were agreed, the troops were ordered to board the waiting buses and they were on their way to their assigned locations.

General Rustom Jamal, Colonel Stevens and Sir Robert Crowford also left in a Mercedes car to meet Prince Sitara Khan at his palace. Colonel Stevens handed over the dossier to the ambassador to pass on to the Crown prince.

They were met warmly by Prince Sitara Khan, who took them to his personal living quarters in the palace. He was visibly nervous and thanked the British government and Colonel Stevens and his soldiers for coming to the aid of Banjar.

The ambassador handed over the intelligence dossier to the prince, and the prince quickly perused the file. He handed the dossier over to General Jamal and asked him in Balochi to ensure that none of the perpetrators got away.

After a brief visit to the palace, the delegation returned to the military base.

Chapter 38

Geneva

Although it had only been two days since he had last seen Rehana, Amir was eager to see her again. It was Friday afternoon and he was counting the minutes until he would be able to see her.

Amir had talked twice to Rehana but had avoided meeting her and exposing them to unnecessary risk. He had also spoken to John Delon, who told him that the German police were now seriously on Richard Bringsen's case and were treating the death as a homicide. Apparently, upon further questioning, both the witnesses, Rudy Stern and Klause Bose, had recanted their stories and admitted they were paid by a Turkish man to give statements to the police. With further pressure, Ahmet Gulay was now singing and admitted that he was asked by his boss, Cemal Dudas, the chief of the Mehwar group, to kill Richard. The police were looking for Cemal Dudas to ascertain the link between the killing and the people who ordered it.

Once the link was established and the police had the perpetrator's name, they would likely issue a press release giving full details. However, John was working with certain friendly journalists in the UK to publish the story of Richard Bringsen's murder, and the editor of the tabloid *People* had agreed to print the story on the front page on Friday under the banner 'British banker Murdered in Germany,' along with Richard Bringsen's picture. The article would carry enough innuendos to indicate that perhaps his death was somehow linked to his job at G&P Bank. The major newspapers promised to run a more detailed story once the press release was issued by the German police.

John also advised that the affidavit to be signed by Danny was now ready and after a final review, it would be submitted to the SIB and the Institute of Chartered Accountants in England and Wales.

Amir told John that he was likely to get very serious evidence of the bank's illegal acts and frauds during the weekend. John suggested he send him the information as soon as possible and visit

London soon thereafter so that matters may progress further. John told him that he had received communication from David Ringbutton and that he was to meet David and a lady by the name of Clare Rocke, a lawyer with the SIB, on Friday to discuss the arrangements for passing the information to the SIB.

Amir had barely done any productive work for the bank in the last couple of days as all his energies and thoughts were now directed towards going after G&P Bank.

He had noticed that Rehmallah packed up around 3.30 p.m. and left. Amir asked Pat if Rehmallah was going to return later. She replied with a wink that Rehmallah had a very important meeting with a high-net-worth client by the name of Poonam in Scotland. Amir felt embarrassed.

At five o'clock sharp, Amir left the bank. He did his usual routine of going around the block and then going into the supermarket. He came out through the backdoor exit, and from there he walked a few metres until he found a telephone booth.

'Hello.' Rehana picked up the telephone on the first ring.

'Hi.' He said.

'Where are you? I'm finding it difficult to wait.' Rehana said.

'I've just come out of the bank and wanted to make sure the coast was clear.'

'Everything and everybody have cleared. Your boss left here at four. He said he would come back on Sunday around lunchtime. The children have gone directly to their friends from the school and will return on Sunday afternoon. I've got a treat that you will never forget.' she said.

'I'll be there in one hour.'

'Why so long? I'm hardly able to breathe without you.'

'I'm going to my apartment first to change and pick up a few things. I'll be there as soon as possible.'

Amir went to a department store and picked up a duffel bag, a bottle of ladies' perfume, a couple of pads of Post-It notes and a basic Polaroid camera. He walked to his apartment, quickly showered, and changed into casual attire. He packed a nightdress, his bathroom kit, the Polaroid camera he had just bought, a regular camera, and the bottle of perfume in the bag and left for Rehmallah's apartment. On the way, he stopped at the florist and bought a bouquet of two dozen red roses.

Amir arrived at Rehmallah's apartment within ten minutes. He went straight up to the third floor. The door to the apartment opened before he could even ring the bell. Rehana had been waiting. She had freshly showered and applied light make-up. She was wearing hot pants and a see-through top without a bra. She looked dazzling.

'Welcome to Casa de Amor,' She said.

Amir handed over the bouquet to Rehana, who took it with both hands and kissed the flowers. Amir could not decide which looked more beautiful, Rehana's lips or the flowers. He decided her lips were more beautiful and took Rehana in his arms and kissed her. She responded eagerly, pushing the door shut.

Amir put his bag to the side and lifted Rehana in his hands. He put her on the couch in the living room, where he tore away her clothes and quickly undressed. They made love on the couch.

'I never knew anybody could make love like you do.' Rehana said.

'I have never met anybody as sweet and delicious as you.' Amir replied.

They sat holding each other, completely naked, for quite some time.

'Let me take a quick shower, and then I'll get the food ready.' Rehana said.

'I can't wait to ravish you again.'

'You have made me very happy tonight, darling.' she kissed Amir again and went to the bedroom.

She came back a few minutes later, still dripping with water. She looked beautiful in a white cotton shalwar kameez.

'This is your home for at least a day and a half, so make yourself comfortable,' she said, bringing out a pair of slippers for him to wear.

'So? How was your day?' she asked.

'Too long. It was very difficult for me to wait for the time to pass so I could come here and be with you.' Amir replied honestly.

'Liar. You don't know how difficult it has been for me. I bet your wait was not half as painful as mine.' Rehana said.

'I have already proved to you how eager I am.' Amir said with a wink.

'You are naughty. Let's have dinner and get to work. I've prepared very special dishes for you.' Rehana led Amir to the dining table.

The table was already set for two, with lighted candles and rose petals floating in water in small crystal bowls. Rehana dimmed the lights in the living room, the effect on the atmosphere was dramatic.

She made Amir sit, held his face in her hands, and kissed him. She then quickly pulled back and went to the kitchen. Amir could barely restrain himself from following her. She brought out several dishes, including a salad, samosas, shami kebab, the famous biryani, karahi gosht, and freshly home-baked round flatbread called roti.

'These are delicious. So many dishes for just two of us? You must have been very busy. You didn't have to do all this, you know? Amir said, complimenting Rehana on her cooking after indulging in all of the Pakistani dishes on the table.

'You are a very, very special person, and I wanted to make special dishes for you. I am happy that you like my cooking. Take some more. You have hardly eaten anything.' Rehana replied.

'I'm really full. I'll burst if I eat anymore!' Amir replied.

The main course was followed by traditional sweets: gulab jaman and shahi tukra. Amir took several pieces of each.

'These are very good.' he said.

'Then you should eat some more. That is the best compliment.' Rehana put some more gulab jamans on Amir's plate.

After dinner, they sat in the living area.

'Coffee?'

'Yes, please. Amir replied.

Rehana brought her coffee and sat down next to Amir. She started caressing him and drank some coffee from his cup.

'Let's finish the job at hand first.' Amir said.

'Yes, let's do it.' Rehana said, leading Amir to a small study next to the bedroom.

There was a large fireproof filing cabinet with a combination lock in the study. As Rehana knew the combination, she put her hand on the dial and turned the numbers on the combination. Amir quickly took out his Polaroid camera and took a picture of the combination she was dialling. She turned the dial several times and the lock clicked open.

She stepped back and said, 'You know what you are looking for. Take your time. I'll clear the table and do the dishes.'

Amir quickly went to work. He opened each drawer carefully and took pictures of its contents so that he could replace the documents exactly as they were stored. In the first drawer, right in the front, were two large black books. Amir opened the first one. Each page was neatly divided into two parts. The first part stated the real name of the account holder, his or her address and identification details. The second part contained his or her alias, the address for the bank's record and a ten-digit account number. Each page also included the account operating instructions and other details of the account holder's preference for managing the account.

The second register contained the same information in the reverse order: the account number followed by an alias, identification indicators, and address for the record. The second part gave the real name, address and personal identification details. Each page of both registers was signed by Masood Qadir and Rehmallah.

Amir was amazed at the creativity and ingenuity of the bank's officials in assigning the aliases and addresses to account holders. For example, one entry read:

Account No.	1011195401
Name	President Eduardo Toridos
Address	Presidential Palace,
	Managua, Nicaragua
Date of birth	10 November 1954
Password	MNP01GA
Wife's name	Isabella Toridos
Identification indicator	Wife's birth date: 15 October 1960
Special instructions	Bank statement and all correspondence

to be retained for collection by the account holder.

Deposits may be received in hard currency through couriers. The bank might have to arrange to pick up from the client's premises. 70% of the funds should be invested immediately in bearer bonds and high-value paintings, jewellery and antiques. The remaining 30% should be retained in liquid money market funds and bank deposits.

Name and address for the record
Account No.   1011195401
Name   Rudyard Kipling
Address   Bateman's Burwash
                          East Sussex
                          England.
Date of birth   30 December 1965
Wife's name   Caroline Kipling

Another account contained the following details:
Account No.   1409197001
Name   General Kwame Odongo
Occupation   Chief of Army staff, Zaire
Address   Army Headquarters,
                          Kinshasa
                          Zaire
Password   KZAC02GA
Date of birth   14 September 1970
Wife's name   Jiji Odongo
Identification Indicator Mother's maiden name: Huluwa

Special instructions
Deposits will normally come in diamonds, precious metals and currency notes. These should be converted quickly and retained in gold holdings, term deposits, and money market funds.

Statements and correspondence to be retained to be collected by the account holder.

Name and address for the record

Account No.	1409197001
Name	David Livingstone
Address	Mikindani, Tanzania.
Date of birth	19 March 1963
Wife's name	Mary Moffat

Amir noted that most of the assigned names were those of famous people who were long dead. The personal details, including the addresses and wives' names, were mostly correct according to the historical record.

He carefully went through the books, attaching the sticky notes to the most prominent ones, which he identified for copying.

He found several pages marked with a slash under Tolbert and Gibbs. For example, one page contained the entry for the account of Charles Ramsey, Senior Banking Partner, Tolbert and Gibbs. He was a borrower instead of a depositor and had taken several loans over the years. His code name was Edgar Hoover with the address of the American Embassy, Berkley Square, London. Similarly, there were accounts in the name of David Finner, a partner in London, and Jacques Regnier, a partner in the Geneva office. Amir quickly pasted a sticky note to these pages.

There were several names of very prominent politicians still holding offices, including ministers in some of the countries in the Indian subcontinent, Europe, the Americas, and the Far East. There were several members of the UK parliament from both parties who had apparently received remittances from unknown sources. There was also a page for an Indian minister still in office. There were names of several American senators who had deposits from remittances directly received from several sources.

As a matter of interest, Amir referred to the name Rafael Dorado, the example mentioned in Richard Bringsen's folder. It was there with Mr. Dorado's address in Panama. He was given the name of Rabindranath Tagore with the address Jorasanko Mansion, Calcutta,

India. His account number was 0705186101. Amir recalled that the actual birth date of Mr. Tagore was 7 May 1861.

One of the interesting names was that of Pedro Sanchez, the famous head of Cali cartel of Columbia. His file clearly mentioned that most of the funds for deposit were to come from the USA from the sale of high-quality Colombian produce. He was given the alias of Joseph Stalin, with an address in the Kremlin, Moscow. Perhaps the alias was appropriate, as Pedro Sanchez was no less powerful than the Soviet dictator.

After identifying many pages for photocopying, Amir systematically listed the names of the account holders and their account numbers on a notepad.

Then, he referred to the account folders, which were neatly filed in the order of the account numbers. Each file contained a copy of the account opening form, which gave full details of the account holder and his business or profession, with a sheet attached with the details of the assigned name and account number for the client. The folder also contained the latest account statement, copies of the instructions received from the client, details of the actions taken by the bank on behalf of the client in response to the client's instructions and any other comments.

The folders gave details of how the funds were received: in suitcases through couriers, initially parked in assets acquired on paper only from unscrupulous merchants and intermediaries, and remitted through dummy accounts to the UK and other parts of the world where they were invested in properties and other high-value assets. The documents clearly indicated that billions of dollars were funnelled into high-value assets in several European countries.

There was a folder for the account of Charles Ramsey of Tolbert and Gibbs. The folder indicated that the account was business sensitive and under no circumstances should the bank press the borrower to settle the outstanding loan. The interest charge was also fixed at three basis points below LIBOR, which in Amir's experience was unheard of. There was no repayment by Mr. Ramsey against several loans of hundreds of thousands of pounds received by him over the last few years. Each paper was signed by Masood and Rehmallah, mentioning the reference of the approval received for each transaction from either Sheikh Tayeb or Azhar Alam. There was also a loan given to Jacques Regnier. Apparently. The loan was given several years back and there was no repayment yet.

Amir swiftly went through the folders for the accounts he had identified from the black book and took them out. There were about thirty such folders, each containing ten to fifteen sheets of paper. He put the black books and the folders into the duffel bag. Rehana had finished the dishes and was watching television.

Amir got up and went to her. She immediately got up and embraced Amir, showering him with kisses.

'Finished? Did you find what you were looking for?' she asked eagerly.

'I'm finished here. I found more than I was looking for. I need to copy some of the documents so they can be presented to the authorities when we make our case,' Amir said.

'Is it safe to take the documents out of the filing cabinet? They might be disturbed, and Rehmallah might come to know. Besides, where would you be able to copy these at this time of the night?' Rehana was worried.

'Don't worry, I've taken precautions to ensure that all the documents will be returned and placed exactly as before. As to the photocopying of the documents, I have made arrangements with the secretarial bureau. They're open twenty-four hours a day.'

'I never knew of any business staying open that late in Switzerland. But, wait, I'll change and come with you.'

'Is it wise? Rehmallah may turn up or somebody might see you outside.' Amir was cautious.

'We are dead if Rehmallah turns up before you return the papers anyway, whether or not I am with you. He'll see that the filing cabinet has been accessed. As for somebody seeing me outside, this is Switzerland, nobody cares.' Rehana said, getting up and going to her bedroom where she quickly changed.

Rehana led Amir to the basement where her Toyota Corolla was parked next to Rehmallah's Mercedes. She was wearing a woollen sweater and pants with high-heeled shoes. It was cold. Rehana quickly got into the car and switched on the engine.

'Where to?'

Amir gave her the address of Bonjour Secretarial Bureau. It wasn't far, they got there in ten minutes. The bureau was open, as promised. Amir quickly went up to the receptionist, identified himself and said that he wanted to make some copies. The secretary showed him the photocopying machine and offered to make the copies for him. Amir declined and said that he would make the copies himself. She advised that there was a photocopy counter on the machine and that he would be charged one Swiss franc per copy. Amir gladly accepted the steep price and went to work.

He made two copies of each document. It took him close to two hours to finish making all of the copies. He was very systematic and ensured that each paper was placed exactly where it was removed from. Rehana was patiently waiting in the reception area, reading magazines and looking busy. Amir loved her for her consideration and care.

After completing the copying, Amir asked the receptionist to give him two large envelopes. He placed one set in each envelope. He marked one for Alan Tipps, care of Bonjour Secretarial Bureau, and put it in the locker assigned to him.

He addressed the other envelope to John Delon in London and asked the receptionist if it could be sent urgently by courier. The receptionist informed him that since it was the weekend, the courier would not come to collect the packages before Monday. However, if it was very urgent, Amir may take the package to the twenty-four-hour DHL centre at route de l'Aéroport. Amir thanked her and paid the bill for photocopying.

'Darling, would it be possible for us to go to the airport?' Amir asked Rehana. 'I don't want to take any chances with these. What I have in my hands is pure dynamite. This could endanger lives.'

'You mean to say that I have been sitting on this stuff all my life without realising the danger it posed to my children and me?' Rehana said.

'Since you were not an interested party and unaware of the danger the documents possessed, you would have been all right. Now, if anybody were to find out that you accessed the cabinet and let me take the documents from there, you and I would both be dead in minutes.' Amir said.

Rehana drove fast. There was not much traffic going toward the airport at that time of the night. They reached the DHL centre within twenty minutes. A very efficient attendant took the package, prepared an airway bill, and gave a copy to Amir. Amir paid the charges in cash.

Only after the package was handed over did Amir start to relax. In the car, he took Rehana's hand and started kissing it. She immediately stopped the car on the side of the road and held Amir. They both started kissing passionately.

'Let's go home. I cannot bear it much longer.' she said, pushing Amir away.

Throughout the drive back, Amir kept holding and kissing Rehana's hand. She responded by putting her hand in Amir's lap. They soon arrived at Rehana's apartment and quickly went upstairs.

As soon as they entered the apartment, Amir rushed to the filing cabinet and systematically inserted the folders back into their respective places. By referring to the notes and photographs he had made, he ensured everything was exactly as before. He closed the cabinet and, referring to the Polaroid picture, ensured that the combination lock was the same as well.

Amir then rushed to Rehana and both of them started hugging and kissing each other. She leaned on Amir's shoulder, put her hand around Amir's waist, and led him to the bedroom. Her bed was sprinkled with flowers. She quickly took off her clothes; Amir did the same, and they jumped into bed.

Once again, they forgot their individual existence and became one, the bed shaking with their movements.

Amir lay on Rehana for quite some time after they finished making love and then slid to the side. Rehana quickly found him and put her head on his chest and slept. Amir also dozed off. When he opened his eyes and checked his watch, it was seven in the morning. Rehana was still asleep with a smile on her face.

Amir got out of bed, went to the bathroom, shaved and showered. Then he went to the kitchen and made breakfast. He took the breakfast to the bedroom, kept the tray on the bedside table, and started caressing and kissing Rehana.

She stirred and held his head and pushed it into her bosom. 'Kiss me, bite me, and make me writhe in pain.'

Amir quickly kissed her breasts and said, 'I have made breakfast, sweetheart.'

She opened her eyes and said, 'This is the first time in my life that somebody has brought me breakfast. Thank you, darling. You are an angel.'

After finishing breakfast in bed, Rehana went to the bathroom for a shower and change. She returned looking even more beautiful and relaxed.

'I have put everything back in the filing cabinet exactly as it was,' he said.

'It better be. Otherwise, I'll meet you in the heaven.' She replied jokingly.

'Don't say such things. You look gorgeous.'

'You have already swept me off my feet. Further flattery won't get you any further.' she replied with a mischievous smile.

'What is on your mind for today?'

'I was thinking of going for a boat ride on Lake Geneva. It's cold, but you will keep me warm. We'll have lunch somewhere nice and then return here in the evening.'

'That sounds fantastic. Let's go.' Amir said, getting up.

They enjoyed the day on the lake and had lunch at a lakeside restaurant. In the evening, Rehana prepared food for both of them while Amir sat down, watching the day's news. After dinner, they sat by each other, caressing and kissing. Soon, they were in bed, making love.

The next morning, Amir got up early and, like the day before, brought breakfast to the bed. He woke Rehana gently with kisses.

'Why don't you also sleep a little longer? Today is Sunday. I was having the most wonderful dream of you and me sitting, holding each other in a cave in the Alps.' Rehana murmured without opening her eyes.

'Yes, but today is Sunday and your family will be here soon.' Amir said.

'Oh, my God! Must you remind me of my misfortunes? I don't mean the children; I mean the husband.' Rehana said, getting up.

'Until we deal with your husband and get you out of his clutches, we have to be careful.'

'What did you say?'

'We'll find a way, so we are always together. I'll get you out of this prison.'

'You will? You promise?'

'I will, and I promise. I won't be able to live without you, so I don't have any alternatives,' Amir said.

'Oh, Amir!' Rehana said, and hugged him. 'I love you so much, darling. If there is only one thing that is true in my life, it is the fact that I will not be able to live without you. I'll die if and when you leave my life. Darling, please, please, never abandon me.'

'I never will. I hope what I am doing succeeds. That might get rid of Mr. Rehmallah and his cronies for a long time.'

After a leisurely breakfast together, Amir kissed Rehana goodbye and walked out of the apartment building. He had a great time and had obtained invaluable information for his project. *Life could not be better*, he thought.

Chapter 39

London

John Delon found the package from Geneva waiting for him when he reached the office on Monday morning.

His secretary walked in and said, 'You have an appointment with Mr. Danial Rafi at eleven a.m. The affidavit and power of attorney you drafted last week are ready for his signature.'

'Good. Let me have it for a final look before Mr. Rafi comes in.'

'You are also to see Mr. David Ringbutton and Ms Clare Rocke of the SIB at 2.30 p.m. at the SIB's offices in Threadneedle Street.'

'I can see it is going to be a very busy day,' John said.

'And in case you've forgotten, the partners' meeting starts in five minutes.'

'Thanks for reminding me. Please get me a copy of the agenda and any other material that has been circulated for the meeting,' John said.

***

It was a small partnership of three partners. They frequently shared information about their clients.

However, Mr. Edward Delon, the senior partner and John's father, insisted on fortnightly formal meetings on the first and third Monday of each month to discuss the firm's affairs and the status of the cases being handled by the firm. Also close to his heart was the firm's working capital. His motto was to bill first and provide service later. He insisted that, except for the very large corporate clients, everybody must pay in advance.

This Monday morning, the two partners joined Edward Delon in his office. He had a small round table for client meetings and for working away from his desk.

'Good morning, gentlemen. All is well, I hope.' he said.

'So far, so good. The business is growing. We all are very busy.' John said to his father, his partner nodding in agreement.

Each partner took turns in briefing on the cases that they were handling. John mentioned the case he was working on for Amir and Danny.

'Sounds pretty sensitive. Might create headlines.' Edward said.

'Yes. That's the reason I've taken it. We might get a lot of free publicity by handling this case. I'm meeting the SIB today and getting papers signed by one of our clients who will spill the beans on Tolbert and Gibbs. I also received a package from Switzerland this morning, which probably contains sufficient material to prosecute G&P Bank. I'd like to have a brainstorming session with you early tomorrow morning after my meetings today.'

'Are you meeting David? Give him my regards.' Edward said.

'From what you've told us, there might be some personal danger to the parties involved, including you. Are you going to be able to handle it?' Peter Tomsky asked with concern.

'There is some personal risk to our clients, and for this reason, I'm trying to keep their identities secret. Both are aware of the risk and are willing to take it. I don't think there is any risk to the firm or me. I don't believe the opposition would dare harm a practicing British lawyer in the city of London.' John Delon replied.

'Be careful, though. Are these clients going to be able to pay our fees?' Edward, ever a businessman, asked.

'Both have given us an advance, which covers the cost of time spent to date. I'll ask for more money when I speak to my client, Amir.'

With that, the partners' meeting concluded.

***

Back in his office, John opened the package he had received from Geneva. He could not believe his eyes when he saw the documents included within. My God, he thought, this, for sure, is going to bring down G&P Bank.

He quickly prepared brief notes for his meeting with the SIB. Then, on an impulse, he consulted the telephone directory and found out that a Mr. Terrence Smith was listed as the chief executive officer of the Institute of Chartered Accountants in England and Wales. John picked up the phone and dialled the institute's number.

'May I speak to Mr. Terrence Smith, please?' he asked when his call was answered.

'Who is speaking, please?' the lady at the other end asked.

'My name is John Delon. I'm a partner in the law firm of Delon, Delon and Tomsky. I need to speak to Mr. Smith on a matter of the greatest importance.'

'Hold on, please.' The telephonist replied.

'Mr. Delon, this is Terrence Smith. What can I do for you?'

'Thank you for taking my call, Mr. Smith. A client of ours has some information that proves that one of the biggest accounting firms in this country was wilfully and knowingly involved in issuing false, unqualified audit reports on a bankrupt organisation. Certain partners personally benefited from financial favours from that organisation. My client wants to go public with the information and has instructed me to pass on this information to a tabloid newspaper. I have, however, convinced my client to let me talk to you first and share the information with you.' John laid it on thick.

'This sounds serious. Please send us the information by mail and we will investigate it thoroughly as is normal protocol with the institute.' Terrance said.

'Mr. Smith, my client's instructions are to release the information to the newspapers by tomorrow. Believe me, once released to the press, there will be monumental damage to the accounting profession in this country and to the institute. The accountants will be a laughing stock and considered to be no different than thieves and robbers. I suggest that we meet today so I can share the information with you. It will be up to you then. We'll be releasing the information to the press tomorrow.'

'Mr. Delon, I don't like your pressure tactics. Of course, you are aware of the libel laws in this country.' Terrence said.

'As a lawyer, I am fully aware of the laws of this country and do not intend to fall foul to any of them. Believe me, the information I have is impeccable and will result in a complete loss of public confidence in accountants and auditors in this country and internationally.' John insisted.

'Okay, Mr. Delon, you have whetted my curiosity. Let me see, the only time I can see you today is around five this afternoon.'

'Five is fine. I'll be at your offices in Moorgate.'

'I'll wait for you. Bye for now.' With that, Terrence was gone.

John relished his conversation with Terrence Smith. He had enjoyed lighting a fire under the pompous Mr. Smith.

At eleven o'clock sharp, Danny arrived at the offices of Delon, Delon and Tomsky. He was directly brought to John's office.

'Thank you for coming on time. I have an extremely busy day today. All for the cause, I assure you.' John said.

'Thank you for seeing me and taking this matter on. I'm ready to sign the affidavit. It is as we drafted, I hope.'

'It is. I'm going to take it to the meeting with the SIB and the Institute of Chartered Accountants in England and Wales, ICAEW. 'I'm meeting their CEO at five this afternoon. Don't worry, I'm not going to reveal your name or the source of information to the SIB or ICAEW. I hope to get a confidentiality and witness protection guarantee from the SIB before handing over any information.' John gave the papers to Danny to sign.

Danny quickly reviewed the papers and signed them in triplicate. John returned one signed copy of the affidavit and power of attorney to Danny.

Danny had brought with him a folder of the copies of the audit working papers and notes of meetings at Tolbert and Gibbs. He gave these to John and explained the details to show the information that clearly indicated the value of several advances and investments made by G&P Bank were seriously impaired, in the opinion of the auditor, permanently, and should have been fully provided for. There were details about TIG and the bank's exposure. The auditor had noted that the bank did not appear to have any security against those advances but they were shown in the bank's books and the balance sheet as fully secured. In the opinion of the audit staff, the bank's biggest client, TIG, was bankrupt, and the bank was exposed to a loss of a couple billion dollars. The discussions at the Tolbert and Gibbs executive meetings were fully documented and clearly showed that all the concerns raised during the field audit

were brushed aside amidst the talk of obtaining large-value assignments from the bank. The partners involved, Charles Ramsey and David Finner, had a totally frivolous and negligent attitude when reviewing the working papers since they had already made up their minds to give a positive opinion on the financial statements of the bank.

John was amazed at the amount of information he received and the level of fraud and other criminal activities committed by G&P Bank. He believed he had all the information he needed to implicate G&P Bank. All he needed was to commence taking action. That would start with the meeting with the SIB that afternoon.

***

John reached the SIB's offices, which were in the same building as the Bank of England on Threadneedle Street, in time for the 2.30 meeting. He told the receptionist that he was there to see Mr. David Ringbutton. She asked John to show an ID, John produced his visiting card and driving licence. She quickly prepared a visitor's pass and gave it to John. She then called David Ringbutton and told him his visitor had arrived.

Within a couple of minutes, David Ringbutton came down and escorted John inside the building. They were allotted a meeting room on the first floor. It was a small, windowless room with a round table and four chairs. Flasks of tea and coffee with a pot of milk and some biscuits were placed on a side table in the corner.

'Thank you for coming. Clare will be here in a minute. She was on a call when you arrived. Can I pour you some tea or coffee?' David asked.

'Coffee is great. Black, no sugar,' John said.

As David passed the cup to John, a smartly dressed lady in her mid-thirties walked in and introduced herself. 'Oh, hello! I'm Clare Rocke, Head of Legal at the SIB.'

'Hi. I'm John Delon, a partner in Delon, Delon and Tomsky. Thank you for seeing me.' John replied.

'I understand you have a source who wishes to divulge information about a bank operating in the UK. Your source believes the bank is involved in fraudulent and other criminal acts and wants to bring this to our attention.' Clare came to the point.

'Yes, that's true. My client has hard evidence to prove his allegations. In fact, I now have two sources, both are connected, though. These sources are afraid that they may come in a harm's way if their identity is disclosed. In my clients' opinion, this bank has a criminal culture and may have already been involved in eliminating staff they suspected of working against them. My clients would like to cooperate with the SIB and any other agency that might need their help, but they cannot afford to be identified nor risk their identity being disclosed to the bank or any other party. They would like a written guarantee from the SIB before they pass on any information.'

'We understand they are scared. We cannot, however, guarantee anything unless we know the quality of the information being passed on to us. In addition, we might have to present your clients as a witness in court for giving evidence.' Clare replied.

'I assure you the information you'll get will stand up in a court of law and there will be no need to call my clients as witnesses. There are documents that would prove all of the crimes committed by the bank.'

'If that is the case, then we may be able to sign an agreement with your clients to protect their identity. However, before we do this, we'd like you to explain the type of crimes you allege have been committed and the evidence your clients have to prove that.' Clare replied.

John opened his briefcase and produced one page from Richard Bringsen's memo in which he described the falsification of the information about accounts and the use of Rabindranath Tagore's name as the account holder for Account No. 075196101. He handed over copies of the page to David and Clare. 'This is just an indication of the type of game being played by the bank. We'll be able to provide you with the account opening form and other documents to prove that Account No. 075196101, in fact, belongs to Mr. Rafael Dorado of Panama, who has been accused by the US government of being involved in the drug cartel.'

'You mean the account belongs to The Mr. Rafael Dorado of Panama? El Presidente?'

'The same. Now you know what we are talking about and why my clients are scared. I want cast-iron guarantees to protect my clients, and if they come into harms' way because of the incompetence or negligence of the SIB, then I will not be afraid to take legal action accordingly.'

'On the basis that the evidence will be documented and would stand up in a court without any need for reference or deposition by your clients, we are ready to give you a guarantee. I'll draft something today and should be able to present the draft to you by tomorrow.'

'That will be fine. Let me caution you, though. There are forces at work in this matter, and there is a possibility that this might explode very soon. So the quicker we move, the better.'

'We will move as swiftly as possible,' Clare assured him.

It was after 4.15 p.m. when John finished his meeting with the SIB. He walked to Bank station and took the underground to Moorgate. He was there in twenty minutes and arrived at the offices of the Institute a few minutes before his scheduled appointment with Mr. Terrence Smith, the CEO.

At the reception, John was asked to go straight up to the third floor. He knocked at the door with the nameplate 'Terrence Smith.' A middle-aged lady was sitting in front of an IBM golf ball typewriter, clicking away at some document.

She looked up and said, 'Good afternoon. What can I do for you?'

'My name is John Delon. I'm here to see Mr. Smith. He is expecting me,' John said.

She picked up the telephone and said, 'Terry, there's a gentleman here to see you; says that you are expecting him.' She looked at John. 'What did you say your name was, Sir?'

'John Delon.'

'You heard. John Delon. Okay, I'll show him in.' She said, getting up from her throne and opening the door to the adjacent room.

Sitting behind a cluttered desk in the room was a man around sixty wearing a dark suit and the Institute's tie. He got up from his chair and said, 'Mr. Delon. Thank you for coming. I'm curious. That is the only reason I'm seeing you at such short notice. I'm afraid I can only give you a few minutes, I have another appointment at 5.30.'

'Thank you for seeing me. Half an hour is more than enough for what I have to share with you. It'll be up to you after that,' John said, presenting his business card. 'A client of mine has clear evidence that a major accounting firm in this country and internationally was involved in a wrongly issued unqualified audit report on the financial statements of a major organisation of public interest. This was done because the partners of the accounting firm obtained personal favours and financial benefits from the client.'

'This is preposterous. I cannot believe what you are saying, particularly since you have not given me any names or evidence in support of what you are talking about. We have a professional ethics committee that initiates stern action against erring members. I suggest you give us all the information in the form of a complaint and we will take it from there.' Mr. Smith was dismissive.

'Just to convince you of the gravity of what I am talking about, I have with me a sworn statement by an individual who has inside information. This might help our discussion.' John showed Mr. Smith a copy of Danny's affidavit in which the name of the deposer, the name of the bank, and all other references were crossed out with a black marker.

Terrence Smith's jaw dropped as he read the affidavit.

'Each and every statement in that affidavit is supported by documents. We are presenting this to a UK government agency tomorrow and will release it to the press simultaneously.' John said, getting up.

'Wait. You know we can't take any action on innuendos and anonymous complaints.'

'I'd be pleased to submit a statement drafted by our firm based on the sworn statement given to us by our client, supporting our statement with full documentary evidence. I'll give it to the president of the institute, the head of the professional ethics committee, and you jointly, under a written guarantee from the institute that my clients' identities will be protected.'

'We don't operate like this, Mr. Delon,' Terrence said.

'I'd prefer this matter be handled through you, so the profession is protected and the institute is seen as taking action. For this purpose, I'll wait until noon tomorrow. I will release the information to the press if I don't hear from you by then. The ball is in your court. I thank you for your time.' John got up.

'I'll speak to our president and see what can be done.' Terrence said, sighing.

'I'll wait for your call until noon tomorrow then.' John said, and walked out.

He was feeling good. Things were moving in the right direction. He took the underground back to Bond Street and from there he walked to his office. There were two messages waiting for him, one was from Ian Softsol, asking him to call urgently, and the other was from Amir, asking him to phone Mr. Alan Tipps on a given number.

John called Ian first.

'Ian, how are you, my friend. John here.' he said.

'You've got me involved in an interesting assignment, I must say. The German police have now established a link between Richard Bringsen's death and a G&P Bank official in Geneva by the name of Oshko. Apparently, Cemal Dudas, the chief of Mehwars, has been cooperating. He has admitted to receiving two hundred thousand dollars from Mr. Oshko to get rid of Richard Bringsen. The German police are getting a warrant for Mr. Oshko as we speak. Since he's still a German citizen, it won't be difficult for the German government to have him brought back to Germany for questioning. My informant tells me that Mr. Oshko comes to Germany for weekends and might be picked up during his next visit here.'

'This is great news. I wonder if we should pass this information on to the press here in the UK.'

'It might be better to wait until the warrant is issued and Mr. Oshko arrested. A report in the press might scare him away.'

'Okay, we'll wait. I appreciate your help in this matter. This is a good development,' John said and rang off.

Then, he called the Geneva number left by Amir and asked the operator to connect him with Mr. Alan Tipps.

'There is a call for you, Sir,' the operator said, transferring the call to Amir, who had parked himself in a small conference room.

'Amir, John.'

'John, I was anxious to find out if you received the package and hear your views on the information.'

'I received the package and went through the information. It's fantastic. I've been very busy today, all on yours' and Danny's affairs.' John told him about his activities and the news from Germany.

'This is wonderful. We are nearing the target. Do we need to do anything in Switzerland? Surely the bank is involved in all sorts of criminal practices here as well.'

'If this German case gets its due attention, then the bank will be in extreme difficulty in Switzerland. They appear to be violating Swiss laws about involvement in criminal activities. I am not an expert on Swiss law. I suggest you go see a good lawyer friend of mine in Geneva. His name is Francois Martin. He works for the law firm of Martin, Vincent and Durrand. They are at 21 Rue du Mont-Blanc. I'll call him and tell him that you will contact him. He might ask you to pay some fees in advance; Swiss lawyers are good but expensive. Speaking of fees, I'd appreciate it if you could remit further two thousand pounds, I have been spending a lot of time on this case and the partners are a little concerned about fees.'

'I must thank you for your support. I'm coming to London this Thursday evening and would like to see you on Friday. I'll pay you then if that's okay. Please give me the telephone number of Francois Martin. I'll call him to set up an appointment.'

'Good. I'd like to see you, as well. In the meantime, I'll continue my contact with the SIB and the institute. I'll give them all the information after obtaining the necessary assurances about confidentiality.' John said, and he gave Amir Francois Martin's telephone number.

Chapter 40

Karachi, Pakistan

Today was the big day for Yakoob Soothar. He was to fly to Amsterdam with the first consignment. On an impulse, he had asked his two brothers, Haroon and Rafik, to join him on the trip. He was feeling generous and thought letting his brothers enjoy an expenses-paid trip to Europe would be a good fence-mending effort. But, of course, he hadn't told them about the consignment he was carrying. That was a secret.

He had accepted only one hundred kilos of the product, as it needed to be packed suitably and transported by air. His Lear jet had a limited capacity to carry weight for long distances. He would pick another one hundred kilos in a couple weeks.

He had also insisted that Salim travel with him, as Salim would be able to handle the cash they would receive in Amsterdam. In order not to raise suspicions, at Salim's suggestion, Yakoob had ordered one hundred model ships emblazoned with TIG markings that were made of aluminium but looked as though they were made of high-quality polished steel. These were ostensibly to be given as gifts to TIG's shipping agents. The ships had hollow cargo holds that were invisibly sealed after stuffing a one-kilogram bag of heroin into each. Fazlullah had arranged for expert welders just for this purpose. Yakoob had to admit that the welders had done a very good job as the ships' bottoms appeared to be one piece of metal, and it was impossible to see that they were joined together.

The jet would have to make stopovers at Tehran, Istanbul, and Rome for refuelling on the way to Amsterdam. The group had no intention of disembarking at any of these airports while the refuelling was done. Yakoob was assured the airport officials would not be interested in them or their aircraft since the jet would be parked away from the passenger terminals.

The plane had arrived from Peshawar only yesterday. Captain Munir, co-pilot Captain Shahzad and the air hostess, Rukhshana, did not know anything about the trip other than that the boss was going to Europe with his brothers and Salim Chaliwala.

The flight plan had already been filed with the Civil Aviation Department, and they were scheduled to take off at 11 a.m. The group arrived at Karachi airport at 10.30. Since they were to fly in a private plane, they were given VIP treatment and cleared through to the aircraft very quickly.

The flight took off at the assigned time of 11 a.m. It was scheduled to reach Schiphol Airport in Amsterdam at eight in the evening.

Yakoob wondered about this new venture he was getting involved in. This trip was essential for TIG, as the group urgently needed funds, and apparently, no funds were available from any other source. No, there was no other way, and there was no risk in what he was doing. He convinced himself that this was the only solution.

Chapter 41

Geneva

Amir arrived at the offices of Martin, Vincent and Durrand at 21 Rue du Mont-Blanc, which was not far from his own office. Although it was after normal office hours, Dr. Francois Martin had agreed to see him. Lawyers seemed to be working all hours in Geneva, and in this case, Dr. Martin had received a call from his old friend, John Delon, so he had to oblige.

After some small talk covering Amir's arrival and work in Switzerland, the weather, and the Swiss and world economy, the lawyer got to the point. 'My friend, John Delon, told me you are his client and may need my assistance in respect to certain matters involving banking regulations in Switzerland. How can I help you?'

'As I told you, I work for G&P Bank. Although I have been transferred to Geneva only recently, I have been with them for some time now. During my time at the bank, I've learnt that they are involved in certain activities which might be described as criminal. I'd like to expose them so they are not able to continue with their activities.'

'I see. This is unusual. Normally, bankers and clients come to us to find a solution to their problems with the authorities and not the other way around. Before going into the details of what you believe to be criminal activities, which might be totally and fully legal in Switzerland, I'd like to know your interest in this matter.' Dr. Martin was no fool.

Amir narrated his ordeal when travelling from Karachi to Geneva. He also expressed his conviction that his friend, Richard Bringsen, was killed at the behest of the bank, and his desire to put a stop to the criminal and illegal activities to protect the bank's honest employees and clients. He admitted that he was acting with the desire for revenge and believed that he had sufficient information to expose the bank and its officials.

'Well, let me tell you how the banking business works and is regulated in Switzerland. All banks here are regulated by the Swiss Financial Market Supervisory Authority or FINMA for short, which derives its authority from a series of federal statutes. The country's tradition of bank secrecy, which dates back to the middle-ages, was first codified in a 1934 law. To override banking secrecy provisions of this law, there must be a substantial criminal allegation before a governmental agency, especially a foreign one, can gain access to account information. Tax evasion, for example, is considered a misdemeanour in Switzerland rather than a crime.

'According to the Swiss Bankers' Association, however, there is also a duty for bankers to provide information to a proper legal authority under certain circumstances. These circumstances are described in this paper.' Dr. Martin gave a piece of paper to Amir.

Amir quickly read the paper. It stated that a bank may disclose the information about its client's affairs in the following cases:
- Civil proceedings (such as inheritance or divorce)
- Debt recovery and bankruptcies
- Criminal proceedings (money laundering, association with a criminal organisation, theft, tax fraud, blackmail, etc.)
- International mutual legal assistance proceedings. Switzerland is required to assist the authorities of foreign states in criminal matters as a result of the 1983 federal law relating to International Mutual Assistance in Criminal Matters. Assets can be frozen and handed over to the foreign authorities concerned. Assistance in criminal matters follows the principles of dual criminality, specialty, and proportionality.

As soon as Amir indicated that he had finished reading the document, Dr. Martin continued, 'From what you have just told me, you claim to have irrefutable evidence to prove that the bank was involved in criminal activities, such as money laundering, association with criminal organisations, theft, et cetera, and that the bank is also involved in assisting clients in accumulating and benefiting from wealth obtained illegally outside Switzerland.

'We in Switzerland are not keen on lending an ear to oblige people acting under personal or emotional compulsions. We do, however, take a very serious view of the banking and financial crimes involving our country, as we do not wish Switzerland's banking business and reputation to be abused or tarnished. We tend to act swiftly and sternly when we find there has been a violation of our ethical and professional standards.

'If you wish, and I am satisfied that your allegations are prima facie true, I am prepared to discuss this case with the president of the Swiss Bankers' Association, who happens to be a good friend. I would, however, like you to prepare a written statement which we would get notarised. The president of the Bankers' Association may guide us to take this further. I believe it should go to the Bank Licensing Authority, who, if satisfied that G&P was involved in the type of activities you have just narrated, might revoke the licence of the bank after following due processes under the Swiss Banking Code. This may also be referred to the public prosecutor to take legal action against the officials of the bank for carrying out criminal activities in Switzerland.'

Amir carefully considered everything he had just heard. 'Thank you. I'll start working on the written statement, giving full details of my findings and provide you with evidence to support my allegations. I should have this ready either tomorrow or the day after. I'll call you as soon as I am ready.'

'Good. Please phone me and we will fix a mutually convenient time. I'll review your statement carefully and make any amendments that may be necessary. I'll then arrange for you to sign it in front of a notary public. In the meantime, I will also speak to my friend, the president of the Swiss Bankers' Association, and sound him out about this case.'

'Excellent. Do I have to sign any contract with your firm to formalise our relationship?'

'Yes, please. We have very strict regulations in Switzerland about accepting clients. I will keep the necessary documents ready for you to sign when you come next. I estimate that our fee for assisting you in this matter may amount to eight thousand Swiss francs. We would like to receive fifty percent in advance.'

'I'll bring cash when I see you next,' Amir said

Amir worked the whole night writing and re-writing the statement. He wanted to get it right. In the end, he had a ten-page statement fully indexed with the evidence, including copies of Richard Bringsen's memo, the registers and account documents obtained from Rehmallah's filing cabinet, and the financial statements of the bank.

The next day, he called the bank to tell them he was not well and would not be coming to work. He then phoned Dr. Martin and told him the information was ready.

'You work fast. It's the fire against this bank in your heart. Okay, I'll be able to see you at eleven. I'll get the documents accepting you as a client ready. Assuming that you've done a good job of piecing everything together, I'll fix a meeting with the notary public for this afternoon. His office is just across the street.'

After making arrangements with Dr. Martin, Amir phoned Rehana. 'Hi, what are you doing?'

'Thinking about you, what else? Thinking about you and waiting for your call has become my life.' Rehana replied.

'Alone?'

'Yes. The children have gone to school. It looks as if something has happened at the bank. You must know. Rehmallah got a call in the middle of the night and left. He said there was a problem, and that he was going to the bank. He hasn't returned. How come you are calling me at this time? You are getting bold.'

'No. I have worked the whole night on the special project, and I'm exhausted. I don't know if there is a problem at the bank. In fact, I haven't gone there and reported sick today. I have an appointment with the lawyer at eleven. If you feel like having a quick refreshment, come over.'

'I'll be there in less than fifteen minutes.' Rehana was excited.

She was there in twelve minutes. As usual, she was stunningly dressed. They made passionate love. Afterward, Amir felt tired and started dozing off. Rehana got up and made him breakfast and brought it to the bed.

'Wake up. You have to see the lawyer.'

He reluctantly pulled himself out of bed, took a shower and quickly got himself ready.

'Where is the lawyer's office?' Rehana asked.

'On Rue du Mont-Blanc. It's not far.'

'I'll drop you there. I brought the car.'

'No, it's too dangerous. I'll take a cab.' Amir insisted.

'Okay, Thanks for making me feel young again. I better go in case Rehmallah phones at home. I'll wait for your call. Please take some more sick leave. Your sickness is healthy for me.' Rehana said teasingly.

Amir reached Dr. Martin's office soon after that. Dr. Martin was waiting for him. 'Good morning. You don't seem to have slept at all last night.'

'I was working on the statement.' Amir said, handing over the folder of papers to Dr. Martin.

'I'll go through these now. Your statement will have to be typed. My secretary can do it very quickly. She'll also give you the papers you need to sign in order to establish our relationship. Would you like some coffee?'

'Yes, please. Black, no sugar,' Amir replied. He watched Dr. Martin pour the coffee into a cup and hand it over to him. 'Do you want me to wait somewhere else while you are going through these?' he asked as he took the coffee.

'No, it's fine. I may need to ask questions and clarify some matters. It's better if you stay here.'

Dr. Martin started going through the papers Amir had handed over. His secretary came in and gave Amir three copies of a set of documents for signing. Amir read the documents and signed each copy. The agreement stated the estimated fee and the requirement of paying fifty percent in advance. Amir returned the signed documents along with four thousand Swiss francs to the secretary, who returned one copy of the documents to Amir, along with the receipt for his payment.

'This is very comprehensive. Let's get this typed up and notarised. Then, I'll take it to the president of the Bankers' Association. I've already spoken to him, and he's happy to see me this afternoon. I think the Swiss Bankers' Association will have no choice but to pass this material on to the Licensing Authority for proceeding against the bank.'

'Do you want me to wait while this is being done?' Amir asked.

'No need. I have fixed an appointment with the notary public at two. Please be here at, let's say, 1.45 p.m. We can go there together and get it notarised.'

Amir looked at his watch. It was past twelve. He'd have over an hour for lunch and organising himself.

'I'll be here,' Amir said and left. Earlier, he had noticed a small Chinese restaurant nearby. He decided to eat lunch there. While walking to the restaurant, he stopped at a news kiosk and picked up a copy of the *International Herald Tribune*.

The restaurant had a lunch buffet. Amir stood in the queue and asked the attendant to give him sweet and sour chicken with egg-fried rice and a Coke. Once his food was ready, he sat down in a corner and opened the newspaper.

Amir was shocked. The front page carried the headline, 'Swiss Banker Arrested for Involvement in the Murder of a Colleague and His Girlfriend in Germany.' In the report, it was mentioned that Mr. Herbert Oshko, working for Growth & Prosperity Bank, commonly known as G&P Bank in Geneva, was arrested in Germany for his involvement in the murder of a British colleague and his girlfriend who were in Speyer to visit the girlfriend's family over the New Year. According to the police, the actual homicide was carried out by a member of a Turkish criminal gang under contract with Mr. Oshko. The murder was apparently committed through a staged accident in which the victim's car was crushed by a lorry. It also mentioned that the German police were staying tight-lipped and not giving further details, saying the matter was still under investigation.

Amir could not eat. He quickly drank his Coke but left the food untouched, and walked out of the restaurant. The situation had become serious. The stakes had risen considerably and although he thought he was ready to deal with the consequences, he was suddenly less sure. If the bank were to know that Amir was behind this development, he would be dead in no time.

He needed to talk to John Delon and brief him on the development if he did not know it already. Amir hailed a taxi and asked the driver to take him to the offices of Bonjour Secretarial Bureau.

The pretty Swiss secretary at the bureau now easily recognised Amir. He asked her to urgently connect him with John Delon in London.

'Mr. Delon is in a meeting. Who is calling, please?' John's secretary attended the call.

'This is Amir Ramli from Geneva. I need to speak to John. It's a life-and-death situation. Please interrupt his meeting and tell him that I need to speak to him immediately.'

'I will see what I can do. Please stay on the line.' replied the secretary.

'Amir? Are you alright?' John Delon came on the line.

'I am okay at the moment but do not know for how long. Have you heard about the arrest in Germany?'

'It's all over the newspapers here, as well. You should see the headlines. The *Times* says "British Banker and Girlfriend Murdered in Germany" on the front page. Ian Softsol called me only a few moments ago and told me that according to his German source, some more arrests are expected as the police now believe the murder was to stop the banker from revealing certain business secrets. It's good, isn't it? We're succeeding. Ian was jubilant. He wants a bonus from you,' John said.

'Yes, it's good, but if the bank finds out I was behind this, then I am dead'

'We knew the risks. There's no turning back now, my friend. I have just handed over the complete documents to the SIB and the Institute of Chartered Accountants. We should see some more fireworks pretty soon.

'Oh, God. This is getting very complicated. Some of the information in the dossier came from a source that can be easily traced. That source might be in danger, too.' Amir was thinking of Rehana. He had exposed Rehana and her daughters to great danger, as Masood and Rehmallah were sure to know there was only one location outside of the bank with the information regarding the secret accounts, and that location was Rehmallah's home.

'The bullet has been fired. I suggest you do everything possible to protect your source. Discuss this with Francois Martin. He may be able to suggest some protection for you and your source. Please feel free to speak to me any time you want. In fact, I might need to speak to you urgently depending upon the reaction we get from the players in the UK, so keep in touch. This is the endgame.'

'Oh, what have I done?' Amir started blaming himself. Rehana was living the life fate had passed her way. He came into her life and turned it upside down. He alienated her from her husband and exposed her to grave danger. *I will not be able to live with myself if anything were to happen to Rehana or her daughters*, Amir told himself.

He asked the telephonist to get Danny in London on the line.

'Hello, there. This is a surprise, you calling me in the office.' Danny said.

'Listen, Danny, shit has started hitting the fan.' Amir briefed Danny about Oshko's arrest and the danger to Danny, Rehana, and himself.

'The fun has started, hasn't it? Good, that's what we wanted. I'm not worried about what happens to you or me. We knew what we were getting into. It was very wrong to exploit this poor lady who probably doesn't understand any of these things. I suggest you do whatever you can to protect her and her children. She won't come under suspicion immediately, as the German case has no connection to her. However, if the information about the accounts comes out from either the Swiss or UK authorities, then her husband and his colleagues will know where the leak came from. You still have a few days, I suppose,' Danny said.

'What should I do?'

'First of all, you should speak to the lady and let her know the situation is getting dangerous. If possible, she should get out from there and take refuge somewhere for a few days until the situation calms down.'

'You mean after her husband has been jailed?'

'Yes. On the other hand, he may be able to avoid prison. In that case, the lady would be in a greater danger. She'll have to act to protect herself and her daughters. This is a mess. You better start moving fast.'

'Thanks, Danny. Sorry, I dragged you into this.'

'All for a good cause. Keep in touch. We'll probably need to speak to each other quite regularly as the situation unfolds.' Danny replied.

After finishing his calls, Amir returned to the offices of Martin, Vincent, and Durrand.

'Had a good lunch?'

'I couldn't eat. Something has happened that you must know.'

'Sit down. You look very pale. Are you okay? Do you need to see a doctor?' The lawyer was concerned.

'No. I'm all right. I don't know if you've seen this,' Amir said, handing over the *International Herald Tribune* to Francois Martin.

Dr. Martin quickly read the article. 'No, I hadn't read this. This sheds new light on the whole situation. What you have deposed in your statement is now supported by the actions of the German police. We'll have to change your statement to include this development. I must say that your case is now stronger.'

'I'm very worried now. Not for myself but for the person who provided me the information included in my deposition. The Bank will know where the information came from and go after the person who supplied it to me.' Amir said.

'We can request the authorities keep your name a secret, as it might endanger your life. However, if the information could only come from one source, then the bank will know either way. In that case, it might be better if the source also gives a deposition and requests the Swiss government to provide him or her protection. Once that happens, then there is very little risk of any physical danger to the person. This is Switzerland, not a banana republic.'

Dr. Martin was trying to find a legal solution in typical Swiss fashion.

'It's more complicated than that. The source is married to one of the culprits and has two daughters. The lives of the daughters, who know nothing about this, may also become hell.' Amir replied.

'It's up to you. As we have not submitted any papers to anybody in Switzerland, it is still possible for you to back off and forget the whole thing. You have already inflicted great damage to the bank by exposing this chap, Oshko, and his involvement in the murder.'

'The information has already gone out. It's already in the hands of the British authorities, and they might be taking action on this matter as we speak.'

'In that case, providing or not providing the information to the Swiss would have no effect on the situation, as action against the bank might have already commenced. You must, however, tell your informant to be alert to any threats that might arise from the spouse or any other source. We should be able to transfer the person to a secret, protected location very quickly. The Swiss authorities will cooperate. Now, if you have not changed your mind, let's finish this.' Dr. Martin said.

Dr. Martin made certain changes to the already prepared statement. These were processed quickly by his secretary. Once the final version was ready, Dr. Martin asked Amir to read it very carefully, which Amir did.

'Okay, let's go. We must see my friend, the notary public.' Dr. Martin said, getting up from his chair.

The meeting with the notary public was handled efficiently. The official asked Amir to produce his passport for identification purposes and asked him to read the statement very carefully. He was asked to confirm that he understood the contents of the statement and was willingly signing it. Amir said yes to all the questions and signed the documents in triplicate. The notary public made entries in various registers and signed and stamped the documents, confirming they were signed in front of him.

After saying goodbye to Dr. Martin, Amir straight away went to his apartment. He was very worried about Rehana. He needed time to think about his next action.

Chapter 42

Ataturk International Airport, Istanbul

The Lear touched down at Istanbul's Ataturk International Airport at 3 p.m. local time. It was to stay there for an hour to refuel and then fly to Leonardo de Vinci airport in Rome en route to Schiphol airport in Amsterdam.

The aircraft was directed by the control tower to go to the far corner of the airport. An airport car arrived as soon as the plane cleared the runway to lead it to its temporary parking spot for refuelling.

The escort car left as soon as the aircraft reached its designated parking slot. A refuelling truck immediately appeared on the side of the plane. The captain opened the door and found that a mobile staircase was already attached to the aircraft. He also saw an official-looking car followed by a Jeep full of soldiers with machine guns approaching the aircraft.

The driver of the refuelling truck approached the aircraft and presented the captain with several forms to be signed for the refuelling. The captain signed the forms and offered his corporate credit card for the fuel payment.

The convoy had now reached the aircraft, and an officer in uniform with stars on his shoulder came out, followed by three others who appeared junior to him in rank. The soldiers in the Jeep also got off and surrounded the plane.

The officer quickly climbed the stairs and peeked into the cabin. 'Good afternoon. Welcome to Istanbul,' he said.

'Good afternoon. Thank you.'

'I am Colonel Ahmet Bazie. We need to inspect the aircraft.'

'We are only transiting and not coming into Istanbul. So, we'll be on our way as soon as the refuelling is done,' the captain replied.

'You are passing through Turkish territory, and it is customary for us to inspect the aircraft transiting here. We will not disturb the passengers. How many have you got there?'

'Four passengers. The owner and some companions are going to Amsterdam. There are three of us: the co-pilot, air hostess and me.'

'We will try not to disturb the passengers. Please convey our apologies to them.' The colonel was very polite. He already had full information about the aircraft's destination, its ownership, and the personal details of the crew and passengers. The Turkish anti-narcotics team had been alerted earlier in the day by American DEA agents based in Peshawar that a Lear Jet carrying a cargo of heroin was flying to Europe via Istanbul. The DEA agents had preferred Istanbul for the interception as Turkey had some of the toughest anti-narcotics laws in the world. The Turkish law enforcement system and prisons were notorious for being very tough.

'Please let me tell the owner that you will carry out a routine inspection of the aircraft, and they will not be disturbed.' The captain said.

'Of course. We will be as unobtrusive as possible. This is routine.' The colonel did not want to alarm anybody.

The captain went into the cabin and spoke to Yakoob. 'Sir, the Turkish authorities want to inspect the aircraft. They say it's routine, and they will try not to disturb you.'

'This is unusual. This has never happened in the past. What do they want? We are only transiting here.' Yakoob was indignant.

'I am afraid we cannot refuse. The authorities may use force if we do not cooperate. Apparently, this is a new procedure at Istanbul Airport.'

'Oh, okay. Ask them to be quick and give them bottles of whisky stored in the back. The Turkish like *baksheesh* (gratuity). They will kiss your hand and disappear quickly.'

'Sure. I'll try to expedite this. This should certainly be over by the time refuelling is done.' The captain was eager not to upset Yakoob.

'My passengers are in a conference. You may inspect the aircraft but please try not to disturb them and be as quick as possible. The owner has asked me to present you with this as a gesture of friendship.' The captain handed the colonel a box of premium whisky.

'Thank you, we really appreciate this. We will try not to disturb the gentlemen. We will start with the cargo hold.' The colonel said as he gestured his team to start checking.

The captain walked out onto the tarmac with the colonel and waited for the checks to be completed.

Soon an officer appeared with a carton full of model ships. 'What are these?' He asked the captain.

'The owner is the chairman of a shipping company. These are the replicas of his ships to be presented to the company's agents in Europe,' the captain explained.

'The base of the ships appears to be hollow. We will need to open at least one to see if there is anything there.' The officer said.

'I hope you do not do any damage to these items. The owner will be very upset. These are for Europe, and Turkey has nothing to do with our cargo,' the captain replied.

'We must see this. The cargo is now passing through Turkey, so we must ensure that everything is proper,' the colonel intervened.

He instructed the officer in Turkish to go ahead and pry open the base of a model ship. The officer took out a pair of shears and carefully cut the replica ship from the top.

'There are packets inside,' the officer said.

'Be careful. We do not want to damage the gift items.' the colonel said cheekily. He was enjoying himself.

Soon, the officer pried two packets, each containing half a kilo of white powder, from the base of the ship.

'What is this, Sir?' The colonel asked the captain.

'I will have to ask the owner. It is his property,' the captain said, and he walked back up to the cabin.

'What is it, Captain? These guys seem to be insistent on bothering us.' Yakoob said.

'Sir, can you please come downstairs? They are examining the replica ships,' the captain said.

'What? Are they mad? Those are gift items. They'll be worthless if damaged,' Yakoob said, getting up. He hoped the Turkish were not smart enough to find out that the ships had the heroin in them.

He was wrong.

He decided to be aggressive. Offence was the best defence, he thought.

'I will go and shoo them off,' he said to Salim and his brothers.

Walking down the staircase, he saw the colonel standing with his officers. The colonel had cleverly put the ship and its contents behind him to achieve an element of surprise.

'What is it, officer? You have caused us enough trouble already. Now stop bothering us so that we can be on our way. I don't want to visit your country, and our gift items are none of your business.' Yakoob walked toward the colonel.

The colonel slowly turned around, picked up the carton of ships that had been opened, and produced the broken ship and pockets of heroin. 'What is it, Sir?' he asked, showing Yakoob the two packets.

'I don't know what it is. We ordered these replica ships from a manufacturer in Pakistan to present to our agents in Europe. Maybe this is some stuffing to keep the ship balanced.' Yakoob was shaken, but he kept his wits.

'Well, let me tell you what it is, Sir. It's heroin. We are now opening all these replica ships to see how much heroin you are carrying.' The colonel was thrilled to teach this smug idiot a lesson.

'I protest and demand to call our embassy here. I am a British subject and entitled to consular assistance.'

'Oh, my God. You do escalate quickly, don't you? All in good time. We are still investigating and not accusing you of any crime,' the colonel said.

Soon, all the boxes were offloaded and every replica ship was pried open.

'We have two hundred packets of what I estimate to be half a kilo each of pure heroin. It seems that all of you are going to be our guests in Turkey for a long time. We are also impounding the aircraft.'

The colonel spoke to his assistants. Immediately, two vehicles were placed behind the aircraft to prevent it from attempting to reverse and take off. The colonel nodded to an officer, who quickly handcuffed Yakoob and the captain. Two officers went up the stairs and dragged the others off the plane. They were all handcuffed and lined up on the tarmac.

'What is happening? Why are they doing this to us?' Haroon turned to Salim and asked.

Salim avoided his gaze and did not reply.

'Look, Sir, there seems to be a conspiracy. We are respectable businessmen. We ordered these ships from a supplier in Pakistan for presentation to our agents in Europe. It seems that the manufacturer of the ships has put this material there, either to get us into trouble or to pass the material on to some parties in Europe.'

'It is good to hear you being polite and not ordering me in my own country. You're a drug smuggler and will be treated as such. Let's go into the terminal so we may complete the paperwork.' The colonel pushed Yakoob.

'What is this, Yakoob? What have these people got against us?' Rafik was trembling with fear.

'Don't be a smartass and pretend that you don't know what's going on. You guys have been smuggling heroin to Europe through Turkey and have now been caught. You will spend a long time in a Turkish prison.'

'Is it true, Yakoob?' Haroon looked as if he might pass out.

'Shut up! You will speak to each other when allowed to do so. Be quiet and walk quickly, otherwise, we will have to drag you to the terminal.'

'What is our fault in this? I, my co-pilot, and the air hostess, had no knowledge of anything here. Why are we being given this treatment?' the captain asked.

'I agree that you may be innocent. I feel sorry for you, particularly the lady who serves food and drinks and looks after this gang of criminals. You may get off quickly if the judge is satisfied that you are innocent, but we have to complete our investigation and make our reports,' the colonel explained.

Inside the terminal building, a group of officers gathered. They all examined, tested, and weighed the packages. Papers were made to charge Yakoob, his brothers, and Salim with smuggling drugs through Turkey, for which the usual punishment was twenty years' hard labour in a Turkish prison. They were then sent to the Istanbul prison and locked up with hardcore criminals.

The crew was taken to a holding centre for suspects, and the pilot and co-pilot were put together in one cell, and the air hostess in a separate cell.

Chapter 43

London, G&P Bank's offices, Knightsbridge

Sheikh Tayeb, Azhar Alam, Shakadir Khan, Mateen Saeed, Masood Qadir, and Rehmallah had gathered in the main conference room to discuss the latest development.

Masood and Rehmallah had flown in from Geneva the previous night with the news of the developments in the case of Richard Bringsen's and his girlfriend's deaths in Speyer and the arrest of Oshko, the bank's security officer in Geneva.

'This is really bad news, and it is attracting a lot of bad publicity for the bank here in the UK and Switzerland. I'd like to learn the full details of what has happened as well as the risk to the bank.' Sheikh Tayeb said.

'We knew that Richard Bringsen was spying and trying to gather material to pass on to people who could harm the bank. I asked Oshko to take care of Mr. Bringsen in a manner without any link to him or the bank. I didn't want to know how he was going to do it. Apparently, the German police have been able to establish some connection between Richard's death in a road accident and Oshko and they have pulled him in for interrogation. I'm sure there is no risk to the bank, as nobody in the bank's senior management was involved in any way in this matter. I'd be surprised if the German police are able to pin anything on Oshko and even if they are able to implicate him, there can be no reason for involving the bank.' Shakadir said.

Masood was worried. 'From what I hear in Switzerland, Oshko gave the contract to get rid of Richard Bringsen to a gang of Turkish criminals. His girlfriend was collateral damage. I don't know what Oshko will tell the police. I hope he doesn't say that he acted on Shakadir's instructions. The British press is having a field day linking the bank to this affair. Since Richard was a British citizen, the British authorities are getting involved. I hear that Scotland Yard is sending a team to Germany to get more details.'

'First of all, I don't think Oshko will involve us. He's a professional. However, even if Oshko says that he acted on my instructions, there won't be anything to prove that he is telling the truth. It will be the word of a criminal against ours.' Shakadir said.

'But the damage will be done. Imagine how the press will play out this story, and its effect on our reputation and business.' Azhar said.

'Is there any way to ensure there is no further damage to the bank arising from this affair?' Sheikh Tayeb asked.

'Any interference by us at this stage may indicate our involvement in this matter,' Azhar said.

'Yes, but it is necessary to assure Oshko that we aren't abandoning him. We should somehow let him know that we will meet all of his legal expenses and continue to pay his salary to whomever he designates while this matter is being sorted out.' Sheikh Tayeb said.

'That's a good idea. I'll try to find an old colleague of his from his days in STASI and get the message to him.' Shakadir offered.

'You do that. You have my authority to spend up to a million dollars on this business to ensure that we aren't affected.' Sheikh Tayeb said.

The red emergency light on the telephone console in the conference room started flashing. Only Sheikh Tayeb's secretary was authorised to interrupt the meeting.

Sheikh Tayeb picked up the phone. 'What is it, Emma?'

'I'm sorry to disturb you, Sir, but there is an urgent telex from Mr. Abu Talib in Karachi. Mr. Talib also phoned me and asked that it should be given to you immediately. He asked me to interrupt the meeting if I had to,' Emma explained.

'Okay, bring in the message. Let's see what the urgency is,' Sheikh Tayeb said. He feared that something very serious must have happened for Abu Talib to do this.

The secretary came in with a long telex, handed it over to Sheikh Tayeb, and left. Sheikh Tayeb put on his reading glasses and started reading it. His face went pale, and his hands started shaking. The telex fell to the ground. He did not bother to pick it up, instead, he covered his face with his hands.

Everybody in the room was stunned. They had never seen him like that before. Azhar went over and picked up the telex. Blood drained from his face as he read it.

'Gentlemen, a serious emergency has arisen. I request that you wait in the adjoining room to allow me to speak to the chairman privately. I will call you in after having a word with the chairman.' Azhar said.

Everybody except Azhar and Sheikh Tayeb left the room.

'This is a disaster. We are finished.' Sheikh Tayeb said, removing his hands from his face after a few minutes.

'What got into these guys to do this?' Azhar asked.

'I don't know. I never trusted Yakoob. But now all the brothers have got themselves locked up in a Turkish prison. They have been caught red-handed smuggling drugs. There isn't anybody to run the group now. TIG will disintegrate. They owe us more than two billion US dollars. How are we going to cover it? We have securities, but both you and I know the securities might not be worth anywhere near the amount of our investment.' Sheikh Tayeb was trembling.

'Please take hold of yourself, Tayeb.' Azhar used the first name of the chairman, which he rarely did. 'You will have a stroke if you do not calm yourself. We need to find a solution to this mess. Coming at the same time as the arrest of Oshko, our problems are compounding. Let's be calm and think.'

'Call the others in and tell them about this disaster.' Sheikh Tayeb said.

Azhar went outside and asked others to join in.

Sheikh Tayeb passed the telex to Mateen, who was sitting next to him. Mateen read it and passed it, without a word, to Masood next to him.

'We know now that we are facing the gravest threat to our existence. These idiots have involved themselves in a totally foolish and senseless act. All the brothers are in a Turkish prison. Their CFO, Salim Chaliwala, is also with them. There is nobody to run the group now. TIG will disintegrate, and with it, G&P Bank.' Sheikh Tayeb had tears in his eyes.

Nobody replied. They all sat with their eyes cast downward, avoiding looking at Sheikh Tayeb.

'We knew they were in difficulties, which appeared temporary. TIG's situation must be worse than they let us know. According to our last assessment, we had considerable collateral in our hands to avoid a disaster for us. We should move quickly. Let's start cashing in securities wherever we can and, if necessary, force a liquidation of the group ourselves to protect our investment.' Azhar said.

'Let's talk to Abu Talib and hear what he says about the situation in Karachi. This news must have jolted the Pakistani markets like an earthquake.' Sheikh Tayeb said.

Azhar dialled Abu Talib's direct number in Karachi.

'Abu Talib, Azhar here. I'm with the chairman and others. You're on speakerphone. We have received your telex. What's the latest?'

'All the major markets, including the stock exchange, closed when the news came in. Everybody is in a shock. If this is not salvaged, it will turn out to be a huge disaster for the local economy. TIG is a huge business group and transacts millions of dollars' worth of business every day. I understand that very senior government officials are meeting in Islamabad as we speak to consider the repercussions on the local economy and to suggest steps to limit the damage. It is, however, generally believed that the group is financially sound and that there should be no major loss to creditors and other stakeholders from this fiasco. We hope to get some indication from the government about how TIG will be managed henceforth, as there is nobody to run the group at the moment. It's expected that the government might appoint a caretaker board. It is also rumoured that the Pakistani government will use its resources to get the brothers out of Turkish prison as soon as possible. The problem is that all three brothers are British subjects and the British government may not want to know them. And the Pakistani government might not be able to do anything in this matter.'

'What is our latest exposure to this group?' Azhar asked.

411

'When we last checked, they owed us more than two billion dollars. This might have changed. Due to the nature and size of the group, it is difficult to get an accurate figure quickly. I have assigned a team of several people to work on this group, and they will update me soon. We have a lot of securities as collateral, but most of these were valued on a going concern basis. On a realisation basis, they may be of much lesser value. Again, we are working on this and should have some figures to share with you by the end of day.' Abu Talib was a professional.

'What do you think we should do to protect our position?' Sheikh Tayeb asked.

'Once we know where we are, we might have to initiate proceedings to get the group declared bankrupt to protect our securities. I will consult lawyers here. As many of the companies in the group are incorporated outside Pakistan, we will have to go to the respective jurisdictions to protect our position. I hope to be able to give you a complete list of the companies and balances outstanding against them, together with the details of securities held by us against each advance. We might also have to talk to the Pakistan government officials in confidence about our actions to ensure that we do not end up on opposite sides.' Abu Talib said.

'Please let us know any information you get from any source and don't worry about time. You may call the chairman or me any time, day or night. You have our access numbers.' Azhar said before disconnecting the line.

Once the call was ended, Azhar addressed the group. 'It might not be as bad as we initially thought. If the group is financially sound and the government is moving quickly to install new interim management to run the group then there should be no problem. In fact, this might be a blessing in disguise, as we may now move to liquidate our investment in the group.' Azhar said.

'Azhar, you are clutching at straws. This is finished. We cannot do anything at this stage and can only hope that the bank will come out of this mess with only a small loss. Let's wait until tomorrow and see what Abu Talib comes up with.' Sheikh Tayeb said.

'This may already be in the financial press and on Reuters. I hope we don't start getting calls from our auditors and regulators to find out what's happening and whether we are covered.' Mateen said.

'You'll have to assure them that the bank is fully covered and doesn't expect to suffer any losses from TIG's situation. After all, the auditors have issued their report only recently, and they must have verified that all the securities were in place.' Azhar said.

Sheikh Tayeb seemed to be losing faith and control. 'Unless some good news comes quickly, I am going to collapse. This is more than I can take in my old age. When is the event in Banjar scheduled?'

'Tomorrow. Everything has been planned meticulously, so at least nothing should go wrong there. I have been assured that the State of Banjar will reinstall G&P Bank to its premier position and invest up to two billion dollars to grow the business once our friends are in power.' Shakadir said.

'I hope everything goes to plan. Yes, Banjar may solve all our problems. Let's hope tomorrow brings better news. I suggest that Azhar, you, Shakadir and Mateen meet me at my place tomorrow early morning for breakfast, say six o'clock. Banjar is five hours ahead of us so it will be eleven in the morning there. We might get some breaking news. I've already ordered a supply of champagne for us to celebrate. I'm very thirsty for success. Masood, I suggest that you and Rehmallah return to Geneva, as you might be needed there to deal with the Oshko affair. Shakadir will join you tomorrow afternoon and then he should go to Germany to ensure that Oshko continues to be loyal.

I am tired and would like to leave. Shakadir, please deal with the Oshko situation. Azhar, I will go to my apartment and rest. Please call me if there is any news.'

With that, Sheikh Tayeb left.

Chapter 44

Geneva

Amir arrived into work at his usual time. He hoped there would be more news about Oshko's affair in Germany. Apparently, there had been a meeting of the bank's inner board in London. Both Masood Qadir and Rehmallah had left for London by the evening flight. Amir had received a call in the middle of the night from Rehana who, speaking in a muffled voice, told him that Rehmallah had been nervous about the London trip. She wondered if he had gone for a liaison with his girlfriend, Poonam. Amir told Rehana of how there were certain serious developments at the bank and Rehmallah had probably gone to London in connection with those.

Yesterday, during the day, the bank had been in turmoil. Everybody was discussing Oshko's involvement and arrest in the murder of Richard Bringsen. There had also been an emergency meeting of the bank's senior officials to consider the effect on the bank's operations in Geneva. Amir had also attended the meeting where Masood Qadir advised that the bank was trying to ascertain the details of the situation and was conducting inquiries into whether there was a personal enmity between Richard Bringsen and Oshko. He also outlined the plan going forward; business as usual.

Amir was thinking about the events of the previous day as he settled in his office. He opened his copy of the *Financial Times* and got a jolt when he noticed the headline in bold letters, **'British Business Tycoons Arrested for Smuggling Drugs in Turkey,'** which outlined the arrest of the Soothar brothers and Salim Chaliwala. The newspaper reported that they had been found with a cache of drugs. He wondered if anybody else in the bank knew about this. On further reflection, he decided there was no need for him to do anything. The bank must know about this and the meeting in London probably dealt with the matter.

The arrest of the Soothars was a very pleasant development as far as Amir was concerned. This was another blow to the bank. He decided to call John Delon and Danny in London. In Oshko's absence, Amir felt brave and called John from his own office.

'John, Amir here. Have you read today's *Financial Times*?' He asked when John picked up the telephone.

'Yes, I have. I also know that your Mr. Oshko is in trouble. Ian tells me he is singing like a canary. The Germans now know everything about Richard Bringsen's activities against the bank and they know about the bank asking Oshko to deal with him. A fellow by the name of Shakadir instructed Oshko.'

'I know both of them. It's good if they are put away for a very long time. The reason I was asking you if you had read today's newspaper is because it appears that the bank's major debtor, TIG, is collapsing. The Soothar brothers, all three of them together with their CFO, have been arrested in Turkey for drug smuggling. There is nobody in TIG to run the group. Don't forget that the group owes G&P Bank over two billion dollars. If TIG goes down, the bank is history.' Amir said.

'I understand that, and I will pass on this information to David Ringbutton at the SIB. The alleged involvement of the bank's officers in Bringsen's murder and the collapse of their major debtor should be sufficient for them to act against the bank. I will also tell the Institute of Chartered Accountants about this, so they are aware that the bank's accounts are now going to be proved wrong, as the TIG investment will turn out to be a bad debt against which no provision was required by the auditors, despite the warning given to the partners by the audit executives.' John replied.

After he finished his call with John, Amir phoned Danny. 'Hi, got the news?'

'Yes. The senior partners have been huddled in a meeting since the morning. They asked me to bring in the working papers and calculate how much the bank was exposed to TIG. I overheard our chairman, Jeffrey Lindor, speaking harshly to David Finner and telling him that he hoped the firm was not too relaxed in issuing the audit report on the bank's financial statements. He also asked Charles Ramsey and David Finner to go through the files to see if the firm was covered. All the working papers have been removed from the filing cabinets and locked up in the chairman's office.' Danny replied.

'Well, it's all finally happening. The thieves are being made to face the music. I hope we don't get hurt as collateral damage.' Amir said.

'It was you who wanted to go after them. It looks as if fate has been helping you, and other issues are also surfacing. A piece of good news – I have now received an offer from Richter Oil Exploration Corporation for the position of chief financial officer. I have already resigned from Tolbert and Gibbs and accepted Richter's offer. Since I didn't get on well with some of the partners recently, they've agreed to waive the notice period and let me finish from here today. I'll join Richter on Monday. You should also think of your future. Come to London; we'll fix you up with a financial institution here.'

'I don't think G&P Bank's goons will let me live if they find out that I was a major player in their demise. In any case, nobody will hire me because I'll have the stigma of G&P Bank on my name.' Amir said.

'You come to London, and we'll see what we can do. Don't go to Pakistan. Your life would be miserable there.' Danny said.

'We'll think about my future once this is over. For the moment, let's keep our heads down and the pressure on.' Amir said.

Amir phoned Dr. Francois Martin and asked if he may see him. Dr. Martin asked him to come after lunch since he was meeting certain Swiss officials in connection with the complaint filed by the Swiss Bankers' Association against G&P Bank.

Amir visited Dr. Martin's offices that afternoon.

'We have made very good progress.' Dr. Martin told him. 'The authorities are furious. They've passed on the information to an investigating magistrate. According to Swiss law, if the investigating magistrate is satisfied that a crime appears to have been committed, he shall pass the case on to the public prosecutor for further investigation and legal action. As part of the investigation, it's possible that there will probably be raids on the bank's offices and some senior officials' residences to collect further evidence.'

'When do you think these raids and arrests will take place?' Amir asked.

'You know these matters move at their own pace. All the legal aspects and procedures need to be looked into and completed. I believe it might take at least a few more days, if not weeks, before the Swiss authorities make a move.' Dr. Martin replied.

'I have some further information for you,' Amir said and passed on the press report about the Soothar brothers' arrest in Turkey. 'This means that the bank's biggest debtor will go bankrupt and might bring the bank down.'

'This is useful. Let me pass this on to my friends in the Bankers' Association.' Dr. Martin said.

Amir was worried. He was worried for Rehana and her children. With the developments taking place, there might be physical and emotional trauma for the family. He had to do something to protect them.

He phoned Rehana. He wanted to update her about the developments and the risks it might pose to her family.

'Hello.' she said.

'Hi, it's me. I am calling you from office.' Amir said.

'This is quite a surprise. You've never phoned me from the office before. Is everything okay?' Rehana sounded worried.

'There are developments which might expose you and your family to difficulties. I'd like to meet you to discuss this in person.'

'There's a coffee shop called Remy's on Rue du Mont-Blanc not far from your office. I'll be there in fifteen minutes,' she said.

'I'll see you there.' Amir said. He left the bank quickly, telling Pat he would be back shortly.

Rehana arrived at the coffee shop soon after Amir reached. He had selected a table in the back for privacy.

Rehana was dressed in a Pakistani shalwar kameez today. She probably did not have time to change. She hugged Amir and kissed him.

'What is it? You've got me worried.' she said.

'It is a matter to worry.' Amir told her about the developments taking place which might get the bank dissolved, expose the bank's officers to criminal proceedings and create personal danger to Rehana and her children as a lot of the information given to the authorities came from the filing cabinet in her apartment.'

'We knew what we were doing might harm the bank and create difficulties for the people there. We also knew Rehmallah might personally get into trouble. I don't care about him; he was getting ready to divorce me and live with Poonam anyway. What we didn't think about was that there might be a raid at our house and the effect this might have on the girls and me. This is worrying. When do you think the raid might take place?' Rehana understood the situation completely.

'I don't know. It's no longer in our hands. The lawyer believes it might take a few days before an action is taken against the bank and its officials in Switzerland.' Amir replied.

'I'll tell Rehmallah that my mother is ill in Karachi and that I want to go there urgently with Sana and Saba for some time. I'm sure he will agree immediately. He wants to spend as much time as possible with Poonam. He'll probably invite Poonam to live in our apartment since her husband doesn't care; he has already given up on his wife.

'I'll phone the school and arrange to get the children's leave approved. The school is very cooperative and is used to parents taking children away at short notice for overseas visits.

'My daughters and I have dual Pakistani and Swiss nationalities. We'll spend a few days in Pakistan and return here after the situation has blown over. I will also call the school and accept the offer to be a teacher. What are your plans?' Rehana was coolly planning for all the contingencies.

'I'll stay here for a while and see how this plays out. I might have to go to London to assist the lawyer there. There will be a huge uproar and chaos if G&P is made to cease operations. I'll have to find another job. I might try to find work in Switzerland and be here with you.' Amir said.

'I'll try to call you from Karachi regularly, normally around midnight your time. My parents will be in bed so it'll be easier for me to talk. However, since communicating on the telephone internationally from Karachi isn't always easy, please take this number. It's my parents' house in Karachi. You may call me on this number for any urgent developments, but please be discreet. People in Karachi are very nosy.' Rehana said, giving Amir the piece of paper with her parents' number on it. Please call me as many times as possible. I will miss you and feel responsible for uprooting you from here. It'd be lovely to be with you without the fear of Rehmallah finding out. Let's pray this thing gets sorted out with minimal hardship to all of us.'

Chapter 45

London: Knightsbridge apartment of Sheikh Tayeb

Azhar Alam, Shakadir Khan and Mateen Saeed arrived on time at six in the morning. They had just finished breakfast with Sheikh Tayeb, who looked very tired but continued to be active. The television was switched on for any news updates, but so far there was no report from Banjar.

'I've received a telex from Habib Jalil in Lagos. He didn't know that we were here, so he sent it to Karachi. My secretary forwarded it to us here,' Azhar said.

'What does Habib want? We have bigger problems here than to worry about Nigeria.' Sheikh Tayeb said.

'He says that our lawyer, Tarimo Akpaka, called him yesterday and advised him that our clients in Nigeria are angry and have decided to take action against the bank. According to Tarimo, they will cancel the licence of the bank, confiscate all assets, and arrest our people on criminal charges. Apparently, the Nigerians are in contact with the regulatory agencies in other countries and there might be concerted action against the bank. Tarimo has also advised Habib that he is not in a position to provide any further services to the bank and was resigning from acting on our behalf. Habib is scared and begging us to do something.'

'What can we do? We don't have eighty million dollars at the moment to give to Nigerians. They want this money transferred to other banks. With all of the problems we have, we don't have the time or the resources to deal with Nigeria. I don't believe Tarimo when he says that the Nigerians are in contact with other countries. The Nigerian deposits with us were illegal in the first place, so how could they now openly admit they had assets with us? I think Tarimo and his friends want to squeeze more money out of us.' Sheikh Tayeb said.

'I hope Banjar comes through.' Azhar said.

'Let's call Abu Talib and find out what's happening there while we wait for news on the Banjar situation,' Sheikh Tayeb said.

Azhar called Abu Talib's direct number.

'Assalam Alaikum. I have the chairman, Shakadir Khan and Mateen Saeed with me here. You are on the speakerphone. We're worried about the developments regarding TIG. What is the situation now?' Azhar asked.

'Waalekum Assalam. My staff and I worked all night to get a handle on the account. According to the information so far, TIG owed us 2.3 billion US. We are still checking the records. It is possible there might be further debts from companies belonging to the group that are not shown as such in our books; TIG might not have declared some companies as a part of the group. TIG's offices in Karachi and elsewhere are closed. The local markets are in turmoil. People believe that TIG's top executives are innocent and have been framed to damage one of the biggest business groups operating from here.' Abu Talib gave a succinct account of the effects of TIG's problems.

'Pakistanis are always in denial and believe in conspiracy theories. What is the government doing to ensure that TIG's business does not go under?' Azhar asked.

'There was a meeting in Islamabad today to consider TIG's situation. It appears that the government has decided to appoint a caretaker board to run the affairs of TIG until the situation clarifies. A formal announcement on the decision is expected shortly, these are still speculations. Fortunately, so far everybody here thinks TIG is financially sound and there is no risk of any serious financial loss to anybody.' Abu Talib replied.

'What about us? Do we have sufficient securities to cover our advances to TIG?' Azhar Alam asked.

'We spent a lot of time in the vault going through the securities kept with us. Unfortunately, it looks like in a lot of cases we have photocopies of title deeds of properties and ships' registration documents but we do not appear to have signed and registered mortgage deeds. We also do not have up-to-date statements of the assets pledged with us. Maybe some of these original documents and mortgage deeds are in London with Mateen Saeed?' Abu Talib asked.

'This is Mateen.' Mateen Saeed spoke. 'We never kept any securities in London for TIG. This group was essentially handled by Karachi. We only intervened if there was a UK angle or to satisfy the auditors. We don't have any security documents with us for TIG.'

'Well, in that case, we'll continue looking for the securities.' Abu Talib continued to sound hopeful.

'We need the security documents. Unless we get assurance from the Pakistan government or the new board that everything is in order and there is no risk of losing our investments, we might need to initiate legal proceedings to protect the bank.' Sheikh Tayeb said.

'We'll prepare the final position of the amount due from the group and continue to look for the documents. I'm worried. Unless we find the original securities and mortgage deeds, we might be in a lot of trouble. The balances are simply too large. Even if we find the security documents, it'll take a while to realise them. We'll have to go through a lot of legal procedures and might have to sell these securities at a fire sale, which might not bring in the full value of these assets. Everybody knows TIG was our major client and people are already talking about G&P's exposure in this debacle.'

'Let's not panic. Find the securities and title deeds first and then we will find some way to keep this under the lid. Keep us posted.' Azhar said, and he ended the call.

Chapter 46

State of Banjar, Banjar City

Normally unable to get out of bed before noon, today Prince Taj Khan was up early. This was the day his rivals would be destroyed, and he would become the Khan of Banjar. All the planning was in place. Colonel Hamza Hassan had arranged everything meticulously. It was decided that the guards at the Khan's and Crown prince's palaces would quietly disappear and the soldiers loyal to Prince Taj would take charge. Similarly, the gunboats patrolling the sea outside the palaces would come ashore under the excuse of attending to some administrative matters. The action was to start soon after mid-day when the faithful had finished the afternoon prayer and reached their homes for rest.

Prince Taj was confident that he would be declared the Khan of Banjar before the day was over. He had already written his speech accepting his ascension to the throne. He had also ordered one hundred cases of vintage Moët & Chandon Cuvée Dom Pérignon Brut for the celebration party to be held once he was declared the Khan.

One of his first visitors that day was Her Highness Farah Naz, the youngest wife of Bulund Khan and a supporter of Prince Taj in his bid to power.

It was just past one in the afternoon when a contingent of nearly twenty Banjari soldiers in armoured carriers led by a captain in a 4x4 appeared at the gates of Prince Taj Khan's palace and asked for the gate to be opened.

Prince Taj was in his audience chamber at that time, chatting with his stepmother to keep his mind busy and to avoid becoming too anxious when he saw several soldiers running toward the entrance of the palace through the window.

He started to get up, thinking that the soldiers were there with the news of the coup and to congratulate him. He was still standing up when the soldiers armed with AK-47s barged into the room.

'We will excuse you for coming here like this if you have brought good news.' he said.

In response, the lead soldier fired a burst from his AK-47, killing the prince, Her Highness, Farah Naz, and the secretary instantaneously. The soldiers quickly spread over the palace and shooting at everybody in sight. The guards at the gate had already been killed and soldiers in armoured carriers were manning the gate.

***

Colonel Hamza Hassan was an early bird but last night he had not slept at all and was out of bed at four in the morning. Today, he was to achieve the power he had been craving his entire adult life. To him, Prince Taj was an imbecile and fool - happy with women and expensive toys. Once Sitara Khan was toppled and Taj Khan was recognised as the Khan of Banjar, it would be Colonel Hassan, who would be the de facto Khan of Banjar. With Banjar's oil wealth and unchallenged power, he would be rich beyond his wildest dreams.

He had meticulously planned this event. His plan was simple. Kill Prince Sitara Khan and his family along with the officers considered loyal to the Crown prince (such as General Jamal), take over the major installations, announce the coup to get rid of what he would label as a corrupt and self-serving government and install Prince Taj as the new Khan of Banjar. He had already received arms and financial support from several sources, including Iran and G&P Bank.

At just about the time Prince Taj's palace was being attacked, Colonel Hassan was in his sprawling villa by the sea. He had several of his loyal commanders and advisers with him. Iran's military attaché from the embassy in the UK and a retired Army general were also present, giving tactical advice. They were going through last-minute preparations before spreading out and mounting the coup.

Suddenly, there was a loud explosion outside that shattered the windowpanes. The chandelier came down from the ceiling with a loud crash. There was smoke in the room, and when it cleared, the colonel and his group were shocked to find themselves facing several soldiers pointing their AK-47s at them. Several armoured vehicles were coming through the gate, which was blown open with a rocket-propelled grenade. Some of the guards assigned to gate duty were putting up a brave defence but they were outnumbered and quickly mowed down.

Colonel Hassan was in shock. *What has gone wrong?* He asked himself. Mustering all of his courage, he got up and said, 'What is the meaning of this?'

The other officers in the room also started to get up. The lead soldier, a major in the Banjari Army, raised his AK-47 and fired a burst above the officers' heads. They quickly sat down.

'I arrest you for treason against the state of Banjar. I strongly advise that you do not resist. Believe me, I'd love to kill the lot of you.' the major said, this time pointing his gun at the head of Colonel Hassan.

'Please don't shoot. I surrender!' Colonel Hassan screamed and raised his hands above his head. All of the other people in the room did the same. 'I cannot be arrested. I demand that I be treated with dignity and respect due to a diplomat. I am Iran's military attaché.'

The major ignored him. The soldiers frisked everybody and took their personal possessions. The group was quickly handcuffed and blindfolded and herded to the waiting buses that had arrived with the armoured carriers.

The attempted coup was over before it began. The forces loyal to Prince Sitara Khan quickly swept through the country, killing or arresting the soldiers loyal to Colonel Hassan before they could make a move.

A military officer in uniform appeared on television and read a statement stating that, due to a threat to the State of Banjar, the government had declared a state of emergency. A curfew was announced and the citizens and residents were asked to stay indoors.

Chapter 47

London: Knightsbridge apartment of Sheikh Tayeb

It was nearly 9.30 a.m. in the UK, 2.30 p.m. in Banjar.

'This should be over by now. I wonder why there is still no news. Maybe there was a change in plans and the event had to be postponed.' Sheikh Tayeb could not bear the tension of waiting.

As if on cue, the television screen displayed the *Breaking News* image, and the news anchor appeared. 'We are getting reports from the small South Asian island nation of Banjar of a possible coup attempt there. Eyewitnesses have reported armoured vehicles and troops on the street. Banjar's television and radio have announced that a state of emergency has been declared by the government and a curfew has been imposed. They are asking the citizens and residents to stay indoors. We will bring you further news as soon as we get it.'

'Congratulations,' Shakadir said to everybody in general. 'It has happened. We have succeeded. We will rule Banjar through those imbeciles, Taj Khan and Hamza Hassan. Our friend, Farah Naz, will be the de facto ruler of Banjar as the old Khan of Banjar is unable to take any cohesive action.'

'Congratulations to you.' Sheikh Tayeb responded. 'You came up with this idea and arranged everything.'

'Desperate situations require desperate solutions. I feel sorry for poor Sitara Khan and his group. They'll be lucky if they are still alive by the end of the day.' Shakadir boasted. The television channel quickly rearranged its schedule for coverage of Banjar. 'Since Banjar is now a success, I must go to Germany and comfort Oshko before he does any damage.' he added.

'Why don't you stay for the lunch? You can go in the afternoon.' Sheikh Tayeb said. He was happy now.

'If I leave now, I'll be in Germany before 2.30 this afternoon. That'll give me enough time to ascertain the situation there and use my contacts to sort things out if needed. I will aim to be back here by tomorrow afternoon.' Shakadir replied.

He phoned the bank and asked Mateen's secretary to get him a first-class seat to Mannheim, which was the nearest airport to Speyer. He was told that Lufthansa had a flight leaving at 12.30 p.m. and that he was already booked.

Shakadir quickly took everybody's leave and departed. Little did he know he would not be returning anywhere for quite a long time.

Chapter 48

London: Bank of England

The meeting of the SIB was called to discuss the latest developments in the affairs of G&P Bank. The attendees were the same as the previous meeting.

'I'll get straight to the point.' Sir Richard Lobs said, starting the meeting. 'We are under pressure to act against G&P Bank. We hear that the US is ready to arrest the bank's officials there and wants us to act against the bank here. There is something more than that meets the eye. It looks as if the bank was involved in some dealings with the American intelligence agencies during the Soviet-Afghan debacle and knows too much. It must be silenced. In fact, we are being pressured by our political leaders to cooperate with the Americans.

'And the bank has not done itself any favours. It is involved in all sorts of activities that should not be tolerated. We're hearing that the bank's management might be involved in the coup attempt in Banjar, which is taking place as we speak.'

'This might not be true. How do we know that the bank is involved in Banjar?' Clare Rocke asked.

'The information was given to me by the Foreign Secretary. Apparently, there is solid evidence to prove that the bank extended financial support to the coup leaders, and the Banjar government is going to act against the bank.'

'If this is true, then the bank cannot be allowed to operate here or anywhere else. This is serious.' Jamie said.

'Exactly. Then there are other matters. There are reports that certain senior officers in the bank's Geneva branch might be implicated in the murder of one of the bank's British staff in Germany. We hear that some of the bank's officials might have been arrested and indicted there.'

'This is a disaster. Does the bank do anything legal?' Jamie was on the offensive.

'G&P's banking business is in dire straits, too. It's possible that the bank might be insolvent. It looks that the owners of the bank's largest debtor, who owe it more than two billion dollars, have been arrested for drug smuggling in Turkey, and the group might face bankruptcy. The information we received indicates that the securities the bank held as collateral from this client might be faulty and the auditors failed to mention this in their report. The financial statements were heavily window-dressed and false. I hear the Institute of Chartered Accountants is already investigating a complaint against the auditors for negligence. I am also planning to issue a notice to the auditors for them to explain their position.

'We have also been advised that Switzerland, Nigeria and Singapore are poised to take action against the bank in their respective countries. From what we hear, the bank has been involved in criminal activities and violations of laws in every country in which they have been operating.

'The countries I just mentioned are requesting that there should be concerted action in all of the countries. Of course, this may mean the end of the bank and may create huge problems for us. Let's not forget that the bank is in the retail banking sector and has thousands of depositors here.' Sir Richard presented a clear picture of the situation and put the problem on the table.

Clare interjected. 'Let's look at the legal situation that should be considered before we propose any action. We'll have to be sure whether any of our laws have been violated. Let's see what G&P Bank could be accused of doing wrong in the UK. To start with, we believe that they are insolvent and presented false information about their financial position in the financial statements and returns submitted to us. Then, the bank's major customer is facing serious financial and legal problems and might be declared bankrupt. This is public knowledge and may seriously impair the bank's ability to continue operations. Also, they have been falsifying their records showing fictitious names of their clients to help them hide their real identities and protect assets, which might have been obtained illegally and through criminal means. And finally, their credibility and creditworthiness are seriously affected by the accusations being levelled against them in other countries. In fact, there are indications that the bank was involved in serious illicit acts involving the state security of Banjar, a friendly nation and a major shareholder in the bank.

'Do these matters give the right to the SIB and The Bank of England to pull the bank's licence in the UK? And if they do, what are our obligations to the depositors and the general public in the UK? Do we need to take further steps or initiate legal and criminal action against the bank's management before acting against the bank itself? These are the questions we need to answer. To be sure of our position, we should at least give the bank's management a chance to explain themselves. We may face even greater trouble if we take unilateral action on the information received from external sources.'

'Okay,' Sir Richard said, nodding his head. 'I suggest that David, you and Clare visit the bank and ask them to clarify some of the questions we have. I'll speak to the president of the Institute of Chartered Accountants and also to the senior partner of Tolbert and Gibbs to inform them that we are not satisfied with the position reported in the bank's financial statements. We need to move very quickly as we are not certain how the events will unfold over the next few days.'

'I'll call the bank today and try to see the senior-most official there.' David Ringbutton said.

Chapter 49

London: Knightsbridge apartment of Sheikh Tayeb.

The group sat down, chatting in a happy banter. The bank's problems were apparently over. The news channel continued to report the turmoil in Banjar, but no outcome was shared.

Soon, a gourmet lunch was served. Keeping to the mood of the group, the cook had prepared dishes enjoyed by Sheikh Tayeb and his wife.

Immediately after lunch, the telephone started ringing. The first call was Shakadir reporting that he was on his way to see some of his contacts to sort out the problem in Germany. Thereafter, a call came in from Mateen's secretary informing him that two officials from the SIB wanted to see him, Sheikh Tayeb, along with Azhar Alam urgently on a critically important matter. Mateen asked her to stall the officials and try to ascertain the reason for their request.

While Mateen was still on the phone, the television screen changed again to *Breaking News*. The anchor appeared on the screen and announced that the latest reports coming from Banjar suggested that Banjar's government had succeeded in quashing a coup attempted by a brother of the Crown prince, other family members, and security forces. Banjar radio and television announced that Crown prince Sitara Khan was in full control of the government and that some perpetrators of the coup had died while others had been arrested. The citizens and residents were advised that there is nothing to fear, as there is no longer a security threat to the country, but they were also instructed to stay indoors so the mopping-up operations by the forces loyal to the government were not hindered. The government promised further news shortly. This report was followed by further reports and analyses of the situation by the experts in the studio in London.

Everybody in the room was stunned. The glass of wine fell off from Sheikh Tayeb's hands onto his expensive Persian carpet. He started shaking badly and collapsed, clutching his chest.

'The chairman seems to be having a heart attack! Call the ambulance, quick! We should take him to Cromwell Hospital. He is registered as a patient there.' Azhar shouted.

Shakila rushed to Sheikh Tayeb's side in a panic and rested his head in her lap. She calmed herself, kissed his forehead, and said, 'Don't worry, you'll be all right.'

Within minutes, the ambulance from Cromwell Hospital had arrived. Sheikh Tayeb was rushed to the emergency cardiac unit of the hospital where a team of doctors took over.

After a wait of a couple of hours, one of the doctors approached Shakila and said, 'He is stable and transferred to the ICU. He had a mild heart attack and fortunately he was brought here quickly. We'll have to do more tests to diagnose the actual condition of his heart muscles. You may see the patient but do not disturb him, and do not stay for more than a minute.'

Hearing the news, Shakila appeared unable to stand up; she sat down on the sofa. She thanked Allah for sparing Sheikh Tayeb's life and opened her bag, taking out several twenty-pound notes. She gave these to Azhar and said, 'Please give these to the poor you find around here. I will do more charity when we get back to the apartment. Allah still wants my husband to continue his work for the poor and needy. My husband will come out stronger from the hospital.'

The group gathered at the hospital sighed in relief. Their chief was okay and not in danger.

Mateen took Azhar aside and whispered, 'My secretary phoned me to say that the SIB team want to see us on an urgent matter. I think we should see them. I have a feeling something serious is taking place.'

'I cannot leave the chairman and Mrs. Tayeb here like this. I suggest you go see what they want.'

'Okay, I'll call as soon as I've spoken to them.'

Mateen phoned his secretary to say that he would be available at the office in an hour's time. He asked her to advise the SIB of his availability if they wanted an urgent meeting. Then, he sat down with Shakila Tayeb and consoled her. He praised Allah for sparing Sheikh Tayeb's life.

***

The bank's London headquarters, Knightsbridge

Mateen went straight to the conference room, where the two SIB officers were waiting for him.

'Good afternoon, Lady, Sir. My name is Mateen Saeed and I am the chief financial officer of G&P Bank in London. I understand you wanted to see me urgently. What can I do for you?' He was in no mood for a social chat so he got directly to the point.

'Thank you for seeing us at such short notice. We would not have insisted if it was not urgent. I am David Ringbutton, and the lady is Ms Clare Rocke. We are both from the SIB. The reason we wanted to see you so urgently is that we have been receiving some very disturbing information about your bank. The information is so substantial and critical that the SIB may have to take urgent action to protect the interests of the banking business in the UK. However, before taking any action, we thought it appropriate to ask you for your comments on the information made available to us.' David laid down the agenda.

'I'm surprised you are giving credence to the information, which might have been passed on to you by people who are certainly not our friends. Nevertheless, I'm interested to hear what the complaints are and to try to satisfy you about the affairs of G&P Bank,' Mateen replied.

'To start with, the prime client of the bank, TIG, who apparently owes your bank very large sums, is in deep financial trouble and its owners have been arrested in Turkey for transporting drugs. I understand TIG might be declared insolvent, which would have serious consequences for your bank.' David fired the opening salvo.

'We have also heard that TIG is in trouble but that shouldn't worry anybody, as our investment is fully secured. We also believe that there is no way TIG can go bankrupt. It is a very sound business group with real assets, and because of this apparent folly of its directors, the group may have to be restructured. I understand that the government of Pakistan is getting involved in appointing a new board of directors to look after the group,' Mateen replied.

'Our information is different. According to our information, the group is bankrupt, and G&P Bank does not have sufficient security to protect your investment. As a matter of fact, we believe that the failure of this one client may be sufficient to ruin the bank. As the regulator of the banking business in this country, we might have to act to protect the depositors and other stakeholders of the bank.' said David.

'This is rubbish. We have recently reviewed our portfolio and made provisions against any doubtful assets. Our financial statements have recently been audited and you have already received a copy of these.'

'We are aware that your financial statements were audited, and you were given a clean bill of health. The amount of work done by the auditors to be able to give a clean report is a different subject and best dealt with them. At this stage, we would like you and your chairman to confirm to the SIB in writing that you've carried out a review of all of the bank's investments, including the advances and loans to TIG, and are satisfied that the bank is sound and there is no reason for any concern.' David said.

'This shouldn't be a problem. We'll have to do some work in order to issue such a categorical statement.'

'We need the letter by tomorrow morning at the latest.'

'But that is ridiculous. You surely don't expect our chairman and myself to sign such confirmation on a few hours' notice. We need to do some work and consult our lawyers to issue such a confirmation.' Mateen retorted.

'I thought you'd be pleased to sign such a letter quite easily. Just now, you informed me that me you were satisfied that the bank was fully protected and all the doubtful assets were fully provided for. In fact, you represented this to your auditors only a few weeks ago.' David went for the kill.

'I'm sure there is nothing to worry about as a result of TIG's troubles, but we have to follow our internal procedures before giving anything to the SIB.' Mateen replied.

'Let me tell you, we have other more worrying information about your bank. We have documents suggesting the bank was willingly falsifying the names of its clients in the bank's record to protect their identities and illicit wealth. We've also been made aware of the bank's involvement in serious cases of money laundering. The SIB is under a lot of pressure to act against your bank. TIG might be the proverbial last straw that broke the camel's back. So, if we do not receive a written assurance of the bank's sound financial position from you and the bank's chairman by tomorrow morning, we might initiate action against your bank. Clare here has been taking notes of our meeting and will confirm under oath that you were given an opportunity to satisfy the SIB about the bank's soundness.' David stood up, Clare also got up, and without shaking hands or saying goodbye they exited the conference room, leaving Mateen feeling paralysed and unable to move.

Mateen remained in shock for quite some time. He was finally shaken out of his state by the telephone.

'Yes?' He said curtly. He was in no mood to be disturbed.

'Sir, Mr. Azhar Alam wants to speak to you urgently,' His secretary said, transferring the line.

'Mateen, I wanted to let you know that the chairman is stable and resting. Thank God there is no more crisis on that front. How did your meeting go?' Azhar said without any preamble.

'Not very well, I'm afraid. We need to talk.'

'Okay, why don't you come to the chairman's apartment? We'll use it as the crisis centre away from the bank's operations.'

'I am on my way.' Mateen replied.

***

He was at Sheikh Tayeb's Knightsbridge apartment within a few minutes. He found it difficult to concentrate and was happy to leave the bank. Azhar and Masood were waiting for him with drinks in their hands.

'A trying day. Everything had to happen today. We need to think and think quickly to deal with the situation. I have asked Abu Talib to join us as soon as possible. He will arrive tomorrow morning. Masood is also staying on longer. Rehmallah is quite capable of looking after Geneva for a short while. I'll phone him and brief him about the situation and ask him to hold the fort there. Tell me, what does the SIB want?' Azhar said as soon as Mateen sat down and poured himself a drink.

'The SIB has learnt about TIG and believes the bank will face difficulties because of that. They seem to believe the bank's advances to TIG are not fully secured and want a letter from the bank, signed by the chairman and me, that affirms that the bank continues to be sound and there is no danger to the bank's health because of the problems faced by TIG.'

'Did you not tell them that the bank's advances are fully secure and there is no risk of any difficulties for the bank, even if TIG is declared insolvent?' Azhar asked.

'Of course, I did. I also told them that the bank's financial statements have been audited, and the auditors were quite satisfied that the bank's assets were stated at a fair value. But they seem to have some inside information. They said they were contacting the auditors also to see what work they did before issuing the clean opinion on the bank's financial statements. They also indicated that they had information in their possession that shows the bank is involved in illegal operations, such as money laundering and hiding the real identities of clients. They seem to be poised to act against the bank and are looking for any excuse to do so.' Mateen said.

'What can they do? Surely, they can't take away our licence or close our operations. Our depositors and investors would kill them. As to the letter they require, we can give them a letter signed by you and me stating at the financial year-end, we did review all our advances and concluded that the assets were valued properly. In view of the latest events, we are reviewing our investments, particularly our advances to TIG, in order to determine whether any further provisions or action to protect our investments are required. As to the other allegations, we should ask them to let us know what information they have, if any, in their possession before they act on it. I believe that fellow Bringsen might have fed them some information. I wish we had dealt with him sooner.' Azhar did not seem to be too disturbed by the demands of the SIB.

'They wanted the letter signed by the chairman.' Mateen said.

'We'll tell them the chairman is ill and in the hospital. I am acting as the chairman and my assurances should be sufficient for the time being.'

'Talking of Bringsen, is there any news from Shakadir?' Mateen asked Masood.

'He must have just reached there. We should get a call from him sometime tonight,' Masood replied

Chapter 50

Geneva

Rehmallah was trying hard to concentrate on the TIG files in front of him. He was going through them in great detail to weed out any documents that might expose the bank to any accusation of negligence or wrongdoing.

The last few days had been hell. TIG owners getting into trouble, Oshko arrested in Germany, and the chairman falling ill at the same time was more than he could handle. There was some good news, though. The previous night, Rehana told him that she had received disturbing news from home. Her mother was seriously ill, and Rehana wanted to go to Karachi to see her as soon as possible. He immediately booked her and the girls on the PIA flight leaving Geneva at 9 pm today. He hoped her mother would not improve for quite some time, so Rehana would stay there for a long while. He looked forward to living with Poonam while Rehana was away.

His relationship with Rehana was over. He did not love her and he had already told her he was going to divorce her and marry Poonam. He felt guilty about the girls but they would have to adjust to reality. He had set aside a tidy sum for the girls' needs.

Jagdish did not mind Poonam moving in with Rehmallah. Poonam's divorce was already in process and should be finalised any day now, but Rehmallah had been slow in filing the papers for his own divorce.

He had a lot to do. Azhar had phoned him from London and asked him to hold the fort. He looked at his watch; it was nearing five in the afternoon. Rehana's flight was at nine. He should take his wife and girls to the airport. He still had a lot to do. He quickly got up and put the TIG files in his briefcase. He'd have to go through them at home.

Rehana and the girls were all packed up and ready to leave when he reached home. Several suitcases were lying ready in the hall, the apartment was clean and organised. Rehana seemed to have prepared herself and the girls for an extended stay in Pakistan. *Good*, he thought. He would be able to relax and enjoy life with Poonam.

'Ready?' He asked, entering the apartment.

'Yes. Everything has been arranged. The school has been notified and I have informed my brother in Karachi. He'll pick us up from the airport. I've cleaned the apartment and stored our clothes and other things properly so they won't get ruined. I've cooked some food for you and put it in the fridge. I'll need some money to spend in Karachi.' Rehana said.

'Oh, yes. I brought you five thousand dollars. Please let me know if you need more.' Rehmallah gave Rehana an envelope containing hundred-dollar bills.

'Do you want a tea or something?' Rehana, the ever a dutiful wife, asked.

'No, let's go. Its rush hour and it will take us time to get to the airport. Now girls, you be good and help your mother. She will be under pressure as your grandma is not well. So, you help her and don't be naughty.' He told Sana and Saba.

'I hope your mother gets well soon. Please give her my best regards, and tell her that I am praying for her recovery.' Rehmallah said, turning to Rehana.

'Yes, please pray for her and for us, too. It's her age. My family gets worried very quickly when something is wrong with her. I hope it's nothing very serious. Anyway, it will be a good change for all of us. Pakistan will be good for the girls, as well. They will get to see their cousins.' Rehana replied.

'Okay, let's go.'

Earlier that day, Rehana had phoned Amir from a public telephone and told him she was leaving that night. Amir wanted to come and see her before she left but she told him not to as she had many things to take care of and the girls were home. They promised that they would get together as soon as the situation permitted.

There was not too much rush at the airport. Rehana and the girls were checked in quickly and went through immigration. Once inside the departure lounge, Rehana called Amir. He was still at the bank.

'Hi, it's me. I'm at the airport. The flight will leave in about an hour.'

'I'm still finishing some paperwork at the office. It seems that things are heating up. I understand Shakadir has gone to Speyer and it's likely that he may be in trouble there. I also hear the Swiss authorities might act against the bank very soon. It's a matter of days rather than weeks now. It's good that you are leaving. Has Rehmallah left the airport?'

'He left as soon as we went through immigration. I'm sure he's hurrying to pick up Poonam. Good. Let them enjoy. I am finished with him.' Rehana said.

'Can I come to see you at the airport?' Amir asked.

'I'm already in the departure lounge. They won't allow me to leave from here. Besides, the girls are here with me. I'll return as soon as things calm down. You may phone me in Karachi on the number I gave you around midnight Karachi time.' Rehana said.

'I'll miss you, my love. Take care and let's stay in touch. I'll phone you as many times as possible. Safe trip and goodbye.' Amir said.

'You look after yourself. Goodbye.' Rehana had a feeling she was going to go through a significant change in her life. She prayed for the change to be for good.

True to Rehana's prediction, Rehmallah called Poonam and told her he'd pick her up in an hour. Despite the problems at the bank, he was feeling relaxed and relieved at his family's departure and looking forward to the opportunity to spend time with Poonam. He stopped at the liquor shop and picked up a bottle of wine. He never brought alcohol home when his family was there, but with Poonam, he would enjoy it.

Chapter 51

London: Bank of England

As the situation regarding G&P was heating up, the SBI was again meeting in an emergency session.

Sir Richard Lobs started the proceedings. 'It looks as though the time for action has come. I hear from the foreign office that Banjar is poised to act. They will nationalise the bank and issue warrants against the senior officials of the bank.

'I also understand that Switzerland has received information indicating the bank was involved in criminal activities and violated the banking laws of the country. There is also this case of the British banker working for the bank in Switzerland who was murdered in Germany. The German police are likely to arrest the bank's security officer for orchestrating the crime. The Swiss are contemplating criminal action against the bank and might cancel the bank's licence.

'We hear that our friends in Nigeria were using the bank's branch as a channel for money laundering. It appears something went wrong there and they have lost assets. They are not happy and want the bank to pay.

'And, of course, the Americans are extremely angry and ready to bulldoze the bank for their own reasons. On top of everything, the bank's biggest borrower has gone bust, and the chairman, who is the real driving force at the bank, has suffered a heart attack. Under the circumstances, it appears that we have no choice but to act and act quickly.' Sir Richard directed his attention to David Ringbutton. 'You and Clare met the bank's CFO yesterday, David. How did it go?'

David apprised the group of his meeting with Mateen Saeed. 'The CFO claimed everything is okay. They reviewed the bank's advances and investments and made the appropriate provisions for any loss a few weeks back for the annual financial statements and audit of the bank. We've asked him to provide us a letter confirming that there was no problem at the bank. He wasn't pleased. We've insisted that the letter should be signed by both the bank's chairman and himself, and should reach us this morning. The letter should be here anytime if he has taken our demand seriously.'

Sir Richard responded, 'About the audit, I have asked for a meeting with Jeffrey Lindor of Tolbert and Gibbs this afternoon. He has a few questions to answer. I fully intend to throw the book at him and warn him that there will be hell to pay if it is found that Tolbert and Gibbs were negligent or wilfully involved in a cover-up of the bank's affairs. Not only will Tolbert and Gibbs be stopped from doing audits of banks or financial institutions in the UK but there might also be criminal action against the firm and the people involved.'

'In view of the developments taking place, it might be appropriate for us to consult the central banks in the countries where the bank is operating and agree on a concerted action plan.' Jamie Lifton advised.

'I agree. I'll speak to the central banks in some of the countries where the bank has operations. Of course, we will not communicate with the places like Columbia and Panama. People in power there are probably more involved in illegal activities than the bank. Let's also see what the bank has to say about its financial position. Their letter may be delivered anytime now. I'm sure they'll assure us that the bank is financially sound and there is nothing to worry about.

'This matter is becoming quite critical. Let's meet tomorrow morning again. If something happens in the meantime, I'll send for you guys and we will meet if necessary.' Sir Richard concluded the meeting.

***

Sheikh Tayeb's apartment, Knightsbridge

A meeting of the senior officials of G&P Bank was also underway at Sheikh Tayeb's residence at the time the SIB was discussing the bank's affairs. Abu Talib had arrived from Karachi early that morning and was tired but alert.

Azhar said, 'Thank you for coming so quickly, Abu Talib. I'm sure you're tired, but the situation is getting critical and we must discuss certain matters before you're able to get some rest.' He went on to provide the latest updates to the group. 'First, I'm pleased to say that the chairman's condition has improved considerably. He is fully conscious and awake. According to the doctors, he may be released today. Of course, he'll have to rest and should not be involved in any stressful situation. Also, Shakadir has reached Speyer. He couldn't go to the police station to see Oshko last night because of the unavailability of his contact there. He'll go there today and try to comfort Oshko. He sounded confident. Now, Abu Talib, please tell us about the situation with TIG.'

Abu Talib provided his update. 'The situation is not good. This fool, Yakoob Soothar, has dropped everybody in shit. Imagine carrying drugs in his personal plane. He must have been crazy. Well, the reports are that the group is completely bankrupt. The authorities everywhere are impounding their ships and other assets for port and other dues. Creditors in several countries have started filing lawsuits for amounts due to them. Hong Kong, where the group had its headquarters, has sealed the company's offices and is sending investigators to examine the company's affairs.

'As of yesterday afternoon, claims aggregating five hundred million dollars have been filed in Pakistan alone. Their staff is deserting them as they were not paid salaries and there is little hope that they will get anything. The government of Pakistan tried to take control of the situation but seeing the magnitude of the problem, they appear to have dropped the idea and are letting events run their course.'

'This is terrible. But we are safe, aren't we? We are fully secured.' Azhar said.

'No, we are not. Over the years, because of our relationship with the family, we continued to extend facilities to the group without fully securing ourselves, thinking the group was prosperous and financially sound. They seemed to be making money. We were making money. We seem to have given loans and advances on the strength of photocopies of title deeds and false statements of inventories as collateral. We never registered any mortgages or charges against the properties deemed to have been given to us as securities.' Abu Talib explained.

'Oh, my God! They have properties in the UK. Do you have proper collateral for the advances given from here?' Azhar looked at Mateen.

'Unfortunately, no. We have the same situation here. They gave us photocopies of title deeds, promising that the originals would follow. They never came. Since we had an excellent relationship with the family and were doing good business, we forgot about following up on these issues.' Mateen replied.

'Didn't the auditors check anything?' Azhar asked.

'You may recall that we had some difficulty with the auditors. However, we succeeded in satisfying them that the provision we made against doubtful assets was adequate. We had to make some people at the auditors happy to accept our assurances.' Mateen said.

'My God. The group owes us 2.3 billion dollars, and we do not seem to have proper securities to cover our investments.'

'We do have some securities and mortgages on certain properties, which I estimate would be worth a couple hundred million dollars. I've already asked our legal team to ensure that our claim is submitted against the assets where we are secured. For the rest, the bank would rank pari-passu with other creditors.'

'That'll happen if the group is declared bankrupt and liquidated.' Azhar said.

'Authorities and stakeholders in the group in several countries are filing for forced liquidation of the group as we speak. Authorities are also moving to confiscate the group's assets, including the ships anchored in their harbours.'

'Aren't the British helping? The Soothars are British subjects.'

'The Brits don't want to know them. I hear the British consulate in Istanbul has even refused to provide consular assistance to the brothers. Let's face it, the group has gone up in smoke.' Abu Talib sounded tired and pessimistic.

'What do we tell the SIB? They're expecting a letter from us today.' Mateen said.

'We'll write the letter as we discussed yesterday. They are buffoons at the SIB. What can they do? Don't worry about them.' Azhar replied.

'We have to do something about Banjar, too. Everybody seems to be sending congratulatory messages to Prince Sitara for successfully crushing the coup. We must also send such a message, apologising for the delay due to the illness of our chairman.' Masood said.

'I'll draft a message of congratulations and offer to visit Banjar at His Highness's convenience. I'll also call him in a couple days; he must be busy sorting out the situation there.' Azhar said.

'The gravity of the situation is such that we should go there. I suggest we leave from here as soon as the circumstances permit.' Abu Talib said.

'We'll go as soon as the chairman is a little more stable and we know that situation in other locations is under control. Masood, we haven't yet heard from Shakadir. I suggest you go to Geneva immediately and see that everything is under control there.' Azhar replied.

'The chairman is stable and it might take a few days before he is back in action. We need to attend to our business needs. The situation for our bank in Banjar was precarious before the current developments. We don't know how these developments will affect us. It might be appropriate for us to visit there immediately to show our solidarity to Prince Sitara Khan. He may consider our support important and might reverse his earlier decisions. I'll go there with you. Mateen will be here to handle any issues that arise.' Abu Talib said.

Azhar considered what Abu Talib suggested. 'If everybody believes that it's important for us to be there, I don't mind going today. Let's find out if there are any flights operating there. I agree, Masood should go to Geneva and be available to handle any questions regarding Bringsen or if Shakadir needs help.'

Masood stood up and prepared to leave the room. 'I'll make arrangements to travel to Geneva today. Do you also want me to find out about the flight situation to Banjar?'

'Yes, please. If there are flights, please book two seats for Abu Talib and myself on the first available flight.' Azhar replied.

Masood returned within minutes. 'I am booked on BA at seven this evening to Geneva. BA is also operating a flight tonight at ten to Banjar. I've booked seats for you and Abu Talib on that flight.'

'Let's phone Yousuf Ali there and ask him to book hotel rooms for us.' Azhar said.

'Telephone connections to Banjar are still not working. You might have to sort out the accommodation once you are there.' Masood said.

Chapter 52

London: Bank of England

An emergency meeting of the SIB was called to discuss certain serious developments that had occurred. Although it was a meeting called by the SIB, the governor of the Bank of England, Sir Edward Townsby, and the director general of MI6, Sir Raymond Weir, were present, in addition to the usual top officials of the SIB.

SIB's Sir Richard was in the chair. 'I thank you all for coming at such a short notice. These are extraordinary circumstances. We have been made aware of certain disturbing developments in connection with G&P Bank which have occurred in the last twenty-four hours. Although we've been trying to deal with the illegal and unethical operations and financially catastrophic situation of the bank in a more systematic manner, recent developments have made it critical that action should be taken against G&P Bank immediately.

'We are grateful that Sir Edward and Sir Raymond are here with us to apprise us of developments and help us formulate an action plan to deal with the situation. I'll first ask Sir Raymond to tell us about the worrying developments. I'll then request Sir Edward for his directions for proceeding further. Sir Edward has been fully updated on our investigations as well as the actions of the last few days in respect to G&P Bank.'

Sir Raymond addressed the group, 'Late last night, we were provided with a copy of the warrants for arrest and extradition of several senior officials of G&P Bank from the government of Banjar. They include chairman Sheikh Tayeb, Azhar Alam, Shakadir Khan, and Abu Talib. We understand that, with the exception of Shakadir Khan, all the named officials are currently present in London. The charges against these officials include participating in the conspiracy to topple Banjar's government. The Banjar government is keeping the warrants secret until we make the arrests here. As soon as they know the accused have been arrested, they will seize the bank's branch in Banjar and confiscate all of their assets and arrest the bank's senior officials there. We thought it appropriate to discuss this with you before acting on Banjar's request; this might affect the bank's operations in the UK.

'We have also learnt that the bank's chief security officer, a fellow by the name of Shakadir Khan, who is also wanted in Banjar, has been arrested in Germany on the charge of involvement in the murder of the British banker, Richard Bringsen. The Germans are keeping the arrest under wraps until the investigations are complete to ensure they get all the players who were involved in the crime.'

Sir Richard replied, 'This is indeed very disturbing, in fact disastrous. If word gets out that the bank's senior officials have been arrested and will be tried for taking part in a conspiracy to topple a sovereign government, the bank might cease to exist. This is in addition to the problems in Germany and elsewhere. We hear that the Swiss are also ready to move against the bank for criminal wrongdoings and violation of the Swiss Banking Code.

'We already know of the bank's precarious financial position and the blow they received because of the potential failure of the bank's biggest client, TIG. We also have information that the Nigerian government is poised to close the bank's operations there. The question is, what should we do and how should we do it? Sir Edward?'

'The way the events are moving, we may already be too late and have no choice but to act immediately. I believe we do not have even twenty-four hours to deal with this matter. Soon the news from Banjar, Germany or Switzerland will hit the press, and then there will be a run on the bank. We'll be accused of criminal inaction, particularly if it came out that we knew of the bank's problems for quite some time and did nothing. I am afraid that we have to move now.'

'How can we do that? The bank will take us to the courts for acting against them maliciously and destroying their business. The events in Banjar, Germany or Switzerland should not be the reason to take action against the bank in the UK.' Clare Rocke never lost sight of the legal implications.

David Ringbutton joined the discussion. 'Let's see what we have here. We have sufficient information with us to indicate that because of the failure of the bank's client, the bank is facing financial insolvency. Although the bank has assured us that they are sound, they have now also said they are re-examining their position. From the information provided to us from other sources, we know that sufficient securities to cover the advances to TIG do not exist. In addition, we know that the bank has been falsifying information to hide the real identity and nature of transactions undertaken by some of its clients.

'We are also aware that action against the bank in many other jurisdictions is imminent. I consider that by tomorrow morning there may be no G&P Bank and the action we face may be from the depositors and investors in this country rather than the bank's officials, who are likely to be in jail.'

'The banking law certainly empowers us to act to safeguard the deposits and investments of bank's customers in the UK. We will be required to appoint financial and legal experts to take charge of the bank's affairs and make an orderly liquidation to protect the bank's clients in the UK.' Again, Clare wanted the SIB to stay on the narrow legal path.

'It would be helpful if authorities in all the jurisdictions were to move simultaneously. That would protect us and the others from being singled out when legal action is initiated by the depositors of the bank, which is bound to happen.' Sir Edward, ever a diplomat, said.

Sir Richard laid out the plan to the group. 'Let's start preparing the documents to announce the withdrawal of G&P Bank's banking licence in the UK and the appointment of liquidators. Clare, I suggest you work with the legal department of the Bank of England to be ready with the documents by this evening. We need to appoint an administrator and a liquidator. We've had bad experiences with the accountants in this matter. Let's appoint the law firm, Gordon Bruise, to be the lead liquidators. They should be assisted by Jardine and Thomas, Chartered Accountants. I know the senior partners in both these firms. I'll talk to them and bring them on board.

'I'll also start working to coordinate action with the central banks in the countries where G&P Bank operates. Fortunately, we are heading into a long weekend, and Monday is a bank holiday. We must act immediately, as I believe that it won't be possible to keep this matter under lids any longer. Action has already started on several fronts, and unless we act now, we'll have a disaster on our hands. I suggest that although it is a Saturday tomorrow, we meet at 9 a.m. to be ready to take action on the cancellation of G&P Bank's licence and to initiate other actions. Clare and David, I request you work together with your teams and be ready with any documents, press releases, et cetera.'

There was no disagreement.

'I'll be in my office early tomorrow morning. Do keep me updated and let me know if you need me to talk to anybody. I'll brief the Chancellor of the Exchequer. He might have to speak to the prime minister as I'm sure there will be a lot of debate and accusations against the BOE and the SIB. We'll all have to face this together.' Sir Edward said.

Sir Raymond added, 'On our part, since we have received a formal request from Banjar, a country with whom we have an extremely cordial relationship and an extradition treaty, to arrest and extradite the bank's officials, we will also go into action tomorrow once you have the pieces from your side in place.'

'I'll make some calls alerting our allies that we are moving against G&P Bank. I understand that the central banks in Banjar, Singapore, Hong Kong, Nigeria and one or two other countries may want to move at the same time as we do.' Sir Richard responded.

The die for the demise of G&P Bank had been cast.

Chapter 53

Geneva: Rehmallah's apartment

It was almost midnight on Friday evening. Earlier that evening, Rehmallah and Poonam had finished the takeaway of chicken biryani, barbecued beef cubes, and wine brought by Rehmallah for the occasion. Now they were in bed, kissing each other passionately. They had already made love twice that evening and were ready for the third time. Although physically exhausted, they were determined to make it a memorable night and did not want to stop. They were interrupted by the sharp ringing of the doorbell and a simultaneous loud knock on the door.

'Open up. Police!' the voice on the other side of the door said.

'This must be some joke. It's not April Fool's tonight, is it? I'll go see who it is.' Rehmallah said, reluctantly disengaging from Poonam. He put on his dressing robe and walked to the door.

Two uniformed police officers and two gentlemen in business suits were at the door. One of the latter had an ID badge in his hand. 'We are officers from the Swiss Federal Police. We have a warrant to search these premises in connection with a federal crime.' He handed Rehmallah a piece of paper that clearly indicated the authority granted by an investigating magistrate to the Geneva Canton Police to search Rehmallah's apartment and confiscate any documents or other material considered appropriate in connection to the investigation of a reported federal crime.

'There must be some mistake, Officer. I live here. I'm a banker and I don't get involved in any criminal activity.' Rehmallah was clearly nervous.

'Sir, we have the correct address and clear instructions to search this apartment. I suggest you move out of our way and let us do our job.' The burly officer said.

'All right. I may need to call the bank's legal officer.'

'Please do. In the meantime, we will do our job.' The officer said, forcing his way into the apartment.

Rehmallah was now very nervous. Poonam was completely naked in the bedroom. It would be embarrassing if her presence in his bedroom was publicised. He rushed to the bedroom to warn her. She was lying on her back with her legs spread.

'Who was it? Come, my darling, let's not waste these wonderful moments.' she said, seeing Rehmallah.

'Poonam, please get up and get dressed. We have visitors.' Rehmallah told her.

'Visitors? At this time of night? Why didn't you tell them to come back some other time?' she said grumpily, getting up and putting on her nightdress.

'I suggest that you get dressed properly and leave. We are being visited by the police. I don't know what for but I don't want them questioning you.'

'Surely there is some mistake. You are a banker, not a drug dealer. And my being here is no crime. I don't care what they ask me. My husband knows I am here and he does not mind. I'm not going anywhere; I'm not leaving you alone here. I'll speak to the officers and clear up the apparent misunderstanding.' Poonam was adamant.

'No, just get dressed quickly and leave. I'll deal with the police.' Rehmallah said.

The Swiss officers were thorough. They quickly looked around the apartment and went to the filing cabinet.

'Those are confidential papers for my employers. I work for G&P Bank. They are protected by the Swiss banking secrecy laws.' Rehmallah protested.

'We have a search warrant and we know what we're looking for.' the officer replied curtly.

Rehmallah thought of calling the bank's lawyer but decided against it to see where the search was leading to.

'Officer, is it okay if my companion leaves?' Rehmallah asked the lead officer.

'We don't need the lady. She may leave if she wants to.' The officer said.

After Poonam left, Rehmallah walked to the telephone and said to the officer, 'Since you are handling the bank's confidential files, I must call the bank's lawyer and let him deal with the situation.'

The officer did not seem to have any objection. Rehmallah dialled the home number of Ralph Torwin, the bank's legal adviser. This was the first time, despite his many years with the bank in Geneva that Rehmallah had ever called Monsieur Torwin at his home, nor had he ever heard of anyone else doing so. He knew that for the Swiss, particularly the French Swiss, their private time was not to be violated. Calling somebody at home for business reasons on a Friday evening was rare in Switzerland.

Rehmallah was surprised when Ralph Torwin picked up on the first ring.

'Hello, Mr. Torwin. This is Rehmallah from G&P Bank. I'm sorry to disturb you so late but a critical situation seems to have arisen. I have a couple of officers from the Swiss police here with a search warrant. They're going through my apartment and handling the confidential files of the bank, which I keep at home.' Rehmallah was very apologetic for disturbing Monsieur Torwin.

'So, they are at your place, too,' Ralph replied.

'What do you mean at my place, too?'

'Well, there is a team at the bank. I have just returned from there. They are also at Masood Qadir's home.'

'Is Masood back?'

'He just returned and got a shock when he reached his residence. The door was open and there were several police officers armed with a search warrant going through his stuff.' Ralph replied.

'What is happening, Ralph?' Rehmallah was now nervous. He dispensed with *Monsieur Torwin* and began calling Ralph by his first name.

'The police seem to have obtained information that the bank is involved in criminal activities and they are now investigating. Apparently, they have a lot of information already. I'm going back to the bank. I've sent an assistant to Masood's place. I'll also send another assistant, Sophie Dollard, to your place to help you in dealing with this matter. It looks like there is nothing we can do to stop the police from taking away anything they want, provided they give us a proper receipt.

'You should also know that, since the Swiss government has gone to the extent of obtaining a search warrant and raiding the bank and your premises, it wouldn't be unusual if your telephone is also tapped and that you and some of the key officials of the bank are unable to leave the country until this matter blows over.'

'This is crazy! We haven't done anything wrong. We've always operated within the banking laws of Switzerland.' Rehmallah was now truly shocked.

'It appears there was an informant at the bank who has given a lot of damaging material to the officials. The police think they have a strong case to investigate. We'll find out in a day or two where all this is going. In the meantime, sit tight and don't do anything which might put you in trouble.' Ralph replied.

'How long do you think this will take to resolve?' Rehmallah asked.

'I don't know. I'll try to see the investigating magistrate dealing with this matter tomorrow. Although since tomorrow is Saturday, he may not be available, but I'll try. We might know something more concrete on Monday.' Ralph replied.

Rehmallah put the telephone down and sat down in a corner, holding his head. This was a catastrophe. He knew that Richard Bringsen was snooping and suspected of gathering information but he had been dead for several weeks. The bank believed they had dealt with Richard Bringsen before he could do any damage.

Chapter 54

Banjar City, State of Banjar

BA flight 137 landed at Banjar International Airport a few minutes earlier than scheduled. The plane was virtually empty, with only a few passengers, mostly Banjari returning home and some government official-type people.

It was one of the first civilian flights landing at the airport after recent events. As there were no people inside the arrivals hall, the incoming passengers were cleared through immigration and customs quickly.

'Looks like we have arrived in a ghost town.' Azhar remarked, picking up his bag from the carousel.

'I hope there's no fighting going on in the city.' Abu Talib replied.

Normally a number of taxis were available outside the airport. Today, there were none.

'Where do you want to go?' A young man in the traditional Banjari attire of long shirt and baggy trousers, accosted them.

'We are looking for a taxi to go to The Empire Hotel.' Azhar replied.

'There are no taxis. I have a car. I'll take you to The Empire Hotel. It will be two hundred dollars.'

'That's too much. Normally we pay fifteen dollars,' Azhar replied.

'You might be waiting for a long time to get somebody to take you to The Empire Hotel for fifteen dollars. Do you want to come or should I go and speak to other passengers?' The Banjari was in no mood for negotiations.

'Okay, we'll go with you.'

'This way.' The man led them to the parking lot, where only a few cars were parked.

As soon as they were seated in his ancient Corolla, the driver said, 'You pay me now.'

'Why? We'll pay you when we get to the hotel,' Abu Talib replied.

'Listen, there are Army checkpoints all over the city. I am a corporal in the Army, so I can go through the checkpoints without trouble, but I'm not taking any passengers without getting paid first. If you don't like it, you may get out of the car now.'

'Okay, here you go.' Azhar handed over two hundred-dollar bills.

The car sped through the deserted streets. There were several checkpoints manned by uniformed soldiers. They all appeared to know the driver and waved him through after a perfunctory look inside the car.

The hotel lobby was crowded with people with cameras and other gear normally carried by journalists, all trying to check-in. There was also a large group trying to check out at the cashier's desk. Apparently, people wanted to get out of Banjar due to the political situation. They were there with their bags, waiting for transport to go to the airport. They wanted to catch the earliest outbound flight available.

The manager of the hotel, who was standing in a corner monitoring the lobby, recognised Azhar and walked up to him.

'Welcome back, Sir. Very unusual situation here. Hopefully, everything is now under control and by tomorrow everything will be normal. These people are panicking and want to leave. As the airport has now started operating, we are doing our best to get them on flights as soon as possible. Staying here long, Sir?' the manager asked politely.

'Just a couple of nights. Sorry, as the telephone lines were not working properly, we couldn't communicate with you about rooms. I hope that you have some available.' Azhar replied.

'Sure, Sir. There will always be room for you here. If you would just step here and sign the form and give us your passports, I'll organise the rest. Would you like a drink?'

'No, we're fine,' Azhar replied, giving his and Abu Talib's passports to the manager.

The manager took the passports and handed them over to the reception. He returned with two keys. 'Both of you will have your usual suites on the top floor. The bellboy has already gone up with your bags. Please let me know if I can be of any further assistance.'

'Are the telephones working?' Azhar asked.

'The local lines are working. The international connections are still difficult, although you get through occasionally.' the manager replied.

Azhar turned to Abu Talib. 'Let's go to my room first. We'll speak to Yousuf Ali and find out what is happening.'

Once inside the room, Azhar tried calling Yousuf's home number but there was no response. He then tried to call other senior staff of the bank whose telephone numbers he had. Again, no response.

'We'll try to contact them tomorrow and if there is no response, we'll go to the bank ourselves. Let's get some rest. I'll see you at breakfast at seven.' Azhar told Abu Talib.

After Abu Talib went to his room, Azhar got into bed and was soon sleeping. He was awakened by a loud knock on the door.

I have overslept, and Abu Talib has come to fetch me, he said to himself, and he put on the light. He was surprised when he checked the time. It was only 4.30 in the morning.

'Who is it?' he asked with some annoyance in his voice.

'Open up! This is the police.'

Azhar quickly dressed and opened the door.

'Police? Is something wrong in the hotel?' He still wasn't fully awake and was trying to grasp the situation.

'I am Major Bashir from the Intelligence Bureau.' The officer showed Azhar his ID. 'You are under arrest for participating in the attempted coup against the government of Banjar. Please come with us.'

'There is a serious mistake! We have just arrived from London. We were not here when there was a coup attempt!' Azhar replied.

'We know. You better come with us now, or I will have to take you forcibly.' The major replied.

'I have a friend in the next suite. I must tell him that I am going with you!' Azhar was in shock.

'Your friend has already left with our team. Please come. No need to take anything from your room. My staff will collect anything of interest.' the major replied.

'This cannot be right. There is some serious mistake. I need to speak to His Highness, Prince Sitara Khan. I'm sure he will be very angry when he finds out about your actions.' Azhar continued to believe this was a serious mistake on the part of the Banjari Intelligence Bureau.

'The order for your arrest came directly from His Highness.' the major replied with a smile.

Chapter 55

Collapse

London – Bank of England

Although it was nine o'clock on a cold, gloomy Saturday morning in London, all the participants of the previous day's meeting were present.

Sir Richard Lobs commenced the proceedings. 'Thank you for taking time out to come here on a weekend. There have been serious and rapid developments in the case of G&P Bank. We have just been informed that two of the bank's senior officials, Azhar Alam and Abu Talib, committed the folly of going to Banjar. They reached there yesterday evening and were promptly taken into custody. We also understand that the local branch manager and other officials of the bank in Banjar have also been taken into custody. The branch in Banjar has been effectively taken over by the Banjar government. They have not made a public announcement at our request for coordinated action.

'The Swiss have also gone into action. I understand they raided the bank's premises and the residences of two senior officials in Geneva and have taken possession of documents that, according to our Swiss colleagues, confirm the bank's criminal activities.

'I've also spoken to the senior partners of both Gordon Bruise and Jardine and Thomas, the law and accounting firms we selected to assist us in dealing with the legal and financial matters related to the bank's cessation of business in the UK. The legal department is now ready with the appropriate announcements, paperwork, and the teams of the SIB officials and police are ready to seal the bank's branches in the UK and take control of the premises.

'The Metropolitan Police's Serious Fraud Office has been advised to initiate criminal proceedings against the bank's officials. I understand the bank's key officials might be served with orders not to leave the United Kingdom until the investigation against the bank is concluded and they are cleared to leave.'

Sir Edward Townsby added, 'I have already briefed the prime minister and chancellor. We have the green light to go ahead when we deem appropriate. The chancellor will schedule a briefing for the commons as soon as we take action. I suggest we go ahead without further delay. Let's do it.'

Following the meeting, the events moved swiftly. A notification announcing the cancellation of the banking licence, the liquidation of its business in the UK, and the appointment of liquidators was sent to the registered offices of G&P Bank and all of its branches. Copies of the notice were affixed on the doors, and security officers were stationed outside all the branches.

Similar action was taken by the authorities in most of the countries where the bank had operations. Banjar, Switzerland, Hong Kong, Singapore and Nigeria. In Nigeria, there had also been arrests of the bank's senior officers present there. Other countries notified the bank's officials not to leave as they were required in connection with the investigation of the bank's affairs.

The following morning, the world woke up to the disaster that struck the banking world. The action against G&P Bank made front-page news across the world. The news items reported that the key officials of the bank were arrested by authorities in several countries. BBC, CNN and other news channels had special presentations involving 'experts' discussing the rise and fall of G&P Bank.

Advertisements announcing the cancellation of licence and forced liquidation of G&P Bank were placed in all of the major newspapers in the UK. Similar announcements appeared in the press around the world.

Growth & Prosperity Bank, commonly known as G&P Bank, which rose on the international banking scene like a meteor, sank faster than the *Titanic*.

Chapter 56

The after-effects

Although it was early afternoon, Amir was still snoozing in bed, blissfully unaware of the disaster his actions had brought to the bank and the banking industry at large when the telephone rang. It was his father in Karachi. A regular listener to BBC, Amir's father had heard the news. Although no action appeared to have been taken against the bank in Pakistan so far, he was shocked and worried.

'What is happening to the bank?' he asked as soon as Amir picked up the phone.

'Hello, Papa. Assalam Alaikum. Is everything okay?' Amir was worried something was wrong, such as a sudden illness in the family. 'And what do you mean, what is happening to the bank?'

'Your bank seems to have been shut down around the world, including in Switzerland. Don't you know?' Amir's father asked.

'What? This is the first I've heard of this. What has happened?' Amir did not want to reveal any prior knowledge of the bank's troubles, even to his own father.

'It's reported on every news service. They say that several senior bank officials are in custody in various countries and may be prosecuted for fraud and more.'

'Well, the bank was operating normally until Friday evening when I left it for the weekend. Let me find out what's happening and I'll call you back,' Amir responded.

'Oh, I am so relieved that you're not in trouble. I was worried you might be among those picked up by the authorities. You are also a senior official of the bank. I'm very concerned for you. This might finish your banking career.' Mr. Ramli was a worrier.

'Don't worry, Papa. There are many things to do in life. I'll find something. But first, let me find out what's happening. I'll call you back.'

Amir quickly switched on the TV. There was a panel of experts discussing the demise of G&P Bank and what led to its downfall.

According to the information shown, the bank's operations were shut down in several countries, and senior bank officials were arrested. The experts were discussing the impact this may have on the banking world and the bank's depositors. Billions of dollars in depositors' funds were going to be frozen and probably lost.

Amir quickly phoned Rehmallah's home number. There was no response. Then he called Masood Qadir. No response there either. Finally, he called Pat, Rehmallah's secretary at home.

'Pat, Amir here. Sorry if I am disturbing you. I just heard of the trouble at the bank. Do you know anything about it?'

'Hello, Amir. Do I know of the bank's troubles? I have just returned from the bank and have been on the phone since four in the morning. They have taken Masood and Rehmallah in. Oshko has been arrested in Germany. Some other bank officials have been arrested in Banjar and other places. Oh, this is a nightmare! I don't know what has happened, but I hear the bank has been closed. You know, I worked with the bank for over twenty years; all my savings and my retirement pension were with the bank.'

'We all are in the same boat. Let me call the Karachi office and find out the reaction there. I'll call you back,' Amir said, and disconnected the line.

He called Danny in London.

'Hello,' came a very sleepy response.

'Danny, Amir.'

'Are you crazy? For me it is still early to get up. I was in bed.' Danny was slowly waking up.

'You haven't heard.'

'What haven't I heard? I have heard nothing. I was enjoying my sleep when you spoilt it.' Danny replied.

'It has happened.'

'For God's sake, don't talk in riddles! What has happened?'

'The bank has collapsed. Its licence has been cancelled and the senior management has been arrested.'

'You're joking. Let me turn on the TV. This should please you. You worked for it.'

'Yes, but it was a rotten apple anyway and was bound to collapse eventually. We only accelerated its demise.'

'Well, congratulations! You must be careful. You're also working for the bank and may be picked up for questioning.'

'Now that this has happened, the reality is sinking in. It's not only the bank's management who is in trouble. We might have ruined the lives of thousands of others – depositors, customers, employees and God knows who else.'

'Well, my friend, the bank was an evil organisation. They were ruined by their management, not you or me. Had they managed their affairs properly and taken care to protect the assets entrusted to them, nobody would have suffered. The bank was ripe for disaster. You did not initiate the downfall of TIG. It was TIG's management who brought it upon themselves. You did not accept photocopies of title deeds for the mortgaged properties. The bank's management did. You did not deceive and manipulate the auditors, the bank did. You only gave the push, which was bound to have come sooner or later. So, clear your conscious on this count and enjoy. Just make sure that you do not get caught up in the blowback.' Danny was quite clear about the people who were responsible for the bank's demise, and it was not Amir nor himself.

After he finished his call with Danny, Amir phoned the number in Karachi that Rehana had given him. Fortunately, Rehana picked up the phone on the first ring.

'Hello.'

'Hi, it's me.'

'I am so happy you called! I hope you're okay. The bank's problems are hot news here. There are all sorts of rumours. I've been trying to speak to Rehmallah but there is no response from the home number or direct line at the bank. The bank's switchboard is also not responding. I was thinking of phoning you as a last resort. Please tell me, what is happening?'

'First, tell me, are you and the girls, okay?' Amir tried to stay calm.

'We are fine but very worried. The girls have also learnt about the problems in the bank and are asking for their father.'

'There has been concerted action against the bank and its management in several countries, including Switzerland, the UK, Germany, and Banjar, and the bank's offices have been sealed, their licences have been suspended or cancelled, and the senior officials have been picked up by the authorities. I understand that there was a raid at your residence. Rehmallah was picked up for questioning by the Swiss police. Nobody has bothered me, perhaps because I am new at the bank.'

'Oh, my God! We created a disaster.'

'Not we, Rehana. The bank. We were not involved in any of the bank's criminal acts. The bank's management is responsible for them. The bank was operating illegally and was bound to fall sometime.'

'You know Pakistan. My family will not be able to live down this stigma. The girls will be ashamed. Soon, we'll have a string of visitors ostensibly to express their sympathies, but in reality, to shame us.'

'I'm sorry that you're finding yourself in this situation but we knew the storm was gathering.'

'Yes, and in a way, I feel relieved. I was a caged bird living with a criminal, and its best that this is ending this way. I am happy that once this is over, I'll be able to live a new and happy life but the next few days will be absolutely horrible.'

'I am sorry. I'm shocked, as well but then I also believe this disaster was going to happen sooner or later. I'm happy that I'll be able to be with you without any fear or interference once this is over. My love, I miss you and really want us to be together as soon as possible.'

'It may be better for me to be in London for a while so the girls and I don't have to confront the emotional and senseless tirade in Pakistan. Pakistanis love to live in denial, so they'll have to blame somebody other than the bank's management for this disaster. I'll think about it and let you know. Please call me after midnight tonight, my time. We'll be able to talk more freely then.' Rehana said.

After finishing the call, Amir quickly got ready and went to the bank. The bank's main door was barred by two Swiss police officers. Amir identified himself as a bank employee and requested to be allowed in.

He was taken to a senior official sitting in a small office on the ground floor of the bank.

'So, you work in the bank. And you are?' The officer said.

'Yes, I joined the bank a few days back. My name is Amir Ramli. I just heard that there was some trouble at the bank and came here to see what was happening.'

'Your name is on the bank's staff list, but you're not identified for any further action. You are, however, not allowed to go in, there is an ongoing investigation.'

'I had plans to travel to London and was wondering if there's any need for me to change those plans.' Amir diplomatically asked if he was free to travel.

'No restrictions, as far as I'm aware. You're a free man. I will, however, make a note that you presented yourself at the bank and informed us of your plans to travel, so there won't be any suspicions if somebody wants to talk to you.' The officer was a gentleman.

Amir returned to his apartment and booked a seat on the BA flight to London that afternoon. Then, he called Danny and told him of his plans to visit London.

Danny was not home, when Amir arrived. He parked himself in his usual small bedroom at the Milton Keynes apartment and poured himself a drink. Soon, Danny arrived.

'So, you have managed to escape the Swiss. I understand they have rounded up quite a few of the bank's officials.'

'They aren't interested in me.' Amir said. 'I spoke to the officer coordinating the investigation; he said I am a free man and that there are no restrictions on me. This has turned out to be a much bigger disaster than what I was playing for. I wanted the bank's officials to be punished. They have cancelled the bank's licence and closed the bank all over the world. Consider the impact on the depositors, employees, and other people involved with the bank. It might destroy the lives of people who were not responsible or in charge.'

'Yes, they have pulled the plug, but not because of the information you provided. The bank was found to be involved in much wider scams and criminal activities than you were aware of. One may be able to deal with money laundering. But getting involved in a coup in a friendly country? Murdering people because they are suspected of whistleblowing? The largest borrower getting caught in drug trafficking? Getting involved in the supply of weapons to nefarious groups all over the world? Relax. What has happened was bound to happen. You and I only made a small contribution by highlighting some of the activities of the bank.

'What you should be worried about is that you might be unemployable for a while. The bank's name might carry a stigma for some time, and nobody may want to know you. You are quite welcome to be a guest in this humble abode as long as you want.' Danny said.

'Yes, I know. Nobody will want to touch me with a barge pole for a while, but it is a big world, and people have short memories. Besides, I haven't been implicated in any way.'

'That's true. Actually, you might find work with the liquidators, who might be able to use somebody with insider knowledge about the bank. I suggest that after a couple of days, you try to contact the liquidation team and see if there is any room for you to work there.'

'Good idea. Let's see how all of this develops,' Amir said.

At 7 p.m. London time, midnight in Karachi, Amir called Rehana. She picked up the telephone immediately.

'Hello, Amir. Thank you for calling. I've been waiting. If anybody comes, I'll pretend that I am speaking to a lady friend in Geneva.'

'How are you, Rehana? How are things there?' Amir enquired.

'Hell. There has been a string of visitors all day. They are all cursing the high street Western banks for conspiring against G&P Bank. I haven't heard a rational voice all day. They all sympathise with us and say that with the right on its side, the bank will be able to defeat these conspiracies. They all believe the charges against the bank are concocted, and the bank is a very sound and beneficial organisation and will come out of this mess unscathed.'

'Wow, this is hot stuff. Do they know Rehmallah has been taken in?'

'No. They don't know anything specifically about Rehmallah, but it is known that the bank's officials have been invited for questioning by government officials in London, Geneva and other places.'

'Invited. That's a nice word. Almost sounds as if they were the VIP guests of governments. Anyway, I visited the bank today but wasn't allowed in. I was told that I was not required and was free to go wherever I wanted. I am now in London with Danny.'

'Oh, good, because I've also decided to travel to London in a couple of days. The atmosphere here will get very hot and emotional and I don't want to face the idiots who come in snooping for information and dishing out fake sympathies.'

'Please let me know what your plans are. I'll pick you up from the airport. I'll also arrange accommodation for you and the girls.'

'I'll let you know the schedule. My cousin, Lubna, has a vacant flat in the Notting Hill Gate area. The flat is only used when her family and she visit London. She has offered me the use of the flat whenever I am in London. I'll ask her to let me use it on the pretext that with the bank's affairs in turmoil, it's necessary for me to go to London and get the girl's education back on track.'

'Good idea. I'll wait for you. Perhaps you and I being together might be the only good thing that comes out of this disaster.'

'You know I am dying for you. I'll let you know when I plan to arrive. You take care of yourself.' Rehana said.

'And you, too.' Amir said.

Following their telephone conversation, Amir started to feel remorse and sadness at the havoc his actions had created. His acts contributed to freeing a monster gripping the lives and livelihood of thousands of people. The revenge did not taste sweet anymore. Depressed, he concentrated on the bright side of seeing Rehana again and spending time with her. At least there was some good coming out of all this.

Rehana reached London after a couple of days. Amir met her at the airport and accompanied her to the flat at the Notting Hill Gate.

It was a nice two-bedroom flat not far from Kensington High Street. Amir stayed with the family for most of the day and returned to Milton Keynes late in the evening.

EPILOGUE

After a period of initial shock, that resulted in acrimonious litigations and accusations by the affected parties against the Bank of England, the SIB, and the bank's management, a sense of stability and direction set in.

The Bank of England caught the flack for its negligence and lack of action in its role to supervise the banking affairs of G&P Bank. An investigation into the handling of this fiasco was undertaken by a select committee of the House of Commons who criticised the SIB and Bank of England for their sluggishness in taking action, but exonerated them from accusations of negligence and ineptitude.

It took the liquidators and accountants several years to sort out the mess of G&P's affairs. The biggest losers were the depositors, who were able to get only ten cents on a dollar after waiting fifteen years. Many depositors who had kept their life savings with the bank were financially destroyed and it was reported that several committed suicides.

The bank's officials in several countries were arrested and charged with criminal wrongdoings. A number of the senior officials changed loyalties and cooperated with the investigators and lawyers in prosecuting the bank's senior management for special deals or reduced sentences.

Sheikh Tayeb, chairman of the bank, was extradited to Banjar where he, along with Azhar Alam and Abu Talib, was tried and convicted of defrauding the state of Banjar and sentenced to twenty-five years in prison. Tayeb died soon afterwards in his prison cell.

Azhar Alam and Abu Talib were released after spending a few years in the Banjar jail and now live in Pakistan, where they do not appear to have a shortage of resources and live a very comfortable life.

Mateen Saeed cooperated with the UK authorities and was therefore not charged. He is living a retired life in a London suburb.

Shakadir Khan was convicted for his role in the murder of Richard Bringsen and was given a ten-year sentence. His whereabouts are unknown.

Masood Qadir and Rehmallah were both charged with violations of the Swiss banking law and other criminal laws. Both are still serving their sentences in Swiss prisons.

Danny accepted a job with Richter Oil Exploration Corporation in London. He continues to live in Milton Keynes with his wife, Seemi, Amir's sister.

Tolbert and Gibbs were destroyed for their role as the auditors of G&P Bank. Their licence to audit financial institutions was revoked, and several lawsuits for criminal negligence and involvement in fraud were filed against the firm and certain partners individually. The chairman, Jeffrey Lindor, and several partners were forced to retire. Two partners, Charles Ramsey and David Finner, were accused of involvement in committing fraud with G&P Bank and were arrested and sentenced to one year in prison. The firm still exists but does not have the professional ranking or reputation it once enjoyed.

TIG was declared bankrupt and liquidated. The three Soothar brothers and their finance director are serving life sentences in a Turkish prison for drug-related offences.

After spending a few days in London, Rehana decided to return to Switzerland; it was easier for her to pick up the threads of life again there. Amir accompanied her.

In Switzerland, Rehana put the children back in their school and accepted a position as a teacher herself. She was able to divorce Rehmallah for infidelity and criminal behaviour, which had severe negative effects on the morale and lives of the children.

Amir found a job with Credit Suisse in Geneva and lives there.

Rehmallah's two daughters, Sana and Saba, are now young ladies who live separately from their mother. Sana works for a bank in Geneva and is married to a Swiss architect. Saba is a lawyer working for a prestigious law firm and living a comfortable single life.

The rise and fall of G&P Bank is a testimony to unbridled greed and the desire for growth at any cost, and the disastrous collapse when things go wrong. The financial world, including the regulators, does not appear to have learnt any lessons from the bank's downfall as is evident from the banking scandals that continue to surface.

THE END.

About the Author

Farooq Mohammad is a qualified financial professional who has worked for over 30 years at major accounting firms across the world. Throughout his career, he has provided assistance and advice to numerous clients from various types of businesses, including banks and financial institutions.

This book was inspired by recent reports of bank failures and scandals, which were caused by greed, ambition, and poor handling by those in authority positions at affected banks. Although many banks have been penalized with heavy fines imposed by regulators for violating banking laws and committing fraud, news of these scandals continues to emerge. In some cases, these practices have resulted in bank failures, causing distress to depositors, employees, and customers.

This book is an attempt to recount the reckless actions of the management of a not-so-large bank that aims to become the number one bank in the world. Although it is a work of fiction, it is not far from many of the horror stories we read about these days.

Ingram Content Group UK Ltd.
Milton Keynes UK
UKHW020711270723
425883UK00016B/673